Apache Spark 2: Data Processing and Real-Time Analytics

Master complex big data processing, stream analytics, and machine learning with Apache Spark

Romeo Kienzler
Md. Rezaul Karim
Sridhar Alla
Siamak Amirghodsi
Meenakshi Rajendran
Broderick Hall
Shuen Mei

BIRMINGHAM - MUMBAI

Apache Spark 2: Data Processing and Real-Time Analytics

First Published: December 2018

Production Reference: 1181218

Published by Packt Publishing Ltd.
Livery Place, 35 Livery Street
Birmingham, B3 2PB, U.K.

ISBN 978-1-78995-920-8

www.packtpub.com

`mapt.io`

Mapt is an online digital library that gives you full access to over 5,000 books and videos, as well as industry-leading tools to help you plan your personal development and advance your career. For more information, please visit our website.

Why Subscribe?

- Spend less time learning and more time coding with practical eBooks and Videos from over 4,000 industry professionals

- Improve your learning with Skill Plans built especially for you

- Get a free eBook or video every month

- Mapt is fully searchable

- Copy and paste, print, and bookmark content

Packt.com

Did you know that Packt offers eBook versions of every book published, with PDF and ePub files available? You can upgrade to the eBook version at `www.packt.com` and as a print book customer, you are entitled to a discount on the eBook copy. Get in touch with us at `customercare@packtpub.com` for more details.

At `www.packt.com`, you can also read a collection of free technical articles, sign up for a range of free newsletters, and receive exclusive discounts and offers on Packt books and eBooks.

Contributors

About the Authors

Romeo Keinzler works as the chief data scientist in the IBM Watson IoT worldwide team, helping clients to apply advanced machine learning at scale on their IoT sensor data. He holds a Master's degree in computer science from the Swiss Federal Institute of Technology, Zurich, with a specialization in information systems, bioinformatics, and applied statistics. His current research focus is on scalable machine learning on Apache Spark. He is a contributor to various open source projects and works as an associate professor for artificial intelligence at Swiss University of Applied Sciences, Berne. He is a member of the IBM Technical Expert Council and the IBM Academy of Technology, IBM's leading brains trust.

Md. Rezaul Karim is a Research Scientist at Fraunhofer FIT, Germany. He is also a PhD candidate at RWTH Aachen University, Aachen, Germany. He holds a BSc and an MSc degree in Computer Science. Before joining Fraunhofer FIT, he worked as a Researcher at Insight Centre for Data Analytics, Ireland. Before this, he worked as a Lead Engineer at Samsung Electronics' distributed R&D Institutes in Korea, India, Turkey, and Bangladesh. Previously, he worked as a Research Assistant at the database lab, Kyung Hee University, Korea. He also worked as an R&D engineer with BMTech21 Worldwide, Korea. Before this, he worked as a Software Engineer with i2SoftTechnology, Dhaka, Bangladesh.

He has more than 8 years' experience in the area of research and development with a solid understanding of algorithms and data structures in C, C++, Java, Scala, R, and Python. He has published several books, articles, and research papers concerning big data and virtualization technologies, such as Spark, Kafka, DC/OS, Docker, Mesos, Zeppelin, Hadoop, and MapReduce. He is also equally competent with deep learning technologies such as TensorFlow, DeepLearning4j, and H2O. His research interests include machine learning, deep learning, the semantic web, linked data, big data, and bioinformatics. Also he is the author of the following book titles:

Large-Scale Machine Learning with Spark (Packt Publishing Ltd.)
Deep Learning with TensorFlow (Packt Publishing Ltd.)
Scala and Spark for Big Data Analytics (Packt Publishing Ltd.)

Sridhar Alla is a big data expert helping companies solve complex problems in distributed computing, large-scale data science and analytics practice. He presents regularly at several prestigious conferences and provides training and consulting to companies. He holds a bachelor's in computer science from JNTU, India.

He loves writing code in Python, Scala, and Java. He also has extensive hands-on knowledge of several Hadoop-based technologies, TensorFlow, NoSQL, IoT, and deep learning.

Siamak Amirghodsi (Sammy) is a world-class senior technology executive leader with an entrepreneurial track record of overseeing big data strategies, cloud transformation, quantitative risk management, advanced analytics, large-scale regulatory data platforming, enterprise architecture, technology road mapping, multi-project execution, and organizational streamlining in Fortune 20 environments in a global setting. Siamak is a hands-on big data, cloud, machine learning, and AI expert, and is currently overseeing the large-scale cloud data platforming and advanced risk analytics build out for a tier-1 financial institution in the United States. Siamak's interests include building advanced technical teams, executive management, Spark, Hadoop, big data analytics, AI, deep learning nets, TensorFlow, cognitive models, swarm algorithms, real-time streaming systems, quantum computing, financial risk management, trading signal discovery, econometrics, long-term financial cycles, IoT, blockchain, probabilistic graphical models, cryptography, and NLP.

Meenakshi Rajendran is a hands-on big data analytics and data governance manager with expertise in large-scale data platforming and machine learning program execution on a global scale. She is experienced in the end-to-end delivery of data analytics and data science products for leading financial institutions. Meenakshi holds a master's degree in business administration and is a certified PMP with over 13 years of experience in global software delivery environments. She not only understands the underpinnings of big data and data science technology but also has a solid understanding of the human side of the equation as well.

Meenakshi's favorite languages are Python, R, Julia, and Scala. Her areas of research and interest are Apache Spark, cloud, regulatory data governance, machine learning, Cassandra, and managing global data teams at scale. In her free time, she dabbles in software engineering management literature, cognitive psychology, and chess for relaxation.

Broderick Hall is a hands-on big data analytics expert and holds a master's degree in computer science with 20 years of experience in designing and developing complex enterprise-wide software applications with real-time and regulatory requirements at a global scale. He has an extensive experience in designing and building real-time financial applications for some of the largest financial institutions and exchanges in USA. He is a deep learning early adopter and is currently working on a large-scale cloud-based data platform with deep learning net augmentation.

Shuen Mei is a big data analytic platforms expert with 15+ years of experience in the financial services industry. He is experienced in designing, building, and executing large-scale, enterprise-distributed financial systems with mission-critical low-latency requirements. He is certified in the Apache Spark, Cloudera Big Data platform, including Developer, Admin, and HBase.

Shuen is also a certified AWS solutions architect with emphasis on peta-byte range real-time data platform systems. Shuen is a skilled software engineer with extensive experience in delivering infrastructure, code, data architecture, and performance tuning solutions in trading and finance for Fortune 100 companies.

Packt Is Searching for Authors Like You

If you're interested in becoming an author for Packt, please visit `authors.packtpub.com` and apply today. We have worked with thousands of developers and tech professionals, just like you, to help them share their insight with the global tech community. You can make a general application, apply for a specific hot topic that we are recruiting an author for, or submit your own idea.

Table of Contents

Preface

Apache Spark is an in-memory, cluster-based data processing system that provides a wide range of functionalities such as big data processing, analytics, machine learning, and more. With this Learning Path, you can take your knowledge of Apache Spark to the next level by learning how to expand Spark's functionality and building your own data flow and machine learning programs on this platform.

You will work with the different modules in Apache Spark, such as interactive querying with Spark SQL, using DataFrames and datasets, implementing streaming analytics with Spark Streaming, and applying machine learning and deep learning techniques on Spark using MLlib and various external tools.

By the end of this elaborately designed Learning Path, you will have all the knowledge you need to master Apache Spark, and build your own big data processing and analytics pipeline quickly and without any hassle.

Who This Book Is For

If you are an intermediate-level Spark developer looking to master the advanced capabilities and use-cases of Apache Spark 2.x, this Learning Path is ideal for you. Big data professionals who want to learn how to integrate and use the features of Apache Spark and build a strong big data pipeline will also find this Learning Path useful. To grasp the concepts explained in this Learning Path, you must know the fundamentals of Apache Spark and Scala.

What This Book Covers

Chapter 1, *A First Taste and What's New in Apache Spark V2*, provides an overview of Apache Spark, the functionality that is available within its modules, and how it can be extended. It covers the tools available in the Apache Spark ecosystem outside the standard Apache Spark modules for processing and storage. It also provides tips on performance tuning.

Chapter 2, *Apache Spark Streaming*, talks about continuous applications using Apache Spark Streaming. You will learn how to incrementally process data and create actionable insights.

Chapter 3, *Structured Streaming*, talks about Structured Streaming – a new way of defining continuous applications using the DataFrame and Dataset APIs.

Chapter 4, *Apache Spark MLlib*, introduces you to MLlib, the de facto standard for machine learning when using Apache Spark.

Chapter 5, *Apache SparkML*, introduces you to the DataFrame-based machine learning library of Apache Spark: the new first-class citizen when it comes to high performance and massively parallel machine learning.

Chapter 6, *Apache SystemML*, introduces you to Apache SystemML, another machine learning library capable of running on top of Apache Spark and incorporating advanced features such as a cost-based optimizer, hybrid execution plans, and low-level operator re-writes.

Chapter 7, *Apache Spark GraphX*, talks about Graph processing with Scala using GraphX. You will learn some basic and also advanced graph algorithms and how to use GraphX to execute them.

Chapter 8, *Spark Tuning*, digs deeper into Apache Spark internals and says that while Spark is great in making us feel as if we are using just another Scala collection, we shouldn't forget that Spark actually runs in a distributed system. Therefore, throughout this chapter, we will cover how to monitor Spark jobs, Spark configuration, common mistakes in Spark app development, and some optimization techniques.

Chapter 9, *Testing and Debugging Spark*, explains how difficult it can be to test an application if it is distributed; then, we see some ways to tackle this. We will cover how to do testing in a distributed environment, and testing and debugging Spark applications.

Chapter 10, *Practical Machine Learning with Spark Using Scala*, covers installing and configuring a real-life development environment with machine learning and programming with Apache Spark. Using screenshots, it walks you through downloading, installing, and configuring Apache Spark and IntelliJ IDEA along with the necessary libraries that would reflect a developer's desktop in a real-world setting. It then proceeds to identify and list over 40 data repositories with real-world datasets that can help the reader in experimenting and advancing even further with the code recipes. In the final step, we run our first ML program on Spark and then provide directions on how to add graphics to your machine learning programs, which are used in the subsequent chapters.

Chapter 11, *Spark's Three Data Musketeers for Machine Learning - Perfect Together,* provides an end-to-end treatment of the three pillars of resilient distributed data manipulation and wrangling in Apache Spark. The chapter comprises detailed recipes covering RDDs, DataFrame, and Dataset facilities from a practitioner's point of view. Through an exhaustive list of 17 recipes, examples, references, and explanation, it lays out the foundation to build a successful career in machine learning sciences. The chapter provides both functional (code) as well as non-functional (SQL interface) programming approaches to solidify the knowledge base reflecting the real demands of a successful Spark ML engineer at tier 1 companies.

Chapter 12, *Common Recipes for Implementing a Robust Machine Learning System,* covers and factors out the tasks that are common in most machine learning systems through 16 short but to-the-point code recipes that the reader can use in their own real-world systems. It covers a gamut of techniques, ranging from normalizing data to evaluating the model output, using best practice metrics via Spark's ML/MLlib facilities that might not be readily visible to the reader. It is a combination of recipes that we use in our day-to-day jobs in most situations but is listed separately to save on space and complexity of other recipes.

Chapter 13, *Recommendation Engine that Scales with Spark,* covers how to explore your data set and build a movie recommendation engine using Spark's ML library facilities. It uses a large dataset and some recipes in addition to figures and write-ups to explore the various methods of recommenders before going deep into collaborative filtering techniques in Spark.

Chapter 14, *Unsupervised Clustering with Apache Spark 2.0,* covers the techniques used in unsupervised learning, such as KMeans, Mixture, and Expectation (EM), Power Iteration Clustering (PIC), and Latent Dirichlet Allocation (LDA), while also covering the why and how to help the reader to understand the core concepts. Using Spark Streaming, the chapter commences with a real-time KMeans clustering recipe to classify the input stream into labeled classes via unsupervised means.

Chapter 15, *Implementing Text Analytics with Spark 2.0 ML Library,* covers the various techniques available in Spark for implementing text analytics at scale. It provides a comprehensive treatment by starting from the basics, such as Term Frequency (TF) and similarity techniques, such as Word2Vec, and moves on to analyzing a complete dump of Wikipedia for a real-life Spark ML project. The chapter concludes with an in-depth discussion and code for implementing Latent Semantic Analysis (LSA) and Topic Modeling with Latent Dirichlet Allocation (LDA) in Spark.

Chapter 16, *Spark Streaming and Machine Learning Library*, starts by providing an introduction to and the future direction of Spark streaming and then proceeds to provide recipes for both RDD-based (DStream) and structured streaming to establish a baseline. The chapter then proceeds to cover all the available ML streaming algorithms in Spark at the time of writing this book. The chapter provides code and shows how to implement streaming DataFrame and streaming data sets, and then proceeds to cover queueStream for debugging before it goes into Streaming KMeans (unsupervised learning) and streaming linear models such as Linear and Logistic regression using real-world datasets.

To Get the Most out of This Book

Operating system: Linux distributions are preferable (including Debian, Ubuntu, Fedora, RHEL, and CentOS) and to be more specific, for Ubuntu it is recommended to have a complete 14.04 (LTS) 64-bit (or later) installation, VMWare player 12, or Virtual box. You can run Spark jobs on Windows (XP/7/8/10) or Mac OS X (10.4.7+).

Hardware configuration: Processor Core i3, Core i5 (recommended), or Core i7 (to get the best results). However, multicore processing will provide faster data processing and scalability. You will need least 8-16 GB RAM (recommended) for a standalone mode and at least 32 GB RAM for a single VM--and higher for a cluster. You will also need enough storage for running heavy jobs (depending on the dataset size you will be handling), and preferably at least 50 GB of free disk storage (for a standalone word missing and for an SQL warehouse).

Along with this, you would require the following:

- VirtualBox 5.1.22 or above
- Hortonworks HDP Sandbox V2.6 or above
- Eclipse Neon or above
- Eclipse Scala Plugin
- Eclipse Git Plugin
- Spark 2.0.0 (or higher)
- Hadoop 2.7 (or higher)
- Java (JDK and JRE) 1.7+/1.8+
- Scala 2.11.x (or higher)
- Python 2.7+/3.4+
- R 3.1+ and RStudio 1.0.143 (or higher)
- Maven Eclipse plugin (2.9 or higher)

- Maven compiler plugin for Eclipse (2.3.2 or higher)
- Maven assembly plugin for Eclipse (2.4.1 or higher)
- Oracle JDK SE 1.8.x
- JetBrain IntelliJ Community Edition 2016.2.X or later version
- Scala plug-in for IntelliJ 2016.2.x
- Jfreechart 1.0.19
- breeze-core 0.12
- Cloud9 1.5.0 JAR
- Bliki-core 3.0.19
- hadoop-streaming 2.2.0
- Jcommon 1.0.23
- Lucene-analyzers-common 6.0.0
- Lucene-core-6.0.0
- Spark-streaming-flume-assembly 2.0.0
- Spark-streaming-kafka-assembly 2.0.0

Download the Example Code Files

You can download the example code files for this book from your account at www.packt.com. If you purchased this book elsewhere, you can visit www.packt.com/support and register to have the files emailed directly to you.

You can download the code files by following these steps:

1. Log in or register at www.packt.com.
2. Select the **SUPPORT** tab.
3. Click on **Code Downloads & Errata**.
4. Enter the name of the book in the **Search** box and follow the onscreen instructions.

Once the file is downloaded, please make sure that you unzip or extract the folder using the latest version of:

- WinRAR/7-Zip for Windows
- Zipeg/iZip/UnRarX for Mac
- 7-Zip/PeaZip for Linux

The code bundle for the book is also hosted on GitHub at `https://github.com/ PacktPublishing/Apache-Spark-2-Data-Processing-and-Real-Time-Analytics`. In case there's an update to the code, it will be updated on the existing GitHub repository.

We also have other code bundles from our rich catalog of books and videos available at `https://github.com/PacktPublishing/`. Check them out!

Conventions Used

In this book, you will find a number of text styles that distinguish between different kinds of information. Here are some examples of these styles and an explanation of their meaning.

Code words in the text, database table names, folder names, filenames, file extensions, pathnames, dummy URLs, user input, and Twitter handles are shown as follows: "The next lines of code read the link and assign it to the to the `BeautifulSoup` function."

A block of code is set as follows:

```
import org.apache.spark.SparkContext
import org.apache.spark.SparkContext._
import org.apache.spark.SparkConf
```

Any command-line input or output is written as follows:

```
$./bin/spark-submit --class com.chapter11.RandomForestDemo \
--master spark://ip-172-31-21-153.us-west-2.compute:7077 \
--executor-memory 2G \
--total-executor-cores 2 \
file:///home/KMeans-0.0.1-SNAPSHOT.jar \
file:///home/mnist.bz2
```

Bold: New terms and important words are shown in bold. Words that you see on the screen, for example, in menus or dialog boxes, appear in the text like this: "Configure **Global Libraries**. Select **Scala SDK** as your global library."

Warnings or important notes appear like this.

 Tips and tricks appear like this.

Get in Touch

Feedback from our readers is always welcome.

General feedback: If you have questions about any aspect of this book, mention the book title in the subject of your message and email us at customercare@packtpub.com.

Errata: Although we have taken every care to ensure the accuracy of our content, mistakes do happen. If you have found a mistake in this book, we would be grateful if you would report this to us. Please visit www.packt.com/submit-errata, selecting your book, clicking on the Errata Submission Form link, and entering the details.

Piracy: If you come across any illegal copies of our works in any form on the Internet, we would be grateful if you would provide us with the location address or website name. Please contact us at copyright@packt.com with a link to the material.

If you are interested in becoming an author: If there is a topic that you have expertise in and you are interested in either writing or contributing to a book, please visit authors.packtpub.com.

Reviews

Please leave a review. Once you have read and used this book, why not leave a review on the site that you purchased it from? Potential readers can then see and use your unbiased opinion to make purchase decisions, we at Packt can understand what you think about our products, and our authors can see your feedback on their book. Thank you!

For more information about Packt, please visit packt.com.

A First Taste and What's New in Apache Spark V2

Apache Spark is a distributed and highly scalable in-memory data analytics system, providing you with the ability to develop applications in Java, Scala, and Python, as well as languages such as R. It has one of the highest contribution/involvement rates among the Apache top-level projects at this time. Apache systems, such as Mahout, now use it as a processing engine instead of MapReduce. It is also possible to use a Hive context to have the Spark applications process data directly to and from Apache Hive.

Initially, Apache Spark provided four main submodules--SQL, MLlib, GraphX, and Streaming. They will all be explained in their own chapters, but a simple overview would be useful here. The modules are interoperable, so data can be passed between them. For instance, streamed data can be passed to SQL and a temporary table can be created. Since version 1.6.0, MLlib has a sibling called SparkML with a different API, which we will cover in later chapters.

The following figure explains how this book will address Apache Spark and its modules:

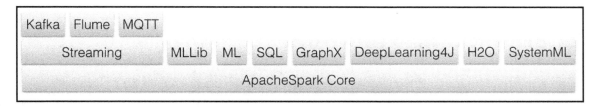

The top two rows show Apache Spark and its submodules. Wherever possible, we will try to illustrate by giving an example of how the functionality may be extended using extra tools.

We infer that Spark is an **in-memory** processing system. When used at scale (it cannot exist alone), the data must reside somewhere. It will probably be used along with the Hadoop toolset and the associated ecosystem.

Luckily, Hadoop stack providers, such as IBM and Hortonworks, provide you with an open data platform, a Hadoop stack, and cluster manager, which integrates with Apache Spark, Hadoop, and most of the current stable toolset fully based on open source.

During this book, we will use **the Hortonworks Data Platform (HDP®) Sandbox 2.6.**

You can use an alternative configuration, but we find that the open data platform provides most of the tools that we need and automates the configuration, leaving us more time for development.

In the following sections, we will cover each of the components mentioned earlier in more detail before we dive into the material starting in the next chapter:

- Spark Machine Learning
- Spark Streaming
- Spark SQL
- Spark Graph Processing
- Extended Ecosystem
- Updates in Apache Spark
- Cluster design
- Cloud-based deployments
- Performance parameters

Spark machine learning

Machine learning is the real reason for Apache Spark because, at the end of the day, you don't want to just ship and transform data from A to B (a process called **ETL** (**Extract Transform Load**)). You want to run advanced data analysis algorithms on top of your data, and you want to run these algorithms at scale. This is where Apache Spark kicks in.

Apache Spark, in its core, provides the runtime for massive parallel data processing, and different parallel machine learning libraries are running on top of it. This is because there is an abundance of machine learning algorithms for popular programming languages like R and Python but they are not scalable. As soon as you load more data to the available main memory of the system, they crash.

Apache Spark, in contrast, can make use of multiple computer nodes to form a cluster and even on a single node can spill data transparently to disk, therefore, avoiding the main memory bottleneck. Two interesting machine learning libraries are shipped with Apache Spark, but in this work, we'll also cover third-party machine learning libraries.

The Spark MLlib module, Classical MLlib, offers a growing but incomplete list of machine learning algorithms. Since the introduction of the **DataFrame**-based machine learning API called **SparkML**, the destiny of MLlib is clear. It is only kept for backward compatibility reasons.

In SparkML, we have a machine learning library in place that can take advantage of these improvements out of the box, using it as an underlying layer.

SparkML will eventually replace MLlib. Apache SystemML introduces the first library running on top of Apache Spark that is not shipped with the Apache Spark distribution. SystemML provides you with an execution environment of R-style syntax with a built-in cost-based optimizer. Massive parallel machine learning is an area of constant change at a high frequency. It is hard to say where that the journey goes, but it is the first time where advanced machine learning at scale is available to everyone using open source and cloud computing.

Deep learning on Apache Spark uses **H20**, **Deeplearning4j**, and **Apache SystemML**, which are other examples of very interesting third-party machine learning libraries that are not shipped with the Apache Spark distribution.

While H20 is somehow complementary to MLlib, Deeplearning4j only focuses on deep learning algorithms. Both use Apache Spark as a means for parallelization of data processing. You might wonder why we want to tackle different machine learning libraries.

The reality is that every library has advantages and disadvantages with the implementation of different algorithms. Therefore, it often depends on your data and Dataset size which implementation you choose for best performance.

However, it is nice that there is so much choice and you are not locked in a single library when using Apache Spark. Open source means openness, and this is just one example of how we are all benefiting from this approach in contrast to a single vendor, single product lock-in. Although recently Apache Spark integrated GraphX, another Apache Spark library into its distribution, we don't expect this will happen too soon. Therefore, it is most likely that Apache Spark as a central data processing platform and additional third-party libraries will co-exist, like Apache Spark being the big data operating system and the third-party libraries are the software you install and run on top of it.

Spark Streaming

Stream processing is another big and popular topic for Apache Spark. It involves the processing of data in Spark as streams and covers topics such as input and output operations, transformations, persistence, and checkpointing, among others.

Apache Spark Streaming will cover the area of processing, and we will also see practical examples of different types of stream processing. This discusses batch and window stream configuration and provides a practical example of checkpointing. It also covers different examples of stream processing, including Kafka and Flume.

There are many ways in which stream data can be used. Other Spark module functionality (for example, SQL, MLlib, and GraphX) can be used to process the stream. You can use Spark Streaming with systems such as **MQTT** or **ZeroMQ.** You can even create custom receivers for your own user-defined data sources.

Spark SQL

From Spark version 1.3, data frames have been introduced in Apache Spark, so that Spark data can be processed in a tabular form and tabular functions (such as `select`, `filter`, and `groupBy`) can be used to process data. The Spark SQL module integrates with Parquet and JSON formats, to allow data to be stored in formats, that better represent the data. This also offers more options to integrate with external systems.

The idea of integrating Apache Spark into the Hadoop Hive big data database can also be introduced. Hive context-based Spark applications can be used to manipulate Hive-based table data. This brings Spark's fast in-memory distributed processing to Hive's big data storage capabilities. It effectively lets Hive use Spark as a processing engine.

Additionally, there is an abundance of additional connectors to access NoSQL databases outside the Hadoop ecosystem directly from Apache Spark.

Spark graph processing

Graph processing is another very important topic when it comes to data analysis. In fact, a majority of problems can be expressed as a graph.

A **graph** is basically, a network of items and their relationships to each other. Items are called **nodes** and relationships are called **edges**. Relationships can be directed or undirected. Relationships, as well as items, can have properties. So a map, for example, can be represented as a graph as well. Each city is a node and the streets between the cities are edges. The distance between the cities can be assigned as properties on the edge.

The **Apache Spark GraphX** module allows Apache Spark to offer fast big data in-memory graph processing. This allows you to run graph algorithms at scale.

One of the most famous algorithms, for example, is the traveling salesman problem. Consider the graph representation of the map mentioned earlier. A salesman has to visit all cities of a region but wants to minimize the distance that he has to travel. As the distances between all the nodes are stored on the edges, a graph algorithm can actually tell you the optimal route. GraphX is able to create, manipulate, and analyze graphs using a variety of built-in algorithms.

It introduces two new data types to support graph processing in Spark--VertexRDD and EdgeRDD--to represent graph nodes and edges. It also introduces graph processing algorithms, such as PageRank and triangle processing.

Extended ecosystem

When examining big data processing systems, we think it is important to look at, not just the system itself, but also how it can be extended and how it integrates with external systems so that greater levels of functionality can be offered. In a book of this size, we cannot cover every option, but by introducing a topic, we can hopefully stimulate the reader's interest so that they can investigate further.

What's new in Apache Spark V2?

Since Apache Spark V2, many things have changed. This doesn't mean that the API has been broken. In contrast, most of the V1.6 Apache Spark applications will run on Apache Spark V2 with or without very little changes, but under the hood, there have been a lot of changes.

Although the **Java Virtual Machine** (**JVM**) is a masterpiece on its own, it is a general-purpose bytecode execution engine. Therefore, there is a lot of JVM object management and **garbage collection** (**GC**) overhead. So, for example, to store a 4-byte string, 48 bytes on the JVM are needed. The GC optimizes on object lifetime estimation, but Apache Spark often knows this better than JVM. Therefore, Tungsten disables the JVM GC for a subset of privately managed data structures to make them L1/L2/L3 Cache-friendly.

In addition, code generation removed the boxing of primitive types polymorphic function dispatching. Finally, a new first-class citizen called Dataset unified the RDD and DataFrame APIs. Datasets are statically typed and avoid runtime type errors. Therefore, Datasets can be used only with Java and Scala. This means that Python and R users still have to stick to DataFrames, which are kept in Apache Spark V2 for backward compatibility reasons.

Cluster design

As we have already mentioned, Apache Spark is a distributed, in-memory, parallel processing system, which needs an associated storage system. So, when you build a big data cluster, you will probably use a distributed storage system such as Hadoop, as well as tools to move data such as Sqoop, Flume, and Kafka.

We wanted to introduce the idea of edge nodes in a big data cluster. These nodes in the cluster will be client-facing, on which reside the client-facing components such as Hadoop NameNode or perhaps the Spark master. Majority of the big data cluster might be behind a firewall. The edge nodes would then reduce the complexity caused by the firewall as they would be the only points of contact accessible from outside. The following figure shows a simplified big data cluster:

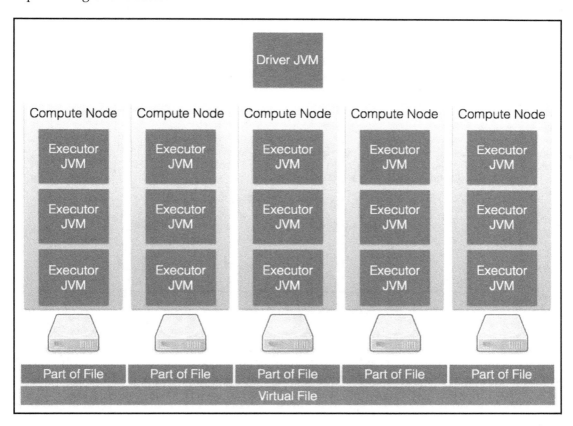

It shows five simplified cluster nodes with executor JVMs, one per CPU core, and the Spark Driver JVM sitting outside the cluster. In addition, you see the disk directly attached to the nodes. This is called the **JBOD (just a bunch of disks)** approach. Very large files are partitioned over the disks and a virtual filesystem such as HDFS makes these chunks available as one large virtual file. This is, of course, stylized and simplified, but you get the idea.

The following simplified component model shows the driver JVM sitting outside the cluster. It talks to the Cluster Manager in order to obtain permission to schedule tasks on the worker nodes, because the Cluster Manager keeps track of resource allocation of all processes running on the cluster.

As we will see later, there is a variety of different cluster managers, some of them also capable of managing other Hadoop workloads or even non-Hadoop applications in parallel to the Spark Executors. Note that the Executor and Driver have bidirectional communication all the time, so network-wise, they should also be sitting close together:

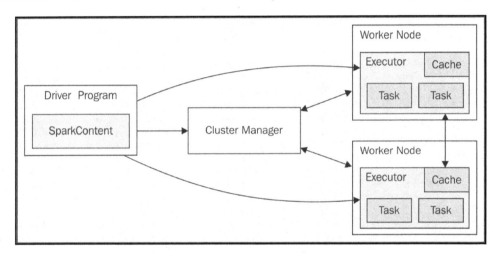

Figure source: https://spark.apache.org/docs/2.0.2/cluster-overview.html

Generally, firewalls, while adding security to the cluster, also increase the complexity. Ports between system components need to be opened up so that they can talk to each other. For instance, Zookeeper is used by many components for configuration. Apache Kafka, the publish/subscribe messaging system, uses Zookeeper to configure its topics, groups, consumers, and producers. So, client ports to Zookeeper, potentially across the firewall, need to be open.

Finally, the allocation of systems to cluster nodes needs to be considered. For instance, if Apache Spark uses Flume or Kafka, then in-memory channels will be used. The size of these channels, and the memory used, caused by the data flow, need to be considered. Apache Spark should not be competing with other Apache components for memory usage. Depending on your data flows and memory usage, it might be necessary to have Spark, Hadoop, Zookeeper, Flume, and other tools on distinct cluster nodes. Alternatively, resource managers such as YARN, Mesos, or Docker can be used to tackle this problem. In standard Hadoop environments, YARN is most likely.

Generally, the edge nodes that act as cluster NameNode servers or Spark master servers will need greater resources than the cluster processing nodes within the firewall. When many Hadoop ecosystem components are deployed on the cluster, all of them will need extra memory on the master server. You should monitor edge nodes for resource usage and adjust in terms of resources and/or application location as necessary. YARN, for instance, is taking care of this.

This section has briefly set the scene, for the big data cluster in terms of Apache Spark, Hadoop, and other tools. However, how might the Apache Spark cluster itself, within the big data cluster, be configured? For instance, it is possible to have many types of Spark cluster manager. The next section will examine this and describe each type of the Apache Spark cluster manager.

Cluster management

The Spark context, as you will see in many of the examples in this book, can be defined via a Spark configuration object and Spark URL. The Spark context connects to the Spark cluster manager, which then allocates resources across the worker nodes for the application. The cluster manager allocates executors across the cluster worker nodes. It copies the application JAR file to the workers and finally allocates tasks.

The following subsections describe the possible Apache Spark cluster manager options available at this time.

Local

By specifying a Spark configuration local URL, it is possible to have the application run locally. By specifying `local[n]`, it is possible to have Spark use *n* threads to run the application locally. This is a useful development and test option because you can also test some sort of parallelization scenarios but keep all log files on a single machine.

Standalone

Standalone mode uses a basic cluster manager that is supplied with Apache Spark. The spark master URL will be as follows:

```
Spark://<hostname>:7077
```

Here, <hostname> is the name of the host on which the Spark master is running. We have specified 7077 as the port, which is the default value, but this is configurable. This simple cluster manager currently supports only **FIFO (first-in-first-out)** scheduling. You can contrive to allow concurrent application scheduling by setting the resource configuration options for each application; for instance, using spark.core.max to share cores between applications.

Apache YARN

At a larger scale, when integrating with Hadoop YARN, the Apache Spark cluster manager can be YARN and the application can run in one of two modes. If the Spark master value is set as yarn-cluster, then the application can be submitted to the cluster and then terminated. The cluster will take care of allocating resources and running tasks. However, if the application master is submitted as yarn-client, then the application stays alive during the life cycle of processing, and requests resources from YARN.

Apache Mesos

Apache Mesos is an open source system, for resource sharing across a cluster. It allows multiple frameworks, to share a cluster by managing and scheduling resources. It is a cluster manager, that provides isolation using Linux containers and allowing multiple systems such as Hadoop, Spark, Kafka, Storm, and more to share a cluster safely. It is highly scalable to thousands of nodes. It is a master/slave-based system and is fault tolerant, using Zookeeper for configuration management.

For a single master node Mesos cluster, the Spark master URL will be in this form:

mesos://<hostname>:5050.

Here, <hostname> is the hostname of the Mesos master server; the port is defined as 5050, which is the default Mesos master port (this is configurable). If there are multiple Mesos master servers in a large-scale high availability Mesos cluster, then the Spark master URL would look as follows:

mesos://zk://<hostname>:2181.

So, the election of the Mesos master server will be controlled by Zookeeper. The <hostname> will be the name of a host in the Zookeeper quorum. Also, the port number, 2181, is the default master port for Zookeeper.

Cloud-based deployments

There are three different abstraction levels of cloud systems--**Infrastructure as a Service (IaaS)**, **Platform as a Service (PaaS)**, and **Software as a Service (SaaS)**. We will see how to use and install Apache Spark on all of these.

The new way to do IaaS is Docker and Kubernetes as opposed to virtual machines, basically providing a way to automatically set up an Apache Spark cluster within minutes. The advantage of Kubernetes is that it can be used among multiple different cloud providers as it is an open standard and also based on open source.

You even can use Kubernetes, in a local data center and transparently and dynamically move workloads between local, dedicated, and public cloud data centers. PaaS, in contrast, takes away from you the burden of installing and operating an Apache Spark cluster because this is provided as a service.

There is an ongoing discussion, whether Docker is IaaS or PaaS but, in our opinion, this is just a form of a lightweight preinstalled virtual machine. This is particularly interesting because the offering is completely based on open source technologies, which enables you to replicate the system on any other data center.

One of the open source components, we'll introduce is Jupyter notebooks; a modern way to do data science, in a cloud-based collaborative environment.

Performance

Before moving on to the rest of the chapters, covering functional areas of Apache Spark and extensions, we will examine the area of performance. What issues and areas need to be considered? What might impact the Spark application performance, starting at the cluster level and finishing with actual Scala code? We don't want to just repeat, what the Spark website says, so take a look at this URL:

```
http://spark.apache.org/docs/<version>/tuning.html
```

Here, `<version>` relates to the version of Spark that you are using; that is, either the latest or something like `1.6.1` for a specific version. So, having looked at this page, we will briefly mention some of the topic areas. We will list some general points in this section without implying an order of importance.

The cluster structure

The size and structure of your big data cluster are going to affect performance. If you have a cloud-based cluster, your IO and latency will suffer, in comparison to an unshared hardware cluster. You will be sharing the underlying hardware, with multiple customers and the cluster hardware may be remote. There are some exceptions to this. The IBM cloud, for instance, offers dedicated bare metal high-performance cluster nodes, with an InfiniBand network connection, which can be rented on an hourly basis.

Additionally, the positioning of cluster components on servers may cause resource contention. For instance, think carefully about locating Hadoop NameNodes, Spark servers, Zookeeper, Flume, and Kafka servers in large clusters. With high workloads, you might consider segregating servers to individual systems. You might also consider using an Apache system such as Mesos that provides better distributions and assignment of resources to the individual processes.

Consider potential parallelism as well. The greater the number of workers in your Spark cluster for large Datasets, the greater the opportunity for parallelism. One rule of thumb is one worker per hyper-thread or virtual core respectively.

Hadoop Distributed File System

You might consider using an alternative to HDFS, depending upon your cluster requirements. For instance, IBM has the **GPFS (General Purpose File System)** for improved performance.

The reason why GPFS might be a better choice is that coming from the high-performance computing background, this filesystem has a full read-write capability, whereas HDFS is designed as a write once, read many filesystems. It offers an improvement in performance over HDFS because it runs at the kernel level as opposed to HDFS, which runs in a **Java Virtual Machine (JVM)** that in turn runs as an operating system process. It also integrates with Hadoop and the Spark cluster tools. IBM runs setups with several hundred petabytes using GPFS.

Another commercial alternative is the **MapR file system** that, besides performance improvements, supports mirroring, snapshots, and high availability.

Ceph is an open source alternative to a distributed, fault-tolerant, and self-healing filesystem for commodity hard drives like HDFS. It runs in the Linux kernel as well and addresses many of the performance issues that HDFS has. Other promising candidates in this space are **Alluxio** (formerly **Tachyon**), **Quantcast**, **GlusterFS**, and **Lustre**.

Finally, **Cassandra** is not a filesystem but a NoSQL key-value store and is tightly integrated with Apache Spark and is therefore traded as a valid and powerful alternative to HDFS--or even to any other distributed filesystem--especially as it supports predicate push-down using `ApacheSparkSQL` and the Catalyst optimizer, which we will cover in the following chapters.

Data locality

The key for good data processing performance is avoidance of network transfers. This was very true a couple of years ago, but is less relevant for tasks with high demands on CPU and low I/O, but for low demand on CPU and high I/O demand data processing algorithms, this still holds.

 We can conclude from this, that HDFS is one of the best ways to achieve data locality, as chunks of files are distributed on the cluster nodes, in most of the cases, using hard drives directly attached to the server systems. This means that those chunks can be processed in parallel using the CPUs on the machines where individual data chunks are located in order to avoid network transfer.

Another way to achieve data locality is using `ApacheSparkSQL`. Depending on the connector implementation, SparkSQL can make use of the data processing capabilities of the source engine. So, for example, when using MongoDB in conjunction with SparkSQL, parts of the SQL statement are preprocessed by MongoDB before data is sent upstream to Apache Spark.

Memory

In order to avoid **OOM** (**Out of Memory**) messages for the tasks on your Apache Spark cluster, please consider a number of questions for the tuning:

- Consider the level of physical memory available on your Spark worker nodes. Can it be increased? Check on the memory consumption of operating system processes during high workloads in order to get an idea of free memory. Make sure that the workers have enough memory.
- Consider data partitioning. Can you increase the number of partitions? As a rule of thumb, you should have at least as many partitions as you have available CPU cores on the cluster. Use the `repartition` function on the RDD API.

- Can you modify the storage fraction and the memory used by the JVM for storage and caching of RDDs? Workers are competing for memory against data storage. Use the **Storage** page on the Apache Spark user interface to see if this fraction is set to an optimal value. Then update the following properties:
- `spark.memory.fraction`
- `spark.memory.storageFraction`
- `spark.memory.offHeap.enabled=true`
- `spark.memory.offHeap.size`

In addition, the following two things can be done in order to improve performance:

- Consider using Parquet as a storage format, which is much more storage effective than CSV or JSON
- Consider using the DataFrame/Dataset API instead of the RDD API as it might resolve in more effective executions (more about this in the next three chapters)

Coding

Try to tune your code, to improve the Spark application performance. For instance, filter your application-based data early in your ETL cycle. One example is, when using raw HTML files, detag them and crop away unneeded parts at an early stage. Tune your degree of parallelism, try to find the resource-expensive parts of your code, and find alternatives.

 ETL is one of the first things you are doing in an analytics project. So you are grabbing data, from third-party systems, either by directly accessing relational or NoSQL databases or by reading exports in various file formats such as, CSV, TSV, JSON or even more exotic ones from local or remote filesystems or from a staging area in HDFS: after some inspections and sanity checks on the files an ETL process in Apache Spark basically reads in the files and creates RDDs or DataFrames/Datasets out of them.

They are transformed, so that they fit the downstream analytics application, running on top of Apache Spark or other applications and then stored back into filesystems as either JSON, CSV or PARQUET files, or even back to relational or NoSQL databases.

Finally, I can recommend the following resource for any performance-related problems with Apache Spark: `https://spark.apache.org/docs/latest/tuning.html`.

Cloud

Although parts of this book will concentrate on examples of Apache Spark installed on physically server-based clusters, we want to make a point, that there are multiple cloud-based options out there that imply many benefits. There are cloud-based systems, that use Apache Spark as an integrated component and cloud-based systems that offer Spark as a service.

Summary

In closing this chapter, we invite you to work your way, through each of the Scala code-based examples in the following chapters. The rate at which Apache Spark has evolved is impressive, and important to note is the frequency of the releases. So even though, at the time of writing, Spark has reached 2.2, we are sure that you will be using a later version.

If you encounter problems, report them at `www.stackoverflow.com` and tag them accordingly; you'll receive feedback within minutes--the user community is very active. Another way of getting information and help is subscribing to the Apache Spark mailing list: `user@apachespark.org`.

By the end of this chapter, you should have a good idea what's waiting for you in this book. We've dedicated our effort to showing you practical examples that are, on the one hand, practical recipes to solve day-to-day problems, but on the other hand, also support you in understanding the details of things taking place behind the scenes. This is very important for writing good data products and a key differentiation from others.

Apache Spark Streaming

2

The Apache Streaming module is a stream processing-based module within Apache Spark. It uses the Spark cluster, to offer the ability to scale to a high degree. Being based on Spark, it is also highly fault tolerant, having the ability to rerun failed tasks by checkpointing the data stream that is being processed. The following topics will be covered in this chapter after an introductory section, which will provide a practical overview of how Apache Spark processes stream-based data:

- Error recovery and checkpointing
- TCP-based stream processing
- File streams
- Kafka stream source

For each topic, we will provide a worked example in Scala and show how the stream-based architecture can be set up and tested.

Overview

The following diagram shows potential data sources for Apache Streaming, such as Kafka, Flume, and HDFS:

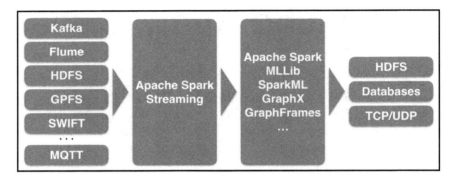

These feed into the Spark Streaming module and are processed as Discrete Streams. The diagram also shows that other Spark module functionality, such as machine learning, can be used to process stream-based data.

The fully processed data can then be an output for HDFS, databases, or dashboards. This diagram is based on the one at the Spark streaming website, but we wanted to extend it to express the Spark module functionality:

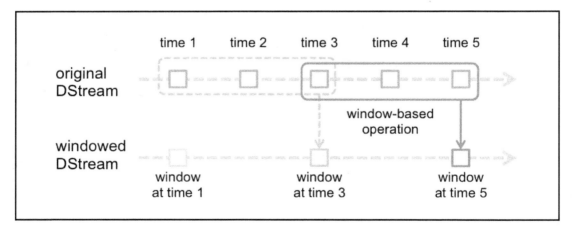

When discussing Spark Discrete Streams, the previous figure, taken from the Spark website at http://spark.apache.org/, is the diagram that we would like to use.

The green boxes in the previous figure show the continuous data stream sent to Spark being broken down into a **Discrete Stream (DStream)**.

 A DStream is nothing other than an ordered set of RDDs. Therefore, Apache Spark Streaming is not real streaming, but micro-batching. The size of the RDDs backing the DStream determines the batch size. This way DStreams can make use of all the functionality provided by RDDs including fault tolerance and the capability of being spillable to disk. The size of each element in the stream is then based on a batch time, which might be two seconds.

It is also possible, to create a window, expressed as the previous red box, over the DStream. For instance, when carrying out trend analysis in real time, it might be necessary to determine the top ten Twitter-based hashtags over a ten-minute window.

So, given that Spark can be used for stream processing, how is a stream created? The following Scala-based code shows how a Twitter stream can be created. This example is simplified because Twitter authorization has not been included, but you get the idea. (The full example code is in the *Checkpointing* section.)

The **Spark Stream Context (SSC)** is created using the Spark Context, sc. A **batch time** is specified when it is created; in this case, 5 seconds. A Twitter-based DStream, called stream, is then created from Streamingcontext using a window of 60 seconds:

```
val ssc    = new StreamingContext(sc, Seconds(5) )
val stream = TwitterUtils.createStream(ssc,None).window( Seconds(60) )
```

Stream processing can be started with the stream context start method (shown next), and the awaitTermination method indicates that it should process until stopped. So, if this code is embedded in a library-based application, it will run until the session is terminated, perhaps with *Crtl + C*:

```
ssc.start()
ssc.awaitTermination()
```

This explains what Spark Streaming is and what it does, but it does not explain error handling or what to do if your stream-based application fails. The next section will examine Spark Streaming error management and recovery.

Errors and recovery

Generally, the question that needs to be asked for your application is: is it critical that you receive and process all the data? If not, then on failure, you might just be able to restart the application and discard the missing or lost data. If this is not the case, then you will need to use checkpointing, which will be described in the next section.

It is also worth noting that your application's error management should be robust and self-sufficient. What we mean by this is that if an exception is non-critical, then manage the exception, perhaps log it, and continue processing. For instance, when a task reaches the maximum number of failures (specified by `spark.task.maxFailures`), it will terminate processing.

 This property, among others, can be set during creation of the `SparkContext` object or as additional command line parameters when invoking `spark-shell` or `spark-submit`.

Checkpointing

On batch processing, we are used to having fault tolerance. This means, in case a node crashed, the job doesn't lose its state and the lost tasks are rescheduled on other workers. Intermediate results are written to persistent storage (which of course has to be fault tolerant as well which is the case for HDFS, GPFS or Cloud Object Storage). Now we want to achieve the same guarantees in streaming as well since it might be crucial that the data stream we are processing is not lost.

It is possible to set up an HDFS-based checkpoint directory to store Apache Spark-based streaming information. In this Scala example, data will be stored in HDFS under `/data/spark/checkpoint`. The following HDFS filesystem `ls` command shows that before starting, the directory does not exist:

```
[hadoop@hc2nn stream]$ hdfs dfs -ls /data/spark/checkpoint
ls: `/data/spark/checkpoint': No such file or directory
```

For replicating the following example, Twitter API credentials are used in order to connect to the Twitter API and obtain a stream of tweets. The following link explains how such credentials are created within the Twitter UI: https://dev.twitter.com/oauth/overview/application-owner-access-tokens.

The following Scala code sample starts by importing Spark Streaming Context and Twitter-based functionality. It then defines an application object named `stream1`:

```
import org.apache.spark._
import org.apache.spark.SparkContext._
import org.apache.spark.streaming._
import org.apache.spark.streaming.twitter._
import org.apache.spark.streaming.StreamingContext._

object stream1 {
```

Next, a method is defined called `createContext`, which will be used to create both the Spark and Streaming contexts. It will also checkpoint the stream to the HDFS-based directory using the streaming context checkpoint method, which takes a directory path as a parameter. The directory path the value (`cpDir`) that was passed to the `createContext` method:

```
def createContext( cpDir : String ) : StreamingContext = {
  val appName = "Stream example 1"
  val conf    = new SparkConf()
  conf.setAppName(appName)
  val sc = new SparkContext(conf)
  val ssc    = new StreamingContext(sc, Seconds(5) )
  ssc.checkpoint( cpDir )
  ssc
}
```

Now, the main method is defined as is the HDFS directory, as well as Twitter access authority and parameters. The Spark Streaming context `ssc` is either retrieved or created using the HDFS checkpoint directory via the `StreamingContext` method--`checkpoint`. If the directory doesn't exist, then the previous method called `createContext` is called, which will create the context and `checkpoint`. Obviously, we have truncated our own Twitter `auth.keys` in this example for security reasons:

```
def main(args: Array[String]) {
  val hdfsDir = "/data/spark/checkpoint"
  val consumerKey       = "QQpxx"
  val consumerSecret    = "0HFzxx"
  val accessToken       = "323xx"
  val accessTokenSecret = "IlQxx"

  System.setProperty("twitter4j.oauth.consumerKey", consumerKey)
  System.setProperty("twitter4j.oauth.consumerSecret", consumerSecret)
  System.setProperty("twitter4j.oauth.accessToken", accessToken)
  System.setProperty("twitter4j.oauth.accessTokenSecret",
accessTokenSecret)
```

```
    val ssc = StreamingContext.getOrCreate(hdfsDir,
        () => { createContext( hdfsDir ) })
    val stream = TwitterUtils.createStream(ssc,None).window( Seconds(60) )
    // do some processing
    ssc.start()
    ssc.awaitTermination()
} // end main
```

Having run this code, which has no actual processing, the HDFS `checkpoint` directory can be checked again. This time, it is apparent that the `checkpoint` directory has been created and the data has been stored:

```
[hadoop@hc2nn stream]$ hdfs dfs -ls /data/spark/checkpoint
Found 1 items
drwxr-xr-x   - hadoop supergroup          0 2015-07-02 13:41
/data/spark/checkpoint/0fc3d94e-6f53-40fb-910d-1eef044b12e9
```

This example, taken from the Apache Spark website, shows you how checkpoint storage can be set up and used. How often is checkpointing carried out? The metadata is stored during each stream batch. The actual data is stored within a period, which is the maximum of the batch interval, or ten seconds. This might not be ideal for you, so you can reset the value using the following method:

```
DStream.checkpoint( newRequiredInterval )
```

Here, `newRequiredInterval` is the new checkpoint interval value that you require; generally, you should aim for a value that is five to ten times your batch interval. Checkpointing saves both the stream batch and metadata (data about the data).

If the application fails, then, when it restarts, the checkpointed data is used when processing is started. The batch data that was being processed at the time of failure is reprocessed along with the batched data since the failure. Remember to monitor the HDFS disk space being used for the checkpointing.

In the next section, we will examine the streaming sources and provide some examples of each type.

Streaming sources

We will not be able to cover all the stream types with practical examples in this section, but where this chapter is too small to include code, we will at least provide a description. In this chapter, we will cover the TCP and file streams and the Flume, Kafka, and Twitter streams. Apache Spark tends only to support this limited set out of the box, but this is not a problem since 3rd party developers provide connectors to other sources as well. We will start with a practical TCP-based example. This chapter examines stream processing architecture.

> For instance, what happens in cases where the stream data delivery rate exceeds the potential data processing rate? Systems such as Kafka provide the possibility of solving this issue by caching data until it is requested with the additional ability to use multiple data topics and consumers (publish-subscribe model).

TCP stream

There is a possibility of using the Spark Streaming Context method called `socketTextStream` to stream data via TCP/IP, by specifying a hostname and port number. The Scala-based code example in this section will receive data on port `10777` that was supplied using the `netcat` Linux command.

> The `netcat` command is a Linux/Unix command which allows you to send and receive data to or from local or remote IP destinations using TCP or UDP. This way every shell script can play the role of a full network client or server. The following is a good tutorial on how to use `netcat`:
> http://www.binarytides.com/netcat-tutorial-for-beginners/.

The code sample starts by importing Spark, the context, and the streaming classes. The object class named `stream2` is defined as it is the main method with arguments:

```
import org.apache.spark._
import org.apache.spark.SparkContext._
import org.apache.spark.streaming._
import org.apache.spark.streaming.StreamingContext._

object stream2 {
  def main(args: Array[String]) {
```

The number of arguments passed to the class is checked to ensure that it is the hostname and port number. A Spark configuration object is created with an application name defined. The Spark and streaming contexts are then created. Then, a streaming batch time of 10 seconds is set:

```
if ( args.length < 2 ) {
  System.err.println("Usage: stream2 <host> <port>")
  System.exit(1)
}

val hostname = args(0).trim
val portnum  = args(1).toInt
val appName  = "Stream example 2"
val conf     = new SparkConf()
conf.setAppName(appName)
val sc  = new SparkContext(conf)
val ssc = new StreamingContext(sc, Seconds(10) )
```

A DStream called `rawDstream` is created by calling the `socketTextStream` method of the streaming context using the `hostname` and port name parameters:

```
val rawDstream = ssc.socketTextStream( hostname, portnum )
```

A top-ten word count is created from the raw stream data by splitting words with spacing. Then, a (key, value) pair is created as (word,1), which is reduced by the key value, this being the word. So now, there is a list of words and their associated counts. The key and value are swapped so the list becomes (count and word). Then, a sort is done on the key, which is now the count. Finally, the top 10 items in the RDD within the DStream are taken and printed out:

```
val wordCount = rawDstream
  .flatMap(line => line.split(" "))
  .map(word => (word,1))
  .reduceByKey(_+_)
  .map(item => item.swap)
  .transform(rdd => rdd.sortByKey(false))
  .foreachRDD( rdd =>
    { rdd.take(10).foreach(x=>println("List : " + x)) }
  )
```

The code closes with the Spark Streaming `start` and `awaitTermination` methods being called to start the stream processing and await process termination:

```
    ssc.start()
      ssc.awaitTermination()
  } // end main
} // end stream2
```

The data for this application is provided, as we stated previously, by the Linux Netcat (`nc`) command. The Linux `cat` command dumps the contents of a log file, which is piped to `nc`. The `lk` options force Netcat to listen for connections and keep on listening if the connection is lost. This example shows that the port being used is `10777`:

```
[root@hc2nn log]# pwd
/var/log
[root@hc2nn log]# cat ./anaconda.storage.log | nc -lk 10777
```

The output from this TCP-based stream processing is shown here. The actual output is not as important as the method demonstrated. However, the data shows, as expected, a list of 10 log file words in descending count order. Note that the top word is empty because the stream was not filtered for empty words:

```
List : (17104,)
List : (2333,=)
List : (1656,:)
List : (1603,;)
List : (1557,DEBUG)
List : (564,True)
List : (495,False)
List : (411,None)
List : (356,at)
List : (335,object)
```

This is interesting if you want to stream data using Apache Spark Streaming based on TCP/IP from a host and port. However, what about more exotic methods? What if you wish to stream data from a messaging system or via memory-based channels? What if you want to use some of the big data tools available today such as Flume and Kafka? The next sections will examine these options, but, first, we will demonstrate how streams can be based on files.

File streams

We have modified the Scala-based code example in the last section to monitor an HDFS-based directory by calling the Spark Streaming Context method called `textFileStream`. We will not display all of the code, given this small change. The application class is now called `stream3`, which takes a single parameter--the HDFS directory. The directory path could be on another storage system as well (all the code samples will be available with this book):

```
val rawDstream = ssc.textFileStream( directory )
```

The stream processing is the same as before. The stream is split into words and the top-ten word list is printed. The only difference this time is that the data must be put in the HDFS directory while the application is running. This is achieved with the HDFS filesystem put command here:

```
[root@hc2nn log]# hdfs dfs -put ./anaconda.storage.log /data/spark/stream
```

As you can see, the HDFS directory used is /data/spark/stream/, and the text-based source log file is anaconda.storage.log (under /var/log/). As expected, the same word list and count is printed:

```
List : (17104,)
List : (2333,=)
...
List : (564,True)
List : (495,False)
List : (411,None)
List : (356,at)
List : (335,object)
```

These are simple streaming methods based on TCP and filesystem data. What if we want to use some of the built-in streaming functionality in Spark Streaming? This will be examined next. The Spark Streaming Flume library will be used as an example.

Flume

Flume is an Apache open source project and product, which is designed to move large amounts of data at a big data scale. It is highly scalable, distributed, and reliable, working on the basis of data source, data sink, and data channels, as shown in the following diagram taken from http://flume.apache.org/:

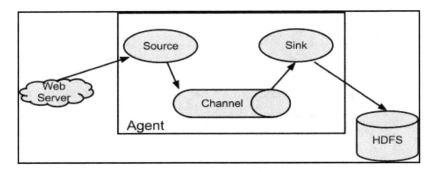

Flume uses agents to process data streams. As can be seen in the previous figure, an agent has a data source, data processing channel, and data sink. A clearer way to describe this flow is via the figure we just saw. The channel acts as a queue for the sourced data and the sink passes the data to the next link in the chain.

Flume agents can form Flume architectures; the output of one agent's sink can be the input to a second agent. Apache Spark allows two approaches to use Apache Flume. The first is an Avro push-based in-memory approach, whereas the second one, still based on Avro, is a pull-based system using a custom Spark sink library. We are using Flume version 1.5 for this example:

```
[root@hc2nn ~]# flume-ng version
Flume 1.5.0-cdh5.3.3
Source code repository: https://git-wip-us.apache.org/repos/asf/flume.git
Revision: b88ce1fd016bc873d817343779dfff6aeea07706
Compiled by jenkins on Wed Apr  8 14:57:43 PDT 2015
From source with checksum 389d91c718e03341a2367bf4ef12428e
```

The Flume-based Spark example that we will initially implement here is the Flume-based push approach, where Spark acts as a receiver and Flume pushes the data to Spark. The following figure represents the structure that we will implement on a single node:

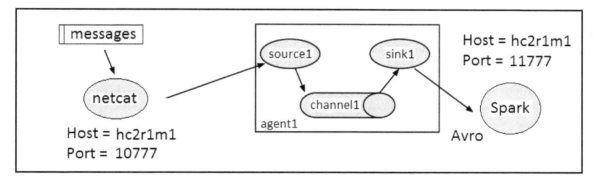

The message data will be sent to port `10777` on a host called `hc2r1m1` using the Linux `netcat` (`nc`) command. This will act as a source (`source1`) for the Flume agent (`agent1`), which will have an in-memory channel called `channel1`. The sink used by `agent1` will be Apache Avro-based, again on a host called `hc2r1m1`, but this time, the port number will be `11777`. The Apache Spark Flume application `stream4` (which we will describe shortly) will listen for Flume stream data on this port.

We start the streaming process by executing the `nc` command against the `10777` port. Now, when we type text in this window, it will be used as a Flume source and the data will be sent to the Spark application:

```
[hadoop@hc2nn ~]$ nc   hc2r1m1.semtech-solutions.co.nz   10777
```

In order to run the Flume agent, `agent1`, we have created a Flume configuration file called `agent1.flume.cfg`, which describes the agent's source, channel, and sink. The contents of the file are as follows. The first section defines the `agent1` source, channel, and sink names.

```
agent1.sources  = source1
agent1.channels = channel1
agent1.sinks    = sink1
```

The next section defines `source1` to be netcat-based, running on the host called `hc2r1m1` and the `10777` port:

```
agent1.sources.source1.channels=channel1
agent1.sources.source1.type=netcat
agent1.sources.source1.bind=hc2r1m1.semtech-solutions.co.nz
agent1.sources.source1.port=10777
```

The `agent1` channel, `channel1`, is defined as a memory-based channel with a maximum event capacity of `1000` events:

```
agent1.channels.channel1.type=memory
agent1.channels.channel1.capacity=1000
```

Finally, the `agent1` sink, `sink1`, is defined as an Apache Avro sink on the host called `hc2r1m1` and the `11777` port:

```
agent1.sinks.sink1.type=avro
agent1.sinks.sink1.hostname=hc2r1m1.semtech-solutions.co.nz
agent1.sinks.sink1.port=11777
agent1.sinks.sink1.channel=channel1
```

We have created a Bash script called `flume.bash` to run the Flume agent, `agent1`. It looks as follows:

```
[hadoop@hc2r1m1 stream]$ more flume.bash
#!/bin/bash
# run the bash agent
flume-ng agent \
    --conf /etc/flume-ng/conf \
    --conf-file ./agent1.flume.cfg \
    -Dflume.root.logger=DEBUG,INFO,console  \
    -name agent1
```

The script calls the Flume executable `flume-ng`, passing the `agent1` configuration file. The call specifies the agent named `agent1`. It also specifies the Flume configuration directory to be `/etc/flume-ng/conf/`, the default value. Initially, we will use a `netcat` Flume source with a Scala-based example to show how data can be sent to an Apache Spark application. Then, we will show how an RSS-based data feed can be processed in a similar way. So initially, the Scala code that will receive the `netcat` data looks like this. The application class name is defined. The necessary classes for Spark and Flume are imported. Finally, the main method is defined:

```
import org.apache.spark._
import org.apache.spark.SparkContext._
import org.apache.spark.streaming._
import org.apache.spark.streaming.StreamingContext._
import org.apache.spark.streaming.flume._

object stream4 {
  def main(args: Array[String]) {
  //The host and port name arguments for the data stream are checked and
extracted:
      if ( args.length < 2 ) {
        System.err.println("Usage: stream4 <host> <port>")
        System.exit(1)
      }
      val hostname = args(0).trim
      val portnum  = args(1).toInt
      println("hostname : " + hostname)
      println("portnum  : " + portnum)
```

The Spark and Streaming contexts are created. Then, the Flume-based data stream is created using the stream context host and port number. The Flume-based class, `FlumeUtils`, has been used to do this by calling its `createStream` method:

```
val appName = "Stream example 4"
val conf    = new SparkConf()
conf.setAppName(appName)
val sc  = new SparkContext(conf)
val ssc = new StreamingContext(sc, Seconds(10) )
val rawDstream = FlumeUtils.createStream(ssc,hostname,portnum)
```

Finally, a stream event count is printed and (for debugging purposes while we test the stream) the stream content is dumped. After this, the stream context is started and configured to run until terminated via the application:

```
rawDstream.count()
        .map(cnt => ">>>> Received events : " + cnt )
        .print()
```

```
        rawDstream.map(e => new String(e.event.getBody.array() ))
                  .print
        ssc.start()
        ssc.awaitTermination()
    } // end main
  } // end stream4
```

Having compiled it, we will run this application using `spark-submit`. In some of the other chapters of this book, we will use a Bash-based script called `run_stream.bash` to execute the job. The script looks as follows:

```
[hadoop@hc2r1m1 stream]$ more run_stream.bash
#!/bin/bash
SPARK_HOME=/usr/local/spark
SPARK_BIN=$SPARK_HOME/bin
SPARK_SBIN=$SPARK_HOME/sbin
JAR_PATH=/home/hadoop/spark/stream/target/scala-2.10/streaming_2.10-1.0.jar
CLASS_VAL=$1
CLASS_PARAMS="${*:2}"
STREAM_JAR=/usr/local/spark/lib/spark-examples-1.3.1-hadoop2.3.0.jar
cd $SPARK_BIN
./spark-submit \
    --class $CLASS_VAL \
    --master spark://hc2nn.semtech-solutions.co.nz:7077  \
    --executor-memory 100M \
    --total-executor-cores 50 \
    --jars $STREAM_JAR \
    $JAR_PATH \
    $CLASS_PARAMS
```

So, this script sets some Spark-based variables and a JAR library path for this job. It takes the Spark class to run as its first parameter. It passes all the other variables as parameters to the Spark application class job. So, the execution of the application looks as follows:

```
[hadoop@hc2r1m1 stream]$ ./run_stream.bash stream4 hc2r1m1 11777
```

This means that the Spark application is ready and is running as a Flume sink on port `11777`. The Flume input is ready, running as a `netcat` task on port `10777`. Now, the Flume agent, `agent1`, can be started using the Flume script called `flume.bash` to send the `netcat` source-based data to the Apache Spark Flume-based sink:

```
[hadoop@hc2r1m1 stream]$ ./flume.bash
```

Now, when the text is passed to the `netcat` session, it should flow through Flume and be processed as a stream by Spark. Let's try it:

```
[hadoop@hc2nn ~]$ nc  hc2r1m1.semtech-solutions.co.nz 10777
```

```
I hope that Apache Spark will print this
OK
I hope that Apache Spark will print this
OK
I hope that Apache Spark will print this
OK
```

Three simple pieces of text have been added to the netcat session and acknowledged with an OK so that they can be passed to Flume. The debug output in the Flume session shows that the events (one per line) have been received and processed:

```
2015-07-06 18:13:18,699 (netcat-handler-0) [DEBUG -
org.apache.flume.source.NetcatSource$NetcatSocketHandler.run(NetcatSource.j
ava:318)] Chars read = 41
  2015-07-06 18:13:18,700 (netcat-handler-0) [DEBUG -
org.apache.flume.source.NetcatSource$NetcatSocketHandler.run(NetcatSource.j
ava:322)] Events processed = 1
  2015-07-06 18:13:18,990 (netcat-handler-0) [DEBUG -
org.apache.flume.source.NetcatSource$NetcatSocketHandler.run(NetcatSource.j
ava:318)] Chars read = 41
  2015-07-06 18:13:18,991 (netcat-handler-0) [DEBUG -
org.apache.flume.source.NetcatSource$NetcatSocketHandler.run(NetcatSource.j
ava:322)] Events processed = 1
  2015-07-06 18:13:19,270 (netcat-handler-0) [DEBUG -
org.apache.flume.source.NetcatSource$NetcatSocketHandler.run(NetcatSource.j
ava:318)] Chars read = 41
  2015-07-06 18:13:19,271 (netcat-handler-0) [DEBUG -
org.apache.flume.source.NetcatSource$NetcatSocketHandler.run(NetcatSource.j
ava:322)] Events processed = 1
```

Finally, in the Spark stream4 application session, three events have been received and processed; in this case, they have been dumped to the session to prove the point that the data arrived. Of course, this is not what you would normally do, but we wanted to prove data transit through this configuration:

```
-------------------------------------------------
Time: 1436163210000 ms
-------------------------------------------------
>>> Received events : 3
-------------------------------------------------
Time: 1436163210000 ms
-------------------------------------------------
I hope that Apache Spark will print this
I hope that Apache Spark will print this
I hope that Apache Spark will print this
```

This is interesting, but it is not really a production-worthy example of Spark Flume data processing. So, in order to demonstrate a potentially real data processing approach, we will change the Flume configuration file source details so that it uses a Perl script, which is executable as follows:

```
agent1.sources.source1.type=exec
agent1.sources.source.command=./rss.perl
```

The Perl script, which has been referenced previously, `rss.perl`, just acts as a source of Reuters science news. It receives the news as XML and converts it into JSON format. It also cleans the data of unwanted noise. First, it imports packages such as LWP and `XML::XPath` to enable XML processing. Then, it specifies a science-based Reuters news data source and creates a new LWP agent to process the data, similar to the following:

```perl
#!/usr/bin/perl
use strict;
use LWP::UserAgent;
use XML::XPath;
my $urlsource="http://feeds.reuters.com/reuters/scienceNews" ;
my  $agent = LWP::UserAgent->new;
#Then an infinite while loop is opened, and an HTTP GET request is carried
out against  the URL. The request is configured, and the agent makes the
request via a call to the  request method:
while()
{
  my  $req = HTTP::Request->new(GET => ($urlsource));
  $req->header('content-type' => 'application/json');
  $req->header('Accept'       => 'application/json');
  my $resp = $agent->request($req);
```

If the request is successful, then the XML data returned is defined as the decoded content of the request. Title information is extracted from the XML via an XPath call using the path called `/rss/channel/item/title`:

```perl
  if ( $resp->is_success )
  {
    my $xmlpage = $resp -> decoded_content;
    my $xp = XML::XPath->new( xml => $xmlpage );
    my $nodeset = $xp->find( '/rss/channel/item/title' );
    my @titles = () ;
    my $index = 0 ;
```

For each node in the extracted title data XML string, data is extracted. It is cleaned of unwanted XML tags and added to a Perl-based array called titles:

```perl
    foreach my $node ($nodeset->get_nodelist) {
      my $xmlstring = XML::XPath::XMLParser::as_string($node) ;
```

```perl
        $xmlstring =~ s/<title>//g;
        $xmlstring =~ s/<\/title>//g;
        $xmlstring =~ s/"//g;
        $xmlstring =~ s/,//g;
        $titles[$index] = $xmlstring ;
        $index = $index + 1 ;
    } # foreach find node
```

The same process is carried out for description-based data in the request response XML. The XPath value used this time is `/rss/channel/item/description/`. There are many more tags to be cleaned from the description data, so there are many more Perl searches and line replacements that act on this data (`s///g`):

```perl
    my $nodeset = $xp->find( '/rss/channel/item/description' );
    my @desc = () ;
    $index = 0 ;
    foreach my $node ($nodeset->get_nodelist) {
        my $xmlstring = XML::XPath::XMLParser::as_string($node) ;
        $xmlstring =~ s/<img.+\/img>//g;
        $xmlstring =~ s/href=".+"//g;
        $xmlstring =~ s/src=".+"//g;
        $xmlstring =~ s/src='.+'//g;
        $xmlstring =~ s/<br.+\/>//g;
        $xmlstring =~ s/<\/div>//g;
        $xmlstring =~ s/<\/a>//g;
        $xmlstring =~ s/<a >\n//g;
        $xmlstring =~ s/<img >//g;
        $xmlstring =~ s/<img \/>//g;
        $xmlstring =~ s/<div.+>//g;
        $xmlstring =~ s/<title>//g;
        $xmlstring =~ s/<\/title>//g;
        $xmlstring =~ s/<description>//g;
        $xmlstring =~ s/<\/description>//g;
        $xmlstring =~ s/&lt;.+>//g;
        $xmlstring =~ s/"//g;
        $xmlstring =~ s/,//g;
        $xmlstring =~ s/\r|\n//g;
        $desc[$index] = $xmlstring ;
        $index = $index + 1 ;
    } # foreach find node
```

Finally, the XML-based title and description data is output in the RSS JSON format using a `print` command. The script then sleeps for 30 seconds and requests more RSS news information to process:

```perl
    my $newsitems = $index ;
    $index = 0 ;
```

```
  for ($index=0; $index < $newsitems; $index++) {
    print "{"category": "science","
              . " "title": "" . $titles[$index] . "","
              . " "summary": "" . $desc[$index] . """
              . "}\n";
    } # for rss items
  } # success ?
  sleep(30) ;
} # while
```

We have created a second Scala-based stream processing code example called `stream5`. It is similar to the `stream4` example, but it now processes the `rss` item data from the stream. Next, `case class` is defined to process the category, title, and summary from the XML RSS information. An HTML location is defined to store the resulting data that comes from the Flume channel:

```
case class RSSItem(category : String, title : String, summary : String) {
  val now: Long = System.currentTimeMillis
  val hdfsdir = "hdfs://hc2nn:8020/data/spark/flume/rss/"
```

The RSS stream data from the Flume-based event is converted to a string. It is then formatted using the case class called `RSSItem`. If there is event data, it is then written to an HDFS directory using the previous `hdfsdir` path:

```
          rawDstream.map(record => {
          implicit val formats = DefaultFormats
          read[RSSItem](new String(record.event.getBody().array()))
       }).foreachRDD(rdd => {
              if (rdd.count() > 0) {
                rdd.map(item => {
                  implicit val formats = DefaultFormats
                  write(item)
                }).saveAsTextFile(hdfsdir+"file_"+now.toString())
              }
       })
```

Running this code sample, it is possible to see that the Perl RSS script is producing data, because the Flume script output indicates that 80 events have been accepted and received:

```
2015-07-07 14:14:24,017 (agent-shutdown-hook) [DEBUG -
org.apache.flume.source.ExecSource.stop(ExecSource.java:219)] Exec source
with command:./news_rss_collector.py stopped.
Metrics:SOURCE:source1{src.events.accepted=80, src.events.received=80,
src.append.accepted=0, src.append-batch.accepted=0, src.open-
connection.count=0, src.append-batch.received=0, src.append.received=0}
The Scala Spark application stream5 has processed 80 events in two batches:
>>>> Received events : 73
```

```
>>>> Received events : 7
```

The events have been stored on HDFS under the expected directory, as the Hadoop filesystem `ls` command shows here:

```
[hadoop@hc2r1m1 stream]$ hdfs dfs -ls /data/spark/flume/rss/
 Found 2 items
 drwxr-xr-x   - hadoop supergroup          0 2015-07-07 14:09
/data/spark/flume/rss/file_1436234439794
 drwxr-xr-x   - hadoop supergroup          0 2015-07-07 14:14
/data/spark/flume/rss/file_1436235208370
```

Also, using the Hadoop filesystem `cat` command, it is possible to prove that the files on HDFS contain `rss` feed news-based data, as shown here:

```
[hadoop@hc2r1m1 stream]$  hdfs dfs -cat
/data/spark/flume/rss/file_1436235208370/part-00000 | head -1
{"category":"healthcare","title":"BRIEF-Aetna CEO says has not had specific
conversations with DOJ on Humana - CNBC","summary":"* Aetna CEO Says Has
Not Had Specific Conversations With Doj About Humana Acquisition - CNBC"}
```

This Spark stream-based example has used Apache Flume to transmit data from an `rss` source, through Flume, to HDFS via a Spark consumer. This is a good example, but what if you want to publish data to a group of consumers? In the next section, we will examine Apache Kafka--a publish/subscribe messaging system--and determine how it can be used with Spark.

Kafka

Apache Kafka (http://kafka.apache.org/) is a top-level open source project in Apache. It is a big data publish/subscribe messaging system that is fast and highly scalable. It uses message brokers for data management and ZooKeeper for configuration so that data can be organized into consumer groups and topics.

Data in Kafka is split into partitions. In this example, we will demonstrate a receiverless Spark-based Kafka consumer so that we don't need to worry about configuring Spark data partitions when compared to our Kafka data. In order to demonstrate Kafka-based message production and consumption, we will use the Perl RSS script from the last section as a data source. The data passing into Kafka and to Spark will be Reuters RSS news data in the JSON format. As topic messages are created by message producers, they are placed in partitions in message order sequence. The messages in the partitions are retained for a configurable time period. Kafka then stores the offset value for each consumer, which is that consumer's position (in terms of message consumption) in that partition.

We are currently using Kafka 0.10.1.0. We have used Kafka message brokers on the Hortonworks HDP 2.6 Sandbox virtual machine. We then set the Kafka broker ID values for each Kafka broker server, giving them a `broker.id` number of 1 through 4. As Kafka uses ZooKeeper for cluster data configuration, we wanted to keep all the Kafka data in a top-level node called kafka in ZooKeeper. In order to do this, we set the Kafka ZooKeeper root value, called `zookeeper.chroot`, to `/kafka`. After making these changes, we restarted the Kafka servers for the changes to take effect.

With Kafka installed, we can check the scripts available to test. The following list shows Kafka-based scripts for message producers and consumers as well as scripts to manage topics and check consumer offsets. These scripts will be used in this section in order to demonstrate Kafka functionality:

```
[hadoop@hc2nn ~]$ ls /usr/bin/kafka*
/usr/bin/kafka-console-consumer        /usr/bin/kafka-run-class
/usr/bin/kafka-console-producer        /usr/bin/kafka-topics
/usr/bin/kafka-consumer-offset-checker
```

In order to run the installed Kafka servers, we need to have the broker server ID's (`broker.id`) values set; otherwise, an error will occur. Once Kafka is running, we will need to prepare a message producer script. The simple Bash script given next, called `kafka.bash`, defines a comma-separated broker list of hosts and ports. It also defines a topic called `rss`. It then calls the Perl script `rss.perl` to generate the RSS-based data. This data is then piped into the Kafka producer script called kafka-console-producer to be sent to Kafka.

```
[hadoop@hc2r1m1 stream]$ more kafka.bash
#!/bin/bash
#BROKER_LIST="hc2r1m1:9092,hc2r1m2:9092,hc2r1m3:9092,hc2r1m4:9092"
BROKER_LIST="hc2r1m1:9092"
TOPIC="rss"
./rss.perl | /usr/bin/kafka-console-producer --broker-list $BROKER_LIST --
topic $TOPIC
```

Notice that we are only running against a single broker, but a link on how to use multiple brokers has been provided as well. Also, notice that we have not mentioned Kafka topics at this point. When a topic is created in Kafka, the number of partitions can be specified. In the following example, the kafka-topics script has been called with the create option. The number of partitions has been set to 5, and the data replication factor has been set to 3. The ZooKeeper server string has been defined as `hc2r1m2-4` with a port number of `2181`. Also, note that the top level ZooKeeper Kafka node has been defined as `/kafka` in the ZooKeeper string:

```
/usr/bin/kafka-topics \
```

```
--create  \
--zookeeper hc2r1m1:2181:2181/kafka \
--replication-factor 3  \
--partitions 5  \
--topic rss
```

We have also created a Bash script called `kafka_list.bash` for use during testing, which checks all the Kafka topics that have been created, and also the Kafka consumer offsets. It calls the Kafka-topics commands with a list option, and a ZooKeeper string to get a list of created topics. It then calls the Kafka script called Kafka-consumer-offset-checker with a ZooKeeper string--the topic name and a group name to get a list of consumer offset values. Using this script, we can check that our topics are created, and the topic data is being consumed correctly:

```
[hadoop@hc2r1m1 stream]$ cat kafka_list.bash
#!/bin/bash
ZOOKEEPER="hc2r1m1:2181:2181/kafka"
TOPIC="rss"
GROUP="group1"
echo ""
echo "==============================="
echo " Kafka Topics "
echo "==============================="
/usr/bin/kafka-topics --list --zookeeper $ZOOKEEPER
echo ""
echo "==============================="
echo " Kafka Offsets "
echo "==============================="
/usr/bin/kafka-consumer-offset-checker \
    --group $GROUP \
    --topic $TOPIC \
    --zookeeper $ZOOKEEPER
```

Next, we need to create the Apache Spark Scala-based Kafka consumer code. As we said, we will create a receiver-less example, so that the Kafka data partitions match in both, Kafka and Spark. The example is called `stream6`. First, the classes are imported for Kafka, spark, context, and streaming. Then, the object class called `stream6`, and the main method are defined. The code looks like this:

```
import kafka.serializer.StringDecoder
import org.apache.spark._
import org.apache.spark.SparkContext._
import org.apache.spark.streaming._
import org.apache.spark.streaming.StreamingContext._
import org.apache.spark.streaming.kafka._

object stream6 {
```

```
def main(args: Array[String]) {
```

Next, the class parameters (broker's string, group ID, and topic) are checked and processed. If the class parameters are incorrect, then an error is printed, and execution stops, else the parameter variables are defined:

```
if ( args.length < 3 ) {
    System.err.println("Usage: stream6 <brokers> <groupid> <topics>\n")
    System.err.println("<brokers> = host1:port1,host2:port2\n")
    System.err.println("<groupid> = group1\n")
    System.err.println("<topics>  = topic1,topic2\n")
    System.exit(1)
}
val brokers = args(0).trim
val groupid = args(1).trim
val topics  = args(2).trim
println("brokers : " + brokers)
println("groupid : " + groupid)
println("topics  : " + topics)
```

The Spark context is defined in terms of an application name. The Spark URL has again been left as the default. The streaming context has been created using the Spark context. We have left the stream batch interval at 10 seconds, which is the same as the last example. However, you can set it using a parameter of your choice:

```
val appName = "Stream example 6"
val conf    = new SparkConf()
conf.setAppName(appName)
val sc  = new SparkContext(conf)
val ssc = new StreamingContext(sc, Seconds(10) )
```

Next, the broker list and group ID are set up as parameters. These values are then used to create a Kafka-based Spark Stream called `rawDstream`:

```
val topicsSet = topics.split(",").toSet
val kafkaParams : Map[String, String] =
  Map("metadata.broker.list" -> brokers,
    "group.id" -> groupid )
val rawDstream = KafkaUtils.createDirectStream[
  String,
  String,
  StringDecoder,
  StringDecoder](ssc, kafkaParams, topicsSet)
```

We have again printed the stream event count for debugging purposes so that we know when the application is receiving and processing the data:

```
rawDstream.count().map(cnt => ">>>>>>>>>>>>>>>> Received events : " + cnt
).print()
```

The HDFS location for the Kafka data has been defined as /data/spark/kafka/rss/. It has been mapped from the DStream into the variable lines. Using the foreachRDD method, a check on the data count is carried out on the lines variable before saving the data in HDFS using the saveAsTextFile method:

```
val now: Long = System.currentTimeMillis
val hdfsdir = "hdfs://hc2nn:8020/data/spark/kafka/rss/"
val lines = rawDstream.map(record => record._2)
lines.foreachRDD(rdd => {
        if (rdd.count() > 0) {
            rdd.saveAsTextFile(hdfsdir+"file_"+now.toString())
        }
    })
```

Finally, the Scala script closes by starting the stream processing and setting the application class to run until terminated with awaitTermination:

```
    ssc.start()
    ssc.awaitTermination()
  } // end main
} // end stream6
```

With all of the scripts explained and the Kafka brokers running, it is time to examine the Kafka configuration, which, if you remember, is maintained by Apache ZooKeeper. (All of the code samples that have been described so far will be released with the book.) We will use the zookeeper-client tool and connect to the ZooKeeper server on the host called hc2r1m2 on the 2181 port. As you can see here, we have received a connected message from the client session:

```
[hadoop@hc2r1m1 stream]$ /usr/bin/zookeeper-client -server hc2r1m2:2181
[zk: hc2r1m2:2181(CONNECTED) 0]
```

If you remember, we specified the top-level ZooKeeper directory for Kafka to be /kafka. If we examine this now via a client session, we can see the Kafka ZooKeeper structure. We will be interested in brokers (the Kafka broker servers) and consumers (the previous Spark Scala code). The ZooKeeper ls command shows that the four Kafka servers are registered with ZooKeeper and are listed by their broker.id configuration values, one to four:

```
[zk: hc2r1m2:2181(CONNECTED) 2] ls /kafka
  [consumers, config, controller, admin, brokers, controller_epoch]
[zk: hc2r1m2:2181(CONNECTED) 3] ls /kafka/brokers
  [topics, ids]
[zk: hc2r1m2:2181(CONNECTED) 4] ls /kafka/brokers/ids
```

```
[3, 2, 1, 4]
```

We will create the topic that we want to use for this test using the Kafka script, `kafka-topics`, with a `create` flag. We do this manually because we want to demonstrate the definition of the data partitions while we do it. Note that we have set the partitions in the Kafka topic `rss` to 5, as shown in the following piece of code. Note also that the ZooKeeper connection string for the command has a comma-separated list of ZooKeeper servers, terminated by the top-level ZooKeeper Kafka directory called `/kafka`. This means that the command puts the new topic in the proper place:

```
[hadoop@hc2nn ~]$ /usr/bin/kafka-topics \
>    --create  \
>    --zookeeper hc2r1m2:2181,hc2r1m3:2181,hc2r1m4:2181/kafka \
>    --replication-factor 3  \
>    --partitions 5  \
>    --topic rss
Created topic "rss".
```

Now, when we use the ZooKeeper client to check the Kafka topic configuration, we can see the correct topic name and the expected number of the partitions:

```
[zk: hc2r1m2:2181(CONNECTED) 5] ls /kafka/brokers/topics
[rss]
[zk: hc2r1m2:2181(CONNECTED) 6] ls /kafka/brokers/topics/rss
[partitions]
[zk: hc2r1m2:2181(CONNECTED) 7] ls /kafka/brokers/topics/rss/partitions
[3, 2, 1, 0, 4]
```

This describes the configuration for the Kafka broker servers in ZooKeeper, but what about the data consumers? Well, the following list shows where the data will be held. Remember that, at this time, there is no consumer running, so it is not represented in ZooKeeper:

```
[zk: hc2r1m2:2181(CONNECTED) 9]  ls /kafka/consumers
[]
[zk: hc2r1m2:2181(CONNECTED) 10] quit
```

In order to start this test, we will run our Kafka data producer and consumer scripts. We will also check the output of the Spark application class and check the Kafka partition offsets and HDFS to make sure that the data has arrived. This is quite complicated, so we will add a diagram here to explain the test architecture:

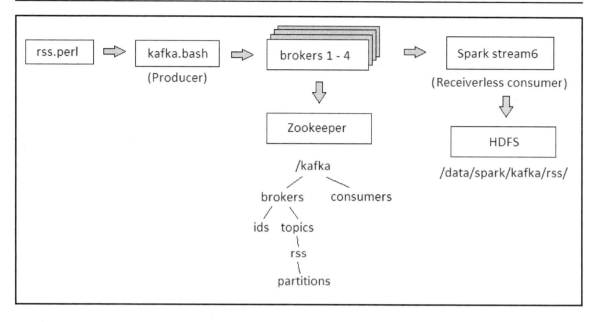

The Perl script called `rss.perl` will be used to provide a data source for a Kafka data producer, which will feed data to the Hortonworks Kafka broker servers. The data will be stored in ZooKeeper, in the structure that has just been examined, under the top-level node called `/kafka`. The Apache Spark Scala-based application will then act as a Kafka consumer and read the data that it will store under HDFS.

In order to try and explain the complexity here, we will examine our method of running the Apache Spark class. It will be started via the `spark-submit` command. Remember that all of these scripts will be released with this book, so you can examine them in your own time. We always use scripts for server test management so that we encapsulate complexity, and command execution is quickly repeatable. The script, `run_stream.bash`, is like many example scripts that have already been used in this chapter and in this book. It accepts a class name and class parameters, and runs the class via `spark-submit`:

```
[hadoop@hc2r1m1 stream]$ more run_stream.bash
#!/bin/bash
SPARK_HOME=/usr/local/spark
SPARK_BIN=$SPARK_HOME/bin
SPARK_SBIN=$SPARK_HOME/sbin
JAR_PATH=/home/hadoop/spark/stream/target/scala-2.10/streaming_2.10-1.0.jar
CLASS_VAL=$1
CLASS_PARAMS="${*:2}"
STREAM_JAR=/usr/local/spark/lib/spark-examples-1.3.1-hadoop2.3.0.jar
cd $SPARK_BIN
```

```
./spark-submit \
  --class $CLASS_VAL \
  --master spark://hc2nn.semtech-solutions.co.nz:7077  \
  --executor-memory 100M \
  --total-executor-cores 50 \
  --jars $STREAM_JAR \
  $JAR_PATH \
  $CLASS_PARAMS
```

We then used a second script, which calls the run_kafka_example.bash script to execute the Kafka consumer code in the previous stream6 application class. Note that this script sets up the full application class name--the broker server list. It also sets up the topic name, called RSS, to use for data consumption. Finally, it defines a consumer group called group1. Remember that Kafka is a publish/subscribe message brokering system. There may be many producers and consumers organized by topic, group, and partition:

```
[hadoop@hc2r1m1 stream]$ more run_kafka_example.bash
#!/bin/bash
RUN_CLASS=nz.co.semtechsolutions.stream6
BROKERS="hc2r1m1:9092,hc2r1m2:9092,hc2r1m3:9092,hc2r1m4:9092"
GROUPID=group1
TOPICS=rss
# run the Apache Spark Kafka example
./run_stream.bash $RUN_CLASS \
                  $BROKERS \
                  $GROUPID \
                  $TOPICS
```

So, we will start the Kafka consumer by running the run_kafka_example.bash script, which, in turn, will run the previous stream6 Scala code using spark-submit. While monitoring Kafka data consumption using the script called kafka_list.bash, we were able to get the kafka-consumer-offset-checker script to list the Kafka-based topics, but for some reason, it will not check the correct path (under /kafka in ZooKeeper) when checking the offsets, as shown here:

```
[hadoop@hc2r1m1 stream]$ ./kafka_list.bash
===============================
  Kafka Topics
===============================
  __consumer_offsets
  rss
===============================
  Kafka Offsets
===============================
Exiting due to: org.apache.zookeeper.KeeperException$NoNodeException:
KeeperErrorCode = NoNode for /consumers/group1/offsets/rss/4.
```

By starting the Kafka producer `rss` feed using the `kafka.bash` script, we can now start feeding the RSS-based data through Kafka into Spark, and then into HDFS. Periodically checking the `spark-submit` session output, it can be seen that events are passing through the Spark-based Kafka DStream. The following output comes from the stream count in the Scala code and shows that, at that point, 28 events were processed:

```
-----------------------------------------------
Time: 1436834440000 ms
-----------------------------------------------
>>>>>>>>>>>>>>>> Received events : 28
```

By checking HDFS under the `/data/spark/kafka/rss/` directory via the Hadoop filesystem `ls` command, it can be seen that there is now data stored on HDFS:

```
[hadoop@hc2r1m1 stream]$ hdfs dfs -ls /data/spark/kafka/rss
Found 1 items
drwxr-xr-x   - hadoop supergroup          0 2015-07-14 12:40
/data/spark/kafka/rss/file_1436833769907
```

By checking the contents of this directory, it can be seen that an HDFS part data file exists, which should contain the RSS-based data from Reuters:

```
[hadoop@hc2r1m1 stream]$ hdfs dfs -ls
/data/spark/kafka/rss/file_1436833769907
 Found 2 items
 -rw-r--r--   3 hadoop supergroup          0 2015-07-14 12:40
/data/spark/kafka/rss/file_1436833769907/_SUCCESS
 -rw-r--r--   3 hadoop supergroup       8205 2015-07-14 12:40
/data/spark/kafka/rss/file_1436833769907/part-00001
```

Using the Hadoop filesystem `cat` Command, we can dump the contents of this HDFS-based file to check its contents. We have used the Linux head command to limit the data to save space. Clearly, this is RSS Reuters science-based information that the Perl script `rss.perl` has converted from XML to RSS JSON format.

```
[hadoop@hc2r1m1 stream]$ hdfs dfs -cat
/data/spark/kafka/rss/file_1436833769907/part-00001 | head -2
{"category": "science", "title": "Bear necessities: low metabolism lets
pandas survive on bamboo", "summary": "WASHINGTON (Reuters) - Giant pandas
eat vegetables even though their bodies are better equipped to eat meat. So
how do these black-and-white bears from the remote misty mountains of
central China survive on a diet almost exclusively of a low-nutrient food
like bamboo?"}
{"category": "science", "title": "PlanetiQ tests sensor for commercial
weather satellites", "summary": "CAPE CANAVERAL (Reuters) - PlanetiQ a
privately owned company is beginning a key test intended to pave the way
for the first commercial weather satellites."}
```

This ends this Kafka example. It can be seen that Kafka brokers have been configured. It shows that an RSS data-based Kafka producer has fed data to the brokers. It has been proved, using the ZooKeeper client, that the Kafka architecture matching the brokers, topics, and partitions has been set up in ZooKeeper. Finally, it has been shown using the Apache Spark-based Scala code in the `stream6` application, that the Kafka data has been consumed and saved to HDFS.

Summary

We could have provided streaming examples for other systems as well, but there was no room in this chapter. Twitter streaming has been examined by example in the *Checkpointing* section. This chapter has provided practical examples of data recovery via checkpointing in Spark Streaming. It has also touched on the performance limitations of checkpointing and shown that the checkpointing interval should be set at five to ten times the Spark stream batch interval.

Checkpointing provides a stream-based recovery mechanism in the case of Spark application failure. This chapter has provided some stream-based worked examples for TCP, File, Flume, and Kafka-based Spark stream coding. All the examples here are based on Scala and compiled with `sbt`. In case you are more familiar with **Maven** the following tutorial explains how to set up a Maven based Scala project: `http://www.scala-lang.org/old/node/345`.

3
Structured Streaming

As you might already have understood from the previous chapters, Apache Spark is currently in transition from RDD-based data processing to a more structured one, backed by DataFrames and Datasets in order to let Catalyst and Tungsten kick in for performance optimizations. This means that the community currently uses a double-tracked approach. While the unstructured APIs are still supported--they haven't even been marked as deprecated yet ,and it is questionable if they ever will--a new set of structured APIs has been introduced for various components with Apache Spark V 2.0, and this is also true for Spark Streaming. Structured Steaming was marked stable in Apache Spark V 2.2. Note that, as of Apache Spark V 2.1 when we started writing this chapter, Structured Streaming is was marked as *alpha*. This is another example of the extreme pace at which Apache Spark is developing.

The following topics will be covered in this chapter:

- The concept of continuous applications
- Unification of batch and stream processing
- Windowing
- Event versus processing time and how to handle late arriving data
- How Catalyst and Tungsten support streaming
- How fault tolerance and end-to-end exactly-once delivery guarantee is achieved
- An example of subscribing to a stream on a message hub
- Stream life cycle management

The concept of continuous applications

Streaming apps tend to grow in complexity. Streaming computations don't run in isolation; they interact with storage systems, batch applications, and machine learning libraries. Therefore, the notion of continuous applications--in contrast to batch processing--emerged, and basically means the composite of batch processing and real-time stream processing with a clear focus of the streaming part being the main driver of the application, and just accessing the data created or processed by batch processes for further augmentation. Continuous applications never stop and continuously produce data as new data arrives.

True unification - same code, same engine

So a continuous application could also be implemented on top of RDDs and DStreams but would require the use of use two different APIs. In Apache Spark Structured Streaming the APIs are unified. This unification is achieved by seeing a structured stream as a relational table without boundaries where new data is continuously appended to the bottom of it. In batch processing on DataFrames using the relational API or SQL, intermediate DataFrames are created. As stream and batch computing are unified on top of the Apache SparkSQL engine, when working with structured streams, intermediate relational tables without boundaries are created.

 It is important to note that one can mix (join) static and incremental data within the same query called a continuous application, which is an application taking static and dynamic data into account and never stops, producing output all the time or, at least when new data arrives. A continuous application doesn't necessarily need access to static data, it can also process streaming data only. But an example for using static data on streams is when getting GPS locations in as a stream and matching those GPS locations to addresses stored in persistent storage. The output of such an operation is a stream of addresses.

Windowing

Open source and commercial streaming engines such as IBM Streams, Apache Storm, or Apache Flink are using the concept of windows.

Windows specify the granularity or number of subsequent records, which are taken into account when executing aggregation functions on streams.

How streaming engines use windowing

There exist five different properties in two dimensions, which is how windows can be defined, where each window definition needs to use one property of each dimension.

The first property is the mode in which subsequent windows of a continuous stream of tuples can be created: sliding and tumbling.

The second is that the number of tuples that fall into a window has to be specified: either count-based, time-based or session-based.

Let's take a look at what they mean:

- **Sliding windows**: A sliding window removes a tuple from it whenever a new tuple is eligible to be included.
- **Tumbling windows**: A tumbling window removes all tuples from it whenever there are enough tuples arriving to create a new window.
- **Count-based windows**: Such windows always have the n newest elements in it. Note that this can be achieved either by a sliding or tumbling tuple update policy.
- **Time-based windows**: This window takes the timestamp of a tuple into account in order to determine whether it belongs to a certain window or not. Such a window can contain the latest n seconds worth of data, for example. Such a window can be sliding and tumbling as well.
  Time-based windows especially are eligible for late arriving data, which is a very interesting concept that Apache Spark Structured Streaming makes possible.
- **Session-based windows**: This window takes a session ID of a tuple into account in order to determine whether it belongs to a certain window or not. Such a window eventually contains all data from a user interaction with an online shop, for example. Such a window can be sliding and tumbling as well, although this notion doesn't make real sense here, because you want eventually act on/react to all data belonging to a specific session.

Time-based and Session-based windows especially are eligible for late arriving data, which is a very interesting concept that Apache Spark Structured Streaming makes possible.

Let's take a look at the following figure, which illustrates tumbling windows:

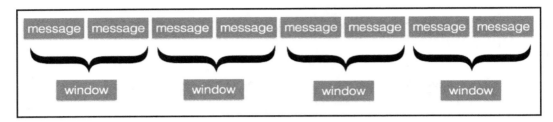

As can be observed, every tuple (or message respectively) ends up in one single window. Now let's have a look at sliding windows:

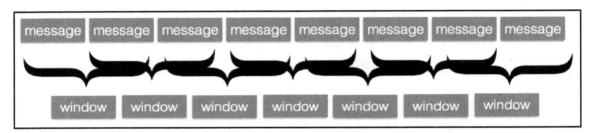

Sliding windows are meant to share tuples among their neighbors. This means that for every tuple arriving, a new window is issued. One example of such a paradigm is the calculation of a moving average once a tuple arrives for the last 100 data points. Now let's consider time-based windows:

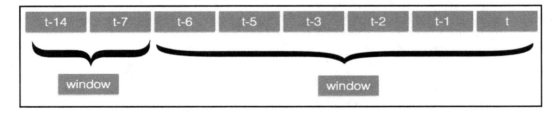

Finally, this last illustration shows time-based windows. It's important to notice that the number of tuples per window can be different as it only depends on how many messages in a certain time frame have arrived; only those will be included in the respective window. So, for example, consider an HTTP server log file to be streamed into Apache Spark Structured Streaming (using Flume as a possible solution). We are grouping tuples (which are the individual lines of the log file) together on a minute basis. Since the number of concurrent users are different at each point in time, during the day the size of the minute windows will also vary depending on it.

How Apache Spark improves windowing

Apache Spark structured streaming is significantly more flexible in the window-processing model. As streams are virtually treated as continuously appended tables, and every row in such a table has a timestamp, operations on windows can be specified in the query itself and each query can define different windows. In addition, if there is a timestamp present in static data, window operations can also be defined, leading to a very flexible stream-processing model.

In other words, Apache Spark windowing is just a sort of special type of grouping on the timestamp column. This makes it really easy to handle late arriving data as well because Apache Spark can include it in the appropriate window and rerun the computation on that window when a certain data item arrives late. This feature is highly configurable.

Event time versus processing time: In time series analysis and especially in stream computing, each record is assigned to a particular timestamp. One way of creating such a timestamp is the arrival time at the stream-processing engine. Often, this is not what you want. Usually, you want to assign an event time for each record at that particular point in time when it was created, for example, when a measurement on an IoT device took place. This allows coping with latency between creating and processing of an event, for example, when an IoT sensor was offline for a certain amount of time, or network congestion caused a delay of data delivery.

The concept of late data is interesting when using event time instead of processing time to assign a unique timestamp to each tuple. Event time is the timestamp when a particular measurement took place, for example. Apache Spark structured streaming can automatically cope with subsets of data arriving at a later point in time transparently.

Late data: If a record arrives at any streaming engine, it is processed immediately. Here, Apache Spark streaming doesn't differ from other engines. However, Apache Spark has the capability of determining the corresponding windows a certain tuple belongs to at any time. If for whatever reason, a tuple arrives late, all affected windows will be updated and all affected aggregate operations based on these updated windows are rerun. This means that results are allowed to change over time in case late data arrives. This is supported out of the box without the programmer worrying about it. Finally, since Apache Spark V2.1, it is possible to specify the amount of time that the system accepts late data using the `withWatermark` method.

The watermark is basically the threshold, used to define how old a late arriving data point is allowed to be in order to still be included in the respective window. Again, consider the HTTP server log file working over a minute length window. If, for whatever reason, a data tuple arrives which is more than 4 hours old it might not make sense to include it in the windows if, for example, this application is used to create a time-series forecast model on an hourly basis to provision or de-provision additional HTTP servers to a cluster. A four-hour-old data point just wouldn't make sense to process, even if it could change the decision, as the decision has already been made.

Increased performance with good old friends

As in Apache SparkSQL for batch processing and, as Apache Spark structured streaming is part of Apache SparkSQL, the Planner (Catalyst) creates incremental execution plans as well for mini-batches. This means that the whole streaming model is based on batches. This is the reason why a unified API for streams and batch processing could be achieved. The price we pay is that Apache Spark streaming sometimes has drawbacks when it comes to very low latency requirements (sub-second, in the range of tens of ms). As the name Structured Streaming and the usage of DataFrames and Datasets implies, we are also benefiting from performance improvements due to project Tungsten, which has been introduced in a previous chapter. To the Tungsten engine itself, a mini batch doesn't look considerably different from an ordinary batch. Only Catalyst is aware of the incremental nature of streams. Therefore, as of Apache Spark V2.2, the following operations are *not* (yet) supported, but they are on the roadmap to be supported eventually:

- Chain of aggregations
- Taking first *n* rows
- Distinct
- Sorting before aggregations
- Outer joins between streaming and static data (only limited support)

As this is constantly changing; it is best to refer to the latest documentation: `http://spark.apache.org/docs/latest/structured-streaming-programming-guide.html`.

How transparent fault tolerance and exactly-once delivery guarantee is achieved

Apache Spark structured streaming supports full crash fault tolerance and exactly-once delivery guarantee without the user taking care of any specific error handling routines. Isn't this amazing? So how is this achieved?

 Full crash fault tolerance and exactly-once delivery guarantee are terms of systems theory. Full crash fault tolerance means that you can basically pull the power plug of the whole data center at any point in time, and no data is lost or left in an inconsistent state. Exactly-once delivery guarantee means, even if the same power plug is pulled, it is guaranteed that each tuple- end-to-end from the data source to the data sink - is delivered - only, and exactly, once. Not zero times and also not more than one time. Of course, those concepts must also hold in case a single node fails or misbehaves (for example- starts throttling).

First of all, states between individual batches and offset ranges (position in a source stream) are kept in-memory but are backed by a **Write Ahead Log** (**WAL**) in a fault-tolerant filesystem such as HDFS. A WAL is basically a log file reflecting the overall stream processing state in a pro-active fashion. This means before data is transformed through an operator, it is first persistently stored in the WAL in a way it can be recovered after a crash. So, in other words, during the processing of an individual mini batch, the regions of the worker memory, as well as the position offset of the streaming source, are persisted to disk. In case the system fails and has to recover, it can re-request chunks of data from the source. Of course, this is only possible if the source supports this semantics.

Replayable sources can replay streams from a given offset

End-to-end exactly-once delivery guarantee requires the streaming source to support some sort of stream replay at a requested position. This is true for file sources and Apache Kafka, for example, as well as the IBM Watson Internet of Things platform, where the following example in this chapter will be based on.

Idempotent sinks prevent data duplication

Another key to end-to-end exactly-once delivery guarantee is idempotent sinks. This basically means that sinks are aware of which particular write operation has succeeded in the past. This means that such a smart sink can re-request data in case of a failure and also drop data in case the same data has been sent multiple times.

State versioning guarantees consistent results after reruns

What about the state? Imagine that a machine learning algorithm maintains a count variable on all the workers. If you replay the exact same data twice, you will end up counting the data multiple times. Therefore, the query planner also maintains a versioned key-value map within the workers, which are persisting their state in turn to HDFS--which is by design fault tolerant.

So, in case of a failure, if data has to be replaced, the planner makes sure that the correct version of the key-value map is used by the workers.

Example - connection to a MQTT message broker

So, let's start with a sample use case. Let's connect to an **Internet of Things (IoT)** sensor data stream. As we haven't covered machine learning so far, we don't analyze the data, we just showcase the concept.

We are using the IBM Watson IoT platform as a streaming source. At its core, the Watson IoT platform is backed by an **MQTT (Message Queue Telemetry Transport)** message broker. MQTT is a lightweight telemetry protocol invented by IBM in 1999 and became-- an **OASIS (Organization for the Advancement of Structured Information Standards**, a global nonprofit consortium that works on the development, convergence, and adoption of standards for security, Internet of Things, energy, content technologies, emergency management, and other areas) standard in 2013--the de facto standard for IoT data integration.

Messaging between applications can be backed by a message queue which is a middleware system supporting asynchronous point to point channels in various delivery modes like **first-in-first-out** (**FIFO**), **last-in-first-out** (**LIFO**) or **Priority Queue** (where each message can be re-ordered by certain criteria).

This is already a very nice feature, but still, couples applications in a certain way because, once a message is read, it is made unavailable to others.

This way N to N communication is hard (but not impossible) to achieve. In a publish/subscribe model applications are completely de-coupled. There doesn't exist any queues anymore but the notion of topics is introduced. Data providers publish messages on specific topics and data consumers subscribe to those topics. This way N to N communication is very straightforward to achieve since it is reflected by the underlying message delivery model. Such a middleware is called a Message Broker in contrast to a Message Queue.

As cloud services tend to change constantly, and cloud, in general, is introduced later in this book, the following tutorial explains how to set up the test data generator in the cloud and connect to the remote MQTT message broker. In this example, we will use the IBM Watson IoT Platform, which is an MQTT message broker available in the cloud. Alternatively one can install an open source message broker like MOSQUITTO which also provides a publicly available test installation on the following URL: `http://test.mosquitto.org/`.

In order to replicate the example, the following steps (1) and (2) are necessary as described in the following tutorial: `https://www.ibm.com/developerworks/library/iot-cognitive-iot-app-machine-learning/index.html`. Please make sure to note down `http_host`, `org`, `apiKey`, and `apiToken` during execution of the tutorial. Those are needed later in order to subscribe to data using Apache Spark Structured Streaming.

As the IBM Watson IoT platform uses the open MQTT standard, no special IBM component is necessary to connect to the platform. Instead, we are using MQTT and Apache Bahir as a connector between MQTT and Apache Spark structured streaming.

 The goal of the Apache Bahir project is to provide a set of source and sink connectors for various data processing engines including Apache Spark and Apache Flink since they are lacking those connectors. In this case, we will use the Apache Bahir MQTT data source for MQTT.

In order to use Apache Bahir, we need to add two dependencies to our local maven repository. A complete pom.xml file is provided in the download section of this chapter. Let's have a look at the dependency section of pom.xml:

```xml
<dependency>
    <groupId>org.apache.bahir</groupId>
    <artifactId>spark-sql-streaming-mqtt_2.11</artifactId>
    <version>2.1.0-SNAPSHOT</version>
</dependency>
<dependency>
    <groupId>org.eclipse.paho</groupId>
    <artifactId>org.eclipse.paho.client.mqttv3</artifactId>
    <version>1.1.0</version>
</dependency>
```

We are basically getting the MQTT Apache structured streaming adapter of Apache Bahir and a dependent package for low-level MQTT processing. A simple mvn dependency:resolve command in the directory of the pom.xml file pulls the required dependencies into our local maven repository, where they can be accessed by the Apache Spark driver and transferred to the Apache Spark workers automatically.

Another way of resolving the dependencies is when using the following command in order to start a spark-shell (spark-submit works the same way); the necessary dependencies are automatically distributed to the workers:

```
Romeos-MacBook-Pro:chapter6 romeokienzler$ spark-shell --packages org.apache.bahir:spark-sql-streaming-mqtt_2.11:2.1.0,org.eclipse.paho:org.eclipse.paho.client.mqttv3:1.1.0
Ivy Default Cache set to: /Users/romeokienzler/.ivy2/cache
The jars for the packages stored in: /Users/romeokienzler/.ivy2/jars
:: loading settings :: url = jar:file:/Users/romeokienzler/Documents/runtimes/spark-2.1.0-bin-hadoop2.7/jars/ivy-2.4.0.jar!/org/apache/ivy/core/settings/ivysettings.xml
org.apache.bahir#spark-sql-streaming-mqtt_2.11 added as a dependency
org.eclipse.paho#org.eclipse.paho.client.mqttv3 added as a dependency
:: resolving dependencies :: org.apache.spark#spark-submit-parent;1.0
	confs: [default]
	found org.apache.bahir#spark-sql-streaming-mqtt_2.11;2.1.0 in local-m2-cache
	found org.apache.spark#spark-tags_2.11;2.1.0 in local-m2-cache
	found org.scalatest#scalatest_2.11;2.2.6 in local-m2-cache
	found org.scala-lang#scala-reflect;2.11.8 in local-m2-cache
	found org.scala-lang.modules#scala-xml_2.11;1.0.2 in local-m2-cache
	found org.spark-project.spark#unused;1.0.0 in local-m2-cache
	found org.eclipse.paho#org.eclipse.paho.client.mqttv3;1.1.0 in central
:: resolution report :: resolve 7237ms :: artifacts dl 8ms
	:: modules in use:
	org.apache.bahir#spark-sql-streaming-mqtt_2.11;2.1.0 from local-m2-cache in [default]
	org.apache.spark#spark-tags_2.11;2.1.0 from local-m2-cache in [default]
	org.eclipse.paho#org.eclipse.paho.client.mqttv3;1.1.0 from central in [default]
	org.scala-lang#scala-reflect;2.11.8 from local-m2-cache in [default]
	org.scala-lang.modules#scala-xml_2.11;1.0.2 from local-m2-cache in [default]
	org.scalatest#scalatest_2.11;2.2.6 from local-m2-cache in [default]
	org.spark-project.spark#unused;1.0.0 from local-m2-cache in [default]
	---------------------------------------------------------------------
	|                  |            modules            ||   artifacts   |
	|       conf       | number| search|dwnlded|evicted|| number|dwnlded|
	---------------------------------------------------------------------
	|     default      |   7   |   1   |   1   |   0   ||   7   |   0   |
	---------------------------------------------------------------------
:: retrieving :: org.apache.spark#spark-submit-parent
	confs: [default]
	0 artifacts copied, 7 already retrieved (0kB/9ms)
Using Spark's default log4j profile: org/apache/spark/log4j-defaults.properties
Setting default log level to "WARN".
To adjust logging level use sc.setLogLevel(newLevel). For SparkR, use setLogLevel(newLevel).
17/07/10 08:37:49 WARN NativeCodeLoader: Unable to load native-hadoop library for your platform... using builtin-java classes where applicable
17/07/10 08:38:08 WARN ObjectStore: Failed to get database global_temp, returning NoSuchObjectException
Spark context Web UI available at http://192.168.0.100:4040
Spark context available as 'sc' (master = local[*], app id = local-1499668675824).
Spark session available as 'spark'.
Welcome to
      ____              __
     / __/__  ___ _____/ /__
    _\ \/ _ \/ _ `/ __/  '_/
   /___/ .__/\_,_/_/ /_/\_\   version 2.1.0
      /_/

Using Scala version 2.11.8 (Java HotSpot(TM) 64-Bit Server VM, Java 1.8.0_65)
Type in expressions to have them evaluated.
Type :help for more information.

scala>
```

Now we need the MQTT credentials that we've obtained earlier. Let's set the values here:

```
val mqtt_host = "pcoyha.messaging.internetofthings.ibmcloud.com"
val org = "pcoyha"
val apiKey = "a-pcoyha-oaigc1k8ub"
val apiToken = "&wuypVX2yNgVLAcLr8"
var randomSessionId = scala.util.Random.nextInt(10000)
```

Now we can start creating a stream connecting to an MQTT message broker. We are telling Apache Spark to use the Apache Bahir MQTT streaming source:

```
val df =
spark.readStream.format("org.apache.bahir.sql.streaming.mqtt.MQTTStreamSour
ceProvider")
```

We need to specify credentials such as `username`, `password`, and `clientId` in order to pull data from the MQTT message broker; the link to the tutorial mentioned earlier explains how to obtain these:

```
.option("username",apiKey)
.option("password",apiToken)
.option("clientId","a:"+org+":"+apiKey)
```

As we are using a publish/subscribe messaging model, we have to provide the topic that we are subscribing to--this topic is used by the test data generator that you've deployed to the cloud before:

```
.option("topic",
"iot-2/type/WashingMachine/id/Washer01/evt/voltage/fmt/json")
```

Once everything is set on the configuration side, we have to provide the endpoint host and port in order to create the stream:

```
.load("tcp://"+mqtt_host+":1883")
```

Interestingly, as can be seen in the following screenshot, this leads to the creation of a DataFrame:

```
scala> :paste
// Entering paste mode (ctrl-D to finish)

val df = spark.readStream
    .format("org.apache.bahir.sql.streaming.mqtt.MQTTStreamSourceProvider")
    .option("username","a-vy0z2s-zfzzckrnqf")
    .option("password","jbusSUaLM5a7v3I-7x")
    .option("clientId","a:vy0z2s:a-vy0z2s-zfzzckrnqf")
    .option("topic", "iot-2/type/TestDeviceType517/id/TestDevice517/evt/lorenz/fmt/json")
    .load("tcp://vy0z2s.messaging.internetofthings.ibmcloud.com:1883")

// Exiting paste mode, now interpreting.

df: org.apache.spark.sql.DataFrame = [value: string, timestamp: timestamp]
```

Note that the schema is fixed to [String, Timestamp] and cannot be changed during stream creation--this is a limitation of the Apache Bahir library. However, using the rich DataFrame API, you can parse the value, a JSON string for example, and create new columns.

As discussed before, this is one of the powerful features of Apache Spark structured streaming, as the very same DataFrame (and Dataset) API now can be used to process historic and real-time data. So let's take a look at the contents of this stream by writing it to the console:

```
val query = df.writeStream.
outputMode("append").
format("console").
start()
```

As output mode, we choose `append` to enforce incremental display and avoid having the complete contents of the historic stream being written to the console again and again. As `format`, we specify `console` as we just want to debug what's happening on the stream:

```
scala> val query = df.writeStream.
     |    outputMode("append").
     |    format("console").
     |    start()
query: org.apache.spark.sql.streaming.StreamingQuery = Streaming Query [id = a2377c24-c274-476e-bc2b-07d57bab1877, runId = 387ca22f-138c-4456-9243-9218766a6f13] [state = ACTIVE]
```

Finally, the `start` method initiates query processing, as can be seen here:

```
-------------------------------------------------
Batch: 332
-------------------------------------------------
+--------------------+--------------------+
|               value|           timestamp|
+--------------------+--------------------+
|{"d":{"voltage":2...|2017-04-26 05:31:...|
|{"d":{"voltage":2...|2017-04-26 05:31:...|
|{"d":{"voltage":2...|2017-04-26 05:31:...|
|{"d":{"voltage":2...|2017-04-26 05:31:...|
|{"d":{"voltage":2...|2017-04-26 05:31:...|
|{"d":{"voltage":2...|2017-04-26 05:31:...|
|{"d":{"voltage":2...|2017-04-26 05:31:...|
|{"d":{"voltage":2...|2017-04-26 05:31:...|
|{"d":{"voltage":2...|2017-04-26 05:31:...|
+--------------------+--------------------+


-------------------------------------------------
Batch: 333
-------------------------------------------------
+--------------------+--------------------+
|               value|           timestamp|
+--------------------+--------------------+
|{"d":{"voltage":2...|2017-04-26 05:31:...|
|{"d":{"voltage":2...|2017-04-26 05:31:...|
|{"d":{"voltage":2...|2017-04-26 05:31:...|
|{"d":{"voltage":2...|2017-04-26 05:31:...|
|{"d":{"voltage":2...|2017-04-26 05:31:...|
|{"d":{"voltage":2...|2017-04-26 05:31:...|
+--------------------+--------------------+


-------------------------------------------------
Batch: 334
-------------------------------------------------
+--------------------+--------------------+
|               value|           timestamp|
+--------------------+--------------------+
|{"d":{"voltage":2...|2017-04-26 05:31:...|
|{"d":{"voltage":2...|2017-04-26 05:31:...|
|{"d":{"voltage":2...|2017-04-26 05:31:...|
|{"d":{"voltage":2...|2017-04-26 05:31:...|
|{"d":{"voltage":2...|2017-04-26 05:31:...|
|{"d":{"voltage":2...|2017-04-26 05:31:...|
+--------------------+--------------------+
```

Controlling continuous applications

Once a continuous application (even a simple one, not taking historic data into account) is started and running, it has to be controlled somehow as the call to the start method immediately starts processing, but also returns without blocking. In case you want your program to block at this stage until the application has finished, one can use the awaitTermination method as follows:

```
query.awaitTermination()
```

This is particularly important when precompiling code and using the spark-submit command. When using spark-shell, the application is not terminated anyway.

More on stream life cycle management

Streaming tends to be used in the creation of continuous applications. This means that the process is running in the background and, in contrast to batch processing, doesn't have a clear stop time; therefore, DataFrames and Datasets backed by a streaming source, support various methods for stream life cycle management, which are explained as follows:

- start: This starts the continuous application. This method doesn't block. If this is not what you want, use awaitTermination.
- stop : This terminates the continuous application.
- awaitTermination : As mentioned earlier, starting a stream using the start method immediately returns, which means that the call is not blocking. Sometimes you want to wait until the stream is terminated, either by someone else calling stop on it or by an error.
- exception: In case a stream stopped because of an error, the cause can be read using this method.
- sourceStatus: This is to obtain real-time meta information on the streaming source.
- sinkStatus : This is to obtain real-time meta information on the streaming sink.

Sinks in Apache Spark streaming are smart in the sense that they support fault tolerance and end-to-end exactly-once delivery guarantee as mentioned before. In addition, Apache Spark needs them to support different output methods. Currently, the following three output methods, append, update, and complete, significantly change the underlying semantics. The following paragraph contains more details about the different output methods.

Different output modes on sinks: Sinks can be specified to handle output in different ways. This is known as `outputMode`. The naive choice would use an incremental approach as we are processing incremental data with streaming anyway. This mode is referred to as `append`. However, there exist requirements where data already processed by the sink has to be changed. One example is the late arrival problem of missing data in a certain time window, which can lead to changing results once the computation for that particular time window is recomputed. This mode is called `complete`.

 Since Version 2.1 of Apache Spark, the `update` mode was introduced that behaves similarly to the `complete` mode but only changes rows that have been altered, therefore saving processing resources and improving speed. Some types of modes do not support all query types. As this is constantly changing, it is best to refer to the latest documentation at `http://spark.apache.org/docs/latest/streaming-programming-guide.html`.

Summary

So why do we have two different streaming engines within the same data processing framework? We hope that after reading this chapter, you'll agree that the main pain points of the classical DStream based engine have been addressed. Formerly, event time-based processing was not possible and only the arrival time of data was considered. Then, late data has simply been processed with the wrong timestamp as only processing time could be used. Also, batch and stream processing required using two different APIs: RDDs and DStreams. Although the API is similar, it is not exactly the same; therefore, the rewriting of code when going back and forth between the two paradigms was necessary. Finally, an end-to-end delivery guarantee was hard to achieve and required lots of user intervention and thinking.

This fault-tolerant end-to-end exactly-once delivery guarantee is achieved through offset tracking and state management in a fault-tolerant Write Ahead Log in conjunction with fault-tolerant sources and sinks. Now let's examine the very interesting topic of machine learning in the next chapter.

4
Apache Spark MLlib

MLlib is the original machine learning library that is provided with Apache Spark, the in-memory cluster-based open source data processing system. This library is still based on the RDD API. In this chapter, we will examine the functionality provided with the MLlib library in terms of areas such as regression, classification, and neural network processing. We will examine the theory behind each algorithm before providing working examples that tackle real problems. The example code and documentation on the web can be sparse and confusing.

We will take a step-by-step approach in describing how the following algorithms can be used and what they are capable of doing:

- Architecture
- Classification with Naive Bayes
- Clustering with K-Means
- Image classification with **artificial neural networks**

Architecture

Remember that, although Spark is used for the speed of its in-memory distributed processing, it doesn't provide storage. You can use the Host (local) filesystem to read and write your data, but if your data volumes are big enough to be described as big data, then it makes sense to use a cloud-based distributed storage system such as OpenStack Swift Object Storage, which can be found in many cloud environments and can also be installed in private data centers.

> In case very high I/O is needed, HDFS would also be an option. More information on HDFS can be found here: http://hadoop.apache.org/docs/current/hadoop-project-dist/hadoop-hdfs/HdfsDesign.html.

The development environment

The Scala language will be used for the coding samples in this book. This is because, as a scripting language, it produces less code than Java. It can also be used from the Spark shell as well as compiled with Apache Spark applications. We will be using the **sbt tool** to compile the Scala code, which we have installed into Hortonworks HDP 2.6 Sandbox as follows:

```
[hadoop@hc2nn ~]# sudo su -
[root@hc2nn ~]# cd /tmp
[root@hc2nn ~]#wget
http://repo.scala-sbt.org/scalasbt/sbt-native-packages/org/scala-sbt/sbt/0.
13.1/sbt.rpm
[root@hc2nn ~]# rpm -ivh sbt.rpm
```

The following URL provides instructions to install sbt on other operating systems including Windows, Linux, and macOS: http://www.scala-sbt.org/0.13/docs/Setup.html.

We used a generic Linux account called **Hadoop**. As the previous commands show, we need to install sbt as the root account, which we have accessed via sudo su -l (switch user). We then downloaded the sbt.rpm file to the /tmp directory from the web-based server called repo.scala-sbt.org using wget. Finally, we installed the rpm file using the rpm command with the options i for install, v for verify, and h to print the hash marks while the package is being installed.

We developed all of the Scala code for Apache Spark in this chapter on the Linux server, using the Linux Hadoop account. We placed each set of code within a subdirectory under /home/hadoop/spark. For instance, the following sbt structure diagram shows that the MLlib Naive Bayes code is stored in a subdirectory called nbayes under the Spark directory. What the diagram also shows is that the Scala code is developed within a subdirectory structure named src/main/scala under the nbayes directory. The files called bayes1.scala and convert.scala contain the Naive Bayes code that will be used in the next section:

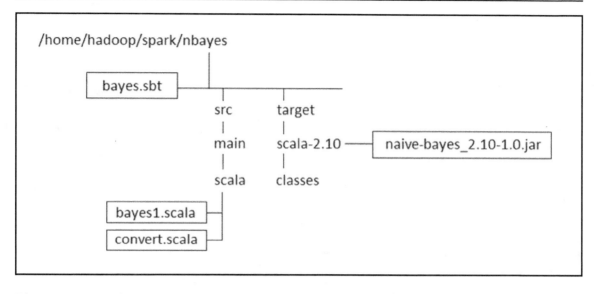

The `bayes.sbt` file is a configuration file used by the `sbt` tool, which describes how to compile the Scala files within the Scala directory. (Note that if you were developing in Java, you would use a path of the `nbayes/src/main/java` form .) The contents of the `bayes.sbt` file are shown next. The `pwd` and `cat` Linux commands remind you of the file location and also remind you to dump the file contents.

The `name`, `version`, and `scalaVersion` options set the details of the project and the version of Scala to be used. The `libraryDependencies` options define where the Hadoop and Spark libraries can be located.

```
[hadoop@hc2nn nbayes]$ pwd
/home/hadoop/spark/nbayes
[hadoop@hc2nn nbayes]$ cat bayes.sbt
name := "Naive Bayes"
version := "1.0"
scalaVersion := "2.11.2"
libraryDependencies += "org.apache.hadoop" % "hadoop-client" % "2.8.1"
libraryDependencies += "org.apache.spark" %% "spark-core" % "2.6.0"
libraryDependencies += "org.apache.spark" %% "spark-mllib" % "2.1.1"
```

The Scala `nbayes` project code can be compiled from the `nbayes` subdirectory using this command:

```
[hadoop@hc2nn nbayes]$ sbt compile
```

The `sbt compile` command is used to compile the code into classes. The classes are then placed in the `nbayes/target/scala-2.10/classes` directory. The compiled classes can be packaged in a JAR file with this command:

```
[hadoop@hc2nn nbayes]$ sbt package
```

The `sbt package` command will create a JAR file under the `nbayes/target/scala-2.10` directory. As we can see in the example in the **sbt structure diagram**, the JAR file named `naive-bayes_2.10-1.0.jar` has been created after a successful compile and package. This JAR file, and the classes that it contains, can then be used in a `spark-submit` command. This will be described later as the functionality in the Apache Spark MLlib module is explored.

Classification with Naive Bayes

This section will provide a working example of the Apache Spark MLlib Naive Bayes algorithm. It will describe the theory behind the algorithm and will provide a step-by-step example in Scala to show how the algorithm may be used.

Theory on Classification

In order to use the Naive Bayes algorithm to classify a dataset, the data must be linearly divisible; that is, the classes within the data must be linearly divisible by class boundaries. The following figure visually explains this with three datasets and two class boundaries shown via the dotted lines:

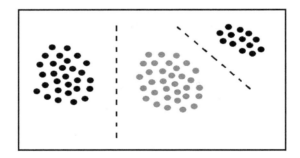

Naive Bayes assumes that the features (or dimensions) within a dataset are independent of one another; that is, they have no effect on each other. The following example considers the classification of e-mails as spam. If you have 100 e-mails, then perform the following:

```
60% of emails are spam
80% of spam emails contain the word buy
20% of spam emails don't contain the word buy
40% of emails are not spam
10% of non spam emails contain the word buy
90% of non spam emails don't contain the word buy
```

Let's convert this example into conditional probabilities so that a Naive Bayes classifier can pick it up:

```
P(Spam) = the probability that an email is spam = 0.6
P(Not Spam) = the probability that an email is not spam = 0.4
P(Buy|Spam) = the probability that an email that is spam has the word buy =
0.8
P(Buy|Not Spam) = the probability that an email that is not spam has the
word buy = 0.1
```

What is the probability that an e-mail that contains the word buy is spam? Well, this would be written as *P (Spam | Buy)*. Naive Bayes says that it is described by the equation in the following figure:

$$P(Spam|Buy) \;=\; \frac{P(Buy|Spam) * P(Spam)}{P(Buy|Spam) * P(Spam) \;+\; P(Buy|Not\ Spam) * P(Not\ Spam)}$$

So, using the previous percentage figures, we get the following:

P(Spam | Buy) = (0.8 * 0.6) / ((0.8 * 0.6) + (0.1 * 0.4)) = (.48) / (.48 + .04)

= .48 / .52 = .923

This means that it is *92* percent more likely that an e-mail that contains the word buy is spam. That was a look at the theory; now it's time to try a real-world example using the Apache Spark MLlib Naive Bayes algorithm.

Naive Bayes in practice

The first step is to choose some data that will be used for classification. We have chosen some data from the UK Government data website at http://data.gov.uk/dataset/road-accidents-safety-data.

The dataset is called **Road Safety - Digital Breath Test Data 2013**, which downloads a zipped text file called DigitalBreathTestData2013.txt. This file contains around half a million rows. The data looks as follows:

```
Reason,Month,Year,WeekType,TimeBand,BreathAlcohol,AgeBand,Gender
Suspicion of Alcohol,Jan,2013,Weekday,12am-4am,75,30-39,Male
Moving Traffic Violation,Jan,2013,Weekday,12am-4am,0,20-24,Male
Road Traffic Collision,Jan,2013,Weekend,12pm-4pm,0,20-24,Female
```

In order to classify the data, we have modified both the column layout and the number of columns. We have simply used Excel, given the data volume. However, if our data size had been in the big data range, we would have had to run some Scala code on top of Apache Spark for **ETL (Extract Transform Load)**. As the following commands show, the data now resides in HDFS in the directory named /data/spark/nbayes. The file name is called DigitalBreathTestData2013- MALE2.csv. The line count from the Linux wc command shows that there are 467,000 rows. Finally, the following data sample shows that we have selected the columns, Gender, Reason, WeekType, TimeBand, BreathAlcohol, and AgeBand to classify. We will try to classify on the Gender column using the other columns as features:

```
[hadoop@hc2nn ~]$ hdfs dfs -cat
/data/spark/nbayes/DigitalBreathTestData2013-MALE2.csv | wc -l
467054
[hadoop@hc2nn ~]$ hdfs dfs -cat
/data/spark/nbayes/DigitalBreathTestData2013-MALE2.csv | head -5
Male,Suspicion of Alcohol,Weekday,12am-4am,75,30-39
Male,Moving Traffic Violation,Weekday,12am-4am,0,20-24
Male,Suspicion of Alcohol,Weekend,4am-8am,12,40-49
Male,Suspicion of Alcohol,Weekday,12am-4am,0,50-59
Female,Road Traffic Collision,Weekend,12pm-4pm,0,20-24
```

The Apache Spark MLlib classification function uses a data structure called LabeledPoint, which is a general purpose data representation defined at http://spark.apache.org/docs/1.0.0/api/scala/index.html#org.apache.spark.mllib.regression. LabeledPoint and https://spark.apache.org/docs/latest/mllib-data-types.html#labeled-point.

This structure only accepts double values, which means that the text values in the previous data need to be classified numerically. Luckily, all of the columns in the data will convert to numeric categories, and we have provided a program in the software package with this book under the chapter2\naive bayes directory to do just that. It is called convert.scala. It takes the contents of the DigitalBreathTestData2013- MALE2.csv file and converts each record into a double vector.

The directory structure and files for an sbt Scala-based development environment have already been described earlier. We are developing our Scala code on the Linux server using the Linux account, Hadoop. Next, the Linux pwd and ls commands show our top-level nbayes development directory with the bayes.sbt configuration file, whose contents have already been examined:

```
[hadoop@hc2nn nbayes]$ pwd
/home/hadoop/spark/nbayes
[hadoop@hc2nn nbayes]$ ls
bayes.sbt        target    project    src
```

The Scala code to run the Naive Bayes example is in the src/main/scala subdirectory under the nbayes directory:

```
[hadoop@hc2nn scala]$ pwd
/home/hadoop/spark/nbayes/src/main/scala
[hadoop@hc2nn scala]$ ls
bayes1.scala convert.scala
```

We will examine the bayes1.scala file later, but first, the text-based data on HDFS must be converted into numeric double values. This is where the convert.scala file is used. The code is as follows:

```
import org.apache.spark.SparkContext
import org.apache.spark.SparkContext._
import org.apache.spark.SparkConf
```

These lines import classes for the Spark context, the connection to the Apache Spark cluster, and the Spark configuration. The object that is being created is called convert1. It is an application as it extends the App class:

```
object convert1 extends App
{
```

The next line creates a function called `enumerateCsvRecord`. It has a parameter called `colData`, which is an array of `Strings` and returns `String`:

```
def enumerateCsvRecord( colData:Array[String]): String =
{
```

The function then enumerates the text values in each column, so, for instance, Male becomes 0. These numeric values are stored in values such as `colVal1`:

```
val colVal1 =
  colData(0) match
  {
    case "Male"                      => 0
    case "Female"                    => 1
    case "Unknown"                   => 2
    case _                           => 99
  }

val colVal2 =
  colData(1) match
  {
    case "Moving Traffic Violation"  => 0
    case "Other"                     => 1
    case "Road Traffic Collision"    => 2
    case "Suspicion of Alcohol"      => 3
    case _                           => 99
  }

val colVal3 =
  colData(2) match
  {
    case "Weekday"                   => 0
    case "Weekend"                   => 0
    case _                           => 99
  }

val colVal4 =
  colData(3) match
  {
    case "12am-4am"                  => 0
    case "4am-8am"                   => 1
    case "8am-12pm"                  => 2
    case "12pm-4pm"                  => 3
    case "4pm-8pm"                   => 4
    case "8pm-12pm"                  => 5
    case _                           => 99
  }
```

```
val colVal5 = colData(4)
val colVal6 =
  colData(5) match
  {
    case "16-19"                          => 0
    case "20-24"                          => 1
    case "25-29"                          => 2
    case "30-39"                          => 3
    case "40-49"                          => 4
    case "50-59"                          => 5
    case "60-69"                          => 6
    case "70-98"                          => 7
    case "Other"                          => 8
    case _                                => 99
  }
```

 A comma-separated string called `lineString` is created from the numeric column values and is then returned. The function closes with the final brace character. Note that the data line created next starts with a label value at column one and is followed by a vector, which represents the data.

The vector is space-separated while the label is separated from the vector by a comma. Using these two separator types allows us to process both--the label and vector--in two simple steps:

```
val lineString = colVal1+","+colVal2+" "+colVal3+" "+colVal4+"
"+colVal5+" "+colVal6
    return lineString
}
```

The main script defines the HDFS server name and path. It defines the input file and the output path in terms of these values. It uses the Spark URL and application name to create a new configuration. It then creates a new context or connection to Spark using these details:

```
val hdfsServer = "hdfs://localhost:8020"
val hdfsPath   = "/data/spark/nbayes/"
val inDataFile = hdfsServer + hdfsPath + "DigitalBreathTestData2013-
MALE2.csv"
val outDataFile = hdfsServer + hdfsPath + "result"
val sparkMaster = "spark://localhost:7077"
val appName = "Convert 1"
val sparkConf = new SparkConf()
sparkConf.setMaster(sparkMaster)
sparkConf.setAppName(appName)
val sparkCxt = new SparkContext(sparkConf)
```

The CSV-based raw data file is loaded from HDFS using the Spark context `textFile` method. Then, a data row count is printed:

```
val csvData = sparkCxt.textFile(inDataFile)
println("Records in : "+ csvData.count() )
```

The CSV raw data is passed line by line to the `enumerateCsvRecord` function. The returned string-based numeric data is stored in the `enumRddData` variable:

```
val enumRddData = csvData.map
{
  csvLine =>
    val colData = csvLine.split(',')
    enumerateCsvRecord(colData)
}
```

Finally, the number of records in the `enumRddData` variable is printed, and the enumerated data is saved to HDFS:

```
println("Records out : "+ enumRddData.count() )
  enumRddData.saveAsTextFile(outDataFile)
} // end object
```

In order to run this script as an application against Spark, it must be compiled. This is carried out with the `sbt package` command, which also compiles the code. The following command is run from the `nbayes` directory:

```
[hadoop@hc2nn nbayes]$ sbt package
Loading /usr/share/sbt/bin/sbt-launch-lib.bash
. . . .
[info] Done packaging.
[success] Total time: 37 s, completed Feb 19, 2015 1:23:55 PM
```

This causes the compiled classes that are created to be packaged into a JAR library, as shown here:

```
[hadoop@hc2nn nbayes]$ pwd
/home/hadoop/spark/nbayes
[hadoop@hc2nn nbayes]$ ls -l target/scala-2.10
total 24
drwxrwxr-x 2 hadoop hadoop 4096 Feb 19 13:23 classes
-rw-rw-r-- 1 hadoop hadoop 17609 Feb 19 13:23 naive-bayes_2.10-1.0.jar
```

The `convert1` application can now be run against Spark using the application name, Spark URL, and full path to the JAR file that was created. Some extra parameters specify memory and the maximum cores that are supposed to be used:

```
spark-submit \
  --class convert1 \
  --master spark://localhost:7077 \
  --executor-memory 700M \
  --total-executor-cores 100 \
  /home/hadoop/spark/nbayes/target/scala-2.10/naive-bayes_2.10-1.0.jar
```

This creates a data directory on HDFS called /data/spark/nbayes/ followed by the result, which contains part files with the processed data:

```
[hadoop@hc2nn nbayes]$ hdfs dfs -ls /data/spark/nbayes
Found 2 items
-rw-r--r--    3 hadoop supergroup    24645166 2015-01-29 21:27
/data/spark/nbayes/DigitalBreathTestData2013-MALE2.csv
drwxr-xr-x    - hadoop supergroup           0 2015-02-19 13:36
/data/spark/nbayes/result
[hadoop@hc2nn nbayes]$ hdfs dfs -ls /data/spark/nbayes/result
Found 3 items
-rw-r--r--    3 hadoop supergroup           0 2015-02-19 13:36
/data/spark/nbayes/result/_SUCCESS
-rw-r--r--    3 hadoop supergroup     2828727 2015-02-19 13:36
/data/spark/nbayes/result/part-00000
-rw-r--r--    3 hadoop supergroup     2865499 2015-02-19 13:36
/data/spark/nbayes/result/part-00001
```

In the following HDFS cat command, we concatenated the part file data into a file called DigitalBreathTestData2013-MALE2a.csv. We then examined the top five lines of the file using the head command to show that it is numeric. Finally, we loaded it in HDFS with the put command:

```
[hadoop@hc2nn nbayes]$ hdfs dfs -cat /data/spark/nbayes/result/part* >
./DigitalBreathTestData2013-MALE2a.csv
[hadoop@hc2nn nbayes]$ head -5 DigitalBreathTestData2013-MALE2a.csv
0,3 0 0 75 3
0,0 0 0 0 1
0,3 0 1 12 4
0,3 0 0 0 5
1,2 0 3 0 1
[hadoop@hc2nn nbayes]$ hdfs dfs -put ./DigitalBreathTestData2013-MALE2a.csv
/data/spark/nbayes
```

The following HDFS ls command now shows the numeric data file stored on HDFS in the nbayes directory:

```
[hadoop@hc2nn nbayes]$ hdfs dfs -ls /data/spark/nbayes
Found 3 items
-rw-r--r--    3 hadoop supergroup    24645166 2015-01-29 21:27
```

```
/data/spark/nbayes/DigitalBreathTestData2013-MALE2.csv
-rw-r--r--   3 hadoop supergroup   5694226 2015-02-19 13:39
/data/spark/nbayes/DigitalBreathTestData2013-MALE2a.csv
drwxr-xr-x - hadoop supergroup       0 2015-02-19 13:36
/data/spark/nbayes/result
```

Now that the data has been converted into a numeric form, it can be processed with the MLlib Naive Bayes algorithm; this is what the Scala file, bayes1.scala, does. This file imports the same configuration and context classes as before. It also imports MLlib classes for Naive Bayes, vectors, and the LabeledPoint structure. The application class that is created this time is called bayes1:

```
import org.apache.spark.SparkContext
import org.apache.spark.SparkContext._
import org.apache.spark.SparkConf
import org.apache.spark.mllib.classification.NaiveBayes
import org.apache.spark.mllib.linalg.Vectors
import org.apache.spark.mllib.regression.LabeledPoint

object bayes1 extends App {
```

The HDFS data file is again defined, and a Spark context is created as before:

```
val hdfsServer = "hdfs://localhost:8020"
val hdfsPath   = "/data/spark/nbayes/"
val dataFile = hdfsServer+hdfsPath+"DigitalBreathTestData2013-MALE2a.csv"
val sparkMaster = "spark://loclhost:7077"
val appName = "Naive Bayes 1"
val conf = new SparkConf()
conf.setMaster(sparkMaster)
conf.setAppName(appName)
val sparkCxt = new SparkContext(conf)
```

The raw CSV data is loaded and split by the separator characters. The first column becomes the label (Male/Female) that the data will be classified on. The final columns separated by spaces become the classification features:

```
val csvData = sparkCxt.textFile(dataFile)
val ArrayData = csvData.map {
  csvLine =>
    val colData = csvLine.split(',')
    LabeledPoint(colData(0).toDouble,
                 Vectors.dense(colData(1)
                     .split('')
                     .map(_.toDouble)
                 )
    )
}
```

```
}
```

The data is then randomly divided into training (70%) and testing (30%) datasets:

```
val divData = ArrayData.randomSplit(Array(0.7, 0.3), seed = 13L)
val trainDataSet = divData(0)
val testDataSet = divData(1)
```

The Naive Bayes MLlib function can now be trained using the previous training set. The trained Naive Bayes model, held in the `nbTrained` variable, can then be used to predict the Male/Female result labels against the testing data:

```
val nbTrained = NaiveBayes.train(trainDataSet)
val nbPredict = nbTrained.predict(testDataSet.map(_.features))
```

Given that all of the data already contained labels, the original and predicted labels for the test data can be compared. An accuracy figure can then be computed to determine how accurate the predictions were, by comparing the original labels with the prediction values:

```
val predictionAndLabel = nbPredict.zip(testDataSet.map(_.label))
val accuracy = 100.0 * predictionAndLabel.filter(x => x._1 ==
x._2).count() /
    testDataSet.count()
println( "Accuracy : " + accuracy );
}
```

So, this explains the Scala Naive Bayes code example. It's now time to run the compiled `bayes1` application using `spark-submit` and determine the classification accuracy. The parameters are the same. It's just the class name that has changed:

```
spark-submit \
  --class bayes1 \
  --master spark://hc2nn.semtech-solutions.co.nz:7077 \
  --executor-memory 700M \
  --total-executor-cores 100 \
  /home/hadoop/spark/nbayes/target/scala-2.10/naive-bayes_2.10-1.0.jar
```

The resulting accuracy given by the Spark cluster is just 43 percent, which seems to imply that this data is not suitable for Naive Bayes:

```
Accuracy: 43.30
```

Luckily we'll introduce artificial neural networks later in the chapter, a more powerful classifier. In the next example, we will use K-Means to try to determine what clusters exist within the data. Remember, Naive Bayes needs the data classes to be linearly separable along the class boundaries. With K-Means, it will be possible to determine both: the membership and centroid location of the clusters within the data.

Clustering with K-Means

This example will use the same test data from the previous example, but we will attempt to find clusters in the data using the MLlib K-Means algorithm.

Theory on Clustering

The K-Means algorithm iteratively attempts to determine clusters within the test data by minimizing the distance between the mean value of cluster center vectors, and the new candidate cluster member vectors. The following equation assumes dataset members that range from *X1* to *Xn*; it also assumes *K* cluster sets that range from *S1* to *Sk*, where *K* <= *n*.

$$\underset{s}{\arg\min} \sum_{i=1}^{K} \sum_{x \in S_i} \left\| x - B_i \right\|^2$$

where B_i is the mean of members of S_i

K-Means in practice

The K-Means MLlib functionality uses the `LabeledPoint` structure to process its data and so it needs numeric input data. As the same data from the last section is being reused, we will not explain the data conversion again. The only change that has been made in data terms in this section, is that processing in HDFS will now take place under the `/data/spark/kmeans/` directory. Additionally, the conversion Scala script for the K-Means example produces a record that is all comma-separated.

The development and processing for the K-Means example has taken place under the /home/hadoop/spark/kmeans directory to separate the work from other development. The sbt configuration file is now called kmeans.sbt and is identical to the last example, except for the project name:

```
name := "K-Means"
```

The code for this section can be found in the software package under chapter7\K-Means. So, looking at the code for kmeans1.scala, which is stored under kmeans/src/main/scala, some similar actions occur. The import statements refer to the Spark context and configuration. This time, however, the K-Means functionality is being imported from MLlib. Additionally, the application class name has been changed for this example to kmeans1:

```
import org.apache.spark.SparkContext
import org.apache.spark.SparkContext._
import org.apache.spark.SparkConf
import org.apache.spark.mllib.linalg.Vectors
import org.apache.spark.mllib.clustering.{KMeans,KMeansModel}

object kmeans1 extends App {
```

The same actions are being taken as in the last example to define the data file--to define the Spark configuration and create a Spark context:

```
val hdfsServer = "hdfs://localhost:8020"
val hdfsPath   = "/data/spark/kmeans/"
val dataFile   = hdfsServer + hdfsPath + "DigitalBreathTestData2013-
MALE2a.csv"
val sparkMaster = "spark://localhost:7077"
val appName = "K-Means 1"
val conf = new SparkConf()
conf.setMaster(sparkMaster)
conf.setAppName(appName)
val sparkCxt = new SparkContext(conf)
```

Next, the CSV data is loaded from the data file and split by comma characters into the VectorData variable:

```
val csvData = sparkCxt.textFile(dataFile)
val VectorData = csvData.map {
  csvLine =>
    Vectors.dense( csvLine.split(',').map(_.toDouble))
}
```

A `KMeans` object is initialized, and the parameters are set to define the number of clusters and the maximum number of iterations to determine them:

```
val kMeans = new KMeans
val numClusters        = 3
val maxIterations      = 50
```

Some default values are defined for the initialization mode, the number of runs, and Epsilon, which we needed for the K-Means call but did not vary for the processing. Finally, these parameters were set against the `KMeans` object:

```
val initializationMode = KMeans.K_MEANS_PARALLEL
val numRuns            = 1
val numEpsilon         = 1e-4
kMeans.setK( numClusters )
kMeans.setMaxIterations( maxIterations )
kMeans.setInitializationMode( initializationMode )
kMeans.setRuns( numRuns )
kMeans.setEpsilon( numEpsilon )
```

We cached the training vector data to improve the performance and trained the `KMeans` object using the vector data to create a trained K-Means model:

```
VectorData.cache
val kMeansModel = kMeans.run( VectorData )
```

We have computed the K-Means cost and number of input data rows, and have to output the results via `println` statements. The cost value indicates how tightly the clusters are packed and how separate the clusters are:

```
val kMeansCost = kMeansModel.computeCost( VectorData )
println( "Input data rows : " + VectorData.count() )
println( "K-Means Cost    : " + kMeansCost )
```

Next, we have used the K-Means Model to print the cluster centers as vectors for each of the three clusters that were computed:

```
kMeansModel.clusterCenters.foreach{ println }
```

Finally, we use the K-Means model to predict function to create a list of cluster membership predictions. We then count these predictions by value to give a count of the data points in each cluster. This shows which clusters are bigger and whether there really are three clusters:

```
val clusterRddInt = kMeansModel.predict( VectorData )
val clusterCount = clusterRddInt.countByValue
  clusterCount.toList.foreach{ println }
} // end object kmeans1
```

So, in order to run this application, it must be compiled and packaged from the kmeans subdirectory as the Linux pwd command shows here:

```
[hadoop@hc2nn kmeans]$ pwd
/home/hadoop/spark/kmeans
[hadoop@hc2nn kmeans]$ sbt package
Loading /usr/share/sbt/bin/sbt-launch-lib.bash
[info] Set current project to K-Means (in build
file:/home/hadoop/spark/kmeans/)
[info] Compiling 2 Scala sources to
/home/hadoop/spark/kmeans/target/scala-2.10/classes...
[info] Packaging /home/hadoop/spark/kmeans/target/scala-2.10/k-
means_2.10-1.0.jar ...
[info] Done packaging.
[success] Total time: 20 s, completed Feb 19, 2015 5:02:07 PM
```

Once this packaging is successful, we check HDFS to ensure that the test data is ready. As in the last example, we convert our data into the numeric form using the convert.scala file, provided in the software package. We will process the DigitalBreathTestData2013-MALE2a.csv data file in the HDFS directory, /data/spark/kmeans, as follows:

```
[hadoop@hc2nn nbayes]$ hdfs dfs -ls /data/spark/kmeans
Found 3 items
-rw-r--r--   3 hadoop supergroup   24645166 2015-02-05 21:11
/data/spark/kmeans/DigitalBreathTestData2013-MALE2.csv
-rw-r--r--   3 hadoop supergroup    5694226 2015-02-05 21:48
/data/spark/kmeans/DigitalBreathTestData2013-MALE2a.csv
drwxr-xr-x   - hadoop supergroup          0 2015-02-05 21:46
/data/spark/kmeans/result
```

The `spark-submit` tool is used to run the K-Means application. The only change in this command is that the class is now `kmeans1`:

```
spark-submit \
  --class kmeans1 \
  --master spark://localhost:7077 \
  --executor-memory 700M \
  --total-executor-cores 100 \
  /home/hadoop/spark/kmeans/target/scala-2.10/k-means_2.10-1.0.jar
```

The output from the Spark cluster run is shown to be as follows:

```
Input data rows : 467054
K-Means Cost    : 5.40312223450789E7
```

The previous output shows the input data volume, which looks correct; it also shows the K-Means cost value. The cost is based on the **Within Set Sum of Squared Errors (WSSSE)** which basically gives a measure of how well the found cluster centroids are matching the distribution of the data points. The better they are matching, the lower the cost. The following link `https://datasciencelab.wordpress.com/2013/12/27/finding-the-k-in-k-means-clustering/` explains WSSSE and how to find a good value for **k** in more detail.

Next, come the three vectors, which describe the data cluster centers with the correct number of dimensions. Remember that these cluster centroid vectors will have the same number of columns as the original vector data:

```
[0.24698249738061878,1.3015883142472253,0.00583011687225 0263,2.917374778855
5207,1.156645130895448,3.4400290524342454]
[0.3321793984152627,1.784137241326256,0.007615970459266097,2.58319870759289
17,119.58366028156011,3.8379106085083468]
[0.25247226760684494,1.702510963969387,0.006384899819416975,2.2314042480006
88,52.202897927594805,3.551509158139135]
```

Finally, cluster membership is given for clusters 1 to 3 with cluster 1 (index 0) having the largest membership at `407539` member vectors:

```
(0,407539)
(1,12999)
(2,46516)
```

So, these two examples show how data can be classified and clustered using Naive Bayes and K-Means. What if I want to classify images or more complex patterns, and use a black box approach to classification? The next section examines Spark-based classification using **ANNs**, or **artificial neural networks**.

Artificial neural networks

The following figure shows a simple biological neuron to the left. The neuron has dendrites that receive signals from other neurons. A cell body controls activation, and an axon carries an electrical impulse to the dendrites of other neurons. The artificial neuron to the right has a series of weighted inputs: a summing function that groups the inputs and a **firing mechanism (F(Net))**, which decides whether the inputs have reached a threshold, and, if so, the neuron will fire:

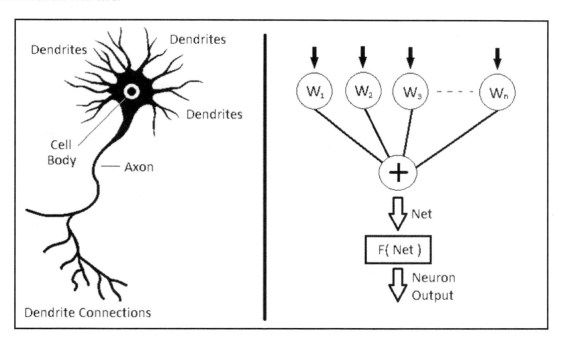

Neural networks are tolerant of noisy images and distortion, and so are useful when a black box classification method is needed for potentially degraded images. The next area to consider is the summation function for the neuron inputs. The following diagram shows the summation function called **Net** for neuron **i**. The connections between the neurons that have the weighting values, contain the stored knowledge of the network. Generally, a network will have an input layer, output layer, and a number of hidden layers. A neuron will fire if the sum of its inputs exceeds a threshold:

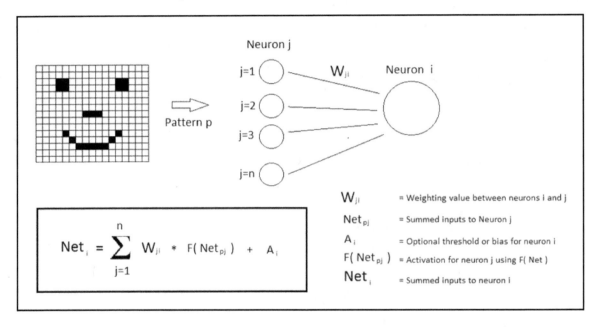

In the previous equation, the diagram and key show that the input values from a pattern **P** are passed to neurons in the input layer of a network. These values become the input layer neuron activation values; they are a special case. The inputs to neuron **i** are the sum of the weighting value for neuron connection **i-j**, multiplied by the activation from neuron **j**. The activation at neuron **j** (if it is not an input layer neuron) is given by **F(Net)**, the squashing function, which will be described next.

A simulated neuron needs a firing mechanism, which decides whether the inputs to the neuron have reached a threshold. Then, it fires to create the activation value for that neuron. This `firing` or `squashing` function can be described by the generalized `sigmoid` function shown in the following figure:

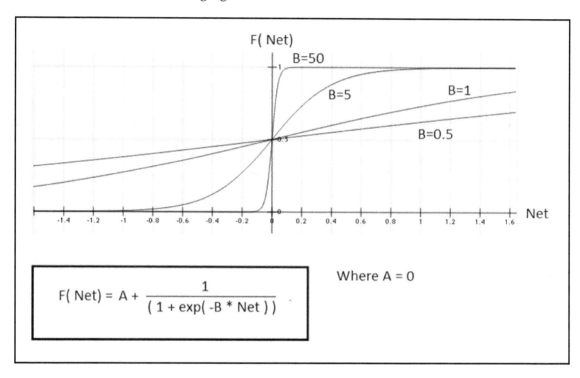

This function has two constants: **A** and **B**; **B** affects the shape of the activation curve as shown in the previous graph. The bigger the value, the more similar a function becomes to an on/off step. The value of **A** sets a minimum for the returned activation. In the previous graph, it is zero.

So, this provides a mechanism to simulate a neuron, create weighting matrices as the neuron connections, and manage the neuron activation. How are the networks organized? The next diagram shows a suggested architecture--the neural network has an input layer of neurons, an output layer, and one or more hidden layers. All neurons in each layer are connected to each neuron in the adjacent layers:

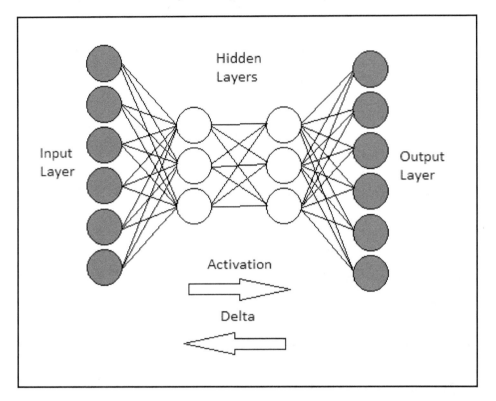

During the training, activation passes from the input layer through the network to the output layer. Then, the error or difference between the expected or actual output causes error deltas to be passed back through the network, altering the weighting matrix values. Once the desired output layer vector is achieved, then the knowledge is stored in the weighting matrices and the network can be further trained or used for classification.

So, the theory behind neural networks has been described in terms of back propagation. Now is the time to obtain some practical knowledge.

ANN in practice

In order to begin ANN training, test data is needed. Given that this type of classification method is supposed to be good at classifying distorted or noisy images, we decided to attempt to classify the images here:

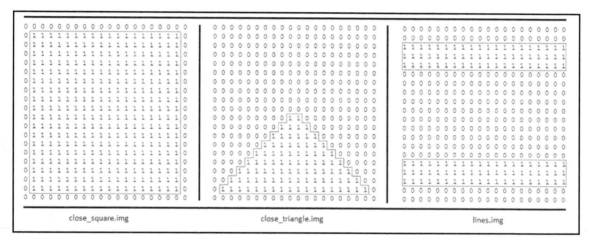

They are hand-crafted text files that contain shaped blocks, created from the characters 1 and 0. When they are stored on HDFS, the carriage return characters are removed so that the image is presented as a single line vector. So, the ANN will be classifying a series of shape images and then will be tested against the same images with noise added to determine whether the classification will still work. There are six training images, and they will each be given an arbitrary training label from 0.1 to 0.6. So, if the ANN is presented with a closed square, it should return a label of 0.1. The following image shows an example of a testing image with noise added.

The noise, created by adding extra zero (0) characters within the image, has been highlighted:

```
0 0 0 0 0 0 0 0 0 0 0 0 0 0 0 0 0 0 0 0
0 1 1 1 1 1 1 1 1 1 1 1 1 1 1 1 1 1 1 0
0 1 ⓪ 1 1 ⓪ 1 1 1 ⓪ 1 1 1 1 1 1 1 1 1 0
0 1 1 1 1 1 1 1 1 1 1 1 1 1 1 1 1 1 1 0
0 1 1 1 1 1 1 1 1 1 1 1 1 1 1 1 1 1 1 0
0 1 1 1 1 1 1 1 1 ⓪ 1 1 1 1 ⓪ 1 1 1 1 0
0 1 1 1 1 1 1 1 1 1 1 1 1 1 1 1 1 1 1 0
0 1 1 1 1 1 1 1 1 1 1 1 1 1 1 1 1 1 1 0
0 1 1 1 1 1 1 1 1 1 1 1 1 1 1 1 1 1 1 0
0 1 1 1 1 1 ⓪ 1 1 1 ⓪ 1 1 1 1 1 1 1 1 0
0 1 1 1 1 1 1 1 1 1 1 1 1 1 1 1 1 1 1 0
0 1 1 1 1 1 1 1 1 1 1 1 1 1 1 1 1 1 1 0
0 1 1 1 1 1 1 1 1 1 1 1 1 ⓪ 1 1 1 1 1 0
0 1 1 1 1 1 ⓪ 1 1 ⓪ 1 1 1 1 1 1 1 1 1 0
0 1 1 ⓪ 1 1 1 1 1 1 1 1 1 1 1 1 1 1 1 0
0 1 1 1 1 1 1 1 1 1 1 1 1 ⓪ 1 1 1 1 1 0
0 1 1 1 1 1 1 1 1 1 1 1 1 1 1 1 1 1 1 0
0 1 1 1 1 ⓪ 1 1 1 1 1 ⓪ 1 1 1 1 1 1 1 0
0 1 1 1 1 1 1 1 1 1 1 1 1 1 1 1 1 1 1 0
0 0 0 0 0 0 0 0 0 0 0 0 0 0 0 0 0 0 0 0
```

close_square_test.img

As before, the ANN code is developed using the Linux Hadoop account in a subdirectory called `spark/ann`. The `ann.sbt` file exists in the `ann` directory:

```
[hadoop@hc2nn ann]$ pwd
/home/hadoop/spark/ann

[hadoop@hc2nn ann]$ ls
ann.sbt    project src target
```

The contents of the `ann.sbt` file have been changed to use full paths of JAR library files for the Spark dependencies:

```
name := "A N N"
version := "1.0"
scalaVersion := "2.11.2"
libraryDependencies += "org.apache.hadoop" % "hadoop-client" % "2.8.1"
```

```
libraryDependencies += "org.apache.spark" % "spark-core" % "2.6.0"
libraryDependencies += "org.apache.spark" % "spark-mllib" % "2.1.1"
libraryDependencies += "org.apache.spark" % "akka" % "2.5.3"
```

As in the previous examples, the actual Scala code to be compiled exists in a subdirectory named src/main/scala. We have created two Scala programs. The first trains using the input data and then tests the ANN model with the same input data. The second tests the trained model with noisy data to test the distorted data classification:

```
[hadoop@hc2nn scala]$ pwd
/home/hadoop/spark/ann/src/main/scala
[hadoop@hc2nn scala]$ ls
test_ann1.scala test_ann2.scala
```

We will examine the first Scala file and then we will just show the extra features of the second file, as the two examples are very similar up to the point of training the ANN. The code examples shown here can be found in the software package provided with this book under the path, chapter2\ANN. So, to examine the first Scala example, the import statements are similar to the previous examples. The Spark context, configuration, vectors, and LabeledPoint are being imported. The RDD class for RDD processing is being imported this time, along with the new ANN class, ANNClassifier. Note that the MLlib/classification routines widely use the LabeledPoint structure for input data, which will contain the features and labels that are supposed to be trained against:

```
import org.apache.spark.SparkContext
import org.apache.spark.SparkContext._
import org.apache.spark.SparkConf
import org.apache.spark.mllib.classification.ANNClassifier
import org.apache.spark.mllib.regression.LabeledPoint
import org.apache.spark.mllib.linalg.Vectors
import org.apache.spark.mllib.linalg._
import org.apache.spark.rdd.RDD

object testann1 extends App {
```

The application class in this example has been called testann1. The HDFS files to be processed have been defined in terms of the HDFS server, path, and file name:

```
val server = "hdfs://localhost:8020"
val path   = "/data/spark/ann/"

val data1 = server + path + "close_square.img"
val data2 = server + path + "close_triangle.img"
val data3 = server + path + "lines.img"
val data4 = server + path + "open_square.img"
val data5 = server + path + "open_triangle.img"
```

```
val data6 = server + path + "plus.img"
```

The Spark context has been created with the URL for the Spark instance, which now has a different port number--8077. The application name is ANN 1. This will appear on the Spark web UI when the application is run:

```
val sparkMaster = "spark://localhost:8077"
val appName = "ANN 1"
val conf = new SparkConf()

conf.setMaster(sparkMaster)
conf.setAppName(appName)

val sparkCxt = new SparkContext(conf)
```

The HDFS-based input training and test data files are loaded. The values on each line are split by space characters, and the numeric values have been converted into doubles. The variables that contain this data are then stored in an array called **inputs**. At the same time, an array called outputs is created, containing the labels from 0.1 to 0.6. These values will be used to classify the input patterns:

```
val rData1 = sparkCxt.textFile(data1).map(_.split("
").map(_.toDouble)).collect
val rData2 = sparkCxt.textFile(data2).map(_.split("
").map(_.toDouble)).collect
val rData3 = sparkCxt.textFile(data3).map(_.split("
").map(_.toDouble)).collect
val rData4 = sparkCxt.textFile(data4).map(_.split("
").map(_.toDouble)).collect
val rData5 = sparkCxt.textFile(data5).map(_.split("
").map(_.toDouble)).collect
val rData6 = sparkCxt.textFile(data6).map(_.split("
").map(_.toDouble)).collect
val inputs = Array[Array[Double]] (
    rData1(0), rData2(0), rData3(0), rData4(0), rData5(0), rData6(0) )
val outputs = Array[Double]( 0.1, 0.2, 0.3, 0.4, 0.5, 0.6 )
```

The input and output data, representing the input data features and labels, are then combined and converted into a LabeledPoint structure. Finally, the data is parallelized in order to partition it for optimal parallel processing:

```
val ioData = inputs.zip( outputs )
val lpData = ioData.map{ case(features,label) =>

  LabeledPoint( label, Vectors.dense(features) )
}
val rddData = sparkCxt.parallelize( lpData )
```

Variables are created to define the hidden layer topology of the ANN. In this case, we have chosen to have two hidden layers, each with 100 neurons. The maximum number of iterations is defined as well as a batch size (six patterns) and convergence tolerance. The tolerance refers to how big the training error can get before we can consider training to have worked. Then, an ANN model is created using these configuration parameters and the input data:

```
val hiddenTopology : Array[Int] = Array( 100, 100 )
val maxNumIterations = 1000
val convTolerance    = 1e-4
val batchSize        = 6
val annModel = ANNClassifier.train(rddData,
                                   batchSize,
                                   hiddenTopology,
                                   maxNumIterations,
                                   convTolerance)
```

In order to test the trained ANN model, the same input training data is used as testing data to obtain prediction labels. First, an input data variable is created called rPredictData. Then, the data is partitioned and, finally, the predictions are obtained using the trained ANN model. For this model to work, it must output the labels, 0.1 to 0.6:

```
val rPredictData = inputs.map{ case(features) =>
  ( Vectors.dense(features) )
}
val rddPredictData = sparkCxt.parallelize( rPredictData )
val predictions = annModel.predict( rddPredictData )
```

The label predictions are printed and the script closes with a closing bracket:

```
predictions.toArray().foreach( value => println( "prediction > " + value )
)
} // end ann1
```

So, in order to run this code sample, it must first be compiled and packaged. By now, you must be familiar with the sbt command, executed from the ann subdirectory:

```
[hadoop@hc2nn ann]$ pwd
/home/hadoop/spark/ann
[hadoop@hc2nn ann]$ sbt package
```

The spark-submit command is then used from within the new spark/spark path using the new Spark-based URL at port 8077 to run the application, testann1:

```
/home/hadoop/spark/spark/bin/spark-submit \
  --class testann1 \
  --master spark://localhost:8077 \
```

```
--executor-memory 700M \
--total-executor-cores 100 \
/home/hadoop/spark/ann/target/scala-2.10/a-n-n_2.10-1.0.jar
```

By checking the Apache Spark web URL at `http://localhost:19080/`, it is now possible to see the application running. The following figure shows the `ANN 1` application running as well as the previously completed executions:

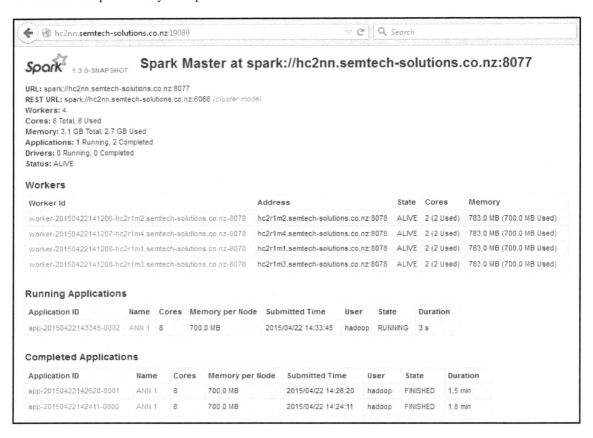

By selecting one of the cluster host worker instances, it is possible to see a list of executors that actually carry out cluster processing for that worker:

ID: app-20150422143345-0002
Name: ANN 1
User: hadoop
Cores: 100 (8 granted, 92 left)
Executor Memory: 700.0 MB
Submit Date: Wed Apr 22 14:33:45 NZST 2015
State: RUNNING
Application Detail UI

Executor Summary

ExecutorID	Worker	Cores	Memory	State	Logs
2	worker-20150422141208-hc2r1m1.semtech-solutions.co.nz-8078	2	700	RUNNING	stdout stderr
1	worker-20150422141208-hc2r1m3.semtech-solutions.co.nz-8078	2	700	RUNNING	stdout stderr
3	worker-20150422141206-hc2r1m2.semtech-solutions.co.nz-8078	2	700	RUNNING	stdout stderr
0	worker-20150422141207-hc2r1m4.semtech-solutions.co.nz-8078	2	700	RUNNING	stdout stderr

Finally, by selecting one of the executors, it is possible to see its history and configuration as well as links to the log file and error information. At this level, with the log information provided, debugging is possible. These log files can be checked to process error messages:

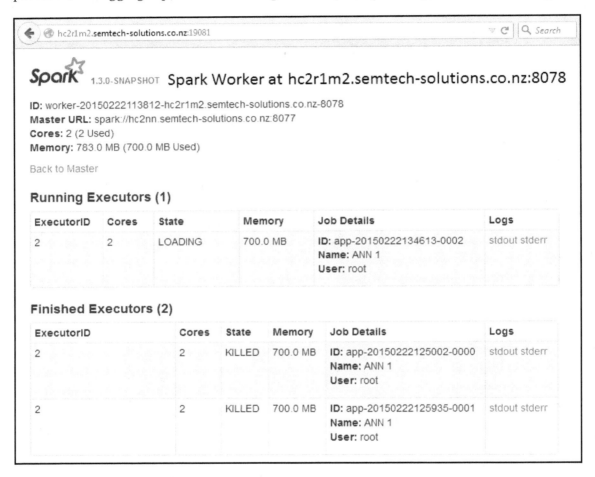

The ANN 1 application provides the following output to show that it has reclassified the same input data correctly. The reclassification has been successful as each of the input patterns has been given the same label that it was trained with:

```
prediction > 0.1
prediction > 0.2
prediction > 0.3
prediction > 0.4
prediction > 0.5
prediction > 0.6
```

So, this shows that ANN training and test prediction will work with the same data. Now, we will train with the same data, but test with distorted or noisy data, an example of which we already demonstrated. This example can be found in the file called `test_ann2.scala` in your software package. It is very similar to the first example, so we will just demonstrate the changed code. The application is now called `testann2`:

```
object testann2 extends App
```

An extra set of testing data is created after the ANN model has been created using the training data. This testing data contains noise:

```
val tData1 = server + path + "close_square_test.img"
val tData2 = server + path + "close_triangle_test.img"
val tData3 = server + path + "lines_test.img"
val tData4 = server + path + "open_square_test.img"
val tData5 = server + path + "open_triangle_test.img"
val tData6 = server + path + "plus_test.img"
```

This data is processed into input arrays and partitioned for cluster processing:

```
val rtData1 = sparkCxt.textFile(tData1).map(_.split("
").map(_.toDouble)).collect
val rtData2 = sparkCxt.textFile(tData2).map(_.split("
").map(_.toDouble)).collect
val rtData3 = sparkCxt.textFile(tData3).map(_.split("
").map(_.toDouble)).collect
val rtData4 = sparkCxt.textFile(tData4).map(_.split("
").map(_.toDouble)).collect
val rtData5 = sparkCxt.textFile(tData5).map(_.split("
").map(_.toDouble)).collect
val rtData6 = sparkCxt.textFile(tData6).map(_.split("
").map(_.toDouble)).collect
val tInputs = Array[Array[Double]] (
    rtData1(0), rtData2(0), rtData3(0), rtData4(0), rtData5(0), rtData6(0)
)

val rTestPredictData = tInputs.map{ case(features) => (
Vectors.dense(features) ) }
val rddTestPredictData = sparkCxt.parallelize( rTestPredictData )
```

It is then used to generate label predictions in the same way as the first example. If the model classifies the data correctly, then the same label values should be printed from 0.1 to 0.6:

```
val testPredictions = annModel.predict( rddTestPredictData )
testPredictions.toArray().foreach( value => println( "test prediction > "
+ value ) )
```

The code has already been compiled, so it can be run using the `spark-submit` command:

```
/home/hadoop/spark/spark/bin/spark-submit \
  --class testann2 \
  --master spark://localhost:8077 \
  --executor-memory 700M \
  --total-executor-cores 100 \
  /home/hadoop/spark/ann/target/scala-2.10/a-n-n_2.10-1.0.jar
```

Here is the cluster output from this script, which shows a successful classification using a trained ANN model and some noisy test data. The noisy data has been classified correctly. For instance, if the trained model had become confused, it might have given a value of 0.15 for the noisy `close_square_test.img` test image in position one, instead of returning `0.1` as it did:

```
test prediction > 0.1
test prediction > 0.2
test prediction > 0.3
test prediction > 0.4
test prediction > 0.5
test prediction > 0.6
```

Summary

This chapter has attempted to provide you with an overview of some of the functionality available within the Apache Spark MLlib module. It has also shown the functionality that will soon be available in terms of ANNs or artificial neural networks. You might have been impressed by how well ANNs work. It is not possible to cover all the areas of MLlib due to the time and space allowed for this chapter. In addition, we now want to concentrate more on the SparkML library in the next chapter, which speeds up machine learning by supporting DataFrames and the underlying Catalyst and Tungsten optimizations.

We saw how to develop Scala-based examples for Naive Bayes classification, K-Means clustering, and ANNs. You learned how to prepare test data for these Spark MLlib routines. You also saw that they all accept the `LabeledPoint` structure, which contains features and labels.

Additionally, each approach takes a training and prediction step to training and testing a model using different datasets. Using the approach shown in this chapter, you can now investigate the remaining functionality in the MLlib library. You can refer to `http://spark.apache.org/` and ensure that you refer to the correct version when checking the documentation.

Having examined the Apache Spark MLlib machine learning library in this chapter, it is now time to consider Apache Spark's SparkML. The next chapter will examine machine learning on top of DataFrames.

Apache SparkML 5

So now that you've learned a lot about MLlib, why another ML API? First of all, it is a common task in data science to work with multiple frameworks and ML libraries as there are always advantages and disadvantages; mostly, it is a trade-off between performance and functionality. R, for instance, is the king when it comes to functionality--there exist more than 6000 R add-on packages. However, R is also one of the slowest execution environments for data science. SparkML, on the other hand, currently has relatively limited functionality but is one of the fastest libraries. Why is this so? This brings us to the second reason why SparkML exists.

The duality between RDD on the one hand and DataFrames and Datasets on the other is like a red thread in this book and doesn't stop influencing the machine learning chapters. As MLlib is designed to work on top of RDDs, SparkML works on top of DataFrames and Datasets, therefore making use of all the new performance benefits that Catalyst and Tungsten bring.

We will cover the following topics in this chapter:

- Introduction to the SparkML API
- The concept of pipelines
- Transformers and estimators
- A working example

What does the new API look like?

When it comes to machine learning on Apache Spark, we are used to transforming data into an appropriate format and data types before we actually feed them to our algorithms. Machine learning practitioners around the globe discovered that the preprocessing tasks on a machine learning project usually follow the same pattern:

- Data preparation
- Training
- Evaluating
- Hyperparameter tuning

Therefore, the new ApacheSparkML API supports this process out of the box. It is called **pipelines** and is inspired by scikit-learn http://scikit-learn.org, a very popular machine learning library for the Python programming language. The central data structure is a DataFrame and all operations run on top of it.

The concept of pipelines

ApacheSparkML pipelines have the following components:

- **DataFrame**: This is the central data store where all the original data and intermediate results are stored in.
- **Transformer**: As the name suggests, a transformer transforms one DataFrame into another by adding additional (feature) columns in most of the cases. Transformers are stateless, which means that they don't have any internal memory and behave exactly the same each time they are used; this is a concept you might be familiar with when using the map function of RDDs.
- **Estimator**: In most of the cases, an estimator is some sort of machine learning model. In contrast to a transformer, an estimator contains an internal state representation and is highly dependent on the history of the data that it has already seen.
- **Pipeline**: This is the glue which is joining the preceding components, DataFrame, Transformer and Estimator, together.
- **Parameter**: Machine learning algorithms have many knobs to tweak. These are called **hyperparameters** and the values learned by a machine learning algorithm to fit data are called parameters. By standardizing how hyperparameters are expressed, ApacheSparkML opens doors to task automation, as we will see later.

Transformers

Let's start with something simple. One of the most common tasks in machine learning data preparation is string indexing and one-hot encoding of categorical values. Let's see how this can be done.

String indexer

Let's assume that we have a DataFrame `df` containing a column called color of categorical labels--red, green, and blue. We want to encode them as integer or float values. This is where `org.apache.spark.ml.feature.StringIndexer` kicks in. It automatically determines the cardinality of the category set and assigns each one a distinct value. So in our example, a list of categories such as red, red, green, red, blue, green should be transformed into 1, 1, 2, 1, 3, 2:

```
import org.apache.spark.ml.feature.StringIndexer
var indexer = new StringIndexer()
  .setInputCol("colors")
  .setOutputCol("colorsIndexed")

var indexed = indexer.fit(df).transform(df)
```

The result of this transformation is a DataFrame called indexed that, in addition to the colors column of the String type, now contains a column called `colorsIndexed` of type double.

OneHotEncoder

We are only halfway through. Although machine learning algorithms are capable of making use of the `colorsIndexed` column, they perform better if we one-hot encode it. This actually means that, instead of having a `colorsIndexed` column containing label indexes between one and three, it is better if we have three columns--one for each color--with the constraint that every row is allowed to set only one of these columns to one, otherwise zero. Let's do it:

```
var encoder = new OneHotEncoder()
  .setInputCol("colorIndexed")
  .setOutputCol("colorVec")

var encoded = encoder.transform(indexed)
```

Intuitively, we would expect that we get three additional columns in the encoded DataFrame, for example, `colorIndexedRed`, `colorIndexedGreen`, and `colorIndexedBlue`. However, this is not the case. In contrast, we just get one additional column in the DataFrame and its type is `org.apache.spark.ml.linalg.Vector`. It uses its internal representation and we basically don't have to care about it, as all ApacheSparkML transformers and estimators are compatible to that format.

VectorAssembler

Before we start with the actual machine learning algorithm, we need to apply one final transformation. We have to create one additional `feature` column containing all the information of the columns that we want the machine learning algorithm to consider. This is done by `org.apache.spark.ml.feature.VectorAssembler` as follows:

```
import org.apache.spark.ml.feature.VectorAssembler
vectorAssembler = new VectorAssembler()
        .setInputCols(Array("colorVec", "field2", "field3","field4"))
        .setOutputCol("features")
```

This transformer adds only one single column to the resulting DataFrame called **features**, which is of the `org.apache.spark.ml.linalg.Vector` type. In other words, this new column called features, created by the `VectorAssembler`, contains all the defined columns (in this case, `colorVec`, `field2`, `field3`, and `field4`) encoded in a single vector object for each row. This is the format the Apache SparkML algorithms are happy with.

Pipelines

Before we dive into estimators--we've already used one in `StringIndexer`--let's first understand the concept of pipelines. As you might have noticed, the transformers add only one single column to a DataFrame and basically omit all other columns not explicitly specified as input columns; they can only be used in conjunction with `org.apache.spark.ml.Pipeline`, which glues individual transformers (and estimators) together to form a complete data analysis process. So let's do this for our two `Pipeline` stages:

```
var transformers = indexer :: encoder :: vectorAssembler :: Nil
var pipeline = new Pipeline().setStages(transformers).fit(df)
var transformed = pipeline.transform(df)
```

The now obtained DataFrame called **transformed** contains all the original columns plus the columns added by the indexer and encoder stages. This is the way in which ApacheSparkML data processing jobs are defined.

Estimators

We've used estimators before in StringIndexer. We've already stated that estimators somehow contain state that changes while looking at data, whereas this is not the case for transformers. So why is StringIndexer an estimator? This is because it needs to remember all the previously seen strings and maintain a mapping table between strings and label indexes.

 In machine learning, it is common to use at least a training and testing subset of your available training data. It can happen that an estimator in the pipeline, such as StringIndexer, has not seen all the string labels while looking at the training dataset. Therefore, you'll get an exception when evaluating the model using the test dataset as the StringIndexer now encounters labels that it has not seen before. This is, in fact, a very rare case and basically could mean that the sample function you use to separate the training and testing datasets is not working; however, there is an option called setHandleInvalid("skip") and your problem is solved.

Another easy way to distinguish between an estimator and a transformer is the additional method called fit on the estimators. Fit actually populates the internal data management structure of the estimators based on a given dataset, which, in the case of StringIndexer, is the mapping table between label strings and label indexes. So now let's take a look at another estimator, an actual machine learning algorithm.

RandomForestClassifier

Let's assume that we are in a binary classification problem setting and want to use RandomForestClassifier. All SparkML algorithms have a compatible API, so they can be used interchangeably. So it really doesn't matter which one we use, but RandomForestClassifier has more (hyper)parameters than more simple models like logistic regression. At a later stage we'll use (hyper)parameter tuning which is also inbuilt in Apache SparkML. Therefore it makes sense to use an algorithm where more knobs can be tweaked. Adding such a binary classifier to our Pipeline is very simple:

```
import org.apache.spark.ml.classification.RandomForestClassifier
```

```
var rf = new RandomForestClassifier()
  .setLabelCol("label")
  .setFeaturesCol("features")

var model = new Pipeline().setStages(transformers :+ rf).fit(df)

var result = model.transform(df)
```

As you can see, `RandomForestClassifier` takes two parameters: the column name of the actual labels (remember that we are in a supervised learning setting) and the features that we've created before. All other parameters are default values and we'll take care of them later. We can just add this machine learning model as a final stage to the `Pipeline`: `transformers :+ rf`. Then, we call fit and transform--always passing our DataFrame as a parameter--and we obtain a final DataFrame called result, which basically contains everything from the `df` DataFrame plus an additional column called predictions. Done! We've created our first machine learning `Pipeline` with Apache SparkML. Now, we want to check how well we are doing against our test dataset. This is also built-in to Apache SparkML.

Model evaluation

As mentioned before, model evaluation is built-in to ApacheSparkML and you'll find all that you need in the `org.apache.spark.ml.evaluation` package. Let's continue with our binary classification. This means that we'll have to use `org.apache.spark.ml.evaluation.BinaryClassificationEvaluator`:

```
import org.apache.spark.ml.evaluation.BinaryClassificationEvaluator
val evaluator = new BinaryClassificationEvaluator()

import org.apache.spark.ml.param.ParamMap
var evaluatorParamMap = ParamMap(evaluator.metricName -> "areaUnderROC")
var aucTraining = evaluator.evaluate(result, evaluatorParamMap)
```

To code previous initialized a `BinaryClassificationEvaluator` function and tells it to calculate the `areaUnderROC`, one of the many possible metrics to assess the prediction performance of a machine learning algorithm.

As we have the actual label and the prediction present in a DataFrame called `result`, it is simple to calculate this score and is done using the following line of code:

```
var aucTraining = evaluator.evaluate(result, evaluatorParamMap)
```

CrossValidation and hyperparameter tuning

We will be looking at one example each of `CrossValidation` and hyperparameter tuning. Let's take a look at `CrossValidation`.

CrossValidation

As stated before, we've used the default parameters of the machine learning algorithm and we don't know if they are a good choice. In addition, instead of simply splitting your data into training and testing, or training, testing, and validation sets, `CrossValidation` might be a better choice because it makes sure that eventually all the data is seen by the machine learning algorithm.

`CrossValidation` basically splits your complete available training data into a number of **k** folds. This parameter **k** can be specified. Then, the whole `Pipeline` is run once for every fold and one machine learning model is trained for each fold. Finally, the different machine learning models obtained are joined. This is done by a voting scheme for classifiers or by averaging for regression.

The following figure illustrates ten-fold `CrossValidation`:

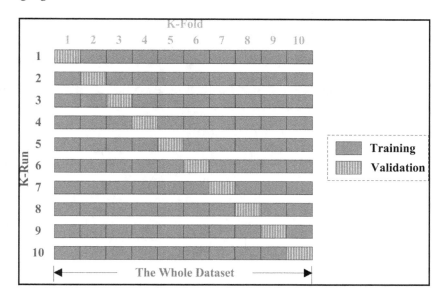

Hyperparameter tuning

`CrossValidation` is often used in conjunction with so-called (hyper)parameter tuning. What are hyperparameters? These are the various knobs that you can tweak on your machine learning algorithm. For example, these are some parameters of the Random Forest classifier:

- Number of trees
- Feature subset strategy
- Impurity
- Maximal number of bins
- Maximal tree depth

Setting these parameters can have a significant influence on the performance of the trained classifier. Often, there is no way of choosing them based on a clear recipe--of course, experience helps--but hyperparameter tuning is considered as black magic. Can't we just choose many different parameters and test the prediction performance? Of course, we can. This feature is also inbuilt in Apache SparkML. The only thing to consider is that such a search can be quite exhaustive. So luckily, Apache Spark is a linearly scalable infrastructure and we can test multiple models very fast.

 Note that the hyperparameters form an n-dimensional space where n is the number of hyperparameters. Every point in this space is one particular hyperparameter configuration, which is a hyperparameter vector. Of course, we can't explore every point in this space, so what we basically do is a grid search over a (hopefully evenly distributed) subset in that space.

All of this is completely integrated and standardized in Apache SparkML; isn't that great? Let's take a look at the following code:

```
import org.apache.spark.ml.param.ParamMap
import org.apache.spark.ml.tuning.{CrossValidator, ParamGridBuilder}
var paramGrid = new ParamGridBuilder()
    .addGrid(rf.numTrees, 3 :: 5 :: 10 :: Nil)
    .addGrid(rf.featureSubsetStrategy, "auto" :: "all" :: Nil)
    .addGrid(rf.impurity, "gini" :: "entropy" :: Nil)
    .addGrid(rf.maxBins, 2 :: 5 :: Nil)
    .addGrid(rf.maxDepth, 3 :: 5 :: Nil)
    .build()
```

In order to perform such a grid search over the hyperparameter space, we need to define it first. Here, the functional programming properties of Scala are quite handy because we just add function pointers and the respective parameters to be evaluated to the parameter grid:

```
var crossValidator = new CrossValidator()
    .setEstimator(new Pipeline().setStages(transformers :+ rf))
    .setEstimatorParamMaps(paramGrid)
    .setNumFolds(5)
.setEvaluator(evaluator)
```

Then we create a `CrossValidator`. Note that in the `setEstimator` method of the `CrossValidator` object, we set our existing `Pipeline`. We are able to do so since the Pipeline by itself turns out to be an estimator as it extends from it. In the `setEstimatorParamMaps` method we set our parameter grid. Finally, we define the number of folds used for `CrossValidation`, pass an instance of our `BinaryClassificationEvaluator`, and we are done:

```
var crossValidatorModel = crossValidator.fit(df)
```

Although there is so much stuff going on behind the scenes, the interface to our `CrossValidator` object stays slim and well-known as `CrossValidator` also extends from `Estimator` and supports the `fit` method. This means that, after calling fit, the complete predefined `Pipeline`, including all feature preprocessing and the RandomForest classifier, is executed multiple times--each time with a different hyperparameter vector.

So let's do some math. How many RandomForest models are executed once this code has run? Basically, this is a number exponentially dependent on the number of parameters to be evaluated and the different parameter values for each parameter. In this case, we have five parameters with parameter values ranging between 2 and 3. So the math is as simple as this: 3 * 2 * 2 * 2 = 24. 24 models have completed, and by just adding additional parameters or parameter values, this number always doubles. So here we are really happy to run on a linearly scalable infrastructure!

So let's evaluate the result:

```
var newPredictions = crossValidatorModel.transform(df)
```

As `CrossValidator` is an `Estimator` returning a model of the `CrossValidatorModel` type, we can use it as an ordinary Apache SparkML model by just calling transform on it in order to obtain predictions. The `CrossValidatorModel` automatically chooses the learned hyperparameters of the underlying model (in this case, `RandomForestClassifier`) to do the prediction. In order to check how well we are doing, we can run our `evaluator` again:

```
evaluator.evaluate(newPredictions, evaluatorParamMap)
```

In case we are curious and want to know the optimal parameters, we can pull the stages from the `Pipeline` and check on the parameters used:

```
var bestModel = crossValidatorModel.bestModel
var bestPipelineModel =
crossValidatorModel.bestModel.asInstanceOf[PipelineModel]
var stages = bestPipelineModel.stages
```

Then we pull `RandomForestClassificationModel` from the best stage and check on the parameters:

```
import org.apache.spark.ml.classification.RandomForestClassificationModel
val rfStage =
stages(stages.length-1).asInstanceOf[RandomForestClassificationModel]
rfStage.getNumTrees
rfStage.getFeatureSubsetStrategy
rfStage.getImpurity
rfStage.getMaxBins
rfStage.getMaxDepth
```

This is enough of theory and it is impossible to cover all transformers, estimators, and helper functions of Apache SparkML but we think this is a very good start. So let's conclude this chapter with a practical example.

The illustrated image is a good example of the pipeline we want to implement:

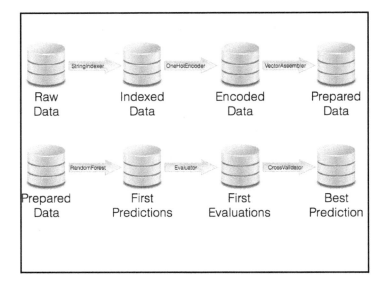

Winning a Kaggle competition with Apache SparkML

Winning a Kaggle competition is an art by itself, but we just want to show you how the Apache SparkML tooling can be used efficiently to do so.

We'll use an archived competition for this offered by BOSCH, a German multinational engineering, and electronics company, on production line performance data. Details for the competition data can be found at `https://www.kaggle.com/c/bosch-production-line-performance/data`.

Data preparation

The challenge data comes in three ZIP packages but we only use two of them. One contains categorical data, one contains continuous data, and the last one contains timestamps of measurements, which we will ignore for now.

If you extract the data, you'll get three large CSV files. So the first thing that we want to do is re-encode them into parquet in order to be more space-efficient:

```
def convert(filePrefix : String) = {
    val basePath = "yourBasePath"
    var df = spark
                .read
                .option("header",true)
                .option("inferSchema", "true")
                .csv("basePath+filePrefix+".csv")
    df = df.repartition(1)
    df.write.parquet(basePath+filePrefix+".parquet")
}

convert("train_numeric")
convert("train_date")
convert("train_categorical")
```

First, we define a function convert that just reads the `.csv` file and rewrites it as a `.parquet` file. As you can see, this saves a lot of space:

train_date.csv	11 Aug 2016, 18:12	2.89 GB	comma-separated values
train_categorical.csv	11 Aug 2016, 17:50	2.68 GB	comma-separated values
train_numeric.csv	11 Aug 2016, 17:41	2.14 GB	comma-separated values
train_date.parquet	26 Apr 2017, 16:52	890.5 MB	Document
train_numeric.parquet	26 Apr 2017, 16:27	257.4 MB	Document
train_categorical.parquet	26 Apr 2017, 17:06	40.6 MB	Document

Now we read the files in again as DataFrames from the `parquet` files:

```
var df_numeric = spark.read.parquet(basePath+"train_numeric.parquet")

var df_categorical =
spark.read.parquet(basePath+"train_categorical.parquet")
```

Here is the output of the same:

```
scala> var df_numeric = spark.read.parquet(basePath+"train_numeric.parquet")
df_numeric: org.apache.spark.sql.DataFrame = [Id: int, L0_S0_F0: double ... 968 more fields]

scala>

scala> var df_date = spark.read.parquet(basePath+"train_date.parquet")
df_date: org.apache.spark.sql.DataFrame = [Id: int, L0_S0_D1: double ... 1155 more fields]

scala>

scala> var df_categorical = spark.read.parquet(basePath+"train_categorical.parquet")
df_categorical: org.apache.spark.sql.DataFrame = [Id: int, L0_S1_F25: string ... 2139 more fields]
```

This is very high-dimensional data; therefore, we will take only a subset of the columns for this illustration:

```
df_categorical.createOrReplaceTempView("dfcat")
var dfcat = spark.sql("select Id, L0_S22_F545 from dfcat")
```

In the following picture, you can see the unique categorical values of that column:

```
scala> dfcat.select("L0_S22_F545").distinct.show
+-----------+
|L0_S22_F545|
+-----------+
|        T16|
|   T12582912|
|       null|
|     T48576|
|   T16777232|
|       T512|
|     T589824|
|      T1372|
|         T8|
|   T16777557|
|        T32|
|      T6553|
|  T-18748192|
|        T96|
+-----------+
```

Now let's do the same with the numerical dataset:

```
df_numeric.createOrReplaceTempView("dfnum")
var dfnum = spark.sql("select Id,L0_S0_F0,L0_S0_F2,L0_S0_F4,Response from
dfnum")
```

Here is the output of the same:

```
scala> dfnum.show
+---+--------+--------+--------+--------+
| Id|L0_S0_F0|L0_S0_F2|L0_S0_F4|Response|
+---+--------+--------+--------+--------+
|  4|    0.03|  -0.034|  -0.197|       0|
|  6|    null|    null|    null|       0|
|  7|   0.088|   0.086|   0.003|       0|
|  9|  -0.036|  -0.064|   0.294|       0|
| 11|  -0.055|  -0.086|   0.294|       0|
| 13|   0.003|   0.019|   0.294|       0|
| 14|    null|    null|    null|       0|
| 16|    null|    null|    null|       0|
| 18|  -0.016|  -0.041|  -0.179|       0|
| 23|    null|    null|    null|       0|
| 26|   0.016|   0.093|  -0.015|       0|
| 27|  -0.062|  -0.153|  -0.197|       0|
| 28|  -0.075|  -0.093|   0.367|       0|
| 31|  -0.003|  -0.093|  -0.161|       0|
| 34|  -0.016|  -0.138|  -0.197|       0|
| 38|   0.252|    0.25|   0.003|       0|
| 41|    null|    null|    null|       0|
| 44|  -0.016|  -0.041|   0.003|       0|
| 47|    null|    null|    null|       0|
| 49|   0.088|   0.033|    0.33|       0|
+---+--------+--------+--------+--------+
only showing top 20 rows
```

Finally, we rejoin these two relations:

```
var df = dfcat.join(dfnum,"Id")
df.createOrReplaceTempView("df")
```

Then we have to do some NA treatment:

```
var df_notnull = spark.sql("""
select
    Response as label,
    case
        when L0_S22_F545 is null then 'NA'
        else L0_S22_F545 end as L0_S22_F545,
    case
        when L0_S0_F0 is null then 0.0
        else L0_S0_F0 end as L0_S0_F0,
    case
        when L0_S0_F2 is null then 0.0
        else L0_S0_F2 end as L0_S0_F2,
    case
        when L0_S0_F4 is null then 0.0
        else L0_S0_F4 end as L0_S0_F4
from df
""")
```

Feature engineering

Now it is time to run the first transformer (which is actually an estimator). It is
`StringIndexer` and needs to keep track of an internal mapping table between strings and
indexes. Therefore, it is not a transformer but an estimator:

```
import org.apache.spark.ml.feature.{OneHotEncoder, StringIndexer}

var indexer = new StringIndexer()
  .setHandleInvalid("skip")
  .setInputCol("L0_S22_F545")
  .setOutputCol("L0_S22_F545Index")

var indexed = indexer.fit(df_notnull).transform(df_notnull)
indexed.printSchema
```

As we can see clearly in the following image, an additional column called
`L0_S22_F545Index` has been created:

```
root
 |-- label: integer (nullable = true)
 |-- L0_S22_F545: string (nullable = true)
 |-- L0_S0_F0: double (nullable = true)
 |-- L0_S0_F2: double (nullable = true)
 |-- L0_S0_F4: double (nullable = true)
 |-- L0_S22_F545Index: double (nullable = true)
```

Finally, let's examine some content of the newly created column and compare it with the
source column.

We can clearly see how the category string gets transformed into a float index:

```
scala> indexed.select("L0_S22_F545","L0_S22_F545Index").distinct.show
+-----------+----------------+
|L0_S22_F545|L0_S22_F545Index|
+-----------+----------------+
|  T12582912|             6.0|
|      T1372|            10.0|
|        T16|             7.0|
|        T32|             9.0|
|      T48576|            2.0|
| T-18748192|             8.0|
|         NA|             0.0|
|  T16777557|             1.0|
|  T16777232|            11.0|
|         T8|             4.0|
|       T512|             3.0|
|    T589824|            13.0|
|      T6553|            12.0|
|        T96|             5.0|
+-----------+----------------+
```

Now we want to apply `OneHotEncoder`, which is a transformer, in order to generate better
features for our machine learning model:

```
var encoder = new OneHotEncoder()
  .setInputCol("L0_S22_F545Index")
  .setOutputCol("L0_S22_F545Vec")

var encoded = encoder.transform(indexed)
```

As you can see in the following figure, the newly created column `L0_S22_F545Vec` contains `org.apache.spark.ml.linalg.SparseVector` objects, which is a compressed representation of a sparse vector:

```
scala> encoded.select("L0_S22_F545Index","L0_S22_F545Vec").distinct.show
+----------------+----------------+
|L0_S22_F545Index|  L0_S22_F545Vec|
+----------------+----------------+
|            11.0|(13,[11],[1.0])|
|             2.0|  (13,[2],[1.0])|
|             8.0|  (13,[8],[1.0])|
|             3.0|  (13,[3],[1.0])|
|            10.0|(13,[10],[1.0])|
|             6.0|  (13,[6],[1.0])|
|             7.0|  (13,[7],[1.0])|
|            12.0|(13,[12],[1.0])|
|             9.0|  (13,[9],[1.0])|
|             4.0|  (13,[4],[1.0])|
|             5.0|  (13,[5],[1.0])|
|             0.0|  (13,[0],[1.0])|
|             1.0|  (13,[1],[1.0])|
|            13.0|      (13,[],[])|
+----------------+----------------+
```

Sparse vector representations: The `OneHotEncoder`, as many other algorithms, returns a sparse vector of the `org.apache.spark.ml.linalg.SparseVector` type as, according to the definition, only one element of the vector can be one, the rest has to remain zero. This gives a lot of opportunity for compression as only the position of the elements that are non-zero has to be known. Apache Spark uses a sparse vector representation in the following format: *(l,[p],[v])*, where *l* stands for length of the vector, *p* for position (this can also be an array of positions), and *v* for the actual values (this can be an array of values). So if we get (13,[10],[1.0]), as in our earlier example, the actual sparse vector looks like this: (0.0,0.0,0.0,0.0,0.0,0.0,0.0,0.0,0.0,0.0,1.0,0.0,0.0,0.0).

So now that we are done with our feature engineering, we want to create one overall sparse vector containing all the necessary columns for our machine learner. This is done using `VectorAssembler`:

```
import org.apache.spark.ml.feature.VectorAssembler
import org.apache.spark.ml.linalg.Vectors

var vectorAssembler = new VectorAssembler()
        .setInputCols(Array("L0_S22_F545Vec", "L0_S0_F0",
"L0_S0_F2","L0_S0_F4"))
```

```
        .setOutputCol("features")

    var assembled = vectorAssembler.transform(encoded)
```

We basically just define a list of column names and a target column, and the rest is done for us:

```
scala> assembled.show
+-----+----------+--------+--------+--------+-----------------+---------------+--------------------+
|label|L0_S22_F545|L0_S0_F0|L0_S0_F2|L0_S0_F4|L0_S22_F545Index|L0_S22_F545Vec|            features|
+-----+----------+--------+--------+--------+-----------------+---------------+--------------------+
|    0|       NA|    0.03|  -0.034|  -0.197|             0.0|(13,[0],[1.0])|(16,[0,13,14,15],...|
|    0|       NA|     0.0|     0.0|     0.0|             0.0|(13,[0],[1.0])|    (16,[0],[1.0])|
|    0|       NA|   0.088|   0.086|   0.003|             0.0|(13,[0],[1.0])|(16,[0,13,14,15],...|
|    0|       NA|  -0.036|  -0.064|   0.294|             0.0|(13,[0],[1.0])|(16,[0,13,14,15],...|
|    0|       NA|  -0.055|  -0.086|   0.294|             0.0|(13,[0],[1.0])|(16,[0,13,14,15],...|
|    0|       NA|   0.003|   0.019|   0.294|             0.0|(13,[0],[1.0])|(16,[0,13,14,15],...|
|    0|       NA|     0.0|     0.0|     0.0|             0.0|(13,[0],[1.0])|    (16,[0],[1.0])|
|    0|       NA|     0.0|     0.0|     0.0|             0.0|(13,[0],[1.0])|    (16,[0],[1.0])|
|    0|       NA|  -0.016|  -0.041|  -0.179|             0.0|(13,[0],[1.0])|(16,[0,13,14,15],...|
|    0|       NA|     0.0|     0.0|     0.0|             0.0|(13,[0],[1.0])|    (16,[0],[1.0])|
|    0|       NA|   0.016|   0.093|  -0.015|             0.0|(13,[0],[1.0])|(16,[0,13,14,15],...|
|    0|       NA|  -0.062|  -0.153|  -0.197|             0.0|(13,[0],[1.0])|(16,[0,13,14,15],...|
|    0|       NA|  -0.075|  -0.093|   0.367|             0.0|(13,[0],[1.0])|(16,[0,13,14,15],...|
|    0|       NA|  -0.003|  -0.093|  -0.161|             0.0|(13,[0],[1.0])|(16,[0,13,14,15],...|
|    0|       NA|  -0.016|  -0.138|  -0.197|             0.0|(13,[0],[1.0])|(16,[0,13,14,15],...|
|    0|       NA|   0.252|    0.25|   0.003|             0.0|(13,[0],[1.0])|    (16,[0],[1.0])|
|    0|       NA|  -0.016|  -0.041|   0.003|             0.0|(13,[0],[1.0])|(16,[0,13,14,15],...|
|    0|       NA|     0.0|     0.0|     0.0|             0.0|(13,[0],[1.0])|    (16,[0],[1.0])|
|    0|       NA|   0.088|   0.033|    0.33|             0.0|(13,[0],[1.0])|(16,[0,13,14,15],...|
+-----+----------+--------+--------+--------+-----------------+---------------+--------------------+
only showing top 20 rows
```

As the view of the `features` column got a bit squashed, let's inspect one instance of the feature field in more detail:

```
scala> assembled.select("features").first.get(0)
res27: Any = (16,[0,13,14,15],[1.0,0.03,-0.034,-0.197])
```

We can clearly see that we are dealing with a sparse vector of length 16 where positions **0, 13, 14,** and **15** are non-zero and contain the following values: `1.0`, `0.03`, `-0.034`, and `-0.197`. Done! Let's create a `Pipeline` out of these components.

Testing the feature engineering pipeline

Let's create a `Pipeline` out of our transformers and estimators:

```
import org.apache.spark.ml.Pipeline
import org.apache.spark.ml.PipelineModel

//Create an array out of individual pipeline stages
var transformers = Array(indexer,encoder,assembled)


var pipeline = new Pipeline().setStages(transformers).fit(df_notnull)

var transformed = pipeline.transform(df_notnull)
```

Note that the `setStages` method of `Pipeline` just expects an array of `transformers` and `estimators`, which we had created earlier. As parts of the `Pipeline` contain estimators, we have to run `fit` on our `DataFrame` first. The obtained `Pipeline` object takes a `DataFrame` in the `transform` method and returns the results of the transformations:

```
scala> transformed.show
+-----+----------+--------+--------+--------+---------------+----------------+--------------------+
|label|L0_S22_F545|L0_S0_F0|L0_S0_F2|L0_S0_F4|L0_S22_F545Index|L0_S22_F545Vec|            features|
+-----+----------+--------+--------+--------+---------------+----------------+--------------------+
|    0|        NA|    0.03|  -0.034|  -0.197|            0.0|(13,[0],[1.0])|(16,[0,13,14,15],...|
|    0|        NA|     0.0|     0.0|     0.0|            0.0|(13,[0],[1.0])|     (16,[0],[1.0])|
|    0|        NA|   0.088|   0.086|   0.003|            0.0|(13,[0],[1.0])|(16,[0,13,14,15],...|
|    0|        NA|  -0.036|  -0.064|   0.294|            0.0|(13,[0],[1.0])|(16,[0,13,14,15],...|
|    0|        NA|  -0.055|  -0.086|   0.294|            0.0|(13,[0],[1.0])|(16,[0,13,14,15],...|
|    0|        NA|   0.003|   0.019|   0.294|            0.0|(13,[0],[1.0])|(16,[0,13,14,15],...|
|    0|        NA|     0.0|     0.0|     0.0|            0.0|(13,[0],[1.0])|     (16,[0],[1.0])|
|    0|        NA|     0.0|     0.0|     0.0|            0.0|(13,[0],[1.0])|     (16,[0],[1.0])|
|    0|        NA|  -0.016|  -0.041|  -0.179|            0.0|(13,[0],[1.0])|(16,[0,13,14,15],...|
|    0|        NA|     0.0|     0.0|     0.0|            0.0|(13,[0],[1.0])|     (16,[0],[1.0])|
|    0|        NA|   0.016|   0.093|  -0.015|            0.0|(13,[0],[1.0])|(16,[0,13,14,15],...|
|    0|        NA|  -0.062|  -0.153|  -0.197|            0.0|(13,[0],[1.0])|(16,[0,13,14,15],...|
|    0|        NA|  -0.075|  -0.093|   0.367|            0.0|(13,[0],[1.0])|(16,[0,13,14,15],...|
|    0|        NA|  -0.003|  -0.093|  -0.161|            0.0|(13,[0],[1.0])|(16,[0,13,14,15],...|
|    0|        NA|  -0.016|  -0.138|  -0.197|            0.0|(13,[0],[1.0])|(16,[0,13,14,15],...|
|    0|        NA|   0.252|    0.25|   0.003|            0.0|(13,[0],[1.0])|(16,[0,13,14,15],...|
|    0|        NA|     0.0|     0.0|     0.0|            0.0|(13,[0],[1.0])|     (16,[0],[1.0])|
|    0|        NA|  -0.016|  -0.041|   0.003|            0.0|(13,[0],[1.0])|(16,[0,13,14,15],...|
|    0|        NA|     0.0|     0.0|     0.0|            0.0|(13,[0],[1.0])|     (16,[0],[1.0])|
|    0|        NA|   0.088|   0.033|    0.33|            0.0|(13,[0],[1.0])|(16,[0,13,14,15],...|
+-----+----------+--------+--------+--------+---------------+----------------+--------------------+
only showing top 20 rows
```

As expected, we obtain the very same DataFrame as we had while running the stages individually in a sequence.

Training the machine learning model

Now it's time to add another component to the `Pipeline`: the actual machine learning algorithm--RandomForest:

```
import org.apache.spark.ml.classification.RandomForestClassifier
var rf = new RandomForestClassifier()
  .setLabelCol("label")
  .setFeaturesCol("features")

var model = new Pipeline().setStages(transformers :+ rf).fit(df_notnull)

var result = model.transform(df_notnull)
```

This code is very straightforward. First, we have to instantiate our algorithm and obtain it as a reference in `rf`. We could have set additional parameters to the model but we'll do this later in an automated fashion in the `CrossValidation` step. Then, we just add the stage to our `Pipeline`, fit it, and finally transform. The `fit` method, apart from running all upstream stages, also calls fit on the `RandomForestClassifier` in order to train it. The trained model is now contained within the `Pipeline` and the `transform` method actually creates our predictions column:

```
scala> result.show
+-----+----------+--------+--------+--------+--------------+--------------+--------------------+--------------------+--------------------+----------+
|label|L0_S22_F545|L0_S0_F0|L0_S0_F2|L0_S0_F4|L0_S22_F545Index|L0_S22_F545Vec|            features|       rawPrediction|         probability|prediction|
+-----+----------+--------+--------+--------+--------------+--------------+--------------------+--------------------+--------------------+----------+
|    0|        NA|    0.03|  -0.034|  -0.197|           0.0|(13,[0],[1.0])|(16,[0,13,14,15],...|[19.8764711847913...|[0.99382355923956...|       0.0|
|    0|        NA|     0.0|     0.0|     0.0|           0.0|(13,[0],[1.0])|      (16,[0],[1.0])|[19.8734515671497...|[0.99367257835748...|       0.0|
|    0|        NA|   0.088|   0.086|   0.003|           0.0|(13,[0],[1.0])|(16,[0,13,14,15],...|[19.8936982048582...|[0.99468491024291...|       0.0|
|    0|        NA|  -0.036|  -0.064|   0.294|           0.0|(13,[0],[1.0])|(16,[0,13,14,15],...|[19.9103667119433...|[0.99551833559716...|       0.0|
|    0|        NA|  -0.055|  -0.086|   0.294|           0.0|(13,[0],[1.0])|(16,[0,13,14,15],...|[19.9128187397603...|[0.99564093698801...|       0.0|
|    0|        NA|   0.003|   0.019|   0.294|           0.0|(13,[0],[1.0])|(16,[0,13,14,15],...|[19.9021809064659...|[0.99510904532329...|       0.0|
|    0|        NA|     0.0|     0.0|     0.0|           0.0|(13,[0],[1.0])|      (16,[0],[1.0])|[19.8734515671497...|[0.99367257835748...|       0.0|
|    0|        NA|  -0.016|  -0.041|  -0.179|           0.0|(13,[0],[1.0])|(16,[0,13,14,15],...|[19.8762685936784...|[0.99381342968392...|       0.0|
|    0|        NA|     0.0|     0.0|     0.0|           0.0|(13,[0],[1.0])|      (16,[0],[1.0])|[19.8734515671497...|[0.99367257835748...|       0.0|
|    0|        NA|   0.016|   0.093|  -0.015|           0.0|(13,[0],[1.0])|(16,[0,13,14,15],...|[19.8393359144095...|[0.99419679572047...|       0.0|
|    0|        NA|  -0.062|  -0.153|  -0.197|           0.0|(13,[0],[1.0])|(16,[0,13,14,15],...|[19.8900653890112...|[0.99450326945056...|       0.0|
|    0|        NA|  -0.075|  -0.093|   0.367|           0.0|(13,[0],[1.0])|(16,[0,13,14,15],...|[19.9155130528803...|[0.99577565264401...|       0.0|
|    0|        NA|  -0.003|  -0.093|  -0.161|           0.0|(13,[0],[1.0])|(16,[0,13,14,15],...|[19.8830065488786...|[0.99415032744393...|       0.0|
|    0|        NA|  -0.016|  -0.138|  -0.197|           0.0|(13,[0],[1.0])|(16,[0,13,14,15],...|[19.8787059668007...|[0.99393529834003...|       0.0|
|    0|        NA|   0.252|    0.25|   0.003|           0.0|(13,[0],[1.0])|(16,[0,13,14,15],...|[19.8899480526405...|[0.99449740263202...|       0.0|
|    0|        NA|     0.0|     0.0|     0.0|           0.0|(13,[0],[1.0])|      (16,[0],[1.0])|[19.8734515671497...|[0.99367257835748...|       0.0|
|    0|        NA|  -0.016|  -0.041|   0.003|           0.0|(13,[0],[1.0])|(16,[0,13,14,15],...|[19.8929538865276...|[0.99464769432638...|       0.0|
|    0|        NA|     0.0|     0.0|     0.0|           0.0|(13,[0],[1.0])|      (16,[0],[1.0])|[19.8734515671497...|[0.99367257835748...|       0.0|
|    0|        NA|   0.088|   0.033|    0.33|           0.0|(13,[0],[1.0])|(16,[0,13,14,15],...|[19.9092368840784...|[0.99546184420392...|       0.0|
+-----+----------+--------+--------+--------+--------------+--------------+--------------------+--------------------+--------------------+----------+
only showing top 20 rows
```

As we can see, we've now obtained an additional column called prediction, which contains the output of the `RandomForestClassifier` model. Of course, we've only used a very limited subset of available features/columns and have also not yet tuned the model, so we don't expect to do very well; however, let's take a look at how we can evaluate our model easily with Apache SparkML.

Model evaluation

Without evaluation, a model is worth nothing as we don't know how accurately it performs. Therefore, we will now use the built-in `BinaryClassificationEvaluator` in order to assess prediction performance and a widely used measure called `areaUnderROC` (going into detail here is beyond the scope of this book):

```
import org.apache.spark.ml.evaluation.BinaryClassificationEvaluator
val evaluator = new BinaryClassificationEvaluator()

import org.apache.spark.ml.param.ParamMap
var evaluatorParamMap = ParamMap(evaluator.metricName -> "areaUnderROC")
var aucTraining = evaluator.evaluate(result, evaluatorParamMap)
```

As we can see, there is a built-in class called `org.apache.spark.ml.evaluation.BinaryClassificationEvaluator` and there are some other classes for other prediction use cases such as `RegressionEvaluator` or `MuliclassClassificationEvaluator`. The `evaluator` takes a parameter map--in this case, we are telling it to use the `areaUnderROC` metric--and finally, the evaluate method evaluates the result:

```
scala> var aucTraining = evaluator.evaluate(result, evaluatorParamMap)
aucTraining: Double = 0.5424418446501833
```

As we can see, `areaUnderROC` is `0.5424418446501833`. An ideal classifier would return a score of one. So we are only doing a bit better than random guesses but, as already stated, the number of features that we are looking at is fairly limited.

 In the previous example, we are using the `areaUnderROC` metric which is used for the evaluation of binary classifiers. There exist an abundance of other metrics used for different disciplines of machine learning such as accuracy, precision, recall, and F1 score. The following provides a good overview http://www.cs.cornell.edu/courses/cs578/2003fa/performance_measures.pdf

This `areaUnderROC` is, in fact, a very bad value. Let's see if choosing better parameters for our `RandomForest` model increases this a bit in the next section.

CrossValidation and hyperparameter tuning

As explained before, a common step in machine learning is cross-validating your model using testing data against training data and also tweaking the knobs of your machine learning algorithms. Let's use Apache SparkML in order to do this for us, fully automated!

First, we have to configure the parameter map and `CrossValidator`:

```
import org.apache.spark.ml.tuning.{CrossValidator, ParamGridBuilder}
var paramGrid = new ParamGridBuilder()
    .addGrid(rf.numTrees, 3 :: 5 :: 10 :: 30 :: 50 :: 70 :: 100 :: 150 ::
Nil)
    .addGrid(rf.featureSubsetStrategy, "auto" :: "all" :: "sqrt" :: "log2"
:: "onethird" :: Nil)
    .addGrid(rf.impurity, "gini" :: "entropy" :: Nil)
    .addGrid(rf.maxBins, 2 :: 5 :: 10 :: 15 :: 20 :: 25 :: 30 :: Nil)
    .addGrid(rf.maxDepth, 3 :: 5 :: 10 :: 15 :: 20 :: 25 :: 30 :: Nil)
    .build()

var crossValidator = new CrossValidator()
      .setEstimator(new Pipeline().setStages(transformers :+ rf))
      .setEstimatorParamMaps(paramGrid)
      .setNumFolds(5)
.setEvaluator(evaluator)
var crossValidatorModel = crossValidator.fit(df_notnull)
var newPredictions = crossValidatorModel.transform(df_notnull)
```

The `org.apache.spark.ml.tuning.ParamGridBuilder` is used in order to define the hyperparameter space where the `CrossValidator` has to search and finally, the `org.apache.spark.ml.tuning.CrossValidator` takes our `Pipeline`, the hyperparameter space of our RandomForest classifier, and the number of folds for the `CrossValidation` as parameters. Now, as usual, we just need to call fit and transform on the `CrossValidator` and it will basically run our `Pipeline` multiple times and return a model that performs the best. Do you know how many different models are trained? Well, we have five folds on `CrossValidation` and five-dimensional hyperparameter space cardinalities between two and eight, so let's do the math: 5 * 8 * 5 * 2 * 7 * 7 = 19600 times!

Using the evaluator to assess the quality of the cross-validated and tuned model

Now that we've optimized our `Pipeline` in a fully automatic fashion, let's see how our best model can be obtained:

```
var bestPipelineModel =
crossValidatorModel.bestModel.asInstanceOf[PipelineModel]
    var stages = bestPipelineModel.stages
import org.apache.spark.ml.classification.RandomForestClassificationModel
    val rfStage =
stages(stages.length-1).asInstanceOf[RandomForestClassificationModel]
rfStage.getNumTrees
rfStage.getFeatureSubsetStrategy
rfStage.getImpurity
rfStage.getMaxBins
rfStage.getMaxDepth
```

The `crossValidatorModel.bestModel` code basically returns the best `Pipeline`. Now we use `bestPipelineModel.stages` to obtain the individual stages and obtain the tuned `RandomForestClassificationModel` using `stages(stages.length-1).asInstanceOf[RandomForestClassificationModel]`. Note that `stages.length-1` addresses the last stage in the `Pipeline`, which is our `RandomForestClassifier`.

So now, we can basically run `evaluator` using the best model and see how it performs:

```
[scala> evaluator.evaluate(newPredictions, evaluatorParamMap)
res6: Double = 0.5362224872557545
```

You might have noticed that `0.5362224872557545` is less than `0.5424418446501833`, as we've obtained before. So why is this the case? Actually, this time we used cross-validation, which means that the model is less likely to over fit and therefore the score is a bit lower.

So let's take a look at the parameters of the best model:

```
scala> rfStage.getNumTrees
res1: Int = 5

scala> rfStage.getFeatureSubsetStrategy
res2: String = auto

scala> rfStage.getImpurity
res3: String = entropy

scala> rfStage.getMaxBins
res4: Int = 5

scala> rfStage.getMaxDepth
res5: Int = 5
```

Note that we've limited the hyperparameter space, so numTrees, maxBins, and maxDepth have been limited to five, and bigger trees will most likely perform better. So feel free to play around with this code and add features, and also use a bigger hyperparameter space, say, bigger trees.

Summary

You've learned that, as in many other places, the introduction of DataFrames leads to the development of complementary frameworks that are not using RDDs directly anymore. This is also the case for machine learning but there is much more to it. Pipeline actually takes machine learning in Apache Spark to the next level as it improves the productivity of the data scientist dramatically.

The compatibility between all intermediate objects and well-thought-out concepts is just awesome. Great! Finally, we've applied the concepts that we discussed on a real dataset from a Kaggle competition, which is a very nice starting point for your own machine learning project with Apache SparkML. The next Chapter covers Apache SystemML, which is a 3rd party machine learning library for Apache Spark. Let's see why it is useful and what the differences are to SparkML.

Apache SystemML

So far, we have only covered components that came along with the standard distribution of Apache Spark (except HDFS, Kafka and Flume, of course). However, Apache Spark can also serve as runtime for third-party components, making it as some sort of operating system for big data applications. In this chapter, we want to introduce Apache SystemML, an amazing piece of technology initially developed by the *IBM Almaden Research Lab* in California. Apache SystemML went through many transformation stages and has now become an Apache top level project.

In this chapter, we will cover the following topics to get a greater insight into the subject:

- Using SystemML for your own machine learning applications on top of Apache Spark
- Learning the fundamental differences between SystemML and other machine learning libraries for Apache Spark
- Discovering the reason why another machine library exists for Apache Spark

Why do we need just another library?

In order to answer this question, we have to know something about SystemML's history, which began ten years ago in 2007 as a research project in the *IBM Almaden Research Lab* in California. The project was driven by the intention to improve the workflow of data scientists, especially those who want to improve and add functionality to existing machine learning algorithms.

So, **SystemML** is a declarative markup language that can transparently distribute work on Apache Spark. It supports Scale-up using multithreading and SIMD instructions on CPUs as well as GPUs and also Scale-out using a cluster, and of course, both together.

Finally, there is a cost-based optimizer in place to generate low-level execution plans taking statistics about the Dataset sizes into account. In other words, **Apache SystemML** is for machine learning, what Catalyst and Tungsten are for DataFrames.

Why on Apache Spark?

Apache Spark solves a lot of common issues in data processing and machine learning, so Apache SystemML can make use of these features. For example, Apache Spark supports the unification of SQL, Graph, Stream, and machine learning data processing on top of a common RDD structure.

In other words, it is a general **DAG** (**directed acyclic graph**) execution engine supporting lazy evaluation and distributed in-memory caching.

The history of Apache SystemML

Apache SystemML is already ten years old. Of course, it went through multiple refactorings and is now a state-of-the-art, and one of the fastest, machine learning libraries in the world.

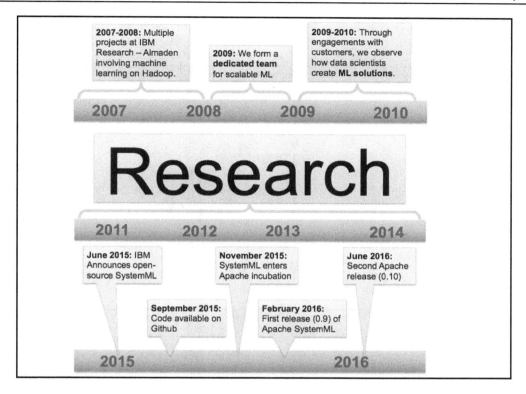

As you can see in the preceding figure, a lot of research has been done for Apache SystemML. It is two years older than Apache Spark and in 2017 it has been turned into a top-level Apache project, leaving **incubator** status. Even during the time SystemML was started, the researchers at *IBM Research Almaden* realized that, very often, out-of-the-box machine learning algorithms perform very poorly on large Datasets.

So, the data analysis pipeline, had to be tuned after a small-scale version of it had been prototyped. The following figure illustrates this:

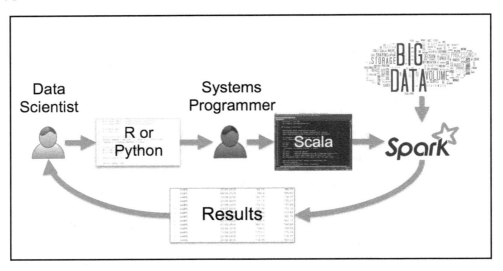

This means that the data scientist will prototype his application in a programming language of his choice, most likely Matlab, R or python and, finally, a systems programmer will pick this up and re-implement this in a JVM language like Java or Scala, which usually turns out to provide better performance and also linearly scales on data parallel framework like Apache Spark.

The scaled version of the prototype will return results on the whole Dataset and the data scientist again is in charge of modifying the prototype and the whole cycle begins again. Not only the IBM Almaden Research staff members have experienced this, but even our team has seen it. So let's make the systems programmer redundant (or at least require him only to take care of our Apache Spark jobs) using Apache SystemML.

A cost-based optimizer for machine learning algorithms

Let's start with an example to exemplify how Apache SystemML works internally. Consider a recommender system.

An example - alternating least squares

A recommender system tries to predict the potential items that a user might be interested in, based on a history from other users.

So let's consider a so-called item-user or product-customer matrix, as illustrated here:

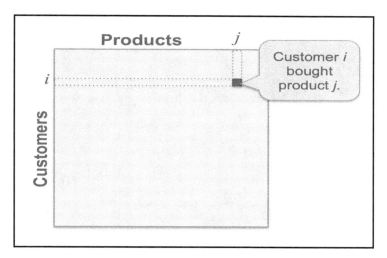

This is a so-called **sparse** matrix because only a couple of cells are populated with non-zero values indicating a match between a customer i and a product j. Either by just putting a **one** in the cell or any other numerical value, for example, indicating the number of products bought or a rating for that particular product j from customer i. Let's call this matrix r_{ui}, where u stands for user and i for item.

Those of you familiar with linear algebra might know that any matrix can be factorized by two smaller matrices. This means that you have to find two matrices p_u and q_i that, when multiplied with each other, reconstruct the original matrix r_{ui}; let's call the reconstruction r_{ui}'. The goal is to find p_u and q_i to reconstruct r_{ui}' such that it doesn't differ too much from r_{ui}. This is done using a sum of squared errors objective.

The following figure illustrates this and the sparsity property of the matrix:

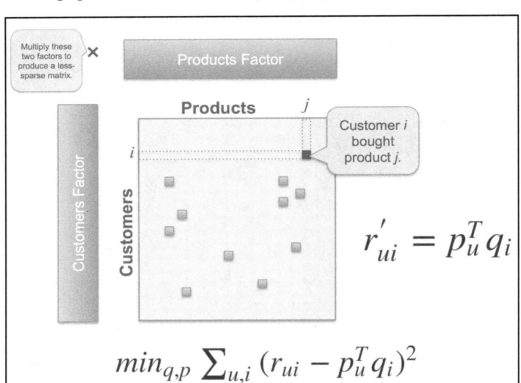

Once we've found good factors p_u and q_i, we can construct r_{ui}' and, finally, new non-zero cells will be present, which become the new predicted product suggestions. In case you haven't understood all the details, don't worry, as we don't need too much of this example to understand the rest of this chapter.

A common algorithm to find p_u and q_i is called **alternating least squares** (**ALS**)--alternating because in each iteration the optimization objective switches from p_u to q_i and vice versa. Don't get bothered with it too much, but this is how it actually works, and, in Apache Spark MLlib, this is just a single line of Scala code:

```
val model = ALS.train(ratings, rank, numIterations, 0.01)
```

So what's wrong with this? Before we explain this, let's take a look at how ALS is implemented in a statistical programming language such as R:

```
U = rand(nrow(X), r, min = -1.0, max = 1.0);
V = rand(r, ncol(X), min = -1.0, max = 1.0);
while(i < mi) {
    i = i + 1; ii = 1;
    if (is_U)
        G = (W * (U %*% V - X)) %*% t(V) + lambda * U;
    else
        G = t(U) %*% (W * (U %*% V - X)) + lambda * V;
    norm_G2 = sum(G ^ 2); norm_R2 = norm_G2;
    R = -G; S = R;
    while(norm_R2 > 10E-9 * norm_G2 & ii <= mii) {
        if (is_U) {
            HS = (W * (S %*% V)) %*% t(V) + lambda * S;
            alpha = norm_R2 / sum (S * HS);
            U = U + alpha * S;
        } else {
            HS = t(U) %*% (W * (U %*% S)) + lambda * S;
            alpha = norm_R2 / sum (S * HS);
            V = V + alpha * S;
        }
        R = R - alpha * HS;
        old_norm_R2 = norm_R2; norm_R2 = sum(R ^ 2);
        S = R + (norm_R2 / old_norm_R2) * S;
        ii = ii + 1;
    }
    is_U = ! is_U;
}
```

Again, don't worry if you don't understand each line, but the purpose of this figure is to show you that in R, this algorithm needs only 27 lines of code to be expressed. If we now take a look at the ALS implementation in MLlib, we'll see that it has more than 800 lines. You can find this implementation at https://github.com/apache/spark/tree/master/mllib/src/main/scala/org/apache/spark/mllib/recommendation.

So why do we need more than 800 lines in Scala on Spark and only 27 in R? This is because of performance optimizations. The ALS implementation in MLlib consists of more than 50% of performance optimization code. So what if we could perform the following?

- Get rid of all performance optimizations in our algorithm implementation
- Port our R code 1:1 to some parallel framework
- In case of changes, just change our R implementation

This is where Apache SystemML kicks in, it supports all this. Apache SystemML's **DSL** (**domain specific language**) is a subset of R syntax, so you can just take the previous example and run it 1:1 without any modification on top of Apache SystemML. In addition, a cost-based performance optimizer generates a physical execution plan on top of Apache Spark in order to minimize execution time based on the size properties of your data. So let's find out how this works.

ApacheSystemML architecture

So the key thing on Apache SystemML is the optimizer. This component turns a high-level description of an algorithm in a domain-specific language into a highly optimized physical execution on Apache Spark, as shown in the following figure:

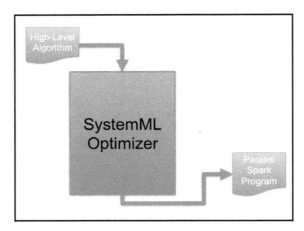

Language parsing

Let's open this black box a bit in order to understand what exactly is going on in the Apache SystemML optimizer. The first thing that the engine does is a compile step on the DSL. So first, syntax checking, then live variable analysis in order to determine which intermediate results are still needed, and finally a semantic check.

High-level operators are generated

Once the previous step is passed, the execution plan using so-called **high-level operators** (**HOPs**) is generated. These are constructed from the **abstract syntax tree** (**AST**) of the DSL. The following important optimization steps are taking place during this phase:

- **Static rewrites**: The DSL offers a rich set of syntactical and semantic features that makes an implementation easy to understand but may result in a non-optimal execution. Apache SystemML detects these branches of the AST and statically rewrites them to a better version, maintaining the semantic equivalency.

- **Dynamic rewrites**: Dynamic rewrites are very similar to static rewrites but are driven by cost-based statistics considering the size of the Datasets to be processed.

The following figure illustrates a static rewrite where a branch of the AST performing a matrix multiplication, is actually rewritten to use a HOP called **wdivmm** (**weighted divide matrix multiplication**), which is a way of computing results of matrix multiplication of that particular form, without materializing a very large intermediate dense matrix in order to save memory:

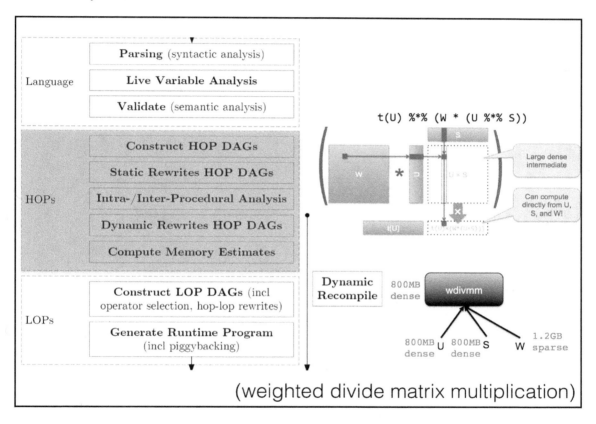

How low-level operators are optimized on

Let's have a look on, how low-level operators are selected and optimized on. We'll stick to the weighted divide matrix multiplication example--a HOP that has been selected before the HOP optimizations process over an ordinary sequence of matrix multiplications. So now the question arises, for example, if it makes sense to use a parallel version of a LOP running parallel on the Apache Spark workers, or whether a local execution is preferable. In this example, Apache SystemML determines that all intermediate results fit into the main memory of the driver node and chooses the local operator, **WDivMM**, over the parallel operator, **MapWDivMM**. The following figure illustrates this process:

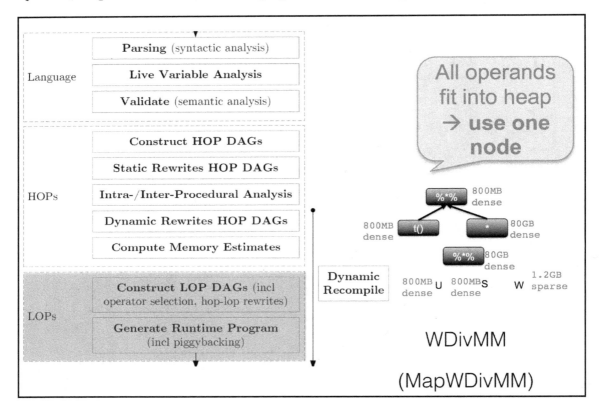

Performance measurements

So is all this effort worth it? Let's take a look at some performance comparisons between a local R script, MLlib, and Apache SystemML:

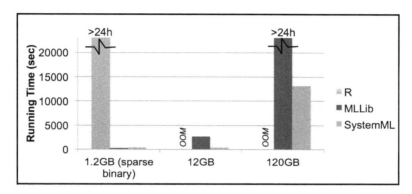

The ALS algorithm has been run on different Datasets with 1.2, 12, and 120 GB size using R, MLlib, and ApacheSystemML. We can clearly see that, even on the smallest Dataset, R is not a feasible solution as it took more than 24 hours, and we are not sure if it would have ever completed. On the 12 GB Dataset, we've noticed that ApacheSystemML runs significantly faster than MLlib, and finally, on the 120 GB Dataset, the ALS implementation of MLlib didn't finish in one day and we gave up.

Apache SystemML in action

So let's take a look at a very simple example. Let's create a script in Apache SystemML DSL--an R-like syntax--in order to multiply two matrices:

```
import org.apache.sysml.api.MLOutput
import org.apache.spark.sql.SQLContext
import org.apache.spark.mllib.util.LinearDataGenerator
import org.apache.sysml.api.MLContext
import
org.apache.sysml.runtime.instructions.spark.utils.{RDDConverterUtilsExt =>
RDDConverterUtils}
import org.apache.sysml.runtime.matrix.MatrixCharacteristics;

val sqlContext = new SQLContext(sc)

val simpleScript =
"""
```

```
fileX = "";
fileY = "";
fileZ = "";

X = read (fileX);
Y = read (fileY);

Z = X %*% Y

write (Z,fileZ);
"""
```

Then, we generate some test data:

```
// Generate data
val rawDataX =
sqlContext.createDataFrame(LinearDataGenerator.generateLinearRDD(sc, 100,
10, 1))
val rawDataY =
sqlContext.createDataFrame(LinearDataGenerator.generateLinearRDD(sc, 10,
100, 1))

// Repartition into a more parallelism-friendly number of partitions
val dataX = rawDataX.repartition(64).cache()
val dataY = rawDataY.repartition(64).cache()
```

In order to use Apache SystemML, we have to create an `MLContext` object:

```
// Create SystemML context
val ml = new MLContext(sc)
```

Now we have to convert our data to a format that Apache SystemML understands:

```
// Convert data to proper format
val mcX = new MatrixCharacteristics()
val mcY = new MatrixCharacteristics()
val X = RDDConverterUtils.vectorDataFrameToBinaryBlock(sc, dataX, mcX,
false, "features")
val Y = RDDConverterUtils.vectorDataFrameToBinaryBlock(sc, dataY, mcY,
false, "features")
```

Now, we pass the data X and Y to the Apache SystemML runtime and also preregister a variable called Z in order to obtain the result from the runtime:

```
// Register inputs & outputs
ml.reset()
ml.registerInput("X", X, mcX)
ml.registerInput("Y", Y, mcY)
ml.registerOutput("Z")
```

Finally, we actually execute the script stored in `simpleScript` with the `executeScript` method and obtain the result from the runtime:

```
val outputs = ml.executeScript(simpleScript)

// Get outputs
val Z = outputs.getDF(sqlContext, "Z")
```

Now Z contains `DataFrame` with the result of the matrix multiplication. Done!

Summary

You've learned that there is room for additional machine learning frameworks and libraries, on top of Apache Spark and that, a cost-based optimizer similar to what we are already using in Catalyst can speed things up tremendously. In addition, separation from performance optimizations code and code for the algorithm facilitates further improvements on the algorithm side without having to care about performance at all.

Additionally, these execution plans are highly adaptable to the size of the data and also to the available hardware configuration based on main memory size and potential accelerators such as GPUs. Apache SystemML dramatically improves on the life cycle of machine learning applications, especially if machine learning algorithms are not used out of the box, but an experienced data scientist works on low-level details on it, in a mathematical or statistical programming language.

In Apache SystemML, this low level, mathematical code can be used out of the box, without any manual transformation or translation to other programming languages. It can be executed on top of Apache Spark.

7
Apache Spark GraphX

In this chapter, we want to examine the Apache Spark GraphX module and graph processing, in general. So, this chapter will cover the topic of implementing graph analysis workflows on top of GraphX. The *GraphX coding* section, written in Scala, will provide a series of graph coding examples. Before writing code in Scala to use the Spark GraphX module, we think it will be useful to provide an overview of what a graph actually is in terms of graph processing. The following section provides a brief introduction using a couple of simple graphs as examples.

In this chapter we will cover:

- Creating a graph from raw data
- Counting
- Filtering
- PageRank
- Triangle count
- Connected components

Overview

A graph can be considered to be a data structure that consists of a group of vertices and edges connecting them. The vertices or nodes in the graph can be anything as long it is an object (so people for example), and the edges are the relationships between them. The edges can be un-directional or directional, meaning that the relationship operates from one node to another. For instance, node **A** is the parent of node **B**.

In the following diagram, the circles represent the vertices or nodes (**A** to **D**), while the thick lines represent the edges or relationships between them (**E1** to **E6**). Each node or edge may have properties, and these values are represented by the associated gray squares (**P1** to **P7**):

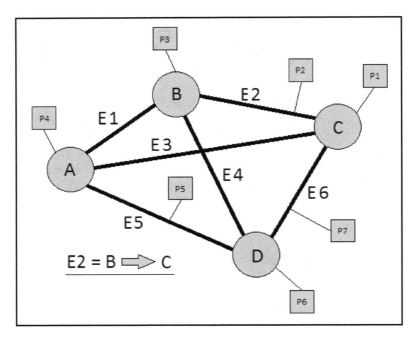

So, if a graph represents a physical route map, the edges might represent minor roads or motorways. The nodes would be motorway junctions or road intersections. Node and edge properties might be road types, speed limits, distance, cost, and grid location.

There are many types of graph implementation, but some examples might be fraud modeling, financial currency transaction modeling, and social modeling as in friend-to-friend connections on Facebook, map processing, web processing, and page ranking.

The preceding diagram shows a generic example of a graph with associated properties. It also shows that edge relationships can be directional, namely edge **E2** acts from node **B** to node **C**.

However, the following example uses family members and the relationships between them to create a graph:

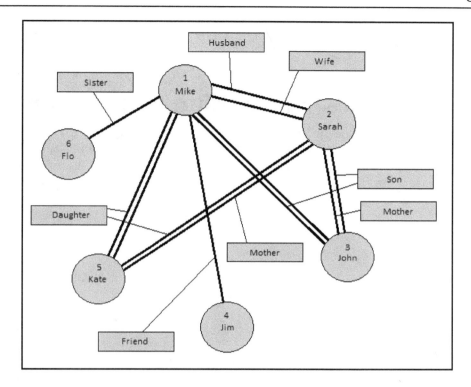

 Note that there can be multiple edges between two nodes or vertices, for instance, the husband and wife relationships between `Mike` and `Sarah`. Also, it is possible that there could be multiple properties on a node or edge.

So, in the preceding example, the `Sister` property acts from node 6 `Flo` to node 1 `Mike`. These are simple graphs to explain the structure of the graph and the element's nature. Real graph applications can reach extreme sizes and require both distributed processing and storage to enable them to be manipulated.

Facebook is able to process graphs containing over 1 trillion edges using Apache Giraph (source Avery Ching Facebook). **Giraph** (`http://giraph.apache.org/`) is an Apache Hadoop ecosystem tool for graph processing, which historically based its processing on MapReduce but now uses TinkerPop (`http://www.tinkerpop.incubator.apache.org/`).

 Although this book concentrates on Apache Spark, that number of the Facebook graph provides a very impressive indicator of the size that a graph can reach.

In the next section, we will examine the use of the Apache Spark GraphX module using Scala.

Graph analytics/processing with GraphX

This section will examine Apache Spark GraphX programming in Scala using the family relationship graph data sample shown in the last section. This data will be accessed as a list of vertices and edges. Although this data set is small, the graphs that you build in this way could be very large. For example, we've been able to analyze 30 TB of financial transaction data of a large bank using only four Apache Spark workers.

The raw data

We are working with two data files. They contain the data that will be used for this section in terms of the vertices and edges that make up a graph:

```
graph1_edges.csv
graph1_vertex.csv
```

The `vertex` file contains just six lines representing the graph used in the last section. Each `vertex` represents a person and has a vertex ID number, a name, and an age value:

```
1,Mike,48
2,Sarah,45
3,John,25
4,Jim,53
5,Kate,22
6,Flo,52
```

The `edge` file contains a set of directed `edge` values in the form source vertex ID, destination vertex ID, and relationship. So, record 1 forms a `Sister` relationship between `Flo` and `Mike`:

```
6,1,Sister
1,2,Husband
2,1,Wife
5,1,Daughter
5,2,Daughter
3,1,Son
3,2,Son
4,1,Friend
1,5,Father
1,3,Father
```

```
2,5,Mother
2,3,Mother
```

Lets, examine some GraphX code samples.

Creating a graph

This section will explain generic Scala code up to the point of creating a GraphX graph from data. This will save time as the same code is reused in each example. Once this is explained, we will concentrate on the actual graph-based manipulation in each code example.

1. The generic code starts by importing Spark context, GraphX, and RDD functionality for use in the Scala code:

   ```
   import org.apache.spark.SparkContext
   import org.apache.spark.SparkContext._
   import org.apache.spark.SparkConf
   import org.apache.spark.graphx._
   import org.apache.spark.rdd.RDD
   ```

2. Then an application is defined, which extends the App class. The application name changes for each example from graph1 to graph5. This application name will be used when running the application using spark-submit:

   ```
   object graph1 extends App {
   ```

3. As already mentioned, there are two data files that contain vertex and edge information:

   ```
   val vertexFile = "graph1_vertex.csv"
   val edgeFile  = "graph1_edges.csv"
   ```

4. The **Spark Master URL** is defined as the application name, which will appear in the Spark user interface when the application runs. A new Spark configuration object is created, and the URL and name are assigned to it:

   ```
   val sparkMaster = "spark://localhost:7077"
   val appName = "Graph 1"
   val conf = new SparkConf()
   conf.setMaster(sparkMaster)
   conf.setAppName(appName)
   ```

5. A new Spark context is created using the configuration that was just defined:

```
val sparkCxt = new SparkContext(conf).
```

6. The `vertex` information from the file is then loaded into an RDD-based structure called vertices using the `sparkCxt.textFile` method. The data is stored as a Long `VertexId` and strings to represent the person's name and age. The data lines are split by commas as this is CSV-based data:

```
val vertices: RDD[(VertexId, (String, String))] =
    sparkCxt.textFile(vertexFile).map { line =>
      val fields = line.split(",")
      ( fields(0).toLong, ( fields(1), fields(2) ) )
}
```

7. Similarly, the `edge` data is loaded into an RDD-based data structure called edges. The CSV-based data is again split by comma values. The first two data values are converted to long values as they represent the source and destination vertex IDs. The final value representing the relationship of the edge is left as `String`. Note that each record in the RDD structure edges is actually now an `Edge` record:

```
val edges: RDD[Edge[String]] =
    sparkCxt.textFile(edgeFile).map { line =>
      val fields = line.split(",")
      Edge(fields(0).toLong, fields(1).toLong, fields(2))
}
```

8. A default value is defined in case a connection or `vertex` is missing; the graph is then constructed from the RDD-based structures vertices and edges and the `default` record:

```
val default = ("Unknown", "Missing")
val graph = Graph(vertices, edges, default)
```

9. This creates a GraphX-based structure called `graph`, which can now be used for each of the examples. Remember that, although these data samples might be small, you could create extremely large graphs using this approach.

Many of these algorithms are iterative applications, for instance, PageRank and triangle count. As a result, the programs will generate many iterative Spark jobs.

Example 1 – counting

The graph has been loaded, and we know the data volumes in the data files. But what about the data content in terms of vertices and edges in the actual graph itself? It is very simple to extract this information using the vertices and edges count function shown as follows:

```
println( "vertices : " + graph.vertices.count )
println( "edges    : " + graph.edges.count )
```

Running the graph1 example using the example name and the .jar file created earlier will provide the count information. The master URL is supplied to connect to the Spark cluster, and some default parameters are supplied for the executor memory and total executor cores:

```
spark-submit \
--class graph1 \
--master spark://localhost:7077 \
--executor-memory 700M \
--total-executor-cores 100 \
/home/hadoop/spark/graphx/target/scala-2.10/graph-x_2.10-1.0.jar
```

The Spark cluster job graph1 provides the following output, which is what would be expected and matches the data files:

```
vertices : 6
edges    : 12
```

Example 2 – filtering

What happens if we need to create a subgraph from the main graph and filter on person age or relationships? The example code from the second example Scala file graph2 shows how this can be done:

```
val c1 = graph.vertices.filter { case (id, (name, age)) => age.toLong > 40
}.count
val c2 = graph.edges.filter { case Edge(from, to, property)
    => property == "Father" | property == "Mother" }.count
println( "Vertices count : " + c1 )
println( "Edges    count : " + c2 )
```

Two example counts have been created from the main graph: the first filters person-based vertices on age only, taking those people who are greater than forty years old. Notice that the age value, which was stored as a string, has been converted to a long for the comparison.

The second example filters the edges on the relationship property of Mother or Father. Two count values c1 and c2 are created and printed as the Spark run output, shown as follows:

```
Vertices count : 4
Edges    count : 4
```

Example 3 – PageRank

The PageRank algorithm provides a ranking value for each of the vertices in a graph. It makes the assumption that the vertices that are connected to the most edges are the most important.

Search engines use PageRank to provide an ordering for page display during a web search as can be seen from the following code:

```
val tolerance = 0.0001
val ranking = graph.pageRank(tolerance).vertices
val rankByPerson = vertices.join(ranking).map {
    case (id, ( (person,age) , rank )) => (rank, id, person)
}
```

The example code creates a tolerance value and calls the graph pageRank method using it. The vertices are then ranked into a new value ranking. In order to make the ranking more meaningful, the ranking values are joined with the original vertices RDD. The rankByPerson value then contains the rank, id, and person name.

The PageRank result held in rankByPerson is then printed record by record using a case statement to identify the record contents and a format statement to print the contents. We did this because we wanted to define the format of the rank value, which can vary:

```
rankByPerson.collect().foreach {
    case (rank, id, person) =>
      println ( f"Rank $rank%1.2f id $id person $person")
}
```

The output from the application is then shown as follows; as expected, `Mike` and `Sarah` have the highest rank as they have the most relationships:

```
Rank 0.15 id 4 person Jim
Rank 0.15 id 6 person Flo
Rank 1.62 id 2 person Sarah
Rank 1.82 id 1 person Mike
Rank 1.13 id 3 person John
Rank 1.13 id 5 person Kate
```

Example 4 – triangle counting

The triangle count algorithm provides a vertex-based count of the number of triangles associated with that vertex. For instance, vertex `Mike` (1) is connected to `Kate` (5), who is connected to `Sarah` (2), `Sarah` is connected to `Mike` (1), and so a triangle is formed. This can be useful for route finding where triangle free minimum spanning tree graphs need to be generated for route planning.

The code to execute a triangle count and print it is simple as shown next. The graph `triangleCount` method is executed for the graph vertices. The result is saved in the value `tCount` and printed:

```
val tCount = graph.triangleCount().vertices
println( tCount.collect().mkString("\n") )
```

The results of the application job show that vertices `Flo` (4) and `Jim` (6) have no triangles, while `Mike` (1) and `Sarah` (2) have the most as expected, as they have the most relationships:

```
(4,0)
(6,0)
(2,4)
(1,4)
(3,2)
(5,2)
```

Example 5 – connected components

When a large graph is created from data, it might contain unconnected subgraphs or subgraphs that are isolated from each other and might contain no bridging or connecting edges between them. These algorithms provide a measure of that connectivity. It might be important depending on your processing to know that all vertices are connected.

The Scala code for this example calls two graph methods, `connectedComponents` and `stronglyConnectedComponents`. The `strong` method required a maximum iteration count, which has been set to `1000`. These counts are acting on the graph vertices:

```
val iterations = 1000
val connected = graph.connectedComponents().vertices
val connectedS = graph.stronglyConnectedComponents(iterations).vertices
```

The `vertex` counts are then joined with the original `vertex` records so that connection counts can be associated with the `vertex` information such as person name:

```
val connByPerson = vertices.join(connected).map {
   case (id, ( (person,age) , conn )) => (conn, id, person)
}
val connByPersonS = vertices.join(connectedS).map {
   case (id, ( (person,age) , conn )) => (conn, id, person)
}
```

The results are then output using a `case` statement and formatted for printing:

```
connByPerson.collect().foreach {
   case (conn, id, person) =>
     println ( f"Weak $conn $id $person" )
}
```

As expected, for the `connectedComponents` algorithm, the results show that, for each `vertex`, there is only one component. That means that all the vertices are members of a single graph as the graph diagram earlier in the chapter showed:

```
Weak 1 4 Jim
Weak 1 6 Flo
Weak 1 2 Sarah
Weak 1 1 Mike
Weak 1 3 John
Weak 1 5 Kate
```

The `stronglyConnectedComponents` method gives a measure of the connectivity in a graph, taking into account the direction of the relationships between them. The results for the `stronglyConnectedComponents` algorithm are output as follows:

```
connByPersonS.collect().foreach {
   case (conn, id, person) =>
     println ( f"Strong $conn $id $person" )
}
```

You might notice from the graph that the relationships `Sister` and `Friend` act from vertices `Flo` (6) and `Jim` (4) to `Mike` (1) as the `edge` and `vertex` data shows:

```
6,1,Sister
4,1,Friend

1,Mike,48
4,Jim,53
6,Flo,52
```

So the `strong` method output shows that, for most vertices, there is only one graph component signified by 1 in the second column. However, vertices 4 and 6 are not reachable due to the direction of their relationship, and so they have a vertex ID instead of a component ID:

```
Strong 4 4 Jim
Strong 6 6 Flo
Strong 1 2 Sarah
Strong 1 1 Mike
Strong 1 3 John
Strong 1 5 Kate
```

Summary

This chapter showed by example how Scala-based code can be used to call GraphX algorithms in Apache Spark. Scala has been used because it requires less code to develop the examples than Java, which saves time. Note that GraphX is not available for Python or R. A Scala-based shell can be used, and the code can be compiled into Spark applications.

The most common graph algorithms have been covered and you should have an idea now on how to solve any graph problem with GraphX. Especially since you've understood that a Graph in GraphX is still represented and backed by RDDs, so you are already familiar with using them. The configuration and code examples from this chapter will also be available for download with the book.

8
Spark Tuning

In this chapter, we will dig deeper into Apache Spark internals and see that while Spark is great in making us feel like we are using just another Scala collection, we don't have to forget that Spark actually runs in a distributed system. Therefore, some extra care should be taken. In a nutshell, the following topics will be covered in this chapter:

- Monitoring Spark jobs
- Spark configuration
- Common mistakes in Spark app development
- Optimization techniques

Monitoring Spark jobs

Spark provides web UI for monitoring all the jobs running or completed on computing nodes (drivers or executors). In this section, we will discuss in brief how to monitor Spark jobs using Spark web UI with appropriate examples. We will see how to monitor the progress of jobs (including submitted, queued, and running jobs). All the tabs in the Spark web UI will be discussed briefly. Finally, we will discuss the logging procedure in Spark for better tuning.

Spark web interface

The web UI (also known as Spark UI) is the web interface for running Spark applications to monitor the execution of jobs on a web browser such as Firefox or Google Chrome. When a SparkContext launches, a web UI that displays useful information about the application gets started on port 4040 in standalone mode. The Spark web UI is available in different ways depending on whether the application is still running or has finished its execution.

Also, you can use the web UI after the application has finished its execution by persisting all the events using `EventLoggingListener`. The `EventLoggingListener`, however, cannot work alone, and the incorporation of the Spark history server is required. Combining these two features, the following facilities can be achieved:

- A list of scheduler stages and tasks
- A summary of RDD sizes
- Memory usage
- Environmental information
- Information about the running executors

You can access the UI at `http://<driver-node>:4040` in a web browser. For example, a Spark job submitted and running as a standalone mode can be accessed at `http://localhost:4040`.

Note that if multiple SparkContexts are running on the same host, they will bind to successive ports beginning with 4040, 4041, 4042, and so on. By default, this information will be available for the duration of your Spark application only. This means that when your Spark job finishes its execution, the binding will no longer be valid or accessible.

As long as the job is running, stages can be observed on Spark UI. However, to view the web UI after the job has finished the execution, you could try setting `spark.eventLog.enabled` as true before submitting your Spark jobs. These forces Spark to log all the events to be displayed in the UI that is already persisted on storage such as local filesystem or HDFS.

In the previous chapter, we saw how to submit a Spark job to a cluster. Let's reuse one of the commands for submitting the k-means clustering, as follows:

```
# Run application as standalone mode on 8 cores
SPARK_HOME/bin/spark-submit \
  --class org.apache.spark.examples.KMeansDemo \
  --master local[8] \
```

```
KMeansDemo-0.1-SNAPSHOT-jar-with-dependencies.jar \
Saratoga_NY_Homes.txt
```

If you submit the job using the preceding command, you will not be able to see the status of the jobs that have finished the execution, so to make the changes permanent, use the following two options:

```
spark.eventLog.enabled=true
spark.eventLog.dir=file:///home/username/log"
```

By setting the preceding two configuration variables, we asked the Spark driver to make the event logging enabled to be saved at `file:///home/username/log`.

In summary, with the following changes, your submitting command will be as follows:

```
# Run application as standalone mode on 8 cores
SPARK_HOME/bin/spark-submit \
  --conf "spark.eventLog.enabled=true" \
  --conf "spark.eventLog.dir=file:///tmp/test" \
  --class org.apache.spark.examples.KMeansDemo \
  --master local[8] \
  KMeansDemo-0.1-SNAPSHOT-jar-with-dependencies.jar \
  Saratoga_NY_Homes.txt
```

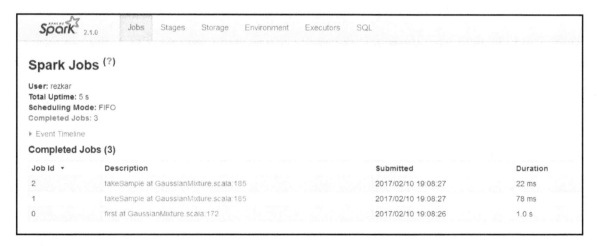

Figure 1: Spark web UI

As shown in the preceding screenshot, Spark web UI provides the following tabs:

- **Jobs**
- **Stages**
- **Storage**
- **Environment**
- **Executors**
- **SQL**

It is to be noted that all the features may not be visible at once as they are lazily created on demand, for example, while running a streaming job.

Jobs

Depending upon the SparkContext, the **Jobs** tab shows the status of all the Spark jobs in a Spark application. When you access the **Jobs** tab on the Spark UI using a web browser at `http://localhost:4040` (for standalone mode), you should observe the following options:

- **User**: This shows the active user who has submitted the Spark job
- **Total Uptime**: This shows the total uptime for the jobs
- **Scheduling Mode**: In most cases, it is first-in-first-out (aka FIFO)
- **Active Jobs**: This shows the number of active jobs
- **Completed Jobs**: This shows the number of completed jobs
- **Event Timeline**: This shows the timeline of a job that has completed its execution

Internally, the **Jobs** tab is represented by the `JobsTab` class, which is a custom **SparkUI** tab with the jobs prefix. The **Jobs** tab uses `JobProgressListener` to access statistics about the Spark jobs to display the above information on the page. Take a look at the following screenshot:

Figure 2: The jobs tab in the Spark web UI

If you further expand the **Active Jobs** option in the **Jobs** tab, you will be able to see the execution plan, status, number of completed stages, and the job ID of that particular job as **DAG Visualization,** as shown in the following:

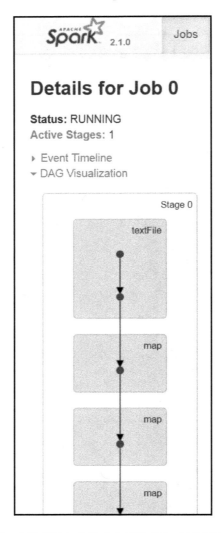

Figure 3: The DAG visualization for task in the Spark web UI (abridged)

When a user enters the code in the Spark console (for example, Spark shell or using Spark submit), Spark Core creates an operator graph. This is basically what happens when a user executes an action (for example, reduce, collect, count, first, take, countByKey, saveAsTextFile) or transformation (for example, map, flatMap, filter, mapPartitions, sample, union, intersection, distinct) on an RDD (which are immutable objects) at a particular node.

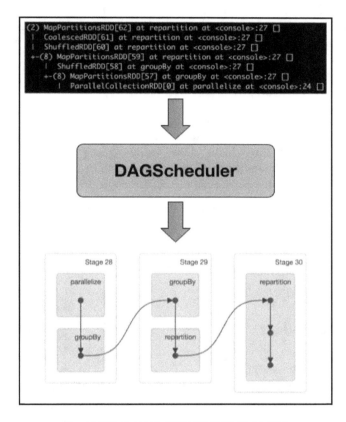

Figure 4: DAG scheduler transforming RDD lineage into stage DAG

During the transformation or action, **Directed Acyclic Graph** (**DAG**) information is used to restore the node to last transformation and actions (refer to *Figure 4* and *Figure 5* for a clearer picture) to maintain the data resiliency. Finally, the graph is submitted to a DAG scheduler.

How does Spark compute the DAG from the RDD and subsequently execute the task?

At a high level, when any action is called on the RDD, Spark creates the DAG and submits it to the DAG scheduler. The DAG scheduler divides operators into stages of tasks. A stage comprises tasks based on partitions of the input data. The DAG scheduler pipelines operators together. For example, many map operators can be scheduled in a single stage. The final result of a DAG scheduler is a set of stages. The stages are passed on to the task scheduler. The task scheduler launches tasks through the cluster manager (Spark Standalone/YARN/Mesos). The task scheduler doesn't know about the dependencies of the stages. The worker executes the tasks on the stage.

The DAG scheduler then keeps track of which RDDs the stage outputs materialized from. It then finds a minimal schedule to run jobs and divides the related operators into stages of tasks. Based on the partitions of the input data, a stage comprises multiple tasks. Then, operators are pipelined together with the DAG scheduler. Practically, more than one map or reduce operator (for example) can be scheduled in a single stage.

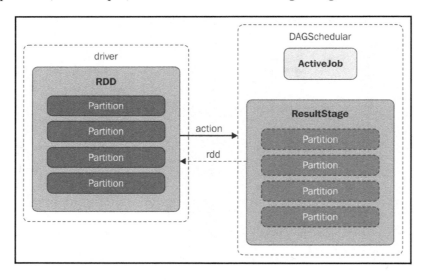

Figure 5: Executing action leads to new ResultStage and ActiveJob in DAGScheduler

Two fundamental concepts in DAG scheduler are jobs and stages. Thus, it has to track them through internal registries and counters. Technically speaking, DAG scheduler is a part of SparkContext's initialization that works exclusively on the driver (immediately after the task scheduler and scheduler backend are ready). DAG scheduler is responsible for three major tasks in Spark execution. It computes an execution DAG, that is, DAG of stages, for a job. It determines the preferred node to run each task on and handles failures due to shuffle output files being lost.

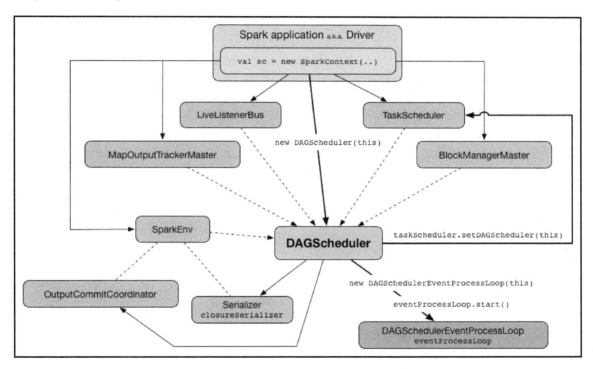

Figure 6: DAGScheduler as created by SparkContext with other services

The final result of a DAG scheduler is a set of stages. Therefore, most of the statistics and the status of the job can be seen using this visualization, for example, execution plan, status, number of completed stages, and the job ID of that particular job.

Stages

The **Stages** tab in Spark UI shows the current status of all stages of all jobs in a Spark application, including two optional pages for the tasks and statistics for a stage and pool details. Note that this information is available only when the application works in a fair scheduling mode. You should be able to access the **Stages** tab at `http://localhost:4040/stages`. Note that when there are no jobs submitted, the tab shows nothing but the title. The Stages tab shows the stages in a Spark application. The following stages can be seen in this tab:

- **Active Stages**
- **Pending Stages**
- **Completed Stages**

For example, when you submit a Spark job locally, you should be able to see the following status:

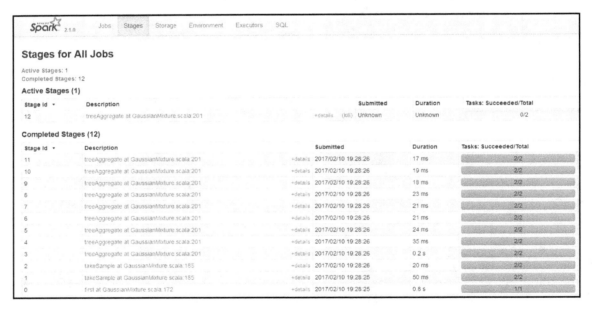

Figure 7: The stages for all jobs in the Spark web UI

In this case, there's only one stage that is an active stage. However, in the upcoming chapters, we will be able to observe other stages when we will submit our Spark jobs to AWS EC2 clusters.

To further dig down to the summary of the completed jobs, click on any link contained in the **Description** column and you should find the related statistics on execution time as metrics. An approximate time of min, median, 25th percentile, 75th percentile, and max for the metrics can also be seen in the following figure:

Summary Metrics for 2 Completed Tasks					
Metric	Min		25th percentile		Median
Duration	0.2 s		0.2 s		0.2 s
GC Time	0 ms		0 ms		0 ms
Input Size / Records	27.6 KB / 1		27.6 KB / 1		28.6 KB / 1

▾ Aggregated Metrics by Executor					
Executor ID ▴	Address	Task Time	Total Tasks	Failed Tasks	Killed Tasks
driver	10.2.17.13:53512	0.5 s	2	0	0

Tasks (2)						
Index ▴	ID	Attempt	Status	Locality Level	Executor ID / Host	Launch Time
0	4	0	SUCCESS	PROCESS_LOCAL	driver / localhost	2017/02/04 12:57:01
1	5	0	SUCCESS	PROCESS_LOCAL	driver / localhost	2017/02/04 12:57:01

Figure 8: The summary for completed jobs on the Spark web UI

Your case might be different as I have executed and submitted only two jobs for demonstration purposes during the writing of this book. You can see other statistics on the executors as well. For my case, I submitted these jobs in the standalone mode by utilizing 8 cores and 32 GB of RAM. In addition to these, information related to the executor, such as ID, IP address with the associated port number, task completion time, number of tasks (including the number of failed tasks, killed tasks, and succeeded tasks), and input size of the dataset per records are shown.

The other section in the image shows other information related to these two tasks, for example, index, ID, attempts, status, locality level, host information, launch time, duration, **Garbage Collection (GC)** time, and so on.

Storage

The **Storage** tab shows the size and memory use for each RDD, DataFrame, or Dataset. You should be able to see the storage-related information of RDDs, DataFrames, or Datasets. The following figure shows storage metadata such as RDD name, storage level, the number of cache partitions, the percentage of a fraction of the data that was cached, and the size of the RDD in the main memory:

Figure 9: Storage tab shows space consumed by an RDD in disk

Note that if the RDD cannot be cached in the main memory, disk space will be used instead. A more detailed discussion will be carried out in a later section of this chapter.

Figure 10: Data distribution and the storage used by the RDD in disk

Environment

The **Environment** tab shows the environmental variables that are currently set on your machine (that is, driver). More specifically, runtime information such as **Java Home**, **Java Version**, and **Scala Version** can be seen under **Runtime Information**. Spark properties such as Spark application ID, app name, and driver host information, driver port, executor ID, master URL, and the schedule mode can be seen. Furthermore, other system-related properties and job properties such as AWT toolkit version, file encoding type (for example, UTF-8), and file encoding package information (for example, sun.io) can be seen under **System Properties**.

Figure 11: Environment tab on Spark web UI

Executors

The **Executors** tab uses `ExecutorsListener` to collect information about executors for a Spark application. An executor is a distributed agent that is responsible for executing tasks. Executors are instantiated in different ways. For example, they can be instantiated when `CoarseGrainedExecutorBackend` receives `RegisteredExecutor` message for Spark Standalone and YARN. The second case is when a Spark job is submitted to Mesos. The Mesos's `MesosExecutorBackend` gets registered. The third case is when you run your Spark jobs locally, that is, `LocalEndpoint` is created. An executor typically runs for the entire lifetime of a Spark application, which is called static allocation of executors, although you can also opt in for dynamic allocation. The executor backends exclusively manage all the executors in a computing node or clusters. An executor reports heartbeat and partial metrics for active tasks to the **HeartbeatReceiver** RPC endpoint on the driver periodically and the results are sent to the driver. They also provide in-memory storage for RDDs that are cached by user programs through block manager. Refer to the following figure for a clearer idea on this:

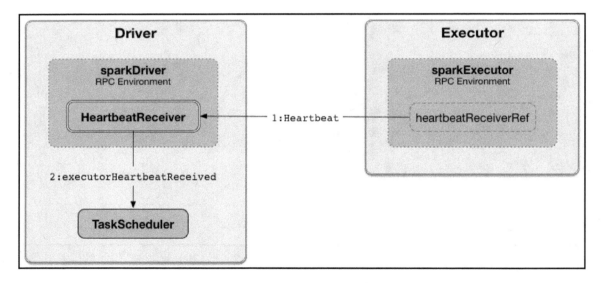

Figure 12: Spark driver instantiates an executor that is responsible for HeartbeatReceiver's Heartbeat message handler

When an executor starts, it first registers with the driver and communicates directly to execute tasks, as shown in the following figure:

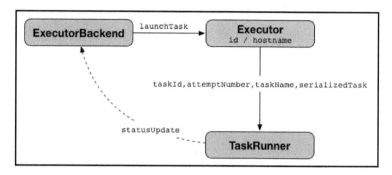

Figure 13: Launching tasks on executor using TaskRunners

You should be able to access the **Executors** tab at `http://localhost:4040/executors`.

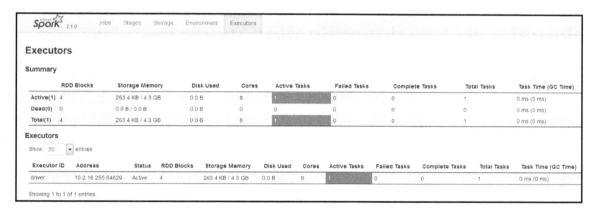

Figure 14: Executor tab on Spark web UI

As shown in the preceding figure, **Executor ID, Address, Status, RDD Blocks, Storage Memory, Disk Used, Cores, Active Tasks, Failed Tasks, Complete Tasks, Total Tasks, Task Time (GC Time), Input, Shuffle Read, Shuffle Write,** and **Thread Dump** about the executor can be seen.

SQL

The **SQL** tab in the Spark UI displays all the accumulator values per operator. You should be able to access the SQL tab at `http://localhost:4040/SQL/`. It displays all the SQL query executions and underlying information by default. However, the SQL tab displays the details of the SQL query execution only after a query has been selected.

A detailed discussion on SQL is out of the scope of this chapter. Interested readers should refer to `http://spark.apache.org/docs/latest/sql-programming-guide.html#sql` for more on how to submit an SQL query and see its result output.

Visualizing Spark application using web UI

When a Spark job is submitted for execution, a web application UI is launched that displays useful information about the application. An event timeline displays the relative ordering and interleaving of application events. The timeline view is available on three levels: across all jobs, within one job, and within one stage. The timeline also shows executor allocation and deallocation.

Figure 15: Spark jobs executed as DAG on Spark web UI

Observing the running and completed Spark jobs

To access and observe the running and the completed Spark jobs, open
`http://spark_driver_host:4040` in a web browser. Note that you will have to replace
`spark_driver_host` with an IP address or hostname accordingly.

> Note that if multiple SparkContexts are running on the same host, they
> will bind to successive ports beginning with 4040, 4041, 4042, and so on.
> By default, this information will be available for the duration of your
> Spark application only. This means that when your Spark job finishes its
> execution, the binding will no longer be valid or accessible.

Now, to access the active jobs that are still executing, click on the **Active Jobs** link and you will see the related information of those jobs. On the other hand, to access the status of the completed jobs, click on **Completed Jobs** and you will see the information as DAG style as discussed in the preceding section.

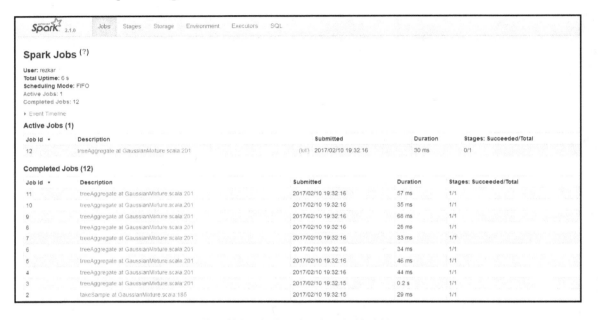

Figure 16: Observing the running and completed Spark jobs

You can achieve these by clicking on the job description link under the **Active Jobs** or **Completed Jobs**.

Debugging Spark applications using logs

Seeing the information about all running Spark applications depends on which cluster manager you are using. You should follow these instructions while debugging your Spark application:

- **Spark Standalone**: Go to the Spark master UI at `http://master:18080`. The master and each worker show cluster and the related job statistics. In addition, a detailed log output for each job is also written to the working directory of each worker. We will discuss how to enable the logging manually using the `log4j` with Spark.

- **YARN**: If your cluster manager is YARN, and suppose that you are running your Spark jobs on the Cloudera (or any other YARN-based platform), then go to the YARN applications page in the Cloudera Manager Admin Console. Now, to debug Spark applications running on YARN, view the logs for the Node Manager role. To make this happen, open the log event viewer and then filter the event stream to choose a time window and log level and to display the Node Manager source. You can access logs through the command as well. The format of the command is as follows:

```
yarn logs -applicationId <application ID> [OPTIONS]
```

For example, the following are the valid commands for these IDs:

```
yarn logs -applicationId application_561453090098_0005
yarn logs -applicationId application_561453090070_0005 userid
```

Note that the user IDs are different. However, this is only true if `yarn.log-aggregation-enable` is true in `yarn-site.xml` and the application has already finished the execution.

Logging with log4j with Spark

Spark uses `log4j` for its own logging. All the operations that happen backend get logged to the Spark shell console (which is already configured to the underlying storage). Spark provides a template of `log4j` as a property file, and we can extend and modify that file for logging in Spark. Move to the `SPARK_HOME/conf` directory and you should see the `log4j.properties.template` file. This could help us as the starting point for our own logging system.

Now, let's create our own custom logging system while running a Spark job. When you are done, rename the file as `log4j.properties` and put it under the same directory (that is, project tree). A sample snapshot of the file can be seen as follows:

```
# Set everything to be logged to the console
log4j.rootCategory=INFO, console
log4j.appender.console=org.apache.log4j.ConsoleAppender
log4j.appender.console.target=System.err
log4j.appender.console.layout=org.apache.log4j.PatternLayout
log4j.appender.console.layout.ConversionPattern=%d{yy/MM/dd HH:mm:ss} %p %c{1}: %m%n

# Set the default spark-shell log level to WARN. When running the spark-shell, the
# log level for this class is used to overwrite the root logger's log level, so that
# the user can have different defaults for the shell and regular Spark apps.
log4j.logger.org.apache.spark.repl.Main=WARN

# Settings to quiet third party logs that are too verbose
log4j.logger.org.spark_project.jetty=WARN
log4j.logger.org.spark_project.jetty.util.component.AbstractLifeCycle=ERROR
log4j.logger.org.apache.spark.repl.SparkIMain$exprTyper=INFO
log4j.logger.org.apache.spark.repl.SparkILoop$SparkILoopInterpreter=INFO
log4j.logger.org.apache.parquet=ERROR
log4j.logger.parquet=ERROR

# SPARK-9183: Settings to avoid annoying messages when looking up nonexistent UDFs in SparkSQL with Hive support
log4j.logger.org.apache.hadoop.hive.metastore.RetryingHMSHandler=FATAL
log4j.logger.org.apache.hadoop.hive.ql.exec.FunctionRegistry=ERROR
```

Figure 17: A snap of the log4j.properties file

By default, everything goes to console and file. However, if you want to bypass all the noise logs to a system file located at, say, `/var/log/sparkU.log`, then you can set these properties in the `log4j.properties` file as follows:

```
log4j.logger.spark.storage=INFO, RollingAppender
log4j.additivity.spark.storage=false
log4j.logger.spark.scheduler=INFO, RollingAppender
log4j.additivity.spark.scheduler=false
log4j.logger.spark.CacheTracker=INFO, RollingAppender
log4j.additivity.spark.CacheTracker=false
log4j.logger.spark.CacheTrackerActor=INFO, RollingAppender
log4j.additivity.spark.CacheTrackerActor=false
log4j.logger.spark.MapOutputTrackerActor=INFO, RollingAppender
log4j.additivity.spark.MapOutputTrackerActor=false
log4j.logger.spark.MapOutputTracker=INFO, RollingAppender
log4j.additivty.spark.MapOutputTracker=false
```

Basically, we want to hide all logs Spark generates so that we don't have to deal with them in the shell. We redirect them to be logged in the filesystem. On the other hand, we want our own logs to be logged in the shell and a separate file so that they don't get mixed up with the ones from Spark. From here, we will point Splunk to the files where our own logs are, which in this particular case is `/var/log/sparkU.log`.

Then the log4j.properties file is picked up by Spark when the application starts, so we don't have to do anything aside from placing it in the mentioned location.

Now let's see how we can create our own logging system. Look at the following code and try to understand what is happening here:

```
import org.apache.spark.{SparkConf, SparkContext}
import org.apache.log4j.LogManager
import org.apache.log4j.Level
import org.apache.log4j.Logger

object MyLog {
  def main(args: Array[String]):Unit= {
    // Stting logger level as WARN
    val log = LogManager.getRootLogger
    log.setLevel(Level.WARN)

    // Creating Spark Context
    val conf = new SparkConf().setAppName("My App").setMaster("local[*]")
    val sc = new SparkContext(conf)

    //Started the computation and printing the logging information
    log.warn("Started")
    val data = sc.parallelize(1 to 100000)
    log.warn("Finished")
  }
}
```

The preceding code conceptually logs only the warning message. It first prints the warning message and then creates an RDD by parallelizing numbers from 1 to 100,000. Once the RDD job is finished, it prints another warning log. However, there is a problem we haven't noticed yet with the earlier code segment.

One drawback of the org.apache.log4j.Logger class is that it is not serializable (refer to the optimization technique section for more details), which implies that we cannot use it inside a *closure* while doing operations on some parts of the Spark API. For example, if you try to execute the following code, you should experience an exception that says Task not serializable:

```
object MyLog {
  def main(args: Array[String]):Unit= {
    // Stting logger level as WARN
    val log = LogManager.getRootLogger
    log.setLevel(Level.WARN)
    // Creating Spark Context
    val conf = new SparkConf().setAppName("My App").setMaster("local[*]")
    val sc = new SparkContext(conf)
```

```
    //Started the computation and printing the logging information
    log.warn("Started")
    val i = 0
    val data = sc.parallelize(i to 100000)
    data.foreach(i => log.info("My number"+ i))
    log.warn("Finished")
  }
}
```

To solve this problem is also easy; just declare the Scala object with `extends Serializable` and now the code looks like the following:

```
class MyMapper(n: Int) extends Serializable{
  @transient lazy val log = org.apache.log4j.LogManager.getLogger
                             ("myLogger")
  def MyMapperDosomething(rdd: RDD[Int]): RDD[String] =
   rdd.map{ i =>
    log.warn("mapping: " + i)
    (i + n).toString
  }
}
```

So what is happening in the preceding code is that the closure can't be neatly distributed to all partitions since it can't close on the logger; hence, the whole instance of type `MyMapper` is distributed to all partitions; once this is done, each partition creates a new logger and uses it for logging.

In summary, the following is the complete code that helps us to get rid of this problem:

```
package com.example.Personal
import org.apache.log4j.{Level, LogManager, PropertyConfigurator}
import org.apache.spark._
import org.apache.spark.rdd.RDD

class MyMapper(n: Int) extends Serializable{
  @transient lazy val log = org.apache.log4j.LogManager.getLogger
                             ("myLogger")
  def MyMapperDosomething(rdd: RDD[Int]): RDD[String] =
   rdd.map{ i =>
    log.warn("Serialization of: " + i)
    (i + n).toString
  }
}

object MyMapper{
  def apply(n: Int): MyMapper = new MyMapper(n)
}
```

```
object MyLog {
  def main(args: Array[String]) {
    val log = LogManager.getRootLogger
    log.setLevel(Level.WARN)
    val conf = new SparkConf().setAppName("My App").setMaster("local[*]")
    val sc = new SparkContext(conf)
    log.warn("Started")
    val data = sc.parallelize(1 to 100000)
    val mapper = MyMapper(1)
    val other = mapper.MyMapperDosomething(data)
    other.collect()
    log.warn("Finished")
  }
}
```

The output is as follows:

```
17/04/29 15:33:43 WARN root: Started
.
.
.
17/04/29 15:31:51 WARN myLogger: mapping: 1
17/04/29 15:31:51 WARN myLogger: mapping: 49992
17/04/29 15:31:51 WARN myLogger: mapping: 49999
17/04/29 15:31:51 WARN myLogger: mapping: 50000
.
.
.
17/04/29 15:31:51 WARN root: Finished
```

We will discuss the built-in logging of Spark in the next section.

Spark configuration

There are a number of ways to configure your Spark jobs. In this section, we will discuss these ways. More specifically, according to Spark 2.x release, there are three locations to configure the system:

- Spark properties
- Environmental variables
- Logging

Spark properties

As discussed previously, Spark properties control most of the application-specific parameters and can be set using a `SparkConf` object of Spark. Alternatively, these parameters can be set through the Java system properties. `SparkConf` allows you to configure some of the common properties as follows:

```
setAppName() // App name
setMaster() // Master URL
setSparkHome() // Set the location where Spark is installed on worker
nodes.
setExecutorEnv() // Set single or multiple environment variables to be used
when launching executors.
setJars() // Set JAR files to distribute to the cluster.
setAll() // Set multiple parameters together.
```

An application can be configured to use a number of available cores on your machine. For example, we could initialize an application with two threads as follows. Note that we run with `local [2]`, meaning two threads, which represents minimal parallelism and using `local [*]`, which utilizes all the available cores in your machine. Alternatively, you can specify the number of executors while submitting Spark jobs with the following spark-submit script:

```
val conf = new SparkConf()
           .setMaster("local[2]")
           .setAppName("SampleApp")
val sc = new SparkContext(conf)
```

There might be some special cases where you need to load Spark properties dynamically when required. You can do this while submitting a Spark job through the spark-submit script. More specifically, you may want to avoid hardcoding certain configurations in `SparkConf`.

Apache Spark precedence:
Spark has the following precedence on the submitted jobs: configs coming from a config file have the lowest priority. The configs coming from the actual code have a higher priority with respect to configs coming from a config file, and configs coming from the CLI through the Spark-submit script have higher priority.

For instance, if you want to run your application with different masters, executors, or different amounts of memory, Spark allows you to simply create an empty configuration object, as follows:

```
val sc = new SparkContext(new SparkConf())
```

Then you can provide the configuration for your Spark job at runtime as follows:

```
SPARK_HOME/bin/spark-submit
  --name "SmapleApp" \
  --class org.apache.spark.examples.KMeansDemo \
  --master mesos://207.184.161.138:7077 \ # Use your IP address
  --conf spark.eventLog.enabled=false
  --conf "spark.executor.extraJavaOptions=-XX:+PrintGCDetails" \
  --deploy-mode cluster \
  --supervise \
  --executor-memory 20G \
  myApp.jar
```

SPARK_HOME/bin/spark-submit will also read configuration options from SPARK_HOME /conf/spark-defaults.conf, in which each line consists of a key and a value separated by whitespace. An example is as follows:

```
spark.master    spark://5.6.7.8:7077
spark.executor.memor y    4g
spark.eventLog.enabled true
spark.serializer org.apache.spark.serializer.KryoSerializer
```

Values that are specified as flags in the properties file will be passed to the application and merged with those ones specified through SparkConf. Finally, as discussed earlier, the application web UI at http://<driver>:4040 lists all the Spark properties under the **Environment** tab.

Environmental variables

Environment variables can be used to set the setting in the computing nodes or machine settings. For example, IP address can be set through the `conf/spark-env.sh` script on each computing node. The following table lists the name and the functionality of the environmental variables that need to be set:

Environment Variable	Meaning
SPARK_MASTER_HOST	Bind the master to a specific hostname or IP address, for example a public one.
SPARK_MASTER_PORT	Start the master on a different port (default: 7077).
SPARK_MASTER_WEBUI_PORT	Port for the master web UI (default: 8080).
SPARK_MASTER_OPTS	Configuration properties that apply only to the master in the form "-Dx=y" (default: none). See below for a list of possible options.
SPARK_LOCAL_DIRS	Directory to use for "scratch" space in Spark, including map output files and RDDs that get stored on disk. This should be on a fast, local disk in your system. It can also be a comma-separated list of multiple directories on different disks.
SPARK_WORKER_CORES	Total number of cores to allow Spark applications to use on the machine (default: all available cores).
SPARK_WORKER_MEMORY	Total amount of memory to allow Spark applications to use on the machine, e.g. 1000m, 2g (default: total memory minus 1 GB); note that each application's *individual* memory is configured using its spark.executor.memory property.
SPARK_WORKER_PORT	Start the Spark worker on a specific port (default: random).
SPARK_WORKER_WEBUI_PORT	Port for the worker web UI (default: 8081).
SPARK_WORKER_DIR	Directory to run applications in, which will include both logs and scratch space (default: SPARK_HOME/work).
SPARK_WORKER_OPTS	Configuration properties that apply only to the worker in the form "-Dx=y" (default: none). See below for a list of possible options.
SPARK_DAEMON_MEMORY	Memory to allocate to the Spark master and worker daemons themselves (default: 1g).
SPARK_DAEMON_JAVA_OPTS	JVM options for the Spark master and worker daemons themselves in the form "-Dx=y" (default: none).
SPARK_PUBLIC_DNS	The public DNS name of the Spark master and workers (default: none).

Figure 18: Environmental variables and their meaning

Logging

Finally, logging can be configured through the `log4j.properties` file under your Spark application tree, as discussed in the preceding section. Spark uses log4j for logging. There are several valid logging levels supported by log4j with Spark; they are as follows:

Log Level	Usages
OFF	This is the most specific, which allows no logging at all
FATAL	This is the most specific one that shows fatal errors with little data
ERROR	This shows only the general errors
WARN	This shows warnings that are recommended to be fixed but not mandatory
INFO	This shows the information required for your Spark job
DEBUG	While debugging, those logs will be printed
TRACE	This provides the least specific error trace with a lot of data
ALL	Least specific message with all data

Table 1: Log level with log4j and Spark

You can set up the default logging for Spark shell in `conf/log4j.properties`. In standalone Spark applications or while in a Spark Shell session, use `conf/log4j.properties.template` as a starting point. In an earlier section of this chapter, we suggested you put the `log4j.properties` file under your project directory while working on an IDE-based environment like Eclipse. However, to disable logging completely, you should use the following `conf/log4j.properties.template` as `log4j.properties`. Just set the `log4j.logger.org` flags as OFF, as follows:

```
log4j.logger.org=OFF
```

In the next section, we will discuss some common mistakes made by the developer or programmer while developing and submitting Spark jobs.

Common mistakes in Spark app development

Common mistakes that happen often are application failure, a slow job that gets stuck due to numerous factors, mistakes in the aggregation, actions or transformations, an exception in the main thread and, of course, **Out Of Memory (OOM)**.

Application failure

Most of the time, application failure happens because one or more stages fail eventually. As discussed earlier in this chapter, Spark jobs comprise several stages. Stages aren't executed independently: for instance, a processing stage can't take place before the relevant input-reading stage. So, suppose that stage 1 executes successfully but stage 2 fails to execute, the whole application fails eventually. This can be shown as follows:

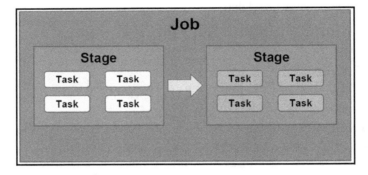

Figure 19: Two stages in a typical Spark job

To show an example, suppose you have the following three RDD operations as stages. The same can be visualized as shown in *Figure 20, Figure 21,* and *Figure 22*:

```
val rdd1 = sc.textFile("hdfs://data/data.csv")
                .map(someMethod)
                .filter(filterMethod)
```

Figure 20: Stage 1 for rdd1

```
val rdd2 = sc.hadoopFile("hdfs://data/data2.csv")
                    .groupByKey()
                    .map(secondMapMethod)
```

Conceptually, this can be shown in *Figure 21*, which first parses the data using the
hadoopFile() method, groups it using the groupByKey() method, and finally, maps it:

Figure 21: Stage 2 for rdd2

```
val rdd3 = rdd1.join(rdd2).map(thirdMapMethod)
```

Conceptually, this can be shown in *Figure 22*, which first parses the data, joins it, and
finally, maps it:

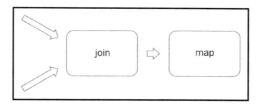

Figure 22: Stage 3 for rdd3

Now you can perform an aggregation function, for example, collect, as follows:

```
rdd3.collect()
```

Well! You have developed a Spark job consisting of three stages. Conceptually, this can be
shown as follows:

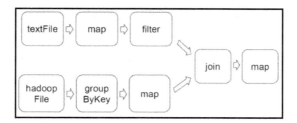

Figure 23: three stages for the rdd3.collect() operation

Now, if one of the stages fails, your job will fail eventually. As a result, the final `rdd3.collect()` statement will throw an exception about stage failure. Moreover, you may have issues with the following four factors:

- Mistakes in the aggregation operation
- Exceptions in the main thread
- OOP
- Class not found exception while submitting jobs using the `spark-submit` script
- Misconception about some API/methods in Spark core library

To get rid of the aforementioned issues, our general suggestion is to ensure that you have not made any mistakes while performing any map, flatMap, or aggregate operations. Second, ensure that there are no flaws in the main method while developing your application with Java or Scala. Sometimes you don't see any syntax error in your code, but it's important that you have developed some small test cases for your application. Most common exceptions that occur in the main method are as follows:

- `java.lang.noclassdeffounderror`
- `java.lang.nullpointerexception`
- `java.lang.arrayindexoutofboundsexception`
- `java.lang.stackoverflowerror`
- `java.lang.classnotfoundexception`
- `java.util.inputmismatchexception`

These exceptions can be avoided with the careful coding of your Spark application. Alternatively, use Eclipse's (or any other IDEs) code debugging features extensively to get rid of the semantic error to avoid the exception. For the third problem, that is, OOM, it's a very common problem. It is to be noted that Spark requires at least 8 GB of main memory, with sufficient disk space available for the standalone mode. On the other hand, to get the full cluster computing facilities, this requirement is often high.

Preparing a JAR file including all the dependencies to execute Spark jobs is of paramount importance. Many practitioners use Google's Guava; it is included in most distributions, yet it doesn't guarantee backward compatibility. This means that sometimes your Spark job won't find a Guava class even if you explicitly provided it; this happens because one of the two versions of the Guava libraries takes precedence over the other, and this version might not include a required class. In order to overcome this issue, you usually resort to shading.

Make sure that you have set the Java heap space with –Xmx parameter with a sufficiently large value if you're coding using IntelliJ, Vim, Eclipse, Notepad, and so on. While working with cluster mode, you should specify the executor memory while submitting Spark jobs using the Spark-submit script. Suppose you have a CSV to be parsed and do some predictive analytics using a random forest classifier, you might need to specify the right amount of memory, say 20 GB, as follows:

```
--executor-memory 20G
```

Even if you receive the OOM error, you can increase this amount to, say, 32 GB or more. Since the random forest is computationally intensive, requiring larger memory, this is just an example of a random forest. You might experience similar issues while just parsing your data. Even a particular stage may fail due to this OOM error. Therefore, make sure that you are aware of this error.

For the `class not found exception`, make sure that you have included your main class in the resulting JAR file. The JAR file should be prepared with all the dependencies to execute your Spark job on the cluster nodes.

For the last issue, we can provide some examples of some misconceptions about the Spark Core library. For example, when you use the `wholeTextFiles` method to prepare RDDs or DataFrames from multiple files, Spark does not run in parallel; in cluster mode for YARN, it may run out of memory sometimes.

Once, I experienced an issue where, at first, I copied six files in my S3 storage to HDFS. Then, I tried to create an RDD, as follows:

```
sc.wholeTextFiles("/mnt/temp") // note the location of the data files is
/mnt/temp/
```

Then, I tried to process those files line by line using a UDF. When I looked at my computing nodes, I saw that only one executor was running per file. However, I then got an error message saying that YARN had run out of memory. Why so? The reasons are as follows:

- The goal of `wholeTextFiles` is to have only one executor for each file to be processed
- If you use `.gz` files, for example, you will have only one executor per file, maximum

Slow jobs or unresponsiveness

Sometimes, if the SparkContext cannot connect to a Spark standalone master, then the driver may display errors such as the following:

```
02/05/17 12:44:45 ERROR AppClient$ClientActor: All masters are
unresponsive! Giving up.
02/05/17 12:45:31 ERROR SparkDeploySchedulerBackend: Application has been
killed. Reason: All masters are unresponsive! Giving up.
02/05/17 12:45:35 ERROR TaskSchedulerImpl: Exiting due to error from
cluster scheduler: Spark cluster looks down
```

At other times, the driver is able to connect to the master node but the master is unable to communicate back to the driver. Then, multiple attempts to connect are made even though the driver will report that it could not connect to the Master's log directory.

Furthermore, you might often experience very slow performance and progress in your Spark jobs. This happens because your driver program is not that fast to compute your jobs. As discussed earlier, sometimes a particular stage may take a longer time than usual because there might be a shuffle, map, join, or aggregation operation involved. Even if the computer is running out of disk storage or main memory, you may experience these issues. For example, if your master node does not respond or you experience unresponsiveness from the computing nodes for a certain period of time, you might think that your Spark job has halted and become stagnant at a certain stage:

```
/11/20 17:20:58 INFO TaskSchedulerImpl: Removed TaskSet 1.0, whose tasks have all completed, from pool
/11/20 17:20:58 INFO TaskSchedulerImpl: Removed TaskSet 2.0, whose tasks have all completed, from pool
/11/20 17:20:58 INFO DAGScheduler: Failed to run collect at ReceiverTracker.scala:270
/11/20 17:20:58 INFO TaskSchedulerImpl: Cancelling stage 1
Exception in thread "Thread-53" org.apache.spark.SparkException: Job aborted due to stage failure: All masters are unresponsive!
Giving up.
        at org.apache.spark.scheduler.DAGScheduler.org$apache$spark$scheduler$DAGScheduler$$failJobAndIndependentStages
(DAGScheduler.scala:1033)
        at org.apache.spark.scheduler.DAGScheduler$$anonfun$abortStage$1.apply(DAGScheduler.scala:1017)
        at org.apache.spark.scheduler.DAGScheduler$$anonfun$abortStage$1.apply(DAGScheduler.scala:1015)
        at scala.collection.mutable.ResizableArray$class.foreach(ResizableArray.scala:59)
        at scala.collection.mutable.ArrayBuffer.foreach(ArrayBuffer.scala:47)
        at org.apache.spark.scheduler.DAGScheduler.abortStage(DAGScheduler.scala:1015)
        at org.apache.spark.scheduler.DAGScheduler$$anonfun$handleTaskSetFailed$1.apply(DAGScheduler.scala:633)
        at org.apache.spark.scheduler.DAGScheduler$$anonfun$handleTaskSetFailed$1.apply(DAGScheduler.scala:633)
        at scala.Option.foreach(Option.scala:236)
        at org.apache.spark.scheduler.DAGScheduler.handleTaskSetFailed(DAGScheduler.scala:633)
        at org.apache.spark.scheduler.DAGSchedulerEventProcessActor$$anonfun$receive$2.applyOrElse(DAGScheduler.scala:1207)
        at akka.actor.ActorCell.receiveMessage(ActorCell.scala:498)
        at akka.actor.ActorCell.invoke(ActorCell.scala:456)
        at akka.dispatch.Mailbox.processMailbox(Mailbox.scala:237)
        at akka.dispatch.Mailbox.run(Mailbox.scala:219)
        at akka.dispatch.ForkJoinExecutorConfigurator$AkkaForkJoinTask.exec(AbstractDispatcher.scala:386)
        at scala.concurrent.forkjoin.ForkJoinTask.doExec(ForkJoinTask.java:260)
        at scala.concurrent.forkjoin.ForkJoinPool$WorkQueue.runTask(ForkJoinPool.java:1339)
        at scala.concurrent.forkjoin.ForkJoinPool.runWorker(ForkJoinPool.java:1979)
        at scala.concurrent.forkjoin.ForkJoinWorkerThread.run(ForkJoinWorkerThread.java:107)
/11/20 17:20:58 INFO DAGScheduler: Failed to run take at DStream.scala:593
/11/20 17:20:58 INFO TaskSchedulerImpl: Cancelling stage 2
/11/20 17:20:58 INFO JobScheduler: Starting job streaming job 1416484202000 ms.0 from job set of time 1416484202000 ms
/11/20 17:20:58 INFO SparkContext: Starting job: take at DStream.scala:593
/11/20 17:20:58 ERROR JobScheduler: Error running job streaming job 1416484200000 ms.0
org.apache.spark.SparkException: Job aborted due to stage failure: All masters are unresponsive! Giving up.
        at org.apache.spark.scheduler.DAGScheduler.org$apache$spark$scheduler$DAGScheduler$$failJobAndIndependentStages
(DAGScheduler.scala:1033)
        at org.apache.spark.scheduler.DAGScheduler$$anonfun$abortStage$1.apply(DAGScheduler.scala:1017)
        at org.apache.spark.scheduler.DAGScheduler$$anonfun$abortStage$1.apply(DAGScheduler.scala:1015)
        at scala.collection.mutable.ResizableArray$class.foreach(ResizableArray.scala:59)
        at scala.collection.mutable.ArrayBuffer.foreach(ArrayBuffer.scala:47)
        at org.apache.spark.scheduler.DAGScheduler.abortStage(DAGScheduler.scala:1015)
```

Figure 24: An example log for executor/driver unresponsiveness

Potential solutions could be several, including the following:

1. Check to make sure that workers and drivers are correctly configured to connect to the Spark master on the exact address listed in the Spark master web UI/logs. Then, explicitly supply the Spark cluster's master URL when starting your Spark shell:

```
$ bin/spark-shell --master spark://master-ip:7077
```

2. Set SPARK_LOCAL_IP to a cluster-addressable hostname for the driver, master, and worker processes.

Sometimes, we experience some issues due to hardware failure. For example, if the filesystem in a computing node closes unexpectedly, that is, an I/O exception, your Spark job will eventually fail too. This is obvious because your Spark job cannot write the resulting RDDs or data to store to the local filesystem or HDFS. This also implies that DAG operations cannot be performed due to the stage failures.

Sometimes, this I/O exception occurs due to an underlying disk failure or other hardware failures. This often provides logs, as follows:

Job Scheduling Information	Diagnostic Info
NA	Job initialization failed: java.io.IOException: Filesystem closed at org.apache.hadoop.hdfs.DFSClient.checkOpen(DFSClient.java:241) at org.apache.hadoop.hdfs.DFSClient.access$800(DFSClient.java:74) at org.apache.hadoop.hdfs.DFSClient$DFSOutputStream.closeInternal(DFSClient.java:3667) at org.apache.hadoop.hdfs.DFSClient$DFSOutputStream.close(DFSClient.java:3626) at org.apache.hadoop.fs.FSDataOutputStream$PositionCache.close(FSDataOutputStream.java:61) at org.apache.hadoop.fs.FSDataOutputStream.close(FSDataOutputStream.java:86) at org.apache.hadoop.security.Credentials.writeTokenStorageFile(Credentials.java:171) at org.apache.hadoop.mapred.JobInProgress.generateAndStoreTokens(JobInProgress.java:3528) at org.apache.hadoop.mapred.JobInProgress.initTasks(JobInProgress.java:696) at org.apache.hadoop.mapred.JobTracker.initJob(JobTracker.java:4207) at org.apache.hadoop.mapred.FairScheduler$JobInitializer$InitJob.run(FairScheduler.java:291) at java.util.concurrent.ThreadPoolExecutor$Worker.runTask(ThreadPoolExecutor.java:886) at java.util.concurrent.ThreadPoolExecutor$Worker.run(ThreadPoolExecutor.java:908) at java.lang.Thread.run(Thread.java:662)

Figure 25: An example filesystem closed

Nevertheless, you often experience slow job computing performance because your Java GC is somewhat busy with, or cannot do, the GC fast. For example, the following figure shows that for task 0, it took 10 hours to finish the GC! I experienced this issue in 2014, when I was new to Spark. Control of these types of issues, however, is not in our hands. Therefore, our recommendation is that you should make the JVM free and try submitting the jobs again.

Task Index	Task ID	Status	Locality Level	Executor	Launch Time	Duration	GC Time
1	0	SUCCESS	NODE_LOCAL		2014/06/13 13:14:16	12.82 h	9.59 h
2	1	SUCCESS	NODE_LOCAL		2014/06/13 13:14:16	12.00 h	8.97 h
3	2	SUCCESS	NODE_LOCAL		2014/06/13 13:14:16	12.39 h	9.16 h
0	3	SUCCESS	NODE_LOCAL		2014/06/13 13:14:16	12.09 h	8.88 h
6	4	SUCCESS	NODE_LOCAL		2014/06/13 13:14:16	11.65 h	8.54 h
4	5	SUCCESS	NODE_LOCAL		2014/06/13 13:14:16	11.68 h	8.62 h
7	6	SUCCESS	NODE_LOCAL		2014/06/13 13:14:16	12.19 h	9.12 h
12	7	SUCCESS	NODE_LOCAL		2014/06/13 13:14:16	11.62 h	8.50 h
8	8	SUCCESS	NODE_LOCAL		2014/06/13 13:14:16	12.57 h	9.40 h
9	9	SUCCESS	NODE_LOCAL		2014/06/13 13:14:16	12.02 h	8.98 h
5	10	SUCCESS	NODE_LOCAL		2014/06/13 13:14:16	12.24 h	9.04 h
11	11	SUCCESS	NODE_LOCAL		2014/06/13 13:14:16	11.11 h	8.15 h
10	12	SUCCESS	NODE_LOCAL		2014/06/13 13:14:16	11.84 h	8.68 h
13	13	SUCCESS	NODE_LOCAL		2014/06/13 13:14:16	11.85 h	8.74 h
18	14	SUCCESS	NODE_LOCAL		2014/06/13 13:14:16	12.26 h	9.17 h

Figure 26: An example where GC stalled in between

The fourth factor could be the slow response or slow job performance is due to the lack of data serialization. This will be discussed in the next section. The fifth factor could be the memory leak in the code that will tend to make your application consume more memory, leaving the files or logical devices open. Therefore, make sure that there is no option that tends to be a memory leak. For example, it is a good practice to finish your Spark application by calling `sc.stop()` or `spark.stop()`. This will make sure that one SparkContext is still open and active. Otherwise, you might get unwanted exceptions or issues. The sixth issue is that we often keep too many open files, and this sometimes creates `FileNotFoundException` in the shuffle or merge stage.

Optimization techniques

There are several aspects of tuning Spark applications toward better optimization techniques. In this section, we will discuss how we can further optimize our Spark applications by applying data serialization by tuning the main memory with better memory management. We can also optimize performance by tuning the data structure in your Scala code while developing Spark applications. The storage, on the other hand, can be maintained well by utilizing serialized RDD storage.

One of the most important aspects is garbage collection, and it's tuning if you have written your Spark application using Java or Scala. We will look at how we can also tune this for optimized performance. For distributed environment- and cluster-based system, a level of parallelism and data locality has to be ensured. Moreover, performance could further be improved by using broadcast variables.

Data serialization

Serialization is an important tuning for performance improvement and optimization in any distributed computing environment. Spark is not an exception, but Spark jobs are often data and computing extensive. Therefore, if your data objects are not in a good format, then you first need to convert them into serialized data objects. This demands a large number of bytes of your memory. Eventually, the whole process will slow down the entire processing and computation drastically.

As a result, you often experience a slow response from the computing nodes. This means that we sometimes fail to make 100% utilization of the computing resources. It is true that Spark tries to keep a balance between convenience and performance. This also implies that data serialization should be the first step in Spark tuning for better performance.

Spark provides two options for data serialization: Java serialization and Kryo serialization libraries:

- **Java serialization:** Spark serializes objects using Java's `ObjectOutputStream` framework. You handle the serialization by creating any class that implements `java.io.Serializable`. Java serialization is very flexible but often quite slow, which is not suitable for large data object serialization.
- **Kryo serialization:** You can also use Kryo library to serialize your data objects more quickly. Compared to Java serialization, Kryo serialization is much faster, with 10x speedup and is compact than that of Java. However, it has one issue, that is, it does not support all the serializable types, but you need to require your classes to be registered.

You can start using Kryo by initializing your Spark job with a `SparkConf` and calling `conf.set(spark.serializer, org.apache.spark.serializer.KryoSerializer)`. To register your own custom classes with Kryo, use the `registerKryoClasses` method, as follows:

```
val conf = new SparkConf()
              .setMaster("local[*]")
              .setAppName("MyApp")
conf.registerKryoClasses(Array(classOf[MyOwnClass1], classOf[MyOwnClass2]))
val sc = new SparkContext(conf)
```

If your objects are large, you may also need to increase the `spark.kryoserializer.buffer` config. This value needs to be large enough to hold the largest object you serialize. Finally, if you don't register your custom classes, Kryo still works; however, the full class name with each object needs to be stored, which is wasteful indeed.

For example, in the logging subsection at the end of the monitoring Spark jobs section, the logging and computing can be optimized using the `Kryo` serialization. At first, just create the `MyMapper` class as a normal class (that is, without any serialization), as follows:

```
class MyMapper(n: Int) { // without any serialization
   @transient lazy val log =
org.apache.log4j.LogManager.getLogger("myLogger")
   def MyMapperDosomething(rdd: RDD[Int]): RDD[String] = rdd.map { i =>
     log.warn("mapping: " + i)
     (i + n).toString
   }
}
```

Now, let's register this class as a `Kyro` serialization class and then set the `Kyro` serialization as follows:

```
conf.registerKryoClasses(Array(classOf[MyMapper])) // register the class
with Kyro
conf.set("spark.serializer", "org.apache.spark.serializer.KryoSerializer")
// set Kayro serialization
```

That's all you need. The full source code of this example is given in the following. You should be able to run and observe the same output, but an optimized one as compared to the previous example:

```
package com.chapter14.Serilazition
import org.apache.spark._
import org.apache.spark.rdd.RDD
class MyMapper(n: Int) { // without any serilization
```

```scala
@transient lazy val log = org.apache.log4j.LogManager.getLogger
                                ("myLogger")
  def MyMapperDosomething(rdd: RDD[Int]): RDD[String] = rdd.map { i =>
    log.warn("mapping: " + i)
    (i + n).toString
  }
}
//Companion object
object MyMapper {
  def apply(n: Int): MyMapper = new MyMapper(n)
}
//Main object
object KyroRegistrationDemo {
  def main(args: Array[String]) {
    val log = LogManager.getRootLogger
    log.setLevel(Level.WARN)
    val conf = new SparkConf()
      .setAppName("My App")
      .setMaster("local[*]")
    conf.registerKryoClasses(Array(classOf[MyMapper2]))
     // register the class with Kyro
    conf.set("spark.serializer", "org.apache.spark.serializer
            .KryoSerializer") // set Kayro serilazation
    val sc = new SparkContext(conf)
    log.warn("Started")
    val data = sc.parallelize(1 to 100000)
    val mapper = MyMapper(1)
    val other = mapper.MyMapperDosomething(data)
    other.collect()
    log.warn("Finished")
  }
}
```

The output is as follows:

```
17/04/29 15:33:43 WARN root: Started
.
.
.
17/04/29 15:31:51 WARN myLogger: mapping: 1
17/04/29 15:31:51 WARN myLogger: mapping: 49992
17/04/29 15:31:51 WARN myLogger: mapping: 49999
17/04/29 15:31:51 WARN myLogger: mapping: 50000
.
.
.
17/04/29 15:31:51 WARN root: Finished
```

Well done! Now let's have a quick look at how to tune the memory. We will look at some advanced strategies to make sure the efficient use of the main memory in the next section.

Memory tuning

In this section, we will discuss some advanced strategies that can be used by users like you to make sure that an efficient use of memory is carried out while executing your Spark jobs. More specifically, we will show how to calculate the memory usages of your objects. We will suggest some advanced ways to improve it by optimizing your data structures or by converting your data objects in a serialized format using Kryo or Java serializer. Finally, we will look at how to tune Spark's Java heap size, cache size, and the Java garbage collector.

There are three considerations in tuning memory usage:

- The amount of memory used by your objects: You may even want your entire dataset to fit in the memory
- The cost of accessing those objects
- The overhead of garbage collection: If you have a high turnover in terms of objects

Although Java objects are fast enough to access, they can easily consume a factor of 2 to 5x more space than the actual (aka raw) data in their original fields. For example, each distinct Java object has 16 bytes of overhead with an object header. A Java string, for example, has almost 40 bytes of extra overhead over the raw string. Furthermore, Java collection classes like `Set`, `List`, `Queue`, `ArrayList`, `Vector`, `LinkedList`, `PriorityQueue`, `HashSet`, `LinkedHashSet`, `TreeSet`, and so on, are also used. The linked data structures, on the other hand, are too complex, occupying too much extra space since there is a wrapper object for each entry in the data structure. Finally, the collections of primitive types frequently store them in the memory as boxed objects, such as `java.lang.Double` and `java.lang.Integer`.

Memory usage and management

Memory usages by your Spark application and underlying computing nodes can be categorized as execution and storage. Execution memory is used during the computation in merge, shuffles, joins, sorts, and aggregations. On the other hand, storage memory is used for caching and propagating internal data across the cluster. In short, this is due to the large amount of I/O across the network.

Technically, Spark caches network data locally. While working with Spark iteratively or interactively, caching or persistence are optimization techniques in Spark. This two help in saving interim partial results so that they can be reused in subsequent stages. Then these interim results (as RDDs) can be kept in memory (default) or more solid storage, such as a disk, and/or replicated. Furthermore, RDDs can be cached using cache operations too. They can also be persisted using a persist operation. The difference between cache and persist operations is purely syntactic. The cache is a synonym of persisting or persists (MEMORY_ONLY), that is, the cache is merely persisted with the default storage level MEMORY_ONLY.

If you go under the Storage tab in your Spark web UI, you should observe the memory/storage used by an RDD, DataFrame, or Dataset object, as shown in *Figure 10*. Although there are two relevant configurations for tuning memory in Spark, users do not need to readjust them. The reason is that the default values set in the configuration files are enough for your requirements and workloads.

spark.memory.fraction is the size of the unified region as a fraction of (JVM heap space - 300 MB) (default 0.6). The rest of the space (40%) is reserved for user data structures, internal metadata in Spark, and safeguarding against OOM errors in case of sparse and unusually large records. On the other hand, spark.memory.storageFraction expresses the size of R storage space as a fraction of the unified region (default is 0.5). The default value of this parameter is 50% of Java heap space, that is, 300 MB.

Now, one question might arise in your mind: which storage level to choose? To answer this question, Spark storage levels provide you with different trade-offs between memory usage and CPU efficiency. If your RDDs fit comfortably with the default storage level (MEMORY_ONLY), let your Spark driver or master go with it. This is the most memory-efficient option, allowing operations on the RDDs to run as fast as possible. You should let it go with this because this is the most memory-efficient option. This also allows numerous operations on the RDDs to be done as fast as possible.

If your RDDs do not fit the main memory, that is, if MEMORY_ONLY does not work out, you should try using MEMORY_ONLY_SER. It is strongly recommended to not spill your RDDs to disk unless your **UDF** (aka **user-defined function** that you have defined for processing your dataset) is too expensive. This also applies if your UDF filters a large amount of the data during the execution stages. In other cases, recomputing a partition, that is, repartition may be faster for reading data objects from disk. Finally, if you want fast fault recovery, use the replicated storage levels.

In summary, there are the following StorageLevels available and supported in Spark 2.x: (number _2 in the name denotes 2 replicas):

- DISK_ONLY: This is for disk-based operation for RDDs
- DISK_ONLY_2: This is for disk-based operation for RDDs for 2 replicas
- MEMORY_ONLY: This is the default for cache operation in memory for RDDs
- MEMORY_ONLY_2: This is the default for cache operation in memory for RDDs with 2 replicas
- MEMORY_ONLY_SER: If your RDDs do not fit the main memory, that is, if MEMORY_ONLY does not work out, this option particularly helps in storing data objects in a serialized form
- MEMORY_ONLY_SER_2: If your RDDs do not fit the main memory, that is, if MEMORY_ONLY does not work out with 2 replicas, this option also helps in storing data objects in a serialized form
- MEMORY_AND_DISK: Memory and disk (aka combined) based RDD persistence
- MEMORY_AND_DISK_2: Memory and disk (aka combined) based RDD persistence with 2 replicas
- MEMORY_AND_DISK_SER: If MEMORY_AND_DISK does not work, it can be used
- MEMORY_AND_DISK_SER_2: If MEMORY_AND_DISK does not work with 2 replicas, this option can be used
- OFF_HEAP: Does not allow writing into Java heap space

Note that cache is a synonym of persist (MEMORY_ONLY). This means that cache is solely persisted with the default storage level, that is, MEMORY_ONLY. Detailed information can be found at https://jaceklaskowski.gitbooks.io/mastering-apache-spark/content/spark-rdd-StorageLevel.html.

Tuning the data structures

The first way to reduce extra memory usage is to avoid some features in the Java data structure that impose extra overheads. For example, pointer-based data structures and wrapper objects contribute to nontrivial overheads. To tune your source code with a better data structure, we provide some suggestions here, which can be useful.

First, design your data structures such that you use arrays of objects and primitive types more. Thus, this also suggests using standard Java or Scala collection classes like `Set`, `List`, `Queue`, `ArrayList`, `Vector`, `LinkedList`, `PriorityQueue`, `HashSet`, `LinkedHashSet`, and `TreeSet` more frequently.

Second, when possible, avoid using nested structures with a lot of small objects and pointers so that your source code becomes more optimized and concise. Third, when possible, consider using numeric IDs and sometimes using enumeration objects rather than using strings for keys. This is recommended because, as we have already stated, a single Java string object creates an extra overhead of 40 bytes. Finally, if you have less than 32 GB of main memory (that is, RAM), set the JVM flag `-XX:+UseCompressedOops` to make pointers 4 bytes instead of 8.

The earlier option can be set in the `SPARK_HOME/conf/spark-env.sh.template`. Just rename the file as `spark-env.sh` and set the value straight away!

Serialized RDD storage

As discussed already, despite other types of memory tuning, when your objects are too large to fit in the main memory or disk efficiently, a simpler and better way of reducing memory usage is storing them in a serialized form.

This can be done using the serialized storage levels in the RDD persistence API, such as `MEMORY_ONLY_SER`. For more information, refer to the previous section on memory management and start exploring available options.

If you specify using MEMORY_ONLY_SER, Spark will then store each RDD partition as one large byte array. However, the only downside of this approach is that it can slow down data access times. This is reasonable and obvious too; fairly speaking, there's no way to avoid it since each object needs to deserialize on the flyback while reusing.

> As discussed previously, we highly recommend using Kryo serialization instead of Java serialization to make data access a bit faster.

Garbage collection tuning

Although it is not a major problem in your Java or Scala programs that just read an RDD sequentially or randomly once and then execute numerous operations on it, **Java Virtual Machine (JVM)** GC can be problematic and complex if you have a large amount of data objects w.r.t RDDs stored in your driver program. When the JVM needs to remove obsolete and unused objects from the old objects to make space for the newer ones, it is mandatory to identify them and remove them from the memory eventually. However, this is a costly operation in terms of processing time and storage. You might be wondering, that the cost of GC is proportional to the number of Java objects stored in your main memory. Therefore, we strongly suggest you tune your data structure. Also, having fewer objects stored in your memory is recommended.

The first step in GC tuning is collecting the related statistics on how frequently garbage collection by JVM occurs on your machine. The second statistic needed in this regard is the amount of time spent on GC by JVM on your machine or computing nodes. This can be achieved by adding -verbose:gc -XX:+PrintGCDetails -XX:+PrintGCTimeStamps to the Java options in your IDE, such as Eclipse, in the JVM startup arguments and specifying a name and location for our GC log file, as follows:

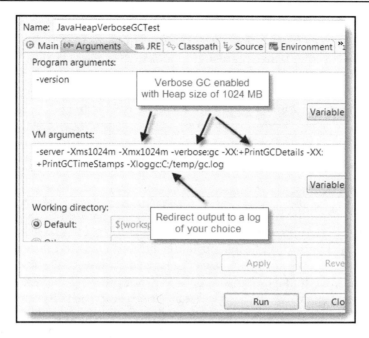

Figure 27: Setting GC verbose on Eclipse

Alternatively, you can specify `verbose:gc` while submitting your Spark jobs using the Spark-submit script, as follows:

```
--conf "spark.executor.extraJavaOptions = -verbose:gc -XX:-PrintGCDetails -
XX:+PrintGCTimeStamps"
```

In short, when specifying GC options for Spark, you must determine where you want the GC options specified, on the executors or on the driver. When you submit your jobs, specify `--driver-java-options -XX:+PrintFlagsFinal -verbose:gc` and so on. For the executor, specify `--conf spark.executor.extraJavaOptions=-XX:+PrintFlagsFinal -verbose:gc` and so on.

Now, when your Spark job is executed, you will be able to see the logs and messages printed in the worker's node at `/var/log/logs` each time a GC occurs. The downside of this approach is that these logs will not be on your driver program but on your cluster's worker nodes.

It is to be noted that `verbose:gc` only prints appropriate message or logs after each GC collection. Correspondingly, it prints details about memory. However, if you are interested in looking for more critical issues, such as a memory leak, `verbose:gc` may not be enough. In that case, you can use some visualization tools, such as that and VisualVM. A better way of GC tuning in your Spark application can be read at `https://databricks.com/blog/2015/05/28/tuning-java-garbage-collection-for-spark-applications.html`.

Level of parallelism

Although you can control the number of map tasks to be executed through optional parameters to the `SparkContext.text` file, Spark sets the same on each file according to its size automatically. In addition to this, for a distributed `reduce` operation such as `groupByKey` and `reduceByKey`, Spark uses the largest parent RDD's number of partitions. However, sometimes, we make one mistake, that is, not utilizing the full computing resources for your nodes in a computing cluster. As a result, the full computing resources will not be fully exploited unless you set and specify the level of parallelism for your Spark job explicitly. Therefore, you should set the level of parallelism as the second argument.

For more on this option, please refer to `https://spark.apache.org/docs/latest/api/scala/index.html#org.apache.spark.rdd.PairRDDFunctions`.

Alternatively, you can do it by setting the config property spark.default.parallelism to change the default. For operations such as parallelizing with no parent RDDs, the level of parallelism depends on the cluster manager, that is, standalone, Mesos, or YARN. For the local mode, set the level of parallelism equal to the number of cores on the local machine. For Mesos or YARN, set the fine-grained mode to 8. In other cases, the total number of cores on all executor nodes or 2, whichever is larger, and in general, 2-3 tasks per CPU core in your cluster is recommended.

Broadcasting

A broadcast variable enables a Spark developer to keep a read-only copy of an instance or class variable cached on each driver program, rather than transferring a copy of its own with the dependent tasks. However, an explicit creation of a broadcast variable is useful only when tasks across multiple stages need the same data in deserialize form.

In Spark application development, using the broadcasting option of SparkContext can reduce the size of each serialized task greatly. This also helps to reduce the cost of initiating a Spark job in a cluster. If you have a certain task in your Spark job that uses large objects from the driver program, you should turn it into a broadcast variable.

To use a broadcast variable in a Spark application, you can instantiate it using `SparkContext.broadcast`. Later on, use the value method from the class to access the shared value as follows:

```
val m = 5
val bv = sc.broadcast(m)
```

Output/log: `bv: org.apache.spark.broadcast.Broadcast[Int] = Broadcast(0)`

```
bv.value()
```

Output/log: `res0: Int = 1`

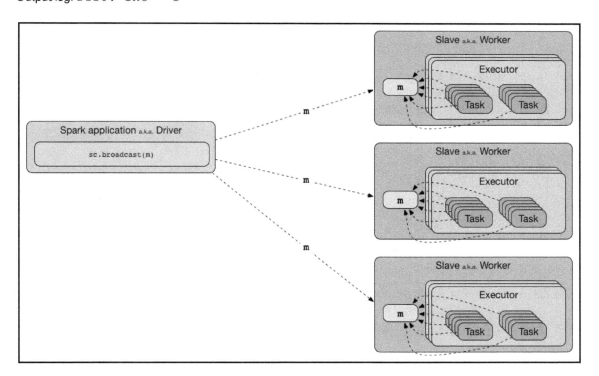

Figure 28: Broadcasting a value from driver to executors

The Broadcast feature of Spark uses the **SparkContext** to create broadcast values. After that, the **BroadcastManager** and **ContextCleaner** are used to control their life cycle, as shown in the following figure:

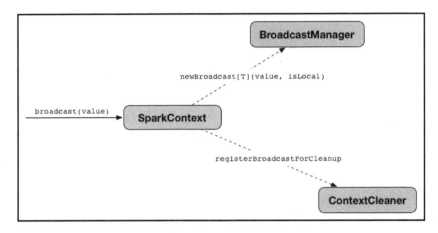

Figure 29: SparkContext broadcasts the variable/value using BroadcastManager and ContextCleaner

Spark application in the driver program automatically prints the serialized size of each task on the driver. Therefore, you can decide whether your tasks are too large to make it parallel. If your task is larger than 20 KB, it's probably worth optimizing.

Data locality

Data locality means how close the data is to the code to be processed. Technically, data locality can have a nontrivial impact on the performance of a Spark job to be executed locally or in cluster mode. As a result, if the data and the code to be processed are tied together, computation is supposed to be much faster. Usually, shipping a serialized code from a driver to an executor is much faster since the code size is much smaller than that of data.

In Spark application development and job execution, there are several levels of locality. In order from closest to farthest, the level depends on the current location of the data you have to process:

Data Locality	Meaning	Special Notes
PROCESS_LOCAL	Data and code are in the same location	Best locality possible
NODE_LOCAL	Data and the code are on the same node, for example, data stored on HDFS	A bit slower than PROCESS_LOCAL since the data has to propagate across the processes and network
NO_PREF	The data is accessed equally from somewhere else	Has no locality preference
RACK_LOCAL	The data is on the same rack of servers over the network	Suitable for large-scale data processing
ANY	The data is elsewhere on the network and not in the same rack	Not recommended unless there are no other options available

Table 2: Data locality and Spark

Spark is developed such that it prefers to schedule all tasks at the best locality level, but this is not guaranteed and not always possible either. As a result, based on the situation in the computing nodes, Spark switches to lower locality levels if available computing resources are too occupied. Moreover, if you would like to have the best data locality, there are two choices for you:

- Wait until a busy CPU gets free to start a task on your data on the same server or same node
- Immediately start a new one, which requires moving data there

Summary

In this chapter, we discussed some advanced topics of Spark toward making your Spark job's performance better. We discussed some basic techniques to tune your Spark jobs. We discussed how to monitor your jobs by accessing Spark web UI. We discussed how to set Spark configuration parameters. We also discussed some common mistakes made by Spark users and provided some recommendations. Finally, we discussed some optimization techniques that help tune Spark applications.

Testing and Debugging Spark

9

In an ideal world, we write perfect Spark codes and everything runs perfectly all the time, right? Just kidding; in practice, we know that working with large-scale datasets is hardly ever that easy, and there are inevitably some data points that will expose any corner cases with your code.

Considering the aforementioned challenges, therefore, in this chapter, we will see how difficult it can be to test an application if it is distributed; then, we will see some ways to tackle this. In a nutshell, the following topics will be cover throughout this chapter:

- Testing in a distributed environment
- Testing Spark application
- Debugging Spark application

Testing in a distributed environment

Leslie Lamport defined the term distributed system as follows:

> *"A distributed system is one in which I cannot get any work done because some machine I have never heard of has crashed."*

Resource sharing through **World Wide Web** (aka **WWW**), a network of connected computers (aka a cluster), is a good example of distributed systems. These distributed environments are often complex and lots of heterogeneity occurs frequently. Testing in these kinds of heterogeneous environments is also challenging. In this section, at first, we will observe some commons issues that are often raised while working with such a system.

Distributed environment

There are numerous definitions of distributed systems. Let's see some definition and then we will try to correlate the aforementioned categories afterward. Coulouris defines a distributed system as *a system in which hardware or software components located at networked computers communicate and coordinate their actions only by message passing*. On the other hand, Tanenbaum defines the term in several ways:

- *A collection of independent computers that appear to the users of the system as a single computer.*
- *A system that consists of a collection of two or more independent Computers which coordinate their processing through the exchange of synchronous or asynchronous message passing.*
- *A distributed system is a collection of autonomous computers linked by a network with software designed to produce an integrated computing facility.*

Now, based on the preceding definition, distributed systems can be categorized as follows:

- Only hardware and software are distributed: The local distributed system is connected through LAN.
- Users are distributed, but there are computing and hardware resources that are running backend, for example, WWW.
- Both users and hardware/software are distributed: Distributed computing cluster that is connected through WAN. For example, you can get these types of computing facilities while using Amazon AWS, Microsoft Azure, Google Cloud, or Digital Ocean's droplets.

Issues in a distributed system

Here we will discuss some major issues that need to be taken care of during the software and hardware testing so that Spark jobs run smoothly in cluster computing, which is essentially a distributed computing environment.

Note that all the issues are unavoidable, but we can at least tune them for betterment. You should follow the instructions and recommendations given in the previous chapter. According to *Kamal Sheel Mishra* and *Anil Kumar Tripathi, Some Issues, Challenges and Problems of Distributed Software System*, in *International Journal of Computer Science and Information Technologies*, Vol. 5 (4), 2014, 4922-4925. URL: https://pdfs.semanticscholar. org/4c6d/c4d739bad13bcd0398e5180c1513f18275d8.pdf, there are several issues that need to be addressed while working with software or hardware in a distributed environment:

- Scalability
- Heterogeneous languages, platform, and architecture
- Resource management
- Security and privacy
- Transparency
- Openness
- Interoperability
- Quality of service
- Failure management
- Synchronization
- Communications
- Software architectures
- Performance analysis
- Generating test data
- Component selection for testing
- Test sequence
- Testing for system scalability and performance
- Availability of source code
- Reproducibility of events
- Deadlocks and race conditions
- Testing for fault tolerance
- Scheduling issue for distributed system
- Distributed task allocation
- Testing distributed software
- Monitoring and control mechanism from the hardware abstraction level

It's true that we cannot fully solve all of these issues, but However, using Spark, we can at least control a few of them that are related to the distributed system. For example, scalability, resource management, quality of service, failure management, synchronization, communications, scheduling issue for distributed system, distributed task allocation, and monitoring and control mechanism in testing distributed software. Most of them were discussed in the previous two chapters. On the other hand, we can address some issues in the testing and software side: such as software architectures, performance analysis, generating test data, component selection for testing, test sequence, testing for system scalability and performance, and availability of source code. These will be covered explicitly or implicitly in this chapter at least.

Challenges of software testing in a distributed environment

There are some common challenges associated with the tasks in an agile software development, and those challenges become more complex while testing the software in a distributed environment before deploying them eventually. Often team members need to merge the software components in parallel after the bugs proliferating. However, based on urgency, often the merging occurs before the testing phase. Sometimes, many stakeholders are distributed across teams. Therefore, there's a huge potential for misunderstanding and teams often lose in between.

For example, Cloud Foundry (`https://www.cloudfoundry.org/`) is an open source heavily distributed PaaS software system for managing deployment and scalability of applications in the Cloud. It promises different features such as scalability, reliability, and elasticity that come inherently to deployments on Cloud Foundry require the underlying distributed system to implement measures to ensure robustness, resiliency, and failover.

The process of software testing is long known to comprise *unit testing, integration testing, smoke testing, acceptance testing, scalability testing, performance testing,* and *quality of service testing*. In Cloud Foundry, the process of testing a distributed system is shown in the following figure:

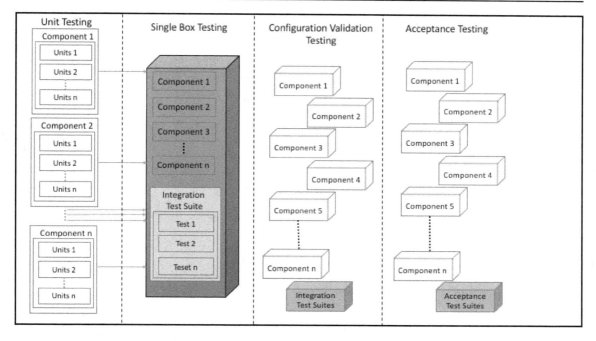

Figure 1: An example of software testing in a distributed environment like Cloud

As shown in the preceding figure (first column), the process of testing in a distributed environment like Cloud starts with running unit tests against the smallest points of contract in the system. Following successful execution of all the unit tests, integration tests are run to validate the behavior of interacting components as part of a single coherent software system (second column) running on a single box (for example, a **Virtual Machine** (**VM**) or bare metal). However, while these tests validate the overall behavior of the system as a monolith, they do not guarantee system validity in a distributed deployment. Once integration tests pass, the next step (third column) is to validate distributed deployment of the system and run the smoke tests.

As you know, that the successful configuration of the software and execution of unit tests prepares us to validate acceptability of system behavior. This verification is done by running acceptance tests (fourth column). Now, to overcome the aforementioned issues and challenges in distributed environments, there are also other hidden challenges that need to be solved by researchers and big data engineers, but those are actually out of the scope of this book.

Now that we know what real challenges are for the software testing in a distributed environment, now let's start testing our Spark code a bit. The next section is dedicated to testing Spark applications.

Testing Spark applications

There are many ways to try to test your Spark code, depending on whether it's Java (you can do basic JUnit tests to test non-Spark pieces) or ScalaTest for your Scala code. You can also do full integration tests by running Spark locally or on a small test cluster. Another awesome choice from Holden Karau is using Spark-testing base. You probably know that there is no native library for unit testing in Spark as of yet. Nevertheless, we can have the following two alternatives to use two libraries:

- ScalaTest
- Spark-testing base

However, before starting to test your Spark applications written in Scala, some background knowledge about unit testing and testing Scala methods is a mandate.

Testing Scala methods

Here, we will see some simple techniques for testing Scala methods. For Scala users, this is the most familiar unit testing framework (you can also use it for testing Java code and soon for JavaScript). ScalaTest supports a number of different testing styles, each designed to support a specific type of testing need. For details, see ScalaTest User Guide at `http://www.scalatest.org/user_guide/selecting_a_style`. Although ScalaTest supports many styles, one of the quickest ways to get started is to use the following ScalaTest traits and write the tests in the **TDD (test-driven development)** style:

1. `FunSuite`
2. `Assertions`
3. `BeforeAndAfter`

Feel free to browse the preceding URLs to learn more about these traits; that will make the rest of this tutorial go smoothly.

It is to be noted that the TDD is a programming technique to develop software, and it states that you should start development from tests. Hence, it doesn't affect how tests are written, but when tests are written. There is no trait or testing style to enforce or encourage TDD in `ScalaTest.FunSuite`, `Assertions`, and `BeforeAndAfter` are only more similar to the xUnit testing frameworks.

There are three assertions available in the ScalaTest in any style trait:

- `assert`: This is used for general assertions in your Scala program.
- `assertResult`: This helps differentiate expected value from the actual values.
- `assertThrows`: This is used to ensure a bit of code throws an expected exception.

The ScalaTest's assertions are defined in the trait `Assertions`, which is further extended by `Suite`. In brief, the `Suite` trait is the super trait for all the style traits. According to the ScalaTest documentation at `http://www.scalatest.org/user_guide/using_assertions`, the `Assertions` trait also provides the following features:

- `assume` to conditionally cancel a test
- `fail` to fail a test unconditionally
- `cancel` to cancel a test unconditionally
- `succeed` to make a test succeed unconditionally
- `intercept` to ensure a bit of code throws an expected exception and then make assertions about the exception
- `assertDoesNotCompile` to ensure a bit of code does not compile
- `assertCompiles` to ensure a bit of code does compile
- `assertTypeError` to ensure a bit of code does not compile because of a type (not parse) error
- `withClue` to add more information about a failure

From the preceding list, we will show a few of them. In your Scala program, you can write assertions by calling `assert` and passing a `Boolean` expression in. You can simply start writing your simple unit test case using `Assertions`. The `Predef` is an object, where this behavior of assert is defined. Note that all the members of the `Predef` get imported into your every Scala source file. The following source code will print `Assertion success` for the following case:

```
package com.chapter16.SparkTesting
object SimpleScalaTest {
  def main(args: Array[String]):Unit= {
    val a = 5
    val b = 5
    assert(a == b)
      println("Assertion success")
  }
}
```

However, if you make a = 2 and b = 1, for example, the assertion will fail and you will experience the following output:

```
Exception in thread "main" java.lang.AssertionError: assertion failed
    at scala.Predef$.assert(Predef.scala:156)
    at com.chapter16.SparkTesting.SimpleScalaTest$.main(SimpleScalaTest.scala:7)
    at com.chapter16.SparkTesting.SimpleScalaTest.main(SimpleScalaTest.scala)
```

Figure 2: An example of assertion fail

If you pass a true expression, assert will return normally. However, assert will terminate abruptly with an Assertion Error if the supplied expression is false. Unlike the AssertionError and TestFailedException forms, the ScalaTest's assert provides more information that will tell you exactly in which line the test case failed or for which expression. Therefore, ScalaTest's assert provides better error messages than Scala's assert.

For example, for the following source code, you should experience TestFailedException that will tell that 5 did not equal 4:

```
package com.chapter16.SparkTesting
import org.scalatest.Assertions._
object SimpleScalaTest {
  def main(args: Array[String]):Unit= {
    val a = 5
    val b = 4
    assert(a == b)
      println("Assertion success")
  }
}
```

The following figure shows the output of the preceding Scala test:

```
Exception in thread "main" org.scalatest.exceptions.TestFailedException: 2 did not equal 1
    at org.scalatest.Assertions$class.newAssertionFailedException(Assertions.scala:500)
    at org.scalatest.Assertions$.newAssertionFailedException(Assertions.scala:1538)
    at org.scalatest.Assertions$AssertionsHelper.macroAssert(Assertions.scala:466)
    at com.chapter16.SparkTesting.SimpleScalaTest$.main(SimpleScalaTest.scala:8)
    at com.chapter16.SparkTesting.SimpleScalaTest.main(SimpleScalaTest.scala)
```

Figure 3: An example of TestFailedException

The following source code explains the use of the `assertResult` unit test to test the result of your method:

```
package com.chapter16.SparkTesting
import org.scalatest.Assertions._
object AssertResult {
  def main(args: Array[String]):Unit= {
    val x = 10
    val y = 6
    assertResult(3) {
      x - y
    }
  }
}
```

The preceding assertion will be failed and Scala will throw an exception `TestFailedException` and prints `Expected 3 but got 4` (*Figure 4*):

```
Exception in thread "main" org.scalatest.exceptions.TestFailedException: Expected 3, but got 4
    at org.scalatest.Assertions$class.newAssertionFailedException(Assertions.scala:495)
    at org.scalatest.Assertions$.newAssertionFailedException(Assertions.scala:1538)
    at org.scalatest.Assertions$class.assertResult(Assertions.scala:1226)
    at org.scalatest.Assertions$.assertResult(Assertions.scala:1538)
    at com.chapter16.SparkTesting.AssertResult$.main(AssertResult.scala:8)
    at com.chapter16.SparkTesting.AssertResult.main(AssertResult.scala)
```

Figure 4: Another example of TestFailedException

Now, let's see a unit testing to show expected exception:

```
package com.chapter16.SparkTesting
import org.scalatest.Assertions._
object ExpectedException {
  def main(args: Array[String]):Unit= {
    val s = "Hello world!"
    try {
      s.charAt(0)
      fail()
    } catch {
      case _: IndexOutOfBoundsException => // Expected, so continue
    }
  }
}
```

If you try to access an array element outside the index, the preceding code will tell you if you're allowed to access the first character of the preceding string `Hello world!`. If your Scala program can access the value in an index, the assertion will fail. This also means that the test case has failed. Thus, the preceding test case will fail naturally since the first index contains the character `H`, and you should experience the following error message (*Figure 5*):

```
Exception in thread "main" org.scalatest.exceptions.TestFailedException
    at org.scalatest.Assertions$class.newAssertionFailedException(Assertions.scala:493)
    at org.scalatest.Assertions$.newAssertionFailedException(Assertions.scala:1538)
    at org.scalatest.Assertions$class.fail(Assertions.scala:1313)
    at org.scalatest.Assertions$.fail(Assertions.scala:1538)
    at com.chapter16.SparkTesting.ExpectedException$.main(ExpectedException.scala:9)
    at com.chapter16.SparkTesting.ExpectedException.main(ExpectedException.scala)
```

Figure 5: Third example of TestFailedException

However, now let's try to access the index at position −1 as follows:

```
package com.chapter16.SparkTesting
import org.scalatest.Assertions._
object ExpectedException {
  def main(args: Array[String]):Unit= {
    val s = "Hello world!"
    try {
      s.charAt(-1)
      fail()
    } catch {
      case _: IndexOutOfBoundsException => // Expected, so continue
    }
  }
}
```

Now the assertion should be true, and consequently, the test case will be passed. Finally, the code will terminate normally. Now, let's check our code snippets if it will compile or not. Very often, you may wish to ensure that a certain ordering of the code that represents emerging "user error" does not compile at all. The objective is to check the strength of the library against the error to disallow unwanted result and behavior. ScalaTest's `Assertions` trait includes the following syntax for that purpose:

```
assertDoesNotCompile("val a: String = 1")
```

If you want to ensure that a snippet of code does not compile because of a type error (as opposed to a syntax error), use the following:

```
assertTypeError("val a: String = 1")
```

A syntax error will still result on a thrown `TestFailedException`. Finally, if you want to state that a snippet of code does compile, you can make that more obvious with the following:

```
assertCompiles("val a: Int = 1")
```

A complete example is shown as follows:

```
package com.chapter16.SparkTesting
import org.scalatest.Assertions._
object CompileOrNot {
  def main(args: Array[String]):Unit= {
    assertDoesNotCompile("val a: String = 1")
    println("assertDoesNotCompile True")
    assertTypeError("val a: String = 1")
    println("assertTypeError True")
    assertCompiles("val a: Int = 1")
    println("assertCompiles True")
    assertDoesNotCompile("val a: Int = 1")
    println("assertDoesNotCompile True")
  }
}
```

The output of the preceding code is shown in the following figure:

```
AssertDoesNotCompile True
AssertTypeError True
AssertCompiles True
Exception in thread "main" org.scalatest.exceptions.TestFailedException: Expected a
compiler error, but got none for code: val a: Int = 1
    at com.chapter16.SparkTesting.CompileOrNot$.main(CompileOrNot.scala:15)
    at com.chapter16.SparkTesting.CompileOrNot.main(CompileOrNot.scala)
```

Figure 6: Multiple tests together

Now we would like to finish the Scala-based unit testing due to page limitation. However, for other unit test cases, you can refer the Scala test guideline at http://www.scalatest.org/user_guide.

Unit testing

In software engineering, often, individual units of source code are tested to determine whether they are fit for use or not. This way of software testing method is also called the unit testing. This testing ensures that the source code developed by a software engineer or developer meets the design specifications and works as intended.

On the other hand, the goal of unit testing is to separate each part of the program (that is, in a modular way). Then try to observe if all the individual parts are working normally. There are several benefits of unit testing in any software system:

- **Find problems early:** It finds bugs or missing parts of the specification early in the development cycle.
- **Facilitates change:** It helps in refactoring and up gradation without worrying about breaking functionality.
- **Simplifies integration:** It makes integration tests easier to write.
- **Documentation:** It provides a living documentation of the system.
- **Design:** It can act as the formal design of the project.

Testing Spark applications

We have already seen how to test your Scala code using built-in `ScalaTest` package of Scala. However, in this subsection, we will see how we could test our Spark application written in Scala. The following three methods will be discussed:

- **Method 1:** Testing Spark applications using JUnit
- **Method 2:** Testing Spark applications using `ScalaTest` package
- **Method 3:** Testing Spark applications using Spark testing base

Methods 1 and 2 will be discussed here with some practical codes. However, a detailed discussion on method 3 will be provided in the next subsection. To keep the understanding easy and simple, we will use the famous word counting applications to demonstrate methods 1 and 2.

Method 1: Using Scala JUnit test

Suppose you have written an application in Scala that can tell you how many words are there in a document or text file as follows:

```
package com.chapter16.SparkTesting
import org.apache.spark._
import org.apache.spark.sql.SparkSession
class wordCounterTestDemo {
  val spark = SparkSession
    .builder
    .master("local[*]")
    .config("spark.sql.warehouse.dir", "E:/Exp/")
    .appName(s"OneVsRestExample")
    .getOrCreate()
  def myWordCounter(fileName: String): Long = {
    val input = spark.sparkContext.textFile(fileName)
    val counts = input.flatMap(_.split(" ")).distinct()
    val counter = counts.count()
    counter
  }
}
```

The preceding code simply parses a text file and performs a flatMap operation by simply splitting the words. Then, it performs another operation to take only the distinct words into consideration. Finally, the myWordCounter method counts how many words are there and returns the value of the counter.

Now, before proceeding into formal testing, let's check if the preceding method works well. Just add the main method and create an object as follows:

```
package com.chapter16.SparkTesting
import org.apache.spark._
import org.apache.spark.sql.SparkSession
object wordCounter {
  val spark = SparkSession
    .builder
    .master("local[*]")
    .config("spark.sql.warehouse.dir", "E:/Exp/")
    .appName("Testing")
    .getOrCreate()
  val fileName = "data/words.txt";
  def myWordCounter(fileName: String): Long = {
    val input = spark.sparkContext.textFile(fileName)
    val counts = input.flatMap(_.split(" ")).distinct()
    val counter = counts.count()
    counter
```

```
    }
    def main(args: Array[String]): Unit = {
      val counter = myWordCounter(fileName)
      println("Number of words: " + counter)
    }
  }
```

If you execute the preceding code, you should observe the following output: `Number of words: 214`. Fantastic! It really works as a local application. Now, test the preceding test case using Scala JUnit test case.

```
package com.chapter16.SparkTesting
import org.scalatest.Assertions._
import org.junit.Test
import org.apache.spark.sql.SparkSession
class wordCountTest {
  val spark = SparkSession
    .builder
    .master("local[*]")
    .config("spark.sql.warehouse.dir", "E:/Exp/")
    .appName(s"OneVsRestExample")
    .getOrCreate()
    @Test def test() {
      val fileName = "data/words.txt"
      val obj = new wordCounterTestDemo()
      assert(obj.myWordCounter(fileName) == 214)
        }
    spark.stop()
}
```

If you see the earlier code carefully, I have used the `Test` annotation before the `test()` method. Inside the `test()` method, I invoked the `assert()` method, where the actual testing occurs. Here we tried to check if the return value of the `myWordCounter()` method is equal to 214. Now run the earlier code as a Scala Unit test as follows (*Figure 7*):

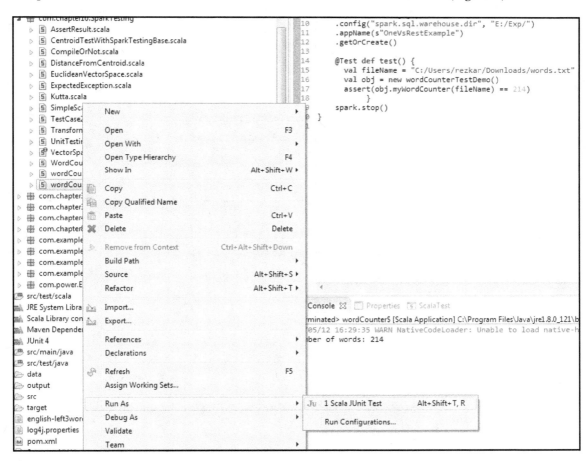

Figure 7: Running Scala code as Scala JUnit Test

Now if the test case passes, you should observe the following output on your Eclipse IDE (*Figure 8*):

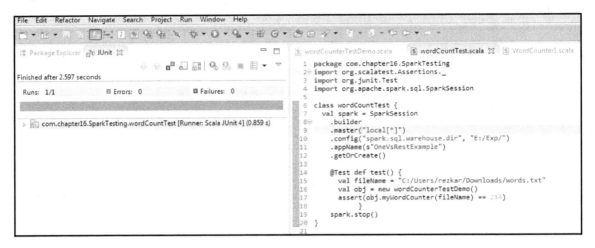

Figure 8: Word count test case passed

Now, for example, try to assert in the following way:

```
assert(obj.myWordCounter(fileName) == 210)
```

If the preceding test case fails, you should observe the following output (*Figure 9*):

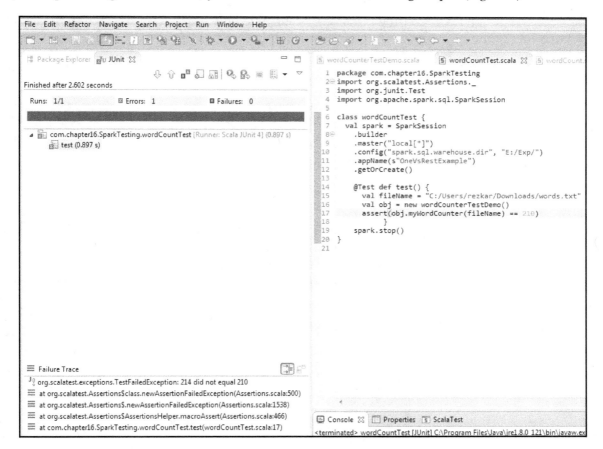

Figure 9: Test case failed

Now let's have a look at method 2 and how it helps us for the betterment.

Method 2: Testing Scala code using FunSuite

Now, let's redesign the preceding test case by returning only the RDD of the texts in the document, as follows:

```
package com.chapter16.SparkTesting
import org.apache.spark._
import org.apache.spark.rdd.RDD
import org.apache.spark.sql.SparkSession
class wordCountRDD {
  def prepareWordCountRDD(file: String, spark: SparkSession): RDD[(String,
Int)] = {
    val lines = spark.sparkContext.textFile(file)
    lines.flatMap(_.split(" ")).map((_, 1)).reduceByKey(_ + _)
  }
}
```

So, the `prepareWordCountRDD()` method in the preceding class returns an RDD of string and integer values. Now, if we want to test the `prepareWordCountRDD()` method's functionality, we can do it more explicit by extending the test class with `FunSuite` and `BeforeAndAfterAll` from the `ScalaTest` package of Scala. The testing works in the following ways:

- Extend the test class with `FunSuite` and `BeforeAndAfterAll` from the `ScalaTest` package of Scala
- Override the `beforeAll()` that creates Spark context
- Perform the test using the `test()` method and use the `assert()` method inside the `test()` method
- Override the `afterAll()` method that stops the Spark context

Based on the preceding steps, let's see a class for testing the preceding `prepareWordCountRDD()` method:

```
package com.chapter16.SparkTesting
import org.scalatest.{ BeforeAndAfterAll, FunSuite }
import org.scalatest.Assertions._
import org.apache.spark.sql.SparkSession
import org.apache.spark.rdd.RDD
class wordCountTest2 extends FunSuite with BeforeAndAfterAll {
  var spark: SparkSession = null
  def tokenize(line: RDD[String]) = {
    line.map(x => x.split(' ')).collect()
  }
  override def beforeAll() {
    spark = SparkSession
```

```
          .builder
          .master("local[*]")
          .config("spark.sql.warehouse.dir", "E:/Exp/")
          .appName(s"OneVsRestExample")
          .getOrCreate()
  }
  test("Test if two RDDs are equal") {
      val input = List("To be,", "or not to be:", "that is the question-",
"William Shakespeare")
      val expected = Array(Array("To", "be,"), Array("or", "not", "to",
"be:"), Array("that", "is", "the", "question-"), Array("William",
"Shakespeare"))
      val transformed = tokenize(spark.sparkContext.parallelize(input))
      assert(transformed === expected)
  }
  test("Test for word count RDD") {
      val fileName = "C:/Users/rezkar/Downloads/words.txt"
      val obj = new wordCountRDD
      val result = obj.prepareWordCountRDD(fileName, spark)
      assert(result.count() === 214)
  }
  override def afterAll() {
      spark.stop()
  }
}
```

The first test says that if two RDDs materialize in two different ways, the contents should be the same. Thus, the first test should get passed. We will see this in the following example. Now, for the second test, as we have seen previously, the word count of RDD is 214, but let's assume it unknown for a while. If it's 214 coincidentally, the test case should pass, which is its expected behavior.

Thus, we are expecting both tests to be passed. Now, on Eclipse, run the test suite as `ScalaTest-File`, as shown in the following figure:

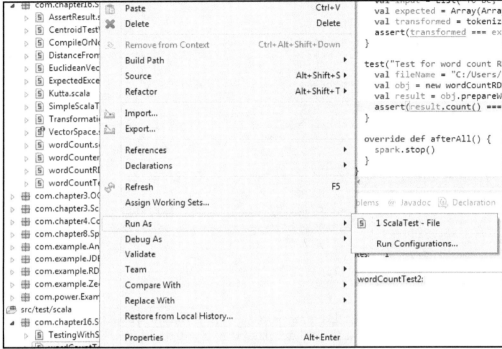

Figure 10: running the test suite as ScalaTest-File

Now you should observe the following output (*Figure 11*). The output shows how many test cases we performed and how many of them passed, failed, canceled, ignored, or was in pending. It also shows the time to execute the overall test.

```
Problems  @ Javadoc  Declaration  Console 23  ScalaTest
<terminated> wordCountTest2.scala [ScalaTest (java runner)] C:\Program Files\Java\jdk1.8.0_10;
Run starting. Expected test count is: 2
wordCountTest2:
17/05/12 20:44:26 WARN NativeCodeLoader: Unable to load native-hadoop li
- Test if two RDDs are equal
- Test for word count RDD
Run completed in 2 seconds, 573 milliseconds.
Total number of tests run: 2
Suites: completed 1, aborted 0
Tests: succeeded 2, failed 0, canceled 0, ignored 0, pending 0
All tests passed.
```

Figure 11: Test result when running the two test suites as ScalaTest-file

Fantastic! The test case passed. Now, let's try changing the compare value in the assertion in the two separate tests using the `test()` method as follows:

```
test("Test for word count RDD") {
  val fileName = "data/words.txt"
  val obj = new wordCountRDD
  val result = obj.prepareWordCountRDD(fileName, spark)
  assert(result.count() === 210)
}
test("Test if two RDDs are equal") {
  val input = List("To be", "or not to be:", "that is the question-",
"William Shakespeare")
  val expected = Array(Array("To", "be,"), Array("or", "not", "to", "be:"),
Array("that", "is", "the", "question-"), Array("William", "Shakespeare"))
  val transformed = tokenize(spark.sparkContext.parallelize(input))
  assert(transformed === expected)
}
```

Now, you should expect that the test case will be failed. Now run the earlier class as `ScalaTest-File` (*Figure 12*):

Figure 12: Test result when running the preceding two test suites as ScalaTest-File

Well done! We have learned how to perform the unit testing using Scala's FunSuite. However, if you evaluate the preceding method carefully, you should agree that there are several disadvantages. For example, you need to ensure an explicit management of `SparkContext` creation and destruction. As a developer or programmer, you have to write more lines of code for testing a sample method. Sometimes, code duplication occurs as the *Before* and the *After* step has to be repeated in all test suites. However, this is debatable since the common code could be put in a common trait.

Now the question is how could we improve our experience? My recommendation is using the Spark testing base to make life easier and more straightforward. We will discuss how we could perform the unit testing the Spark testing base.

Method 3: Making life easier with Spark testing base

Spark testing base helps you to test your most of the Spark codes with ease. So, what are the pros of this method then? There are many in fact. For example, using this the code is not verbose but we can get a very succinct code. The API is itself richer than that of ScalaTest or JUnit. Multiple languages support, for example, Scala, Java, and Python. It has the support of built-in RDD comparators. You can also use it for testing streaming applications. And finally and most importantly, it supports both local and cluster mode testings. This is most important for testing in a distributed environment.

 The GitHub repo is located at `https://github.com/holdenk/spark-testing-base`.

Before starting the unit testing with Spark testing base, you should include the following dependency in the Maven friendly `pom.xml` file in your project tree for Spark 2.x as follows:

```
<dependency>
   <groupId>com.holdenkarau</groupId>
   <artifactId>spark-testing-base_2.10</artifactId>
   <version>2.0.0_0.6.0</version>
</dependency>
```

For SBT, you can add the following dependency:

```
"com.holdenkarau" %% "spark-testing-base" % "2.0.0_0.6.0"
```

Note that it is recommended to add the preceding dependency in the `test` scope by specifying `<scope>test</scope>` for both the Maven and SBT cases. In addition to these, there are other considerations such as memory requirements and OOMs and disabling the parallel execution. The default Java options in the SBT testing are too small to support for running multiple tests. Sometimes it's harder to test Spark codes if the job is submitted in local mode! Now you can naturally understand how difficult it would be in a real cluster mode -i.e. YARN or Mesos.

To get rid of this problem, you can increase the amount of memory in your `build.sbt` file in your project tree. Just add the following parameters as follows:

```
javaOptions ++= Seq("-Xms512M", "-Xmx2048M", "-XX:MaxPermSize=2048M", "-XX:+CMSClassUnloadingEnabled")
```

However, if you are using Surefire, you can add the following:

```
<argLine>-Xmx2048m -XX:MaxPermSize=2048m</argLine>
```

In your Maven-based build, you can make it by setting the value in the environmental variable. For more on this issue, refer to https://maven.apache.org/configure.html.

This is just an example to run spark testing base's own tests. Therefore, you might need to set bigger value. Finally, make sure that you have disabled the parallel execution in your SBT by adding the following line of code:

```
parallelExecution in Test := false
```

On the other hand, if you're using surefire, make sure that `forkCount` and `reuseForks` are set as 1 and true, respectively. Let's see an example of using Spark testing base. The following source code has three test cases. The first test case is the dummy that compares if 1 is equal to 1 or not, which obviously will be passed. The second test case counts the number of words from the sentence, say `Hello world! My name is Reza`, and compares if this has six words or not. The final and the last test case tries to compare two RDDs:

```scala
package com.chapter16.SparkTesting
import org.scalatest.Assertions._
import org.apache.spark.rdd.RDD
import com.holdenkarau.spark.testing.SharedSparkContext
import org.scalatest.FunSuite
class TransformationTestWithSparkTestingBase extends FunSuite with
SharedSparkContext {
  def tokenize(line: RDD[String]) = {
    line.map(x => x.split(' ')).collect()
  }
  test("works, obviously!") {
    assert(1 == 1)
  }
  test("Words counting") {
    assert(sc.parallelize("Hello world My name is Reza".split("\\W")).map(_
+ 1).count == 6)
  }
  test("Testing RDD transformations using a shared Spark Context") {
    val input = List("Testing", "RDD transformations", "using a shared",
"Spark Context")
    val expected = Array(Array("Testing"), Array("RDD", "transformations"),
Array("using", "a", "shared"), Array("Spark", "Context"))
    val transformed = tokenize(sc.parallelize(input))
    assert(transformed === expected)
  }
}
```

From the preceding source code, we can see that we can perform multiple test cases using Spark testing base. Upon successful execution, you should observe the following output (*Figure 13*):

```
Console 23   Problems
<terminated> TransformationTestWithSparkTestingBase.scala [ScalaTest (java runner)] C:\Program Files\Java\jdk1.8.0_102\bin\javaw.exe (19 Feb 2017, 00:49:48)
Run starting. Expected test count is: 3
TransformationTestWithSparkTestingBase:
17/02/19 00:49:49 WARN NativeCodeLoader: Unable to load native-hadoop library for your platform... using builtin-java classes where applicable
- works, obviously!

[Stage 0:>                                                    (0 + 0) / 8]
                                                                    - broken
- Testing RDD transformations using a shared Spark Context
Run completed in 2 seconds, 534 milliseconds.
Total number of tests run: 3
Suites: completed 1, aborted 0
Tests: succeeded 3, failed 0, canceled 0, ignored 0, pending 0
All tests passed.
```

```
Console   Problems   ScalaTest 23
Tests:     3/3            Succeeded:  3        Failed:    0
Ignored:   0             Pending:    0        Canceled:  0
Suites:    1             Aborted:    0

> TransformationTestWithSparkTestingBase (2.179 s)                    ≡ Stack Trace
```

Figure 13: A successful execution and passed test using Spark testing base

Configuring Hadoop runtime on Windows

We have already seen how to test your Spark applications written in Scala on Eclipse or IntelliJ, but there is another potential issue that should not be overlooked. Although Spark works on Windows, Spark is designed to be run on the UNIX-like operating system. Therefore, if you are working in a Windows environment, then extra care needs to be taken.

While using Eclipse or IntelliJ to develop your Spark applications for solving data analytics, machine learning, data science, or deep learning applications on Windows, you might face an I/O exception error and your application might not compile successfully or may be interrupted. Actually, the thing is that Spark expects that there is a runtime environment for Hadoop on Windows too. For example, if you run a Spark application, say KMeansDemo.scala, on Eclipse for the first time, you will experience an I/O exception saying the following:

> **17/02/26 13:22:00 ERROR Shell: Failed to locate the winutils binary in the hadoop binary path java.io.IOException: Could not locate executable null\bin\winutils.exe in the Hadoop binaries.**

The reason is that by default, Hadoop is developed for the Linux environment, and if you are developing your Spark applications on Windows platform, a bridge is required that will provide an environment for the Hadoop runtime for Spark to be properly executed. The details of the I/O exception can be seen in the following figure:

```
17/02/26 13:22:00 ERROR Shell: Failed to locate the winutils binary in the hadoop binary path
java.io.IOException: Could not locate executable null\bin\winutils.exe in the Hadoop binaries.
        at org.apache.hadoop.util.Shell.getQualifiedBinPath(Shell.java:278)
        at org.apache.hadoop.util.Shell.getWinUtilsPath(Shell.java:300)
        at org.apache.hadoop.util.Shell.<clinit>(Shell.java:293)
        at org.apache.hadoop.util.StringUtils.<clinit>(StringUtils.java:76)
        at org.apache.hadoop.mapred.FileInputFormat.setInputPaths(FileInputFormat.java:362)
        at org.apache.spark.SparkContext$$anonfun$hadoopFile$1$$anonfun$30.apply(SparkContext.scala:1014)
        at org.apache.spark.SparkContext$$anonfun$hadoopFile$1$$anonfun$30.apply(SparkContext.scala:1014)
        at org.apache.spark.rdd.HadoopRDD$$anonfun$getJobConf$6.apply(HadoopRDD.scala:179)
        at org.apache.spark.rdd.HadoopRDD$$anonfun$getJobConf$6.apply(HadoopRDD.scala:179)
        at scala.Option.foreach(Option.scala:257)
        at org.apache.spark.rdd.HadoopRDD.getJobConf(HadoopRDD.scala:179)
        at org.apache.spark.rdd.HadoopRDD.getPartitions(HadoopRDD.scala:198)
        at org.apache.spark.rdd.RDD$$anonfun$partitions$2.apply(RDD.scala:252)
        at org.apache.spark.rdd.RDD$$anonfun$partitions$2.apply(RDD.scala:250)
        at scala.Option.getOrElse(Option.scala:121)
        at org.apache.spark.rdd.RDD.partitions(RDD.scala:250)
        at org.apache.spark.rdd.MapPartitionsRDD.getPartitions(MapPartitionsRDD.scala:35)
        at org.apache.spark.rdd.RDD$$anonfun$partitions$2.apply(RDD.scala:252)
        at org.apache.spark.rdd.RDD$$anonfun$partitions$2.apply(RDD.scala:250)
        at scala.Option.getOrElse(Option.scala:121)
        at org.apache.spark.rdd.RDD.partitions(RDD.scala:250)
        at org.apache.spark.rdd.MapPartitionsRDD.getPartitions(MapPartitionsRDD.scala:35)
        at org.apache.spark.rdd.RDD$$anonfun$partitions$2.apply(RDD.scala:252)
        at org.apache.spark.rdd.RDD$$anonfun$partitions$2.apply(RDD.scala:250)
        at scala.Option.getOrElse(Option.scala:121)
        at org.apache.spark.rdd.RDD.partitions(RDD.scala:250)
        at org.apache.spark.rdd.MapPartitionsRDD.getPartitions(MapPartitionsRDD.scala:35)
        at org.apache.spark.rdd.RDD$$anonfun$partitions$2.apply(RDD.scala:252)
        at org.apache.spark.rdd.RDD$$anonfun$partitions$2.apply(RDD.scala:250)
        at scala.Option.getOrElse(Option.scala:121)
        at org.apache.spark.rdd.RDD.partitions(RDD.scala:250)
        at org.apache.spark.rdd.MapPartitionsRDD.getPartitions(MapPartitionsRDD.scala:35)
        at org.apache.spark.rdd.RDD$$anonfun$partitions$2.apply(RDD.scala:252)
        at org.apache.spark.rdd.RDD$$anonfun$partitions$2.apply(RDD.scala:250)
        at scala.Option.getOrElse(Option.scala:121)
```

Figure 14: I/O exception occurred due to the failure of not to locate the winutils binary in the Hadoop binary path

Now, how to get rid of this problem then? The solution is straightforward. As the error message says, we need to have an executable, namely `winutils.exe`. Now download the `winutils.exe` file from `https://github.com/steveloughran/winutils/tree/master/hadoop-2.7.1/bin`, paste it in the Spark distribution directory, and configure Eclipse. More specifically, suppose your Spark distribution containing Hadoop is located at `C:/Users/spark-2.1.0-bin-hadoop2.7`. Inside the Spark distribution, there is a directory named bin. Now, paste the executable there (that is, `path = C:/Users/spark-2.1.0-binhadoop2.7/bin/`).

The second phase of the solution is going to Eclipse and then selecting the main class (that is, KMeansDemo.scala in this case), and then going to the **Run** menu. From the **Run** menu, go to the **Run Configurations** option and from there select the **Environment** tab, as shown in the following figure:

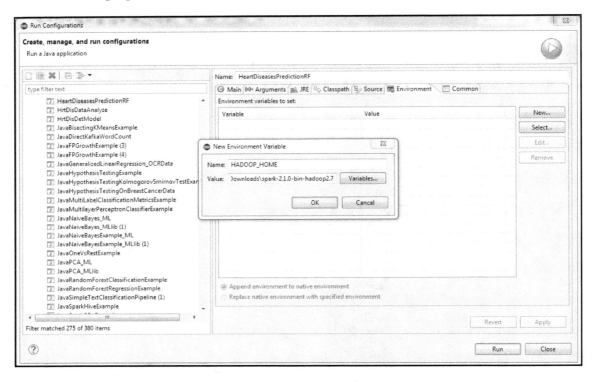

Figure 15: Solving the I/O exception occurred due to the absence of winutils binary in the Hadoop binary path

If you select the tab, you a will have the option to create a new environmental variable for Eclipse using the JVM. Now create a new environmental variable named HADOOP_HOME and put the value as C:/Users/spark-2.1.0-bin-hadoop2.7/. Now press on **Apply** button and rerun your application, and your problem should be resolved.

It is to be noted that while working with Spark on Windows in a PySpark, the winutils.exe file is required too.

Please make a note that the preceding solution is also applicable in debugging your applications. Sometimes, even if the preceding error occurs, your Spark application will run properly. However, if the size of the dataset is large, it is most likely that the preceding error will occur.

Debugging Spark applications

In this section, we will see how to debug Spark applications that are running locally (on Eclipse or IntelliJ), standalone or cluster mode in YARN or Mesos. However, before diving deeper, it is necessary to know about logging in the Spark application.

Logging with log4j with Spark recap

As stated earlier, Spark uses log4j for its own logging. If you configured Spark properly, Spark gets logged all the operation to the shell console. A sample snapshot of the file can be seen from the following figure:

```
# Set everything to be logged to the console
log4j.rootCategory=INFO, console
log4j.appender.console=org.apache.log4j.ConsoleAppender
log4j.appender.console.target=System.err
log4j.appender.console.layout=org.apache.log4j.PatternLayout
log4j.appender.console.layout.ConversionPattern=%d{yy/MM/dd HH:mm:ss} %p %c{1}: %m%n

# Set the default spark-shell log level to WARN. When running the spark-shell, the
# log level for this class is used to overwrite the root logger's log level, so that
# the user can have different defaults for the shell and regular Spark apps.
log4j.logger.org.apache.spark.repl.Main=WARN

# Settings to quiet third party logs that are too verbose
log4j.logger.org.spark_project.jetty=WARN
log4j.logger.org.spark_project.jetty.util.component.AbstractLifeCycle=ERROR
log4j.logger.org.apache.spark.repl.SparkIMain$exprTyper=INFO
log4j.logger.org.apache.spark.repl.SparkILoop$SparkILoopInterpreter=INFO
log4j.logger.org.apache.parquet=ERROR
log4j.logger.parquet=ERROR

# SPARK-9183: Settings to avoid annoying messages when looking up nonexistent UDFs in SparkSQL with Hive support
log4j.logger.org.apache.hadoop.hive.metastore.RetryingHMSHandler=FATAL
log4j.logger.org.apache.hadoop.hive.ql.exec.FunctionRegistry=ERROR
```

Figure 16: A snap of the log4j.properties file

Set the default spark-shell log level to WARN. When running the spark-shell, the log level for this class is used to overwrite the root logger's log level so that the user can have different defaults for the shell and regular Spark apps. We also need to append JVM arguments when launching a job executed by an executor and managed by the driver. For this, you should edit the `conf/spark-defaults.conf`. In short, the following options can be added:

```
spark.executor.extraJavaOptions=-
Dlog4j.configuration=file:/usr/local/spark-2.1.1/conf/log4j.properties
spark.driver.extraJavaOptions=-
Dlog4j.configuration=file:/usr/local/spark-2.1.1/conf/log4j.properties
```

To make the discussion clearer, we need to hide all the logs generated by Spark. We then can redirect them to be logged in the file system. On the other hand, we want our own logs to be logged in the shell and a separate file so that they don't get mixed up with the ones from Spark. From here, we will point Spark to the files where our own logs are, which in this particular case is `/var/log/sparkU.log`. This `log4j.properties` file is then picked up by Spark when the application starts, so we don't have to do anything aside of placing it in the mentioned location:

```scala
package com.chapter14.Serilazition
import org.apache.log4j.LogManager
import org.apache.log4j.Level
import org.apache.spark.sql.SparkSession
object myCustomLog {
  def main(args: Array[String]): Unit = {
    val log = LogManager.getRootLogger
    //Everything is printed as INFO once the log level is set to INFO
untill you set the level to new level for example WARN.
    log.setLevel(Level.INFO)
    log.info("Let's get started!")
    // Setting logger level as WARN: after that nothing prints other than
WARN
    log.setLevel(Level.WARN)
    // Creating Spark Session
    val spark = SparkSession
      .builder
      .master("local[*]")
      .config("spark.sql.warehouse.dir", "E:/Exp/")
      .appName("Logging")
      .getOrCreate()
    // These will note be printed!
    log.info("Get prepared!")
    log.trace("Show if there is any ERROR!")
    //Started the computation and printing the logging information
    log.warn("Started")
```

```
spark.sparkContext.parallelize(1 to 20).foreach(println)
log.warn("Finished")
  }
}
```

In the preceding code, everything is printed as INFO once the log level is set to INFO until you set the level to a new level for example WARN. However, after that no info or trace and so on, that will not be printed. In addition to that, there are several valid logging levels supported by log4j with Spark. The successful execution of the preceding code should generate the following output:

```
17/05/13 16:39:14 INFO root: Let's get started!
17/05/13 16:39:15 WARN root: Started
4
1
2
5
3
17/05/13 16:39:16 WARN root: Finished
```

You can also set up the default logging for Spark shell in conf/log4j.properties. Spark provides a template of the log4j as a property file, and we can extend and modify that file for logging in Spark. Move to the SPARK_HOME/conf directory and you should see the log4j.properties.template file. You should use the following conf/log4j.properties.template after renaming it to log4j.properties. While developing your Spark application, you can put the log4j.properties file under your project directory while working on an IDE-based environment such as Eclipse. However, to disable logging completely, just set the log4j.logger.org flags as OFF as follows:

```
log4j.logger.org=OFF
```

So far, everything is very easy. However, there is a problem we haven't noticed yet in the preceding code segment. One drawback of the org.apache.log4j.Logger class is that it is not serializable, which implies that we cannot use it inside a closure while doing operations on some parts of the Spark API. For example, suppose we do the following in our Spark code:

```
object myCustomLogger {
  def main(args: Array[String]):Unit= {
    // Setting logger level as WARN
    val log = LogManager.getRootLogger
    log.setLevel(Level.WARN)
    // Creating Spark Context
    val conf = new SparkConf().setAppName("My App").setMaster("local[*]")
    val sc = new SparkContext(conf)
```

```
    //Started the computation and printing the logging information
    //log.warn("Started")
    val i = 0
    val data = sc.parallelize(i to 100000)
    data.map{number =>
      log.info("My number"+ i)
      number.toString
    }
    //log.warn("Finished")
  }
}
```

You should experience an exception that says `Task` not serializable as follows:

```
org.apache.spark.SparkException: Job aborted due to stage failure: Task not
serializable: java.io.NotSerializableException: ...
Exception in thread "main" org.apache.spark.SparkException: Task not
serializable
Caused by: java.io.NotSerializableException:
org.apache.log4j.spi.RootLogger
Serialization stack: object not serializable
```

At first, we can try to solve this problem in a naive way. What you can do is just make the Scala class (that does the actual operation) `Serializable` using `extends Serializable`. For example, the code looks as follows:

```
class MyMapper(n: Int) extends Serializable {
  @transient lazy val log =
org.apache.log4j.LogManager.getLogger("myLogger")
  def logMapper(rdd: RDD[Int]): RDD[String] =
    rdd.map { i =>
      log.warn("mapping: " + i)
      (i + n).toString
    }
  }
```

This section is intended for carrying out a discussion on logging. However, we take the opportunity to make it more versatile for general purpose Spark programming and issues. In order to overcome the task not serializable error in a more efficient way, the compiler will try to send the whole object (not only the lambda) by making it serializable and forces SPark to accept that. However, it increases shuffling significantly, especially for big objects! The other ways are making the whole class Serializable or by declaring the instance only within the lambda function passed in the map operation. Sometimes, keeping the not Serializable objects across the nodes can work. Lastly, use the forEachPartition() or mapPartitions() instead of just map() and create the not Serializable objects. In summary, these are the ways to solve the problem around:

- Serializable the class
- Declare the instance only within the lambda function passed in the map
- Make the NotSerializable object as a static and create it once per machine
- Call the forEachPartition () or mapPartitions() instead of map() and create the NotSerializable object

In the preceding code, we have used the annotation @transient lazy, which marks the Logger class to be nonpersistent. On the other hand, an object containing the method apply (i.e. MyMapperObject) that instantiate the object of the MyMapper class is as follows:

```
//Companion object
object MyMapper {
  def apply(n: Int): MyMapper = new MyMapper(n)
}
```

Finally, the object containing the main() method is as follows:

```
//Main object
object myCustomLogwithClosureSerializable {
  def main(args: Array[String]) {
    val log = LogManager.getRootLogger
    log.setLevel(Level.WARN)
    val spark = SparkSession
      .builder
      .master("local[*]")
      .config("spark.sql.warehouse.dir", "E:/Exp/")
      .appName("Testing")
```

```
        .getOrCreate()
    log.warn("Started")
    val data = spark.sparkContext.parallelize(1 to 100000)
    val mapper = MyMapper(1)
    val other = mapper.logMapper(data)
    other.collect()
    log.warn("Finished")
}
```

Now, let's see another example that provides better insight to keep fighting the issue we are talking about. Suppose we have the following class that computes the multiplication of two integers:

```
class MultiplicaitonOfTwoNumber {
  def multiply(a: Int, b: Int): Int = {
    val product = a * b
    product
  }
}
```

Now, essentially, if you try to use this class for computing the multiplication in the lambda closure using map(), you will get the Task Not Serializable error that we described earlier. Now we simply can use foreachPartition() and the lambda inside as follows:

```
val myRDD = spark.sparkContext.parallelize(0 to 1000)
    myRDD.foreachPartition(s => {
      val notSerializable = new MultiplicaitonOfTwoNumber
      println(notSerializable.multiply(s.next(), s.next()))
    })
```

Now, if you compile it, it should return the desired result. For your ease, the complete code with the main() method is as follows:

```
package com.chapter16.SparkTesting
import org.apache.spark.sql.SparkSession
class MultiplicaitonOfTwoNumber {
  def multiply(a: Int, b: Int): Int = {
    val product = a * b
    product
  }
}
```

```
object MakingTaskSerilazible {
  def main(args: Array[String]): Unit = {
    val spark = SparkSession
      .builder
      .master("local[*]")
      .config("spark.sql.warehouse.dir", "E:/Exp/")
      .appName("MakingTaskSerilazible")
      .getOrCreate()
 val myRDD = spark.sparkContext.parallelize(0 to 1000)
    myRDD.foreachPartition(s => {
      val notSerializable = new MultiplicaitonOfTwoNumber
      println(notSerializable.multiply(s.next(), s.next()))
    })
  }
}
```

The output is as follows:

```
0
5700
1406
156
4032
7832
2550
650
```

Debugging the Spark application

In this section, we will discuss how to debug Spark applications running on locally on Eclipse or IntelliJ, as standalone or cluster mode in YARN or Mesos. Before getting started, you can also read the debugging documentation at https://hortonworks.com/hadoop-tutorial/setting-spark-development-environment-scala/.

Debugging Spark application on Eclipse as Scala debug

To make this happen, just configure your Eclipse to debug your Spark applications as a regular Scala code debug. To configure select **Run** | **Debug Configuration** | **Scala Application** as shown in the following figure:

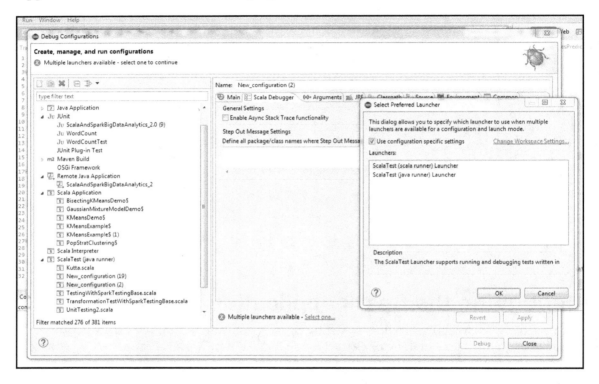

Figure 17: Configuring Eclipse to debug Spark applications as a regular Scala code debug

Suppose we want to debug our `KMeansDemo.scala` and ask Eclipse (you can have similar options on InteliJ IDE) to start the execution at line 56 and set the breakpoint in line 95. To do so, run your Scala code as debugging and you should observe the following scenario on Eclipse:

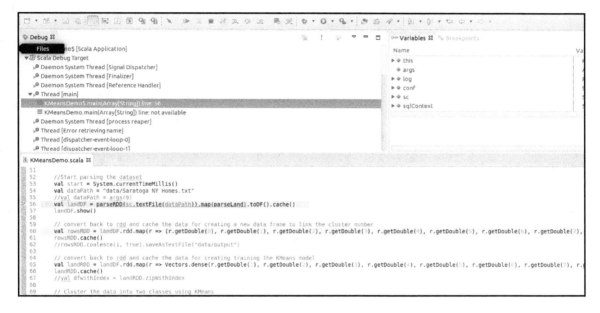

Figure 18: Debugging Spark applications on Eclipse

Then, Eclipse will pause on the line you ask it to stop the execution in line 95, as shown in the following screenshot:

```
▼ ⊞ <terminated>KMeansDemo$ [Scala Application]
   ⊞ <terminated, exit value: 0>/usr/lib/jvm/java-8-oracle/bin/java (Feb 19, 2017, 12:34:48 PM)
```

```
 KMeansDemo.scala ⊠
 81    val end = System.currentTimeMillis()
 82    println("Model building and prediction time: "+ {end - start} + "ms")
 83
 84    // Compute and print the prediction accuracy for each house
 85    model.predict(landRDD).foreach(println)
 86    landDF.show()
 87
 88    // Get the prediction from the model with the ID so we can link them back to other information
 89    val predictions = rowsRDD.map{r => (r._1, model.predict(Vectors.dense(r._2, r._3, r._4, r._5, r._6, r._7, r._
 90    val conMat = predictions.collect().toMap.values
 91    println(conMat)
 92
 93
 94    // convert the rdd to a dataframe
 95    val predCluster = predictions.toDF("Price", "CLUSTER")
 96    predCluster.show()
 97
 98
 99    // Join the prediction DataFrame with the old dataframe to know the individual cluster number for each house
 100   val newDF = landDF.join(predCluster, "Price")
```

```
 Console ⊠    Tasks   Scala Expression Evaluator
<terminated> KMeansDemo$ [Scala Application] /usr/lib/jvm/java-8-oracle/bin/java (Feb 19, 2017, 12:34:48 PM)
|253750.0|      3|
| 60000.0|      2|
| 87500.0|      2|
+--------+-------+
only showing top 20 rows

MapLike(2, 2, 2, 1, 0, 2, 0, 0, 0, 0, 2, 1, 3, 3, 2, 3, 0, 2, 2, 0, 3, 2, 2, 2, 1, 0, 0, 0, 3, 2, 3, 3, 3, 2, 0, 1, 3,
17/02/19 12:35:09 WARN root: Finshed
```

Figure 19: Debugging Spark applications on Eclipse (breakpoint)

In summary, to simplify the preceding example, if there is any error between line 56 and line 95, Eclipse will show where the error actually occurs. Otherwise, it will follow the normal workflow if not interrupted.

Debugging Spark jobs running as local and standalone mode

While debugging your Spark application locally or as standalone mode, you should know that debugging the driver program and debugging one of the executors is different since using these two types of nodes requires different submission parameters passed to spark-submit. Throughout this section, I'll use port 4000 as the address. For example, if you want to debug the driver program, you can add the following to your spark-submit command:

```
--driver-java-options -
agentlib:jdwp=transport=dt_socket,server=y,suspend=y,address=4000
```

After that, you should set your remote debugger to connect to the node where you have submitted the driver program. For the preceding case, port number 4000 was specified. However, if something (that is, other Spark jobs, other applications or services, and so on) is already running on that port, you might also need to customize that port, that is, change the port number.

On the other hand, connecting to an executor is similar to the preceding option, except for the address option. More specifically, you will have to replace the address with your local machine's address (IP address or hostname with the port number). However, it is always a good practice and recommended to test that you can access your local machine from the Spark cluster where the actual computing occurs. For example, you can use the following options to make the debugging environment enable to your spark-submit command:

```
--num-executors 1\
--executor-cores 1 \
--conf "spark.executor.extraJavaOptions=-
agentlib:jdwp=transport=dt_socket,server=n,address=localhost:4000,suspend=n
"
```

In summary, use the following command to submit your Spark jobs (the KMeansDemo application in this case):

```
$ SPARK_HOME/bin/spark-submit \
--class "com.chapter13.Clustering.KMeansDemo" \
--master spark://ubuntu:7077 \
--num-executors 1\
--executor-cores 1 \
--conf "spark.executor.extraJavaOptions=-
agentlib:jdwp=transport=dt_socket,server=n,address=
host_name_to_your_computer.org:5005,suspend=n" \
--driver-java-options -
```

```
agentlib:jdwp=transport=dt_socket,server=y,suspend=y,address=4000 \
 KMeans-0.0.1-SNAPSHOT-jar-with-dependencies.jar \
Saratoga_NY_Homes.txt
```

Now, start your local debugger in a listening mode and start your Spark program. Finally, wait for the executor to attach to your debugger. You will observe the following message on your terminal:

```
Listening for transport dt_socket at address: 4000
```

It is important to know that you need to set the number of executors to 1 only. Setting multiple executors will all try to connect to your debugger and will eventually create some weird problems. It is to be noted that sometimes setting the SPARK_JAVA_OPTS helps in debugging your Spark applications that are running locally or as standalone mode. The command is as follows:

```
$ export SPARK_JAVA_OPTS=-
agentlib:jdwp=transport=dt_socket,server=y,address=4000,suspend=y,onuncaugh
t=n
```

However, since Spark release 1.0.0, SPARK_JAVA_OPTS has been deprecated and replaced by spark-defaults.conf and command line arguments to Spark-submit or Spark-shell. It is also to be noted that setting spark.driver.extraJavaOptions and spark.executor.extraJavaOptions, which we saw in the previous section, in spark-defaults.conf is not a replacement for SPARK_JAVA_OPTS. But to be frank, SPARK_JAVA_OPTS, it still works pretty well and you can try as well.

Debugging Spark applications on YARN or Mesos cluster

When you run a Spark application on YARN, there is an option that you can enable by modifying yarn-env.sh:

```
YARN_OPTS="-
agentlib:jdwp=transport=dt_socket,server=y,suspend=n,address=4000
$YARN_OPTS"
```

Now, the remote debugging will be available through port 4000 on your Eclipse or IntelliJ IDE. The second option is by setting the SPARK_SUBMIT_OPTS. You can use either Eclipse or IntelliJ to develop your Spark applications that can be submitted to be executed on remote multinode YARN clusters. What I do is that I create a Maven project on Eclipse or IntelliJ and package my Java or Scala application as a jar file and then submit it as a Spark job. However, in order to attach your IDE such as Eclipse or IntelliJ debugger to your Spark application, you can define all the submission parameters using the SPARK_SUBMIT_OPTS environment variable as follows:

```
$ export SPARK_SUBMIT_OPTS=-
agentlib:jdwp=transport=dt_socket,server=y,suspend=y,address=4000
```

Then submit your Spark job as follows (please change the values accordingly based on your requirements and setup):

```
$ SPARK_HOME/bin/spark-submit \
--class "com.chapter13.Clustering.KMeansDemo" \
--master yarn \
--deploy-mode cluster \
--driver-memory 16g \
--executor-memory 4g \
--executor-cores 4 \
--queue the_queue \
--num-executors 1\
--executor-cores 1 \
--conf "spark.executor.extraJavaOptions=-
agentlib:jdwp=transport=dt_socket,server=n,address=
host_name_to_your_computer.org:4000,suspend=n" \
--driver-java-options -
agentlib:jdwp=transport=dt_socket,server=y,suspend=y,address=4000 \
 KMeans-0.0.1-SNAPSHOT-jar-with-dependencies.jar \
Saratoga_NY_Homes.txt
```

After running the preceding command, it will wait until you connect your debugger, as shown in the following: `Listening for transport dt_socket at address: 4000`. Now you can configure your Java remote application (Scala application will work too) on the IntelliJ debugger, as shown in the following screenshot:

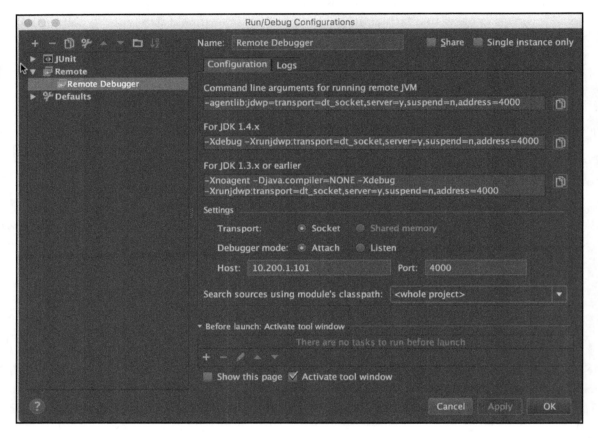

Figure 20: Configuring remote debugger on IntelliJ

For the preceding case, 10.200.1.101 is the IP address of the remote computing node where your Spark job is basically running. Finally, you will have to start the debugger by clicking on Debug under IntelliJ's Run menu. Then, if the debugger connects to your remote Spark app, you will see the logging info in the application console on IntelliJ. Now if you can set the breakpoints and the rests of them are normal debugging.

The following figure shows an example how will you see on the IntelliJ when pausing a Spark job with a breakpoint:

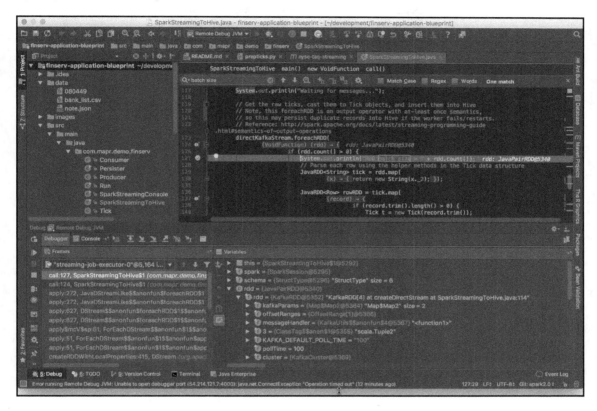

Figure 21: An example how will you see on the IntelliJ when pausing a Spark job with a breakpoint

Although it works well, sometimes I experienced that using `SPARK_JAVA_OPTS` won't help you much in the debug process on Eclipse or even IntelliJ. Instead, use and export `SPARK_WORKER_OPTS` and `SPARK_MASTER_OPTS` while running your Spark jobs on a real cluster (YARN, Mesos, or AWS) as follows:

```
$ export SPARK_WORKER_OPTS="-Xdebug -
Xrunjdwp:server=y,transport=dt_socket,address=4000,suspend=n"
$ export SPARK_MASTER_OPTS="-Xdebug -
Xrunjdwp:server=y,transport=dt_socket,address=4000,suspend=n"
```

Then start your Master node as follows:

```
$ SPARKH_HOME/sbin/start-master.sh
```

Now open an SSH connection to your remote machine where the Spark job is actually running and map your localhost at 4000 (aka `localhost:4000`) to `host_name_to_your_computer.org:5000`, assuming the cluster is at `host_name_to_your_computer.org:5000` and listening on port 5000. Now that your Eclipse will consider that you're just debugging your Spark application as a local Spark application or process. However, to make this happen, you will have to configure the remote debugger on Eclipse, as shown in the following figure:

Figure 22: Connecting remote host on Eclipse for debugging Spark application

That's it! Now you can debug on your live cluster as if it were your desktop. The preceding examples are for running with the Spark Master set as YARN-client. However, it should also work when running on a Mesos cluster. If you're running using YARN-cluster mode, you may have to set the driver to attach to your debugger rather than attaching your debugger to the driver since you won't necessarily know in advance what mode the driver will be executing on.

Debugging Spark application using SBT

The preceding setting works mostly on Eclipse or IntelliJ using the Maven project. Suppose that you already have your application done and are working on your preferred IDEs such as IntelliJ or Eclipse as follows:

```
object DebugTestSBT {
  def main(args: Array[String]): Unit = {
    val spark = SparkSession
      .builder
      .master("local[*]")
      .config("spark.sql.warehouse.dir", "C:/Exp/")
      .appName("Logging")
      .getOrCreate()
    spark.sparkContext.setCheckpointDir("C:/Exp/")
    println("------------Attach debugger now!-------------")
    Thread.sleep(8000)
    // code goes here, with breakpoints set on the lines you want to pause
  }
}
```

Now, if you want to get this job to the local cluster (standalone), the very first step is packaging the application with all its dependencies into a fat JAR. For doing this, use the following command:

```
$ sbt assembly
```

This will generate the fat JAR. Now the task is to submit the Spark job to a local cluster. You need to have a spark-submit script somewhere on your system:

```
$ export SPARK_JAVA_OPTS=-
agentlib:jdwp=transport=dt_socket,server=y,suspend=n,address=5005
```

The preceding command exports a Java argument that will be used to start Spark with the debugger:

```
$ SPARK_HOME/bin/spark-submit --class Test --master local[*] --driver-
memory 4G --executor-memory 4G /path/project-assembly-0.0.1.jar
```

In the preceding command, `--class` needs to point to a fully qualified class path to your job. Upon successful execution of this command, your Spark job will be executed without breaking at the breakpoints. Now to get the debugging facility on your IDE, say IntelliJ, you need to configure to connect to the cluster. For more details on the official IDEA documentation, refer to http://stackoverflow.com/questions/21114066/attach-intellij-idea-debugger-to-a-running-java-process.

It is to be noted that if you just create a default remote run/debug configuration and leave the default port of 5005, it should work fine. Now, when you submit the job for the next time and see the message to attach the debugger, you have eight seconds to switch to IntelliJ IDEA and trigger this run configuration. The program will then continue to execute and pause at any breakpoint you defined. You can then step through it like any normal Scala/Java program. You can even step into Spark functions to see what it's doing under the hood.

Summary

In this chapter, you saw how difficult the testing and debugging your Spark applications are. These can even be more critical in a distributed environment. We also discussed some advanced ways to tackle them altogether. In summary, you learned the way of testing in a distributed environment. Then you learned a better way of testing your Spark application. Finally, we discussed some advanced ways of debugging Spark applications.

This is more or less the end of our little journey with advanced topics on Spark. Now, a general suggestion from our side to you as readers or if you are relatively newer to the data science, data analytics, machine learning, Scala, or Spark is that you should at first try to understand what types of analytics you want to perform. To be more specific, for example, if your problem is a machine learning problem, try to guess what type of learning algorithms should be the best fit, that is, classification, clustering, regression, recommendation, or frequent pattern mining. Then define and formulate the problem, and after that, you should generate or download the appropriate data based on the feature engineering concept of Spark that we have discussed earlier. On the other hand, if you think that you can solve your problem by using deep learning algorithms or APIs, you should use other third-party algorithms and integrate with Spark and work straight away.

Our final recommendation to the readers is to browse the Spark website (at `http://spark.apache.org/`) regularly to get the updates and also try to incorporate the regular Spark-provided APIs with other third-party applications or tools to get the best result of the collaboration.

10
Practical Machine Learning with Spark Using Scala

In this chapter, we will cover:

- Configuring IntelliJ to work with Spark and run Spark ML sample codes
- Running a sample ML code from Spark
- Identifying data sources for practical machine learning
- Running your first program using Apache Spark 2.0 with the IntelliJ IDE
- How to add graphics to your Spark program

Introduction

With the recent advancements in cluster computing coupled with the rise of big data, the field of machine learning has been pushed to the forefront of computing. The need for an interactive platform that enables data science at scale has long been a dream that is now a reality.

The following three areas together have enabled and accelerated interactive data science at scale:

- **Apache Spark**: A unified technology platform for data science that combines a fast compute engine and fault-tolerant data structures into a well-designed and integrated offering
- **Machine learning**: A field of artificial intelligence that enables machines to mimic some of the tasks originally reserved exclusively for the human brain
- **Scala**: A modern JVM-based language that builds on traditional languages, but unites functional and object-oriented concepts without the verboseness of other languages

First, we need to set up the development environment, which will consist of the following components:

- Spark
- IntelliJ community edition IDE
- Scala

The recipes in this chapter will give you detailed instructions for installing and configuring the IntelliJ IDE, Scala plugin, and Spark. After the development environment is set up, we'll proceed to run one of the Spark ML sample codes to test the setup.

Apache Spark

Apache Spark is emerging as the de facto platform and trade language for big data analytics and as a complement to the **Hadoop** paradigm. Spark enables a data scientist to work in the manner that is most conducive to their workflow right out of the box. Spark's approach is to process the workload in a completely distributed manner without the need for **MapReduce** (**MR**) or repeated writing of the intermediate results to a disk.

Spark provides an easy-to-use distributed framework in a unified technology stack, which has made it the platform of choice for data science projects, which more often than not require an iterative algorithm that eventually merges toward a solution. These algorithms, due to their inner workings, generate a large amount of intermediate results that need to go from one stage to the next during the intermediate steps. The need for an interactive tool with a robust native distributed **machine learning library** (**MLlib**) rules out a disk-based approach for most of the data science projects.

Spark has a different approach toward cluster computing. It solves the problem as a technology stack rather than as an ecosystem. A large number of centrally managed libraries combined with a lightning-fast compute engine that can support fault-tolerant data structures has poised Spark to take over Hadoop as the preferred big data platform for analytics.

Spark has a modular approach, as depicted in the following diagram:

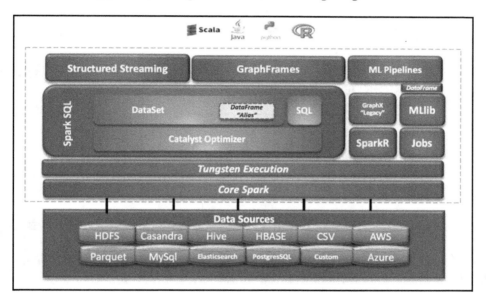

Machine learning

The aim of machine learning is to produce machines and devices that can mimic human intelligence and automate some of the tasks that have been traditionally reserved for a human brain. Machine learning algorithms are designed to go through very large data sets in a relatively short time and approximate answers that would have taken a human much longer to process.

The field of machine learning can be classified into many forms and at a high level, it can be classified as supervised and unsupervised learning. Supervised learning algorithms are a class of ML algorithms that use a training set (that is, labeled data) to compute a probabilistic distribution or graphical model that in turn allows them to classify the new data points without further human intervention. Unsupervised learning is a type of machine learning algorithm used to draw inferences from datasets consisting of input data without labeled responses.

Out of the box, Spark offers a rich set of ML algorithms that can be deployed on large datasets without any further coding. The following figure depicts Spark's MLlib algorithms as a mind map. Spark's MLlib is designed to take advantage of parallelism while having fault-tolerant distributed data structures. Spark refers to such data structures as **Resilient Distributed Datasets** or **RDDs**:

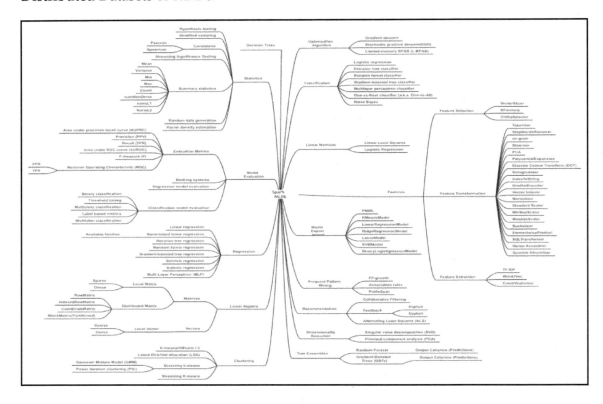

Scala

Scala is a modern programming language that is emerging as an alternative to traditional programming languages such as **Java** and **C++**. Scala is a JVM-based language that not only offers a concise syntax without the traditional boilerplate code, but also incorporates both object-oriented and functional programming into an extremely crisp and extraordinarily powerful type-safe language.

Scala takes a flexible and expressive approach, which makes it perfect for interacting with Spark's MLlib. The fact that Spark itself is written in Scala provides a strong evidence that the Scala language is a full-service programming language that can be used to create sophisticated system code with heavy performance needs.

Scala builds on Java's tradition by addressing some of its shortcomings, while avoiding an all-or-nothing approach. Scala code compiles into Java bytecode, which in turn makes it possible to coexist with rich Java libraries interchangeably. The ability to use Java libraries with Scala and vice versa provides continuity and a rich environment for software engineers to build modern and complex machine learning systems without being fully disconnected from the Java tradition and code base.

Scala fully supports a feature-rich functional programming paradigm with standard support for lambda, currying, type interface, immutability, lazy evaluation, and a pattern-matching paradigm reminiscent of Perl without the cryptic syntax. Scala is an excellent match for machine learning programming due to its support for algebra-friendly data types, anonymous functions, covariance, contra-variance, and higher-order functions.

Here's a hello world program in Scala:

```
object HelloWorld extends App {
   println("Hello World!")
 }
```

Compiling and running `HelloWorld` in Scala looks like this:

```
Siamaks-MBP:~ Siamak$ scalac HelloWorld.scala
Siamaks-MBP:~ Siamak$ scala HelloWorld
Hello World!
Siamaks-MBP:~ Siamak$ 
```

The Apache Spark Machine Learning Cookbook takes a practical approach by offering a multi-disciplinary view with the developer in mind. This book focuses on the interactions and cohesiveness of **machine learning, Apache Spark**, and **Scala**. We also take an extra step and teach you how to set up and run a comprehensive development environment familiar to a developer and provide code snippets that you have to run in an interactive shell without the modern facilities that an IDE provides:

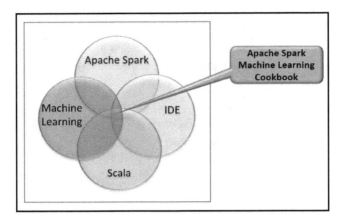

Software versions and libraries used in this book

The following table provides a detailed list of software versions and libraries used in this book. If you follow the installation instructions covered in this chapter, it will include most of the items listed here. Any other JAR or library files that may be required for specific recipes are covered via additional installation instructions in the respective recipes:

Core systems	Version
Spark	2.0.0
Java	1.8
IntelliJ IDEA	2016.2.4
Scala-sdk	2.11.8

Miscellaneous JARs that will be required are as follows:

Miscellaneous JARs	Version
bliki-core	3.0.19
breeze-viz	0.12
Cloud9	1.5.0
Hadoop-streaming	2.2.0
JCommon	1.0.23
JFreeChart	1.0.19
lucene-analyzers-common	6.0.0
Lucene-Core	6.0.0
scopt	3.3.0
spark-streaming-flume-assembly	2.0.0
spark-streaming-kafka-0-8-assembly	2.0.0

We have additionally tested all the recipes in this book on Spark 2.1.1 and found that the programs executed as expected. It is recommended for learning purposes you use the software versions and libraries listed in these tables.

To stay current with the rapidly changing Spark landscape and documentation, the API links to the Spark documentation mentioned throughout this book point to the latest version of Spark 2.x.x, but the API references in the recipes are explicitly for Spark 2.0.0.

All the Spark documentation links provided in this book will point to the latest documentation on Spark's website. If you prefer to look for documentation for a specific version of Spark (for example, Spark 2.0.0), look for relevant documentation on the Spark website using the following URL:

```
https://spark.apache.org/documentation.html
```

We've made the code as simple as possible for clarity purposes rather than demonstrating the advanced features of Scala.

Configuring IntelliJ to work with Spark and run Spark ML sample codes

We need to run some configurations to ensure that the project settings are correct before being able to run the samples that are provided by Spark or any of the programs listed this book.

Getting ready

We need to be particularly careful when configuring the project structure and global libraries. After we set everything up, we proceed to run the sample ML code provided by the Spark team to verify the setup. Sample code can be found under the Spark directory or can be obtained by downloading the Spark source code with samples.

How to do it...

The following are the steps for configuring IntelliJ to work with Spark MLlib and for running the sample ML code provided by Spark in the examples directory. The examples directory can be found in your home directory for Spark. Use the Scala samples to proceed:

1. Click on the **Project Structure...** option, as shown in the following screenshot, to configure project settings:

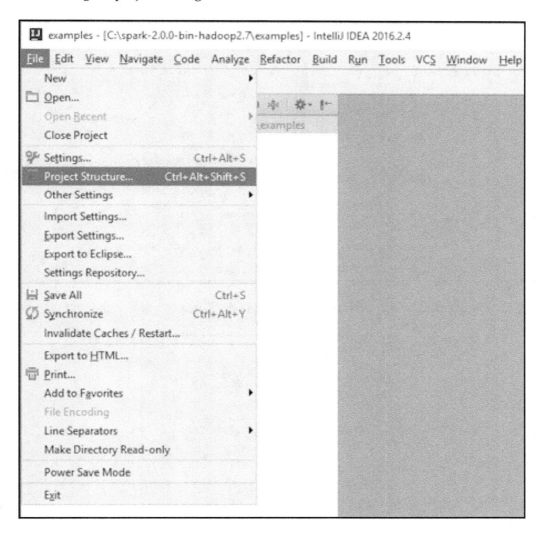

2. Verify the settings:

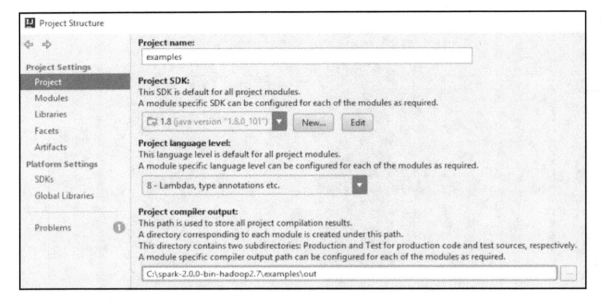

3. Configure **Global Libraries**. Select **Scala SDK** as your global library:

4. Select the JARs for the new Scala SDK and let the download complete:

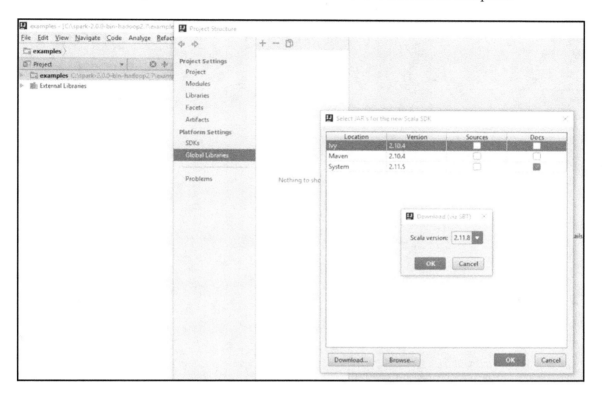

5. Select the project name:

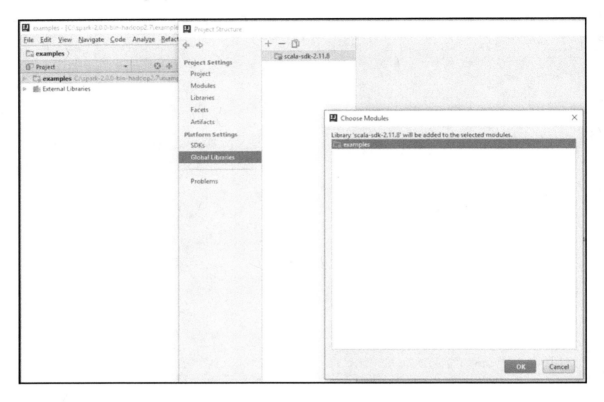

6. Verify the settings and additional libraries:

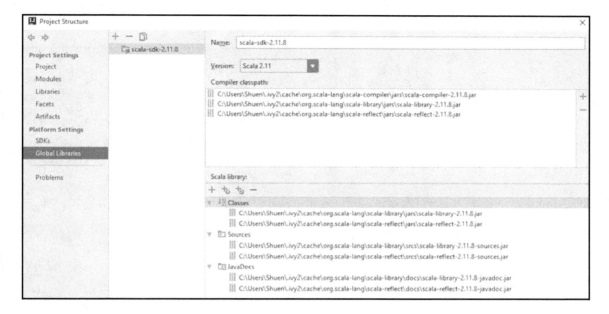

7. Add dependency JARs. Select modules under the **Project Settings** in the left-hand pane and click on dependencies to choose the required JARs, as shown in the following screenshot:

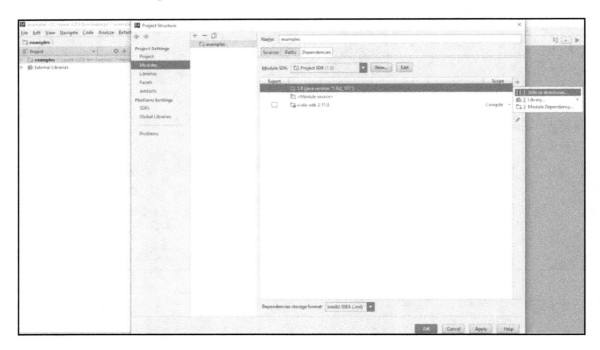

8. Select the JAR files provided by Spark. Choose Spark's default installation directory and then select the `lib` directory:

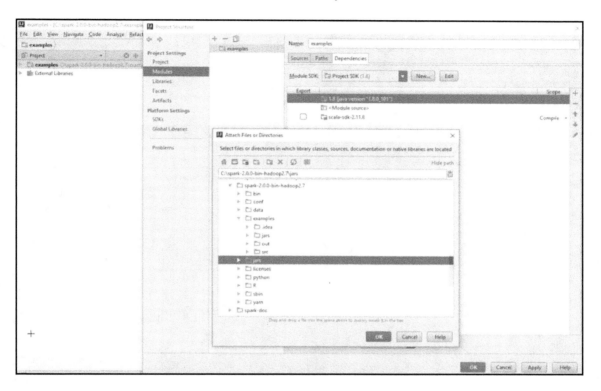

9. We then select the JAR files for examples that are provided for Spark out of the box.

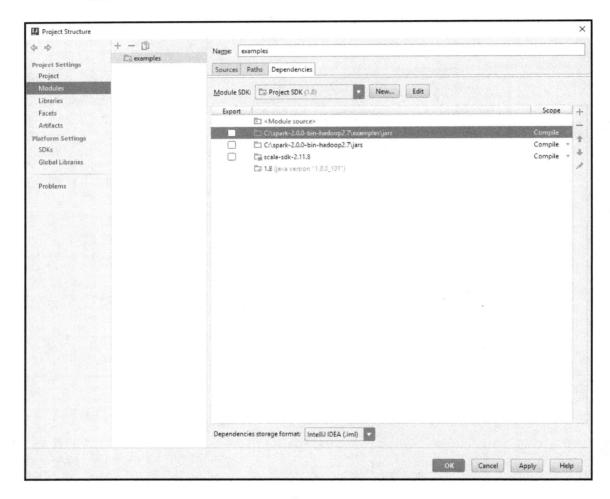

10. Add required JARs by verifying that you selected and imported all the JARs listed under `External Libraries` in the left-hand pane:

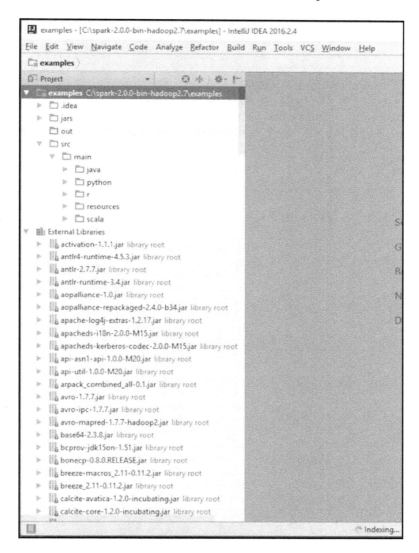

11. Spark 2.0 uses Scala 2.11. Two new streaming JARs, Flume and Kafka, are needed to run the examples, and can be downloaded from the following URLs:

- `https://repo1.maven.org/maven2/org/apache/spark/spark-streaming-flume-assembly_2.11/2.0.0/spark-streaming-flume-assembly_2.11-2.0.0.jar`

- `https://repo1.maven.org/maven2/org/apache/spark/spark-streaming-kafka-0-8-assembly_2.11/2.0.0/spark-streaming-kafka-0-8-assembly_2.11-2.0.0.jar`

The next step is to download and install the Flume and Kafka JARs. For the purposes of this book, we have used the Maven repo:

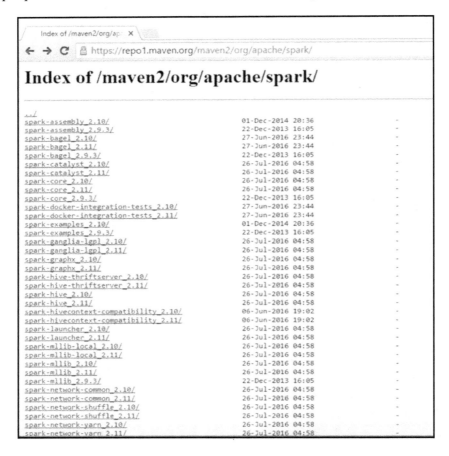

12. Download and install the Kafka assembly:

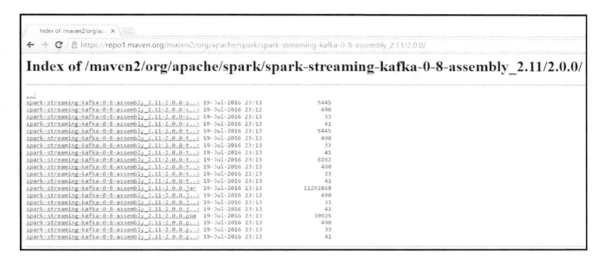

13. Download and install the Flume assembly:

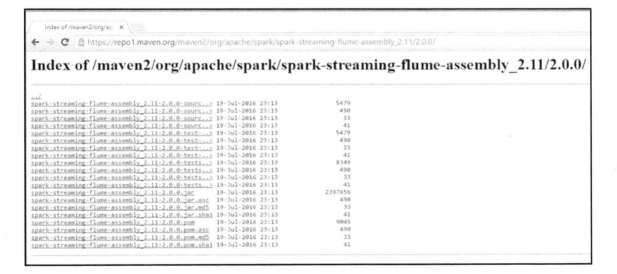

14. After the download is complete, move the downloaded JAR files to the `lib` directory of Spark. We used the `C` drive when we installed Spark:

15. Open your IDE and verify that all the JARs under the `External Libraries` folder on the left, as shown in the following screenshot, are present in your setup:

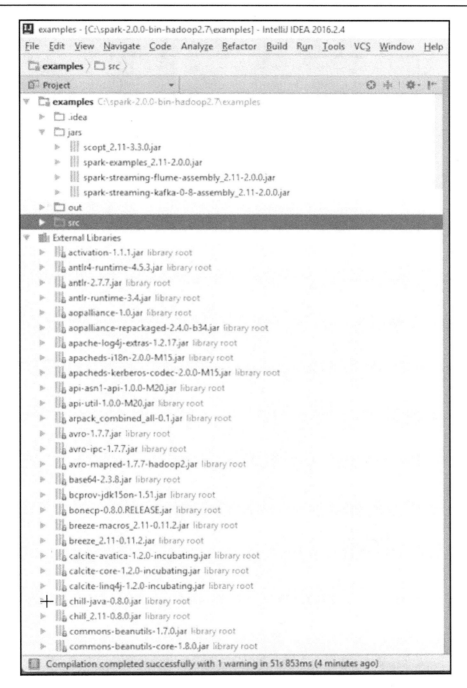

16. Build the example projects in Spark to verify the setup:

17. Verify that the build was successful:

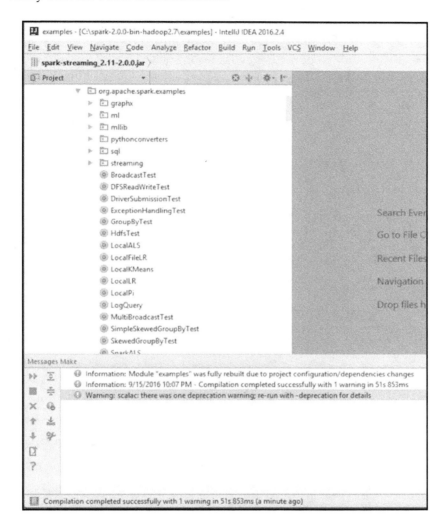

There's more...

Prior to Spark 2.0, we needed another library from Google called **Guava** for facilitating I/O and for providing a set of rich methods of defining tables and then letting Spark broadcast them across the cluster. Due to dependency issues that were hard to work around, Spark 2.0 no longer uses the Guava library. Make sure you use the Guava library if you are using Spark versions prior to 2.0 (required in version 1.5.2). The Guava library can be accessed at the following URL:

```
https://github.com/google/guava/wiki
```

You may want to use Guava version 15.0, which can be found here:

```
https://mvnrepository.com/artifact/com.google.guava/guava/15.0
```

If you are using installation instructions from previous blogs, make sure to exclude the Guava library from the installation set.

See also

If there are other third-party libraries or JARs required for the completion of the Spark installation, you can find those in the following Maven repository:

```
https://repo1.maven.org/maven2/org/apache/spark/
```

Running a sample ML code from Spark

We can verify the setup by simply downloading the sample code from the Spark source tree and importing it into IntelliJ to make sure it runs.

Getting ready

We will first run the logistic regression code from the samples to verify installation. In the next section, we proceed to write our own version of the same program and examine the output in order to understand how it works.

How to do it...

1. Go to the source directory and pick one of the ML sample code files to run. We've selected the logistic regression example.

If you cannot find the source code in your directory, you can always download the Spark source, unzip, and then extract the examples directory accordingly.

2. After selecting the example, select **Edit Configurations...**, as shown in the following screenshot:

3. In the **Configurations** tab, define the following options:
   - **VM options**: The choice shown allows you to run a standalone Spark cluster
   - **Program arguments**: What we are supposed to pass into the program

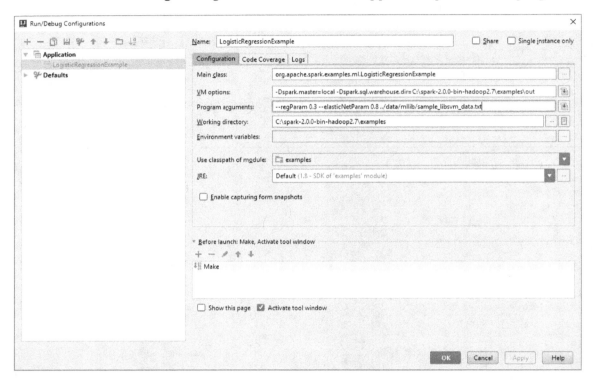

4. Run the logistic regression by going to **Run 'LogisticRegressionExample'**, as shown in the following screenshot:

5. Verify the exit code and make sure it is as shown in the following screenshot:

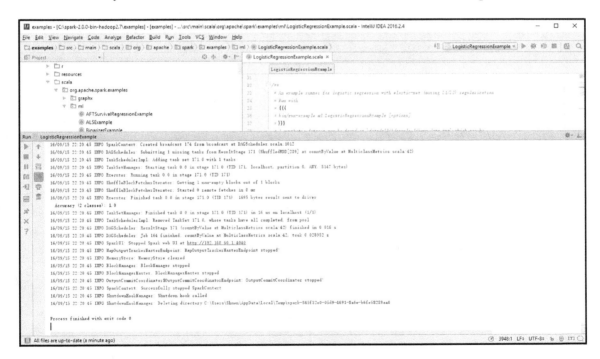

Identifying data sources for practical machine learning

Getting data for machine learning projects was a challenge in the past. However, now there is a rich set of public data sources specifically suitable for machine learning.

Getting ready

In addition to the university and government sources, there are many other open sources of data that can be used to learn and code your own examples and projects. We will list the data sources and show you how to best obtain and download data for each chapter.

How to do it...

The following is a list of open source data worth exploring if you would like to develop applications in this field:

- *UCI machine learning repository*: This is an extensive library with search functionality. At the time of writing, there were more than 350 datasets. You can click on the `https://archive.ics.uci.edu/ml/index.html` link to see all the datasets or look for a specific set using a simple search (*Ctrl + F*).
- *Kaggle datasets*: You need to create an account, but you can download any sets for learning as well as for competing in machine learning competitions. The `https://www.kaggle.com/competitions` link provides details for exploring and learning more about Kaggle, and the inner workings of machine learning competitions.
- *MLdata.org*: A public site open to all with a repository of datasets for machine learning enthusiasts.
- *Google Trends*: You can find statistics on search volume (as a proportion of total search) for any given term since 2004 on `http://www.google.com/trends/explore`.
- *The CIA World Factbook*: The `https://www.cia.gov/library/publications/the-world-factbook/` link provides information on the history, population, economy, government, infrastructure, and military of 267 countries.

See also

Other sources for machine learning data:

- SMS spam data: `http://www.dt.fee.unicamp.br/~tiago/smsspamcollection/`
- Financial dataset from Lending Club
  `https://www.lendingclub.com/info/download-data.action`
- Research data from Yahoo `http://webscope.sandbox.yahoo.com/index.php`
- Amazon AWS public dataset `http://aws.amazon.com/public-data-sets/`
- Labeled visual data from Image Net `http://www.image-net.org`
- Census datasets `http://www.census.gov`
- Compiled YouTube dataset `http://netsg.cs.sfu.ca/youtubedata/`
- Collected rating data from the MovieLens site
  `http://grouplens.org/datasets/movielens/`
- Enron dataset available to the public `http://www.cs.cmu.edu/~enron/`
- Dataset for the classic book elements of statistical learning
  `http://statweb.stanford.edu/~tibs/ElemStatLearn/data.htmlIMDB`
- Movie dataset `http://www.imdb.com/interfaces`
- Million Song dataset `http://labrosa.ee.columbia.edu/millionsong/`
- Dataset for speech and audio `http://labrosa.ee.columbia.edu/projects/`
- Face recognition data `http://www.face-rec.org/databases/`
- Social science data `http://www.icpsr.umich.edu/icpsrweb/ICPSR/studies`
- Bulk datasets from Cornell University `http://arxiv.org/help/bulk_data_s3`
- Project Guttenberg datasets
  `http://www.gutenberg.org/wiki/Gutenberg:Offline_Catalogs`
- Datasets from World Bank `http://data.worldbank.org`
- Lexical database from World Net `http://wordnet.princeton.edu`
- Collision data from NYPD `http://nypd.openscrape.com/#/`
- Dataset for congressional row calls and others `http://voteview.com/dwnl.htm`
- Large graph datasets from Stanford
  `http://snap.stanford.edu/data/index.html`
- Rich set of data from datahub `https://datahub.io/dataset`
- Yelp's academic dataset `https://www.yelp.com/academic_dataset`
- Source of data from GitHub
  `https://github.com/caesar0301/awesome-public-datasets`
- Dataset archives from Reddit `https://www.reddit.com/r/datasets/`

There are some specialized datasets (for example, text analytics in Spanish, and gene and IMF data) that might be of some interest to you:

- Datasets from Colombia (in Spanish):
  `http://www.datos.gov.co/frm/buscador/frmBuscador.aspx`
- Dataset from cancer studies
  `http://www.broadinstitute.org/cgi-bin/cancer/datasets.cgi`
- Research data from Pew `http://www.pewinternet.org/datasets/`
- Data from the state of Illinois/USA `https://data.illinois.gov`
- Data from freebase.com `http://www.freebase.com`
- Datasets from the UN and its associated agencies `http://data.un.org`
- International Monetary Fund datasets `http://www.imf.org/external/data.htm`
- UK government data `https://data.gov.uk`
- Open data from Estonia
  `http://pub.stat.ee/px-web.2001/Dialog/statfile1.asp`
- Many ML libraries in R containing data that can be exported as CSV
  `https://www.r-project.org`
- Gene expression datasets `http://www.ncbi.nlm.nih.gov/geo/`

Running your first program using Apache Spark 2.0 with the IntelliJ IDE

The purpose of this program is to get you comfortable with compiling and running a recipe using the Spark 2.0 development environment you just set up. We will explore the components and steps in later chapters.

We are going to write our own version of the Spark 2.0.0 program and examine the output so we can understand how it works. To emphasize, this short recipe is only a simple RDD program with Scala sugar syntax to make sure you have set up your environment correctly before starting to work with more complicated recipes.

How to do it...

1. Start a new project in IntelliJ or in an IDE of your choice. Make sure that the necessary JAR files are included.

2. Download the sample code for the book, find the myFirstSpark20.scala file, and place the code in the following directory.

   We installed Spark 2.0 in the C:\spark-2.0.0-bin-hadoop2.7\ directory on a Windows machine.

3. Place the myFirstSpark20.scala file in the C:\spark-2.0.0-bin-hadoop2.7\examples\src\main\scala\spark\ml\cookbook\chapter1 directory:

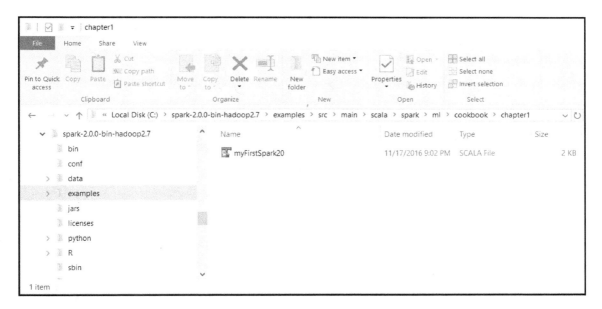

Mac users note that we installed Spark 2.0 in the /Users/USERNAME/spark/spark-2.0.0-bin-hadoop2.7/ directory on a Mac machine.

Place the myFirstSpark20.scala file in the /Users/USERNAME/spark/spark-2.0.0-bin-hadoop2.7/examples/src/main/scala/spark/ml/cookbook/chapter1 directory.

4. Set up the package location where the program will reside:

    ```
    package spark.ml.cookbook.chapter1
    ```

5. Import the necessary packages for the Spark session to gain access to the cluster and `log4j.Logger` to reduce the amount of output produced by Spark:

    ```
    import org.apache.spark.sql.SparkSession
    import org.apache.log4j.Logger
    import org.apache.log4j.Level
    ```

6. Set output level to ERROR to reduce Spark's logging output:

    ```
    Logger.getLogger("org").setLevel(Level.ERROR)
    ```

7. Initialize a Spark session by specifying configurations with the builder pattern, thus making an entry point available for the Spark cluster:

    ```
    val spark = SparkSession
    .builder
    .master("local[*]")
    .appName("myFirstSpark20")
    .config("spark.sql.warehouse.dir", ".")
    .getOrCreate()
    ```

    The `myFirstSpark20` object will run in local mode. The previous code block is a typical way to start creating a `SparkSession` object.

8. We then create two array variables:

    ```
    val x =
    Array(1.0,5.0,8.0,10.0,15.0,21.0,27.0,30.0,38.0,45.0,50.0,64.0)
    val y =
    Array(5.0,1.0,4.0,11.0,25.0,18.0,33.0,20.0,30.0,43.0,55.0,57.0)
    ```

9. We then let Spark create two RDDs based on the array created before:

    ```
    val xRDD = spark.sparkContext.parallelize(x)
    val yRDD = spark.sparkContext.parallelize(y)
    ```

10. Next, we let Spark operate on the RDD; the `zip()` function will create a new RDD from the two RDDs mentioned before:

    ```
    val zipedRDD = xRDD.zip(yRDD)
    zipedRDD.collect().foreach(println)
    ```

In the console output at runtime (more details on how to run the program in the IntelliJ IDE in the following steps), you will see this:

```
(1.0,5.0)
(5.0, 1.0)
(8.0,4.0)
(10.0,11.0)
(15.0,25.0)
(21.0,18.0)
(27.0,33.0)
(30.0,20.0)
(38.0,30.0)
(45.0,43.0)
(50.0,55.0)
(64.0,57.0)
```

11. Now, we sum up the value for xRDD and yRDD and calculate the new `zipedRDD` sum value. We also calculate the item count for `zipedRDD`:

```
val xSum = zipedRDD.map(_._1).sum()
val ySum = zipedRDD.map(_._2).sum()
val xySum= zipedRDD.map(c => c._1 * c._2).sum()
val n= zipedRDD.count()
```

12. We print out the value calculated previously in the console:

```
println("RDD X Sum: " +xSum)
println("RDD Y Sum: " +ySum)
println("RDD X*Y Sum: "+xySum)
println("Total count: "+n)
```

Here's the console output:

```
RDD X Sum: 314.0
RDD Y Sum: 302.0
RDD X*Y Sum: 11869.0
Total count: 12
```

13. We close the program by stopping the Spark session:

```
spark.stop()
```

14. Once the program is complete, the layout of `myFirstSpark20.scala` in the IntelliJ project explorer will look like the following:

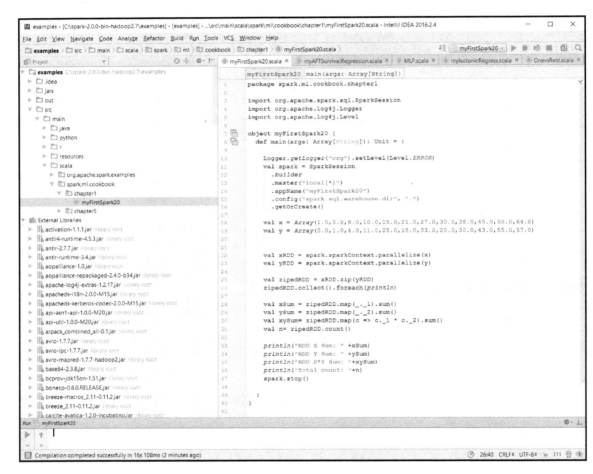

15. Make sure there is no compiling error. You can test this by rebuilding the project:

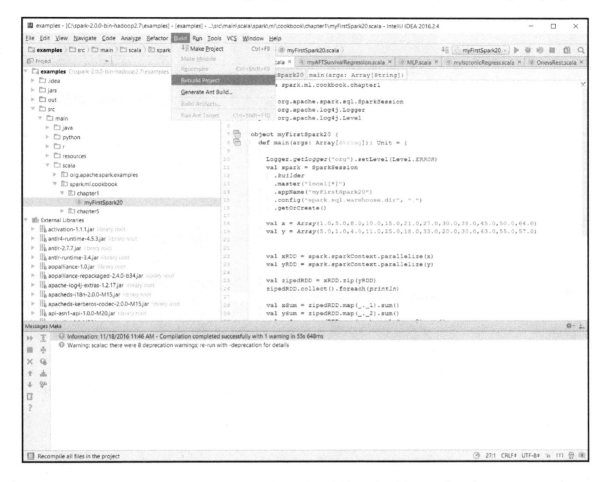

Once the rebuild is complete, there should be a build completed message on the console:

```
Information: November 18, 2016, 11:46 AM - Compilation completed
successfully with 1 warning in 55s 648ms
```

16. You can run the previous program by right-clicking on `the myFirstSpark20` object in the project explorer and selecting the context menu option (shown in the next screenshot) called `Run myFirstSpark20`.

You can also use the **Run** menu from the menu bar to perform the same action.

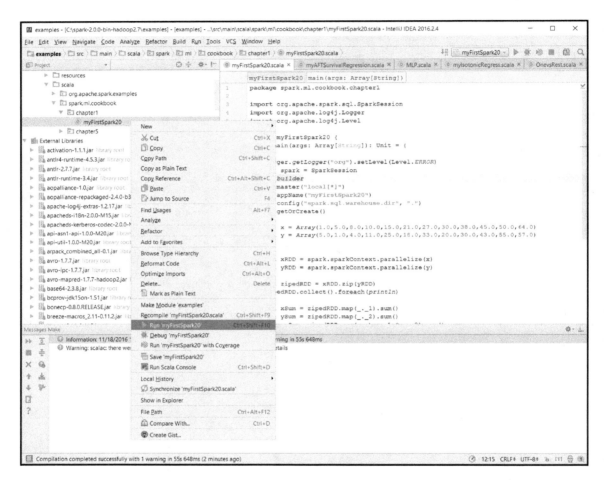

17. Once the program is successfully executed, you will see the following message:

```
Process finished with exit code 0
```

This is also shown in the following screenshot:

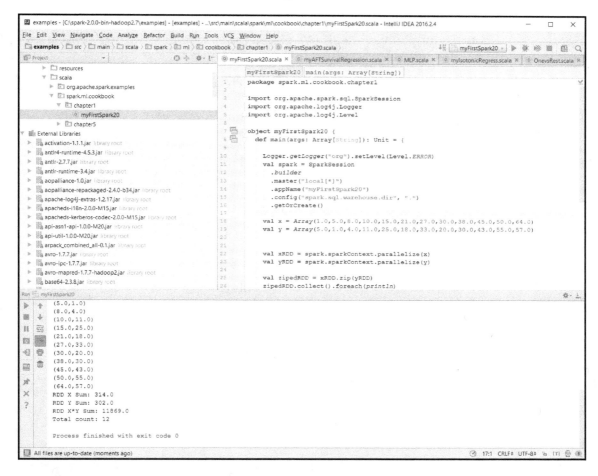

18. Mac users with IntelliJ will be able to perform this action using the same context menu.

Place the code in the correct path.

How it works...

In this example, we wrote our first Scala program, `myFirstSpark20.scala`, and displayed the steps to execute the program in IntelliJ. We placed the code in the path described in the steps for both Windows and Mac.

In the `myFirstSpark20` code, we saw a typical way to create a `SparkSession` object and how to configure it to run in local mode using the `master()` function. We created two RDDs out of the array objects and used a simple `zip()` function to create a new RDD.

We also did a simple sum calculation on the RDDs that were created and then displayed the result in the console. Finally, we exited and released the resource by calling `spark.stop()`.

There's more...

Spark can be downloaded from `http://spark.apache.org/downloads.html`.

Documentation for Spark 2.0 related to RDD can be found at `http://spark.apache.org/docs/latest/programming-guide.html#rdd-operations`.

See also

- More information about JetBrain IntelliJ can be found at `https://www.jetbrains.com/idea/`.

How to add graphics to your Spark program

In this recipe, we discuss how to use JFreeChart to add a graphic chart to your Spark 2.0.0 program.

How to do it...

1. Set up the JFreeChart library. JFreeChart JARs can be downloaded from the `https://sourceforge.net/projects/jfreechart/files/` site.

2. The JFreeChart version we have covered in this book is JFreeChart 1.0.19, as can be seen in the following screenshot. It can be downloaded from the `https://sourceforge.net/projects/jfreechart/files/1.%20JFreeChart/ 1.0.19/jfreechart-1.0.19.zip/download` site:

3. Once the ZIP file is downloaded, extract it. We extracted the ZIP file under `C:\` for a Windows machine, then proceed to find the `lib` directory under the extracted destination directory.

4. We then find the two libraries we need (JFreeChart requires JCommon), `JFreeChart-1.0.19.jar` and `JCommon-1.0.23`:

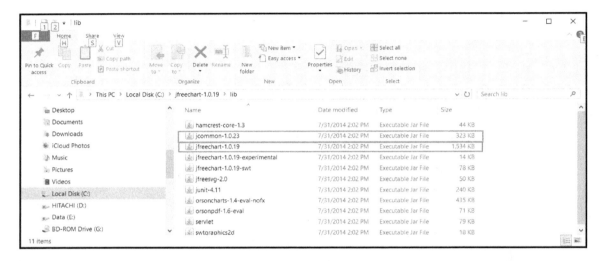

5. Now we copy the two previously mentioned JARs into the `C:\spark-2.0.0-bin-hadoop2.7\examples\jars\` directory.

6. This directory, as mentioned in the previous setup section, is in the classpath for the IntelliJ IDE project setting:

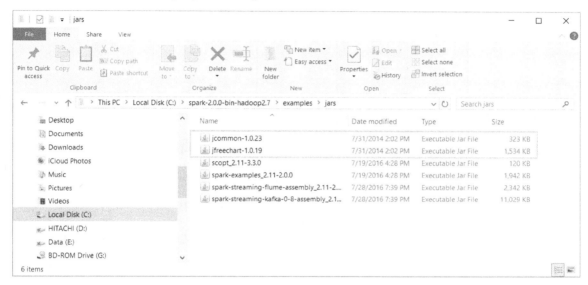

 In macOS, you need to place the previous two JARs in the `/Users/USERNAME/spark/spark-2.0.0-bin-hadoop2.7/examples\jars\` directory.

7. Start a new project in IntelliJ or in an IDE of your choice. Make sure that the necessary JAR files are included.

8. Download the sample code for the book, find `MyChart.scala`, and place the code in the following directory.

9. We installed Spark 2.0 in the `C:\spark-2.0.0-bin-hadoop2.7\` directory in Windows. Place `MyChart.scala` in the `C:\spark-2.0.0-bin-hadoop2.7\examples\src\main\scala\spark\ml\cookbook\chapter1` directory.

10. Set up the package location where the program will reside:

```
package spark.ml.cookbook.chapter1
```

11. Import the necessary packages for the Spark session to gain access to the cluster and `log4j.Logger` to reduce the amount of output produced by Spark.

12. Import necessary JFreeChart packages for the graphics:

```
import java.awt.Color
import org.apache.log4j.{Level, Logger}
import org.apache.spark.sql.SparkSession
import org.jfree.chart.plot.{PlotOrientation, XYPlot}
import org.jfree.chart.{ChartFactory, ChartFrame, JFreeChart}
import org.jfree.data.xy.{XYSeries, XYSeriesCollection}
import scala.util.Random
```

13. Set the output level to ERROR to reduce Spark's logging output:

```
Logger.getLogger("org").setLevel(Level.ERROR)
```

14. Initialize a Spark session specifying configurations with the builder pattern, thus making an entry point available for the Spark cluster:

```
val spark = SparkSession
  .builder
  .master("local[*]")
  .appName("myChart")
  .config("spark.sql.warehouse.dir", ".")
  .getOrCreate()
```

15. The `myChart` object will run in local mode. The previous code block is a typical start to creating a `SparkSession` object.

16. We then create an RDD using a random number and ZIP the number with its index:

```
val data = spark.sparkContext.parallelize(Random.shuffle(1 to
15).zipWithIndex)
```

17. We print out the RDD in the console:

```
data.foreach(println)
```

Here is the console output:

```
(14,10)
(6,2)
(7,7)
(8,12)
(13,5)
(15,13)
(10,8)
(4,3)
(3,11)
(1,0)
(2,4)
(11,9)
(12,14)
(9,6)
(5,1)
```

18. We then create a data series for JFreeChart to display:

```
val xy = new XYSeries("")
data.collect().foreach{ case (y: Int, x: Int) => xy.add(x,y) }
val dataset = new XYSeriesCollection(xy)
```

19. Next, we create a chart object from JFreeChart's ChartFactory and set up the basic configurations:

```
val chart = ChartFactory.createXYLineChart(
  "MyChart",  // chart title
  "x",                // x axis label
  "y",                // y axis label
  dataset,            // data
  PlotOrientation.VERTICAL,
  false,              // include legend
  true,               // tooltips
  false               // urls
)
```

20. We get the plot object from the chart and prepare it to display graphics:

```
val plot = chart.getXYPlot()
```

21. We configure the plot first:

```
configurePlot(plot)
```

22. The `configurePlot` function is defined as follows; it sets up some basic color schema for the graphical part:

```
def configurePlot(plot: XYPlot): Unit = {
  plot.setBackgroundPaint(Color.WHITE)
  plot.setDomainGridlinePaint(Color.BLACK)
  plot.setRangeGridlinePaint(Color.BLACK)
  plot.setOutlineVisible(false)
}
```

23. We now show the `chart`:

```
show(chart)
```

24. The `show()` function is defined as follows. It is a very standard frame-based graphic-displaying function:

```
def show(chart: JFreeChart) {
  val frame = new ChartFrame("plot", chart)
  frame.pack()
  frame.setVisible(true)
}
```

25. Once `show(chart)` is executed successfully, the following frame will pop up:

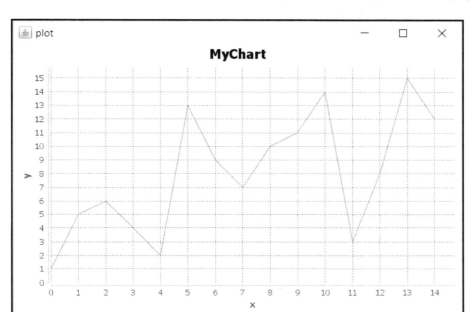

26. We close the program by stopping the Spark session:

```
spark.stop()
```

How it works...

In this example, we wrote `MyChart.scala` and saw the steps for executing the program in IntelliJ. We placed code in the path described in the steps for both Windows and Mac.

In the code, we saw a typical way to create the `SparkSession` object and how to use the `master()` function. We created an RDD out of an array of random integers in the range of 1 to 15 and zipped it with the Index.

We then used JFreeChart to compose a basic chart that contains a simple x and y axis, and supplied the chart with the dataset we generated from the original RDD in the previous steps.

We set up the schema for the chart and called the `show()` function in JFreeChart to show a Frame with the *x* and *y* axes displayed as a linear graphical chart.

Finally, we exited and released the resource by calling `spark.stop()`.

There's more...

More about JFreeChart can be found here:

- `http://www.jfree.org/jfreechart/`
- `http://www.jfree.org/jfreechart/api/javadoc/index.html`

See also

Additional examples about the features and capabilities of JFreeChart can be found at the following website:

`http://www.jfree.org/jfreechart/samples.html`

11
Spark's Three Data Musketeers for Machine Learning - Perfect Together

In this chapter, we will cover the following recipes:

- Creating RDDs with Spark 2.0 using internal data sources
- Creating RDDs with Spark 2.0 using external data sources
- Transforming RDDs with Spark 2.0 using the filter() API
- Transforming RDDs with the super useful flatMap() API
- Transforming RDDs with set operation APIs
- RDD transformation/aggregation with groupBy() and reduceByKey()
- Transforming RDDs with the zip() API
- Join transformation with paired key-value RDDs
- Reduce and grouping transformation with paired key-value RDDs
- Creating DataFrames from Scala data structures
- Operating on DataFrames programmatically without SQL
- Loading DataFrames and setup from an external source
- Using DataFrames with standard SQL language - SparkSQL
- Working with the Dataset API using a Scala sequence
- Creating and using Datasets from RDDs and back again
- Working with JSON using the Dataset API and SQL together
- Functional programming with the Dataset API using domain objects

Introduction

The three workhorses of Spark for efficient processing of data at scale are RDD, DataFrames, and the Dataset API. While each can stand on its own merit, the new paradigm shift favors Dataset as the unifying data API to meet all data wrangling needs in a single interface.

The new Spark 2.0 Dataset API is a type-safe collection of domain objects that can be operated on via transformation (similar to RDDs' filter, `map`, `flatMap()`, and so on) in parallel using functional or relational operations. For backward compatibility, Dataset has a view called **DataFrame**, which is a collection of rows that are untyped. In this chapter, we demonstrate all three API sets. The figure ahead summarizes the pros and cons of the key components of Spark for data wrangling:

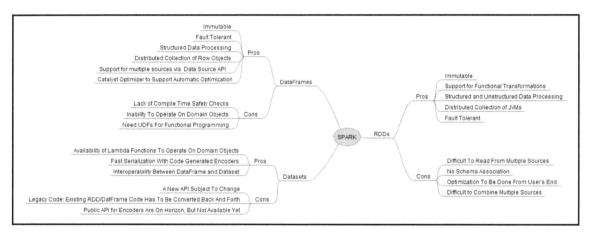

An advanced developer in machine learning must understand and be able to use all three API sets without any issues, for algorithmic augmentation or legacy reasons. While we recommend that every developer should migrate toward the high-level Dataset API, you will still need to know RDDs for programming against the Spark core system. For example, it is very common for investment banking and hedge funds to read leading journals in machine learning, mathematical programming, finance, statistics, or artificial intelligence and then code the research in low-level APIs to gain competitive advantage.

RDDs - what started it all...

The RDD API is a critical toolkit for Spark developers since it favors low-level control over the data within a functional programming paradigm. What makes RDDs powerful also makes it harder to work with for new programmers. While it may be easy to understand the RDD API and manual optimization techniques (for example, `filter()` before a `groupBy()` operation), writing advanced code would require consistent practice and fluency.

When data files, blocks, or data structures are converted to RDDs, the data is broken down into smaller units called **partitions** (similar to splits in Hadoop) and distributed among the nodes so they can be operated on in parallel at the same time. Spark provides this functionality right out of the box at scale without any additional coding. The framework will take care of all the details for you and you can concentrate on writing code without worrying about the data.

To appreciate the genius and yet the elegance of the underlying RDDs, one must read the original paper on this subject, which was deemed as the best work on this subject. The paper can be accessed here:

`https://www.usenix.org/system/files/conference/nsdi12/nsdi12-final138.pdf`

There are many types of RDDs in Spark that can simplify programming. The following mind map depicts a partial taxonomy of RDDs. It is suggested that a programmer on Spark know the types of RDDs available out of the box at minimum, even the less-known ones such as **RandomRDD ,VertexRDD, HadoopRDD, JdbcRDD,** and **UnionRDD,** in order to avoid unnecessary coding.

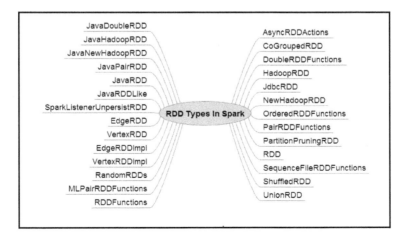

DataFrame - a natural evolution to unite API and SQL via a high-level API

The Spark developer community has always strived to provide an easy-to-use high-level API for the community starting from the AMPlab days at Berkley. The next evolution in the Data API materialized when Michael Armbrust gave the community the SparkSQL and Catalyst optimizer, which made data virtualization possible with Spark using a simple and well-understood SQL interface. The DataFrame API was a natural evolution to take advantage of SparkSQL by organizing data into named columns like relational tables.

The DataFrame API made data wrangling via SQL available to a multitude of data scientists and developers familiar with DataFrames in R (data.frame) or Python/Pandas (pandas.DataFrame).

Dataset - a high-level unifying Data API

A dataset is an immutable collection of objects which are modelled/mapped to a traditional relational schema. There are four attributes that distinguish it as the preferred method going forward. We particularly find the Dataset API appealing since we find it familiar to RDDs with the usual transformational operators (for example, `filter()`, `map()`, `flatMap()`, and so on). The Dataset will follow a lazy execution paradigm similar to RDD. The best way to try to reconcile DataFrames and Datasets is to think of a DataFrame as an alias that can be thought of as `Dataset[Row]`.

- **Strong type safety**: We now have both compile-time (syntax errors) and runtime safety in a unified Data API, which helps the ML developer not only during development, but can also help guard against mishaps during runtime. Developers hit by unexpected runtime errors using DataFrame or RDD Lambda either in Scala or Python (due to flaws in data) will better understand and appreciate this new contribution from the Spark community and Databricks (`https://databricks.com`).

- **Tungsten Memory Management enabled**: Tungsten brings Apache Spark closer to bare metal (that is, leveraging the `sun.misc.Unsafe interface`). The encoders facilitate mapping of JVM objects to tabular format (see the following figure). If you use the Dataset API, Spark will map the JVM objects to internal Tungsten off-heap binary format, which is more efficient. While the details of Tungsten internals are beyond the scope of a cookbook on machine learning, it is worth mentioning that the benchmarking shows significant improvement using off-head memory management versus JVM objects. It is noteworthy to mention that the concept of off-heap memory management has always been intrinsic in Apache Flink before it became available in Spark. Spark developers realized the importance of project Tungsten since Spark 1.4, 1.5, and 1.6 to its current state in Spark 2.0+. Again, we emphasize that even though DataFrame will be supported as of writing this, and has been covered in detail (most prod systems are still pre-Spark 2.0), we encourage you to start thinking in the Dataset paradigm. The following figure shows how RDD, DataFrame, and DataSet relate to the project Tungsten evolutionary roadmap:

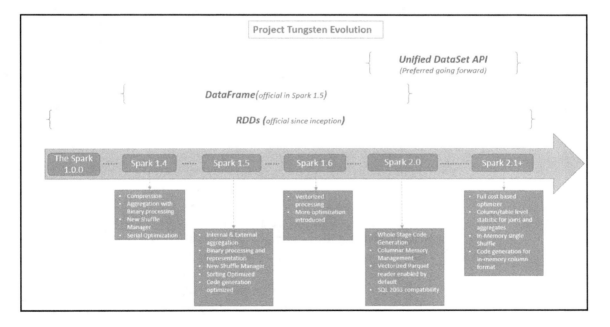

- **Encoders**: Encoders are Spark's serialization and deserialization (that is, SerDe) framework in Spark 2.0. Encoders seamlessly handle the mapping of JVM objects to tabular format that you can get under the cover and modify if desired (expert level).

    - Unlike standard Java serialization and other serialization schemes (for example, Kryo), the encoders do not use runtime reflection to discover object internals to serialize on the fly. Instead, encoder code is generated and compiled during compile time to bytecode for a given object, which will result in much faster operation (no reflection is used) to serialize and de-serialize the object. The reflection at runtime for object internals (for example, lookup of fields and their format) imposes extra overhead that is not present using Spark 2.0. The ability to use Kryo, standard java serialization, or any other serialization technique still remains an option (edge cases and backward compatibility) if needed.

    - The encoders for standard data types and objects (made of standard data types) are available in Tungsten out of the box. Using a quick informal program benchmark, serializing objects back and forth using Kryo serialization, which is popular with Hadoop MapReduce developers, versus encoders, revealed a significant 4x to 8x improvement. When we looked at the source code and probed under the covers, we realized that the encoders actually use runtime code generation (at bytecode level!) to pack and unpack objects. For completeness, we mention that the objects also seemed to be smaller, but further details and the reasons as to why it is so, is beyond the scope of this book.

    - The Encoder[T] is an internal artifact made of the DataSet[T], which is just a schema of records. You can create your own custom encoders as needed in Scala using tuples of underlying data (for example, Long, Double, and Int). Before you embark on the custom encoder journey (for example, want to store custom objects in DataSet[T]), make sure you take a look at `Encoders.scala` and `SQLImplicits.scala` in Spark's source directory. The plan and strategic direction for Spark is to provide a public API in future releases.

- **Catalyst optimizer friendly**: Using Catalyst, the API gestures are translated into logical query plans which use a catalog (user-defined functions) and ultimately translate the logical plan to a physical plan, which is often much more efficient than proposed by the original scheme (even if you try to put `groupBy()` before `filter()`, it is smart enough to arrange it the other way around). For better clarity, see the following figure:

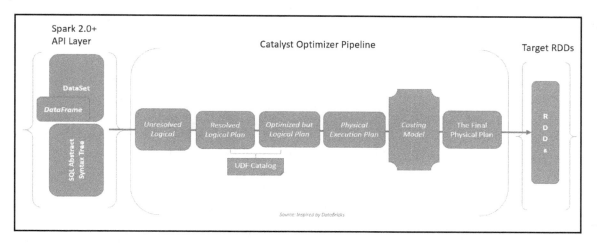

Noteworthy for pre-Spark 2.0 users:

- `SparkSession` is now the single entry point into the system. SQLContext and HiveContext are replaced by SparkSession.
- For Java users, be sure to replace DataFrame with `Dataset<Row>`
- Use the new catalog interface via `SparkSession` to execute `cacheTable()`, `dropTempView()`, `createExternalTable()`, `ListTable()`, and so on.
- DataFrame and DataSet API:
  - `unionALL()` is deprecated; you should use now `union()`
  - `explode()` should be replaced by `functions.explode()` plus `select()` or `flatMap()`
  - `registerTempTable` has been deprecated and replaced by `createOrReplaceTempView()`

Creating RDDs with Spark 2.0 using internal data sources

There are four ways to create RDDs in Spark. They range from the `parallelize()` method for simple testing and debugging within the client driver code to streaming RDDs for near-realtime responses. In this recipe, we provide you with several examples to demonstrate RDD creation using internal sources.

How to do it...

1. Start a new project in IntelliJ or in an IDE of your choice. Make sure the necessary JAR files are included.

2. Set up the package location where the program will reside:

   ```
   package spark.ml.cookbook.chapter3
   ```

3. Import the necessary packages:

   ```
   import breeze.numerics.pow
   import org.apache.spark.sql.SparkSession
   import Array._
   ```

4. Import the packages for setting up logging level for `log4j`. This step is optional, but we highly recommend it (change the level appropriately as you move through the development cycle).

   ```
   import org.apache.log4j.Logger
   import org.apache.log4j.Level
   ```

5. Set up the logging level to warning and error to cut down on output. See the previous step for package requirements.

   ```
   Logger.getLogger("org").setLevel(Level.ERROR)
   Logger.getLogger("akka").setLevel(Level.ERROR)
   ```

6. Set up the Spark context and application parameter so Spark can run:

```
val spark = SparkSession
  .builder
  .master("local[*]")
  .appName("myRDD")
  .config("Spark.sql.warehouse.dir", ".")
  .getOrCreate()
```

7. We declare two local data structures to hold the data prior to using any distributed RDDs. It should be noted that the data here will be held in the driver's heap space via local data structures. We make an explicit mention here, due to the multitude of problems programmers encounter when using large data sets for testing using the `parallelize()` technique. Ensure that you have enough space to hold the data locally in the driver if you use this technique.

```
val SignalNoise: Array[Double] =
Array(0.2,1.2,0.1,0.4,0.3,0.3,0.1,0.3,0.3,0.9,1.8,0.2,3.5,0.5,0.3,0
.3,0.2,0.4,0.5,0.9,0.1)
val SignalStrength: Array[Double] =
Array(6.2,1.2,1.2,6.4,5.5,5.3,4.7,2.4,3.2,9.4,1.8,1.2,3.5,5.5,7.7,9
.3,1.1,3.1,2.1,4.1,5.1)
```

8. We use the `parallelize()` function to take the local data and distribute it across the cluster.

```
val parSN=spark.sparkContext.parallelize(SignalNoise) //
parallelized signal noise RDD
val parSS=spark.sparkContext.parallelize(SignalStrength)  //
parallelized signal strength
```

9. Let's take a look at the difference between the two data structures as seen by Spark. This can be done by printing the two data structure handles: a local array and a cluster parallel collection (that is, RDD).

The output will be as follows:

```
Signal Noise Local Array , [D@2ab0702e)
RDD Version of Signal Noise on the cluster
,ParallelCollectionRDD[0] at parallelize at myRDD.scala:45)
```

10. Spark tries to set the number of partitions (that is, splits in Hadoop) itself based on the configuration of the cluster, but there are times when we need to set the number of partitions manually. The `parallelize()` function offers a second parameter that allows you to set the number of partitions manually.

```
val parSN=spark.sparkContext.parallelize(SignalNoise) //
parallelized signal noise RDD set with default partition
val parSS=spark.sparkContext.parallelize(SignalStrength) //
parallelized signal strength set with default partition
val parSN2=spark.sparkContext.parallelize(SignalNoise,4) //
parallelized signal noise set with 4 partition
val parSS2=spark.sparkContext.parallelize(SignalStrength,8) //
parallelized signal strength set with 8 partition
println("parSN partition length ", parSN.partitions.length )
println("parSS partition length ", parSS.partitions.length )
println("parSN2 partition length ",parSN2.partitions.length )
println("parSS2 partition length ",parSS2.partitions.length )
```

The output will be as follows:

```
parSN partition length ,2
parSS partition length ,2
parSN2 partition length ,4
parSS2 partition length ,8
```

In the first two lines, Spark has chosen two partitions by default, and, in the next two lines, we have set the number of partitions to 4 and 8, respectively.

How it works...

The data held in the client driver is parallelized and distributed across the cluster using the number of portioned RDDs (the second parameter) as the guideline. The resulting RDD is the magic of Spark that started it all (refer to Matei Zaharia's original white paper).

The resulting RDDs are now fully distributed data structures with fault tolerance and lineage that can be operated on in parallel using Spark framework.

We read a text file `A Tale of Two Cities by Charles Dickens` from `http://www.gutenberg.org/` into Spark RDDs. We then proceed to split and tokenize the data and print the number of total words using Spark's operators (for example, `map`, `flatMap()`, and so on).

Creating RDDs with Spark 2.0 using external data sources

In this recipe, we provide you with several examples to demonstrate RDD creation using external sources.

How to do it...

1. Start a new project in IntelliJ or in an IDE of your choice. Make sure the necessary JAR files are included.

2. Set up the package location where the program will reside:

```
package spark.ml.cookbook.chapter3
```

3. Import the necessary packages:

```
import breeze.numerics.pow
import org.apache.spark.sql.SparkSession
import Array._
```

4. Import the packages for setting up logging level for log4j. This step is optional, but we highly recommend it (change the level appropriately as you move through the development cycle).

```
import org.apache.log4j.Logger
import org.apache.log4j.Level
```

5. Set up the logging level to warning and error to cut down on output. See the previous step for package requirements.

```
Logger.getLogger("org").setLevel(Level.ERROR)
Logger.getLogger("akka").setLevel(Level.ERROR)
```

6. Set up the Spark context and application parameter so Spark can run.

```
val spark = SparkSession
  .builder
  .master("local[*]")
  .appName("myRDD")
  .config("Spark.sql.warehouse.dir", ".")
  .getOrCreate()
```

7. We obtain the data from the Gutenberg project. This is a great source for accessing actual text, ranging from the complete works of *Shakespeare* to *Charles Dickens*.

8. Download the text from the following sources and store it in your local directory:
   - Source: `http://www.gutenberg.org`
   - Selected book: *A Tale of Two Cities by Charles Dickens*
   - URL: `http://www.gutenberg.org/cache/epub/98/pg98.txt`

9. Once again, we use `SparkContext`, available via `SparkSession`, and its function `textFile()` to read the external data source and parallelize it across the cluster. Remarkably, all the work is done for the developer behind the scenes by Spark using one single call to load a wide variety of formats (for example, text, S3, and HDFS), which parallelizes the data across the cluster using the `protocol:filepath` combination.

10. To demonstrate, we load the book, which is stored as ASCII, text using the `textFile()` method from `SparkContext` via `SparkSession`, which, in turn, goes to work behind the scenes and creates portioned RDDs across the cluster.

```
val book1 =
spark.sparkContext.textFile("../data/sparkml2/chapter3/a.txt")
```

The output will be as follows:

```
Number of lines = 16271
```

11. Even though we have not covered the Spark transformation operator, we'll look at a small code snippet which will break the file into words using blanks as a separator. In a real-life situation, a regular expression will be needed to cover all the edge cases with all the whitespace variations (refer to the *Transforming RDDs with Spark using filter() APIs* recipe in this chapter).
   - We use a lambda function to receive each line as it is read and split it into words using blanks as separator.
   - We use a flatMap to break the array of lists of words (that is, each group of words from a line corresponds to a distinct array/list for that line). In short, what we want is a list of words and not a list of a list of words for each line.

```
val book2 = book1.flatMap(l => l.split(" "))
println(book1.count())
```

The output will be as follows:

```
Number of words = 143228
```

How it works...

We read a text file A Tale of Two Cities by Charles Dickens from http://www.gutenberg.org/ into an RDD and then proceed to tokenize the words by using whitespace as the separator in a lambda expression using .split() and .flatmap() of RDD itself. We then proceed to use the .count() method of RDDs to output the total number of words. While this is simple, you have to bear in mind that the operation takes place using the distributed parallel framework of Spark with only a couple of lines.

There's more...

Creating RDDs with external data sources, whether it is a text file, Hadoop HDFS, sequence file, Casandra, or Parquet file is remarkably simple. Once again, we use SparkSession (SparkContext prior to Spark 2.0) to get a handle to the cluster. Once the function (for example, textFile Protocol: file path) is executed, the data is broken into smaller pieces (partitions) and automatically flows to the cluster, which becomes available to the computations as fault-tolerant distributed collections that can be operated on in parallel.

1. There are a number of variations that one must consider when working with real-life situations. The best advice based on our own experience is to consult the documentation before writing your own functions or connectors. Spark either supports your data source right out of the box, or the vendor has a connector that can be downloaded to do the same.

2. Another situation that we often see is many small files that are generated (usually within HDFS directories) that need to be parallelized as RDDs for consumption. SparkContext has a method named wholeTextFiles() which lets you read a directory containing multiple files and returns each of them as (filename, content) key-value pairs. We found this to be very useful in multi-stage machine learning situations using lambda architecture, where the model parameters are calculated as a batch and then updated in Spark every day.

In this example, we read multiple files and then print the first file for examination.

The `spark.sparkContext.wholeTextFiles()` function is used to read a large number of small files and present them as (K,V), or key-value:

```
val dirKVrdd =
spark.sparkContext.wholeTextFiles("../data/sparkml2/chapter3/*.txt") //
place a large number of small files for demo
println ("files in the directory as RDD ", dirKVrdd)
println("total number of files ", dirKVrdd.count())
println("Keys ", dirKVrdd.keys.count())
println("Values ", dirKVrdd.values.count())
dirKVrdd.collect()
println("Values ", dirKVrdd.first())
```

On running the previous code, you will get the following output:

```
files in the directory as RDD ,../data/sparkml2/chapter3/*.txt
WholeTextFileRDD[10] at wholeTextFiles at myRDD.scala:88)
total number of files 2
Keys ,2
Values ,2
Values ,(file:/C:/spark-2.0.0-bin-
hadoop2.7/data/sparkml2/chapter3/a.txt,
The Project Gutenberg EBook of A Tale of Two Cities,
by Charles Dickens
```

See also

Spark documentation for the `textFile()` and `wholeTextFiles()` functions:

```
http://spark.apache.org/docs/latest/api/scala/index.html#org.apache.spark.Spark
Context
```

The `textFile()` API is a single abstraction for interfacing to external data sources. The formulation of protocol/path is enough to invoke the right decoder. We'll demonstrate reading from an ASCII text file, Amazon AWS S3, and HDFS with code snippets that the user would leverage to build their own system.

- The path can be expressed as a simple path (for example, local text file) to a complete URI with the required protocol (for example, s3n for AWS storage buckets) to complete resource path with server and port configuration (for example, to read HDFS file from a Hadoop cluster).

- The `textFile()` method supports full directories, regex wildcards, and compressed formats as well. Take a look at this example code:

  ```
  val book1 = spark.sparkContext.textFile("C:/xyz/dailyBuySel/*.tif")
  ```

- The `textFile()` method has an optional parameter at the end that defines the minimum number of partitions required by RDDs.

For example, we explicitly direct Spark to break the file into 13 partitions:

```
val book1 = spark.sparkContext.textFile("../data/sparkml2/chapter3/a.txt",
13)
```

You also have the option of specifying a URI to read and create RDDs from other sources such as HDFS, and S3 by specifying a complete URI (protocol:path). The following examples demonstrate the point:

1. Reading and creating files from Amazon S3 buckets. A word of caution is that the AWS inline credentials in the URI will break if the AWS secret key has a forward slash. See this sample file:

   ```
   spark.sparkContext.hadoopConfiguration.set("fs.s3n.awsAccessKeyId",
   "xyz")
   spark.sparkContext.hadoopConfiguration.set("fs.s3n.awsSecretAccessK
   ey", "....xyz...")
   S3Rdd = spark.sparkContext.textFile("s3n://myBucket01/MyFile01")
   ```

2. Reading from HDFS is very similar. In this example, we are reading from a local Hadoop cluster, but, in a real-world situation, the port number will be different and set by the administrator.

   ```
   val hdfsRDD =
   spark.sparkContext.textFile("hdfs:///localhost:9000/xyz/top10Vector
   s.txt")
   ```

Transforming RDDs with Spark 2.0 using the filter() API

In this recipe, we explore the `filter()` method of RDD which is used to select a subset of the base RDD and return a new filtered RDD. The format is similar to `map()`, but a lambda function selects which members are to be included in the resulting RDD.

How to do it...

1. Start a new project in IntelliJ or in an IDE of your choice. Make sure the necessary JAR files are included.

2. Set up the package location where the program will reside:

```
package spark.ml.cookbook.chapter3
```

3. Import the necessary packages:

```
import breeze.numerics.pow
import org.apache.spark.sql.SparkSession
import Array._
```

4. Import the packages for setting up the logging level for `log4j`. This step is optional, but we highly recommend it (change the level appropriately as you move through the development cycle).

```
import org.apache.log4j.Logger
import org.apache.log4j.Level
```

5. Set up the logging level to warning and error to cut down on output. See the previous step for package requirements.

```
Logger.getLogger("org").setLevel(Level.ERROR)
Logger.getLogger("akka").setLevel(Level.ERROR)
```

6. Set up the Spark context and application parameter so Spark can run.

```
val spark = SparkSession
  .builder
  .master("local[*]")
  .appName("myRDD")
  .config("Spark.sql.warehouse.dir", ".")
  .getOrCreate()
```

7. Add the following lines for the examples to compile. The `pow()` function will allow us to raise any number to any power (for example, square the number):

```
import breeze.numerics.pow
```

8. We create some data and `parallelize()` it to get our base RDD. We also use `textFile()` to create the initial (for example, base RDD) from our text file that we downloaded earlier from the `http://www.gutenberg.org/cache/epub/98/pg98.txt` link:

```
val num : Array[Double] = Array(1,2,3,4,5,6,7,8,9,10,11,12,13)
  val numRDD=sc.parallelize(num)
  val book1 =
spark.sparkContext.textFile("../data/sparkml2/chapter3/a.txt")
```

9. We apply the `filter()` function to the RDDs to demonstrate the `filter()` function transformation. We use the `filter()` function to select the odd members from the original RDD.

10. The `filter()` function iterates (in parallel) through members of the RDD and applies the mod function (%) and compares it to 1. In short, if there is a reminder after dividing by 2, then it must be an odd number.

```
val myOdd= num.filter( i => (i%2) == 1)
```

This is a second variation of the previous line, but here we demonstrate the use of _ (underscore), which acts as a wildcard. We use this notation in Scala to abbreviate the obvious:

```
val myOdd2= num.filter(_ %2 == 1) // 2nd variation using scala
notation
myOdd.take(3).foreach(println)
```

On running the previous code, you will get the following output:

```
1.0
3.0
5.0
```

11. Another example combines map and filter together. This code snippet first squares every number and then applies the `filter` function to select the odd numbers from the original RDD.

```
val myOdd3= num.map(pow(_,2)).filter(_ %2 == 1)
myOdd3.take(3).foreach(println)
```

The output will be as follows:

```
1.0
9.0
25.0
```

12. In this example, we use the `filter()` method to identify the lines that are fewer than 30 characters. The resulting RDD will only contain the short lines. A quick examination of counts and output verify the results. The RDD transformation functions can be chained together, as long as the format complies with the function syntax.

```
val shortLines = book1.filter(_.length < 30).filter(_.length > 0)
   println("Total number of lines = ", book1.count())
   println("Number of Short Lines = ", shortLines.count())
   shortLines.take(3).foreach(println)
```

On running the previous code, you will get the following output:

```
(Total number of lines = 16271)
(Number of Short Lines = 1424)
Title: A Tale of Two Cities
Author: Charles Dickens
Language: English
```

13. In this example we use the `contain()` method to filter out sentences that contain the word `two` in any upper/lowercase combination. We use several methods chained together to find the desired sentences.

```
val theLines =
book1.map(_.trim.toUpperCase()).filter(_.contains("TWO"))
println("Total number of lines = ", book1.count())
println("Number of lines with TWO = ", theLines.count())
theLines.take(3).foreach(println)
```

How it works...

The `filter()` API is demonstrated using several examples. In the first example we went through an RDD and output odd numbers by using a lambda expression `.filter ( i => (i%2) == 1)` which takes advantage of the mod (modulus) function.

In the second example we made it a bit interesting by mapping the result to a square function using a lambda expression `num.map(pow(_,2)).filter(_ %2 == 1)`.

In the third example, we went through the text and filtered out short lines (for example, lines under 30 character) using the lambda expression `.filter(_.length < 30).filter(_.length > 0)` to print short versus total number of lines (`.count()`) as output.

There's more...

The `filter()` API walks through the parallelized distributed collection (that is, RDDs) and applies the selection criteria supplied to `filter()` as a lambda in order to include or exclude the element from the resulting RDD. The combination uses `map()`, which transforms each element and `filter()`, which selects a subset is a powerful combination in Spark ML programming.

We will see later with the `DataFrame` API how a similar `Filter()` API can be used to achieve the same effect using a higher-level framework used in R and Python (pandas).

See also

- Documentation for `.filter()`, which is a method call of RDD, is available at http://spark.apache.org/docs/latest/api/scala/index.html#org.apache. spark.api.java.JavaRDD.
- Documentation for `BloomFilter()`--for the sake of completeness, be aware that there is also a bloom filter function already in existence and it is suggested that you avoid coding by yourselves. The link for this same is http://spark.apache.org/docs/latest/api/scala/index.html#org.apache. spark.util.sketch.BloomFilter.

Transforming RDDs with the super useful flatMap() API

In this recipe, we examine the `flatMap()` method which is often a source of confusion for beginners; however, on closer examination we demonstrate that it is a clear concept that applies the lambda function to each element just like map, and then flattens the resulting RDD as a single structure (rather than having a list of lists, we create a single list made of all sublist with sublist elements).

How to do it...

1. Start a new project in IntelliJ or in an IDE of your choice. Make sure the necessary JAR files are included.

2. Set up the package location where the program will reside

   ```
   package spark.ml.cookbook.chapter3
   ```

3. Import the necessary packages

   ```
   import breeze.numerics.pow
   import org.apache.spark.sql.SparkSession
   import Array._
   ```

4. Import the packages for setting up the logging level for log4j. This step is optional, but we highly recommend it (change the level appropriately as you move through the development cycle).

   ```
   import org.apache.log4j.Logger
   import org.apache.log4j.Level
   ```

5. Set up the logging level to warning and error to cut down on output. See the previous step for package requirements.

   ```
   Logger.getLogger("org").setLevel(Level.ERROR)
   Logger.getLogger("akka").setLevel(Level.ERROR)
   ```

6. Set up the Spark context and application parameter so Spark can run.

   ```
   val spark = SparkSession
     .builder
     .master("local[*]")
     .appName("myRDD")
     .config("Spark.sql.warehouse.dir", ".")
     .getOrCreate()
   ```

7. We use textFile() function to create the initial (that is, base RDD) from our text file that we downloaded earlier from
   http://www.gutenberg.org/cache/epub/98/pg98.txt:

   ```
   val book1 =
   spark.sparkContext.textFile("../data/sparkml2/chapter3/a.txt")
   ```

8. We apply the map function to the RDDs to demonstrate the `map()` function transformation. To start with, we are doing it the wrong way to make a point: we first attempt to separate all the words based on the regular expression *[\s\W]+]* using just `map()` to demonstrate that the resulting RDD is a list of lists in which each list corresponds to a line and the tokenized word within that line. This example demonstrates what could cause confusion for beginners when using `flatMap()`.

9. The following line trims each line and then splits the line into words. The resulting RDD (that is, wordRDD2) will be a list of lists of words rather than a single list of words for the whole file.

```
val wordRDD2 = book1.map(_.trim.split("""[\s\W]+""")
).filter(_.length > 0)
wordRDD2.take(3) foreach(println(_))
```

On running the previous code, you will get the following output.

```
[Ljava.lang.String;@1e60b459
[Ljava.lang.String;@717d7587
[Ljava.lang.String;@3e906375
```

10. We use the `flatMap()` method to not only map, but also flatten the list of lists so we end up with an RDD which is made of words themselves. We trim and split the words (that is, tokenize) and then filter for words greater than zero and then map it to upper case.

```
val wordRDD3 = book1.flatMap(_.trim.split("""[\s\W]+""")
).filter(_.length > 0).map(_.toUpperCase())
println("Total number of lines = ", book1.count())
println("Number of words = ", wordRDD3.count())
```

In this case, after flattening the list using `flatMap()`, we can get a list of the words back as expected.

```
wordRDD3.take(5) foreach(println(_))
```

The output is as follows:

```
Total number of lines = 16271
Number of words = 141603
THE
PROJECT
GUTENBERG
EBOOK
OF
```

How it works...

In this short example, we read a text file and then split the words (that is, tokenize it) using the `flatMap(_.trim.split("""[\s\W]+""")` lambda expression to have a single RDD with the tokenized content. Additionally we use the `filter ()` API `filter(_.length > 0)` to exclude the empty lines and the lambda expression `.map(_.toUpperCase())` in a `.map()` API to map to uppercase before outputting the results.

There are cases where we do not want to get a list back for every element of base RDD (for example, get a list for words corresponding to a line). We sometimes prefer to have a single flattened list that is flat and corresponds to every word in the document. In short, rather than a list of lists, we want a single list containing all the elements.

There's more...

The function `glom()` is a function that lets you model each partition in the RDD as an array rather than a row list. While it is possible to produce the results in most cases, `glom()` allows you to reduce the shuffling between partitions.

While at the surface, both method 1 and 2 mentioned in the text below look similar for calculating the minimum numbers in an RDD, the `glom()` function will cause much less data shuffling across the network by first applying `min()` to all the partitions, and then sending over the resulting data. The best way to see the difference is to use this on 10M+ RDDs and watch the IO and CPU usage accordingly.

- The first method is to find the minimum value without using `glom()`:

```
val minValue1= numRDD.reduce(_ min _)
println("minValue1 = ", minValue1)
```

On running the preceding code, you will get the following output:

```
minValue1 = 1.0
```

- The second method is to find the minimum value using `glom(`, which causes a local application of the min function to a partition and then sends the results across via a shuffle.

```
val minValue2 = numRDD.glom().map(_.min).reduce(_ min _)
println("minValue2 = ", minValue2)
```

On running the preceding code, you will get the following output:

```
minValue1 = 1.0
```

See also

- Documentation for `flatMap()`, `PairFlatMap()`, and other variations under RDD is available
  at http://spark.apache.org/docs/latest/api/scala/index.html#org.apache.spark.api.java.JavaRDD
- Documentation for the `FlatMap()` function under RDD is available
  at http://spark.apache.org/docs/latest/api/scala/index.html#org.apache.spark.api.java.function.FlatMapFunction
- Documentation for the `PairFlatMap()` function - very handy variation for paired data elements is available
  at http://spark.apache.org/docs/latest/api/scala/index.html#org.apache.spark.api.java.function.PairFlatMapFunction
- The `flatMap()` method applies the supplied function (lambda or named function via def) to every element, flattens the structure, and produces a new RDD.

Transforming RDDs with set operation APIs

In this recipe, we explore set operations on RDDs, such as `intersection()`, `union()`, `subtract()`, and `distinct()` and `Cartesian()`. Let's implement the usual set operations in a distributed manner.

How to do it...

1. Start a new project in IntelliJ or in an IDE of your choice. Make sure the necessary JAR files are included.

2. Set up the package location where the program will reside

```
package spark.ml.cookbook.chapter3
```

3. Import the necessary packages

```
import breeze.numerics.pow
import org.apache.spark.sql.SparkSession
import Array._
```

4. Import the packages for setting up the logging level for `log4j`. This step is optional, but we highly recommend it (change the level appropriately as you move through the development cycle).

```
import org.apache.log4j.Logger
import org.apache.log4j.Level
```

5. Set up the logging level to warning and error to cut down on output. See the previous step for package requirements.

```
Logger.getLogger("org").setLevel(Level.ERROR)
Logger.getLogger("akka").setLevel(Level.ERROR)
```

6. Set up the Spark context and application parameter so Spark can run.

```
val spark = SparkSession
  .builder
  .master("local[*]")
  .appName("myRDD")
  .config("Spark.sql.warehouse.dir", ".")
  .getOrCreate()
```

7. Set up the data structures and RDD for the example:

```
val num : Array[Double]     = Array(1,2,3,4,5,6,7,8,9,10,11,12,13)
val odd : Array[Double]     = Array(1,3,5,7,9,11,13)
val even : Array[Double]    = Array(2,4,6,8,10,12)
```

8. We apply the `intersection()` function to the RDDs to demonstrate the transformation:

```
val intersectRDD = numRDD.intersection(oddRDD)
```

On running the previous code, you will get the following output:

```
1.0
3.0
5.0
```

9. We apply the `union()` function to the RDDs to demonstrate the transformation:

```
val unionRDD = oddRDD.union(evenRDD)
```

On running the previous code, you will get the following output:

```
1.0
2.0
3.0
4.0
```

10. We apply the `subtract()` function to the RDDs to demonstrate the transformation:

```
val subtractRDD = numRDD.subtract(oddRDD)
```

On running the previous code, you will get the following output:

```
2.0
4.0
6.0
8.0
```

11. We apply the `distinct()` function to the RDDs to demonstrate the transformation:

```
val namesRDD = spark.sparkContext.parallelize(List("Ed","Jain",
"Laura", "Ed"))
val ditinctRDD = namesRDD.distinct()
```

On running the previous code, you will get the following output:

```
"ED"
"Jain"
"Laura"
```

12. We apply the `distinct()` function to the RDDs to demonstrate the transformation

```
val cartesianRDD = oddRDD.cartesian(evenRDD)
cartesianRDD.collect.foreach(println)
```

On running the previous code, you will get the following output:

```
(1.0,2.0)
(1.0,4.0)
(1.0,6.0)
(3.0,2.0)
(3.0,4.0)
(3.0,6.0)
```

How it works...

In this example, we started with three sets of number Arrays (odd, even, and their combo) and then proceeded to pass them as parameters into the set operation API. We covered how to use `intersection()`, `union()`, `subtract()`, `distinct()`, and `cartesian()` RDD operators.

See also

While the RDD set operators are easy to use, one must be careful with the data shuffling that Spark has to perform in the background to complete some of these operations (for example, intersection).

It is worth noting that the union operator does not remove duplicates from the resulting RDD set.

RDD transformation/aggregation with groupBy() and reduceByKey()

In this recipe, we explore the `groupBy()` and `reduceBy()` methods, which allow us to group values corresponding to a key. It is an expensive operation due to internal shuffling. We first demonstrate `groupby()` in more detail and then cover `reduceBy()` to show the similarity in coding these while stressing the advantage of the `reduceBy()` operator.

How to do it...

1. Start a new project in IntelliJ or in an IDE of your choice. Make sure the necessary JAR files are included.

2. Set up the package location where the program will reside:

   ```
   package spark.ml.cookbook.chapter3
   ```

3. Import the necessary packages:

   ```
   import breeze.numerics.pow
   import org.apache.spark.sql.SparkSession
   import Array._
   ```

4. Import the packages for setting up the logging level for `log4j`. This step is optional, but we highly recommend it (change the level appropriately as you move through the development cycle):

   ```
   import org.apache.log4j.Logger
   import org.apache.log4j.Level
   ```

5. Set up the logging level to warning and error to cut down on output. See the previous step for package requirements.

   ```
   Logger.getLogger("org").setLevel(Level.ERROR)
   Logger.getLogger("akka").setLevel(Level.ERROR)
   ```

6. Set up the Spark context and application parameter so Spark can run:

   ```
   val spark = SparkSession
     .builder
     .master("local[*]")
     .appName("myRDD")
     .config("Spark.sql.warehouse.dir", ".")
     .getOrCreate()
   ```

7. Set up the data structures and RDD for the example. In this example, we create an RDD using range facilities and divide them into three partitions (that is, explicit parameter set). It simply creates numbers 1 through 12 and puts them into 3 partitions.

   ```
   val rangeRDD=sc.parallelize(1 to 12,3)
   ```

8. We apply the `groupBy()` function to the RDDs to demonstrate the transformation. In the example, we take the partitioned RDD of ranges and label them as odd/even using the `mod` function.

```
val groupByRDD= rangeRDD.groupBy( i => {if (i % 2 == 1) "Odd"
  else "Even"}).collect
groupByRDD.foreach(println)
```

On running the previous code, you will get the following output:

```
groupByRDD=
(Odd, CompactBuffer (1, 3, 5, 7, 9, 11))
(Even, CompactBuffer (2, 4, 6, 8, 10, 12))
```

9. Now that we have seen how to code `groupBy()`, we switch gears and demonstrate `reduceByKey()`.

10. To see the difference in coding, while producing the same output more efficiently, we set up an array with two letters (that is, a and b) so we can show aggregation by summing them up.

```
val alphabets = Array("a", "b", "a", "a", "a", "b") // two type
only to make it simple
```

11. In this step, we use a Spark context to produce a parallelized RDD:

```
val alphabetsPairsRDD =
spark.sparkContext.parallelize(alphabets).map(alphabets =>
(alphabets, 1))
```

12. We apply the `groupBy()` function first using the usual Scala syntax `(_+_)` to traverse the RDD and sum up, while aggregating by the type of alphabet (that is, considered key):

```
val countsUsingGroup = alphabetsPairsRDD.groupByKey()
  .map(c => (c._1, c._2.sum))
  .collect()
```

13. We apply the `reduceByKey()` function first using the usual Scala syntax `(_+_)` to traverse the RDD and sum up while aggregating by type of alphabet (that is, considered key)

```
val countsUsingReduce = alphabetsPairsRDD
  .reduceByKey(_ + _)
  .collect()
```

14. We output the results:

```
println("Output for  groupBy")
countsUsingGroup.foreach(println(_))
println("Output for  reduceByKey")
countsUsingReduce.foreach(println(_))
```

On running the previous code, you will get the following output:

```
Output for groupBy
(b,2)
(a,4)
Output for reduceByKey
(b,2)
(a,4)
```

How it works...

In this example, we created numbers one through twelve and placed them in three partitions. We then proceeded to break them into odd/even using a simple mod operation while. The `groupBy()` is used to aggregate them into two groups of odd/even. This is a typical aggregation problem that should look familiar to SQL users. Later in this chapter, we revisit this operation using `DataFrame` which also takes advantage of the better optimization techniques provided by the SparkSQL engine. In the later part, we demonstrate the similarity of `groupBy()` and `reduceByKey()`. We set up an array of alphabets (that is, `a` and `b`) and then convert them into RDD. We then proceed to aggregate them based on key (that is, unique letters - only two in this case) and print the total in each group.

There's more...

Given the direction for Spark which favors the Dataset/DataFrame paradigm over low-level RDD coding, one must seriously consider the reasoning for doing `groupBy()` on an RDD. While there are legitimate situations for which the operation is needed, the readers are advised to reformulate their solution to take advantage of the SparkSQL subsystem and its optimizer called **Catalyst**.

The Catalyst optimizer takes into account Scala's powerful features such as **pattern matching** and **quasiquotes** while building an optimized query plan.

- The documentation on Scala pattern matching is available at http://docs.scala-lang.org/tutorials/tour/pattern-matching.html
- The documentation on Scala quasiquotes is available at http://docs.scala-lang.org/overviews/quasiquotes/intro.html

Runtime efficiency consideration: The groupBy() function groups data by keys. The operation causes internal shuffling which can explode the execution time; one must always prefer to use the reduceByKey() family of operations to a straight groupBy() method call. The groupBy() method is an expensive operation due to shuffling. Each group is made of keys and items that belong to that key. The ordering of values corresponding to the key will not be guaranteed by Spark.

For an explanation of the two operations, see the Databricks knowledge base blog:

https://databricks.gitbooks.io/databricks-Spark-knowledge-base/content/best_practices/prefer_reducebykey_over_groupbykey.html

See also

Documentation for groupBy() and reduceByKey() operations under RDD:

http://spark.apache.org/docs/latest/api/scala/index.html#org.apache.spark.api.java.JavaRDD

Transforming RDDs with the zip() API

In this recipe we explore the zip() function. For those of us working in Python or Scala, zip() is a familiar method that lets you pair items before applying an inline function. Using Spark, it can be used to facilitate RDD arithmetic between pairs. Conceptually, it combines the two RDDs in such a way that each member of one RDD is paired with the second RDD that occupies the same position (that is, it lines up the two RDDs and makes pairs out of the members).

How to do it...

1. Start a new project in IntelliJ or in an IDE of your choice. Make sure the necessary JAR files are included.

2. Set up the package location where the program will reside

   ```
   package spark.ml.cookbook.chapter3
   ```

3. Import the necessary packages

   ```
   import org.apache.spark.sql.SparkSession
   ```

4. Import the packages for setting up the logging level for log4j. This step is optional, but we highly recommend it (change the level appropriately as you move through the development cycle).

   ```
   import org.apache.log4j.Logger
   import org.apache.log4j.Level
   ```

5. Set up the logging level to warning and error to cut down on output. See the previous step for package requirements.

   ```
   Logger.getLogger("org").setLevel(Level.ERROR)
   Logger.getLogger("akka").setLevel(Level.ERROR)
   ```

6. Set up the Spark context and application parameter so Spark can run.

   ```
   val spark = SparkSession
   .builder
   .master("local[*]")
   .appName("myRDD")
   .config("Spark.sql.warehouse.dir", ".")
   .getOrCreate()
   ```

7. Set up the data structures and RDD for the example. In this example we create two RDDs from Array[] and let Spark decide on the number of partitions (that is, the second parameter in the parallize() method is not set).

   ```
   val SignalNoise: Array[Double] =
   Array(0.2,1.2,0.1,0.4,0.3,0.3,0.1,0.3,0.3,0.9,1.8,0.2,3.5,0.5,0.3,0
   .3,0.2,0.4,0.5,0.9,0.1)
   val SignalStrength: Array[Double] =
   Array(6.2,1.2,1.2,6.4,5.5,5.3,4.7,2.4,3.2,9.4,1.8,1.2,3.5,5.5,7.7,9
   .3,1.1,3.1,2.1,4.1,5.1)
   val parSN=spark.sparkContext.parallelize(SignalNoise) //
   parallelized signal noise RDD
   ```

```
val parSS=spark.sparkContext.parallelize(SignalStrength)   //
parallelized signal strength
```

8. We apply the `zip()` function to the RDDs to demonstrate the transformation. In the example, we take the partitioned RDD of ranges and label them as odd/even using the mod function. We use the `zip()` function to pair elements from the two RDDs (SignalNoiseRDD and SignalStrengthRDD) so we can apply a `map()` function and compute their ratio (noise to signal ratio). We can use this technique to perform almost all types of arithmetic or non-arithmetic operations involving individual members of two RDDs.

9. The pairing of two RDD members act as a tuple or a row. The individual members of the pair created by `zip()` can be accessed by their position (for example, `._1` and `._2`)

```
val zipRDD= parSN.zip(parSS).map(r => r._1 / r._2).collect()
println("zipRDD=")
zipRDD.foreach(println)
```

On running the previous code, you will get the following output:

```
zipRDD=
0.03225806451612903
1.0
0.08333333333333334
0.0625
0.05454545454545454
```

How it works...

In this example, we first set up two arrays representing signal noise and signal strength. They are simply a set of measured numbers that we could have received from the IoT platform. We then proceeded to pair the two separate arrays so each member looks like they have been input originally as a pair of (x, y). We then proceed to divide the pair and produce the noise to signal ratio using the following code snippet:

```
val zipRDD= parSN.zip(parSS).map(r => r._1 / r._2)
```

The `zip()` method has many variations that involve partitions. The developers should familiarize themselves with variations of the `zip()` method with partition (for example, `zipPartitions`).

See also

- Documentation for `zip()` and `zipPartitions()` operations under RDD is available
  at `http://spark.apache.org/docs/latest/api/scala/index.html#org.apache.spark.api.java.JavaRDD`

Join transformation with paired key-value RDDs

In this recipe, we introduce the `KeyValueRDD` pair RDD and the supporting join operations such as `join()`, `leftOuterJoin` and `rightOuterJoin()`, and `fullOuterJoin()` as an alternative to the more traditional and more expensive set operations available via the set operation API, such as `intersection()`, `union()`, `subtraction()`, `distinct()`, `cartesian()`, and so on.

We'll demonstrate `join()`, `leftOuterJoin` and `rightOuterJoin()`, and `fullOuterJoin()`, to explain the power and flexibility of key-value pair RDDs.

```
println("Full Joined RDD = ")
val fullJoinedRDD = keyValueRDD.fullOuterJoin(keyValueCity2RDD)
fullJoinedRDD.collect().foreach(println(_))
```

How to do it...

1. Set up the data structures and RDD for the example:

```
val keyValuePairs =
List(("north",1),("south",2),("east",3),("west",4))
val keyValueCity1 =
List(("north","Madison"),("south","Miami"),("east","NYC"),("west","SanJose"))
val keyValueCity2 = List(("north","Madison"),("west","SanJose"))
```

2. Turn the List into RDDs:

```
val keyValueRDD = spark.sparkContext.parallelize(keyValuePairs)
val keyValueCity1RDD =
spark.sparkContext.parallelize(keyValueCity1)
val keyValueCity2RDD =
spark.sparkContext.parallelize(keyValueCity2)
```

3. We can access the `keys` and `values` inside a pair RDD.

```
val keys=keyValueRDD.keys
val values=keyValueRDD.values
```

4. We apply the `mapValues()` function to the pair RDDs to demonstrate the transformation. In this example we use the map function to lift up the value by adding 100 to every element. This is a popular technique to introduce noise to the data (that is, jittering).

```
val kvMappedRDD = keyValueRDD.mapValues(_+100)
kvMappedRDD.collect().foreach(println(_))
```

On running the previous code, you will get the following output:

```
(north,101)
(south,102)
(east,103)
(west,104)
```

5. We apply the `join()` function to the RDDs to demonstrate the transformation. We use `join()` to join the two RDDs. We join the two RDDs based on keys (that is, north, south, and so on).

```
println("Joined RDD = ")
val joinedRDD = keyValueRDD.join(keyValueCity1RDD)
joinedRDD.collect().foreach(println(_))
```

On running the previous code, you will get the following output:

```
(south, (2,Miami))
(north, (1,Madison))
(west, (4,SanJose))
(east, (3,NYC))
```

6. We apply the `leftOuterJoin()` function to the RDDs to demonstrate the transformation. The `leftOuterjoin` acts like a relational left outer join. Spark replaces the absence of a membership with `None` rather than `NULL`, which is common in relational systems.

```
println("Left Joined RDD = ")
val leftJoinedRDD = keyValueRDD.leftOuterJoin(keyValueCity2RDD)
leftJoinedRDD.collect().foreach(println(_))
```

On running the previous code, you will get the following output:

```
(south, (2,None))
(north, (1,Some(Madison)))
(west, (4,Some(SanJose)))
(east, (3,None))
```

7. We'll apply `rightOuterJoin()` to the RDDs to demonstrate the transformation. This is similar to a right outer join in relational systems.

```
println("Right Joined RDD = ")
val rightJoinedRDD = keyValueRDD.rightOuterJoin(keyValueCity2RDD)
rightJoinedRDD.collect().foreach(println(_))
```

On running the previous code, you will get the following output:

```
(north, (Some(1),Madison))
(west, (Some(4),SanJose))
```

8. We then apply the `fullOuterJoin()` function to the RDDs to demonstrate the transformation. This is similar to full outer join in relational systems.

```
val fullJoinedRDD = keyValueRDD.fullOuterJoin(keyValueCity2RDD)
fullJoinedRDD.collect().foreach(println(_))
```

On running the previous code, you will get the following output:

```
Full Joined RDD =
(south, (Some(2),None))
(north, (Some(1),Some(Madison)))
(west, (Some(4),Some(SanJose)))
(east, (Some(3),None))
```

How it works...

In this recipe, we declared three lists representing typical data available in relational tables, which could be imported using a connector to Casandra or RedShift (not shown here to simplify the recipe). We used two of the three lists representing city names (that is, data tables) and joined them with the first list, which represents directions (for example, defining tables). The first step is to define three lists of paired values. We then parallelized them into key-value RDDs so we can perform join operations between the first RDD (that is, directions) and the other two RDDs representing city names. We applied the join function to the RDDs to demonstrate the transformation.

We demonstrated `join()`, `leftOuterJoin` and `rightOuterJoin()`, and `fullOuterJoin()` to show the power and flexibility when combined with key-value pair RDDs.

There's more...

Documentation for `join()` and its variations under RDD is available at `http://spark.apache.org/docs/latest/api/scala/index.html#org.apache.spark.api.java.JavaRDD`.

Reduce and grouping transformation with paired key-value RDDs

In this recipe, we explore reduce and group by key. The `reduceByKey()` and `groupbyKey()` operations are much more efficient and preferred to `reduce()` and `groupBy()` in most cases. The functions provide convenient facilities to aggregate values and combine them by key with less shuffling, which is problematic on large data sets.

How to do it...

1. Start a new project in IntelliJ or in an IDE of your choice. Make sure the necessary JAR files are included.

2. Set up the package location where the program will reside

   ```
   package spark.ml.cookbook.chapter3
   ```

3. Import the necessary packages

```
import org.apache.spark.sql.SparkSession
```

4. Import the packages for setting up the logging level for `log4j`. This step is optional, but we highly recommend it (change the level appropriately as you move through the development cycle).

```
import org.apache.log4j.Logger
import org.apache.log4j.Level
```

5. Set up the logging level to warning and error to cut down on output. See the previous step for package requirement:

```
Logger.getLogger("org").setLevel(Level.ERROR)
Logger.getLogger("akka").setLevel(Level.ERROR)
```

6. Set up the Spark context and application parameter so Spark can run.

```
val spark = SparkSession
  .builder
  .master("local[*]")
  .appName("myRDD")
  .config("Spark.sql.warehouse.dir", ".")
  .getOrCreate()
```

7. Set up the data structures and RDD for the example:

```
val signaltypeRDD =
spark.sparkContext.parallelize(List(("Buy",1000),("Sell",500),("Buy",600),("Sell",800)))
```

8. We apply `groupByKey()` to demonstrate the transformation. In this example, we group all the buy and sell signals together while operating in a distributed setting.

```
val signaltypeRDD =
spark.sparkContext.parallelize(List(("Buy",1000),("Sell",500),("Buy",600),("Sell",800)))
val groupedRDD = signaltypeRDD.groupByKey()
groupedRDD.collect().foreach(println(_))
```

On running the previous code, you will get the following output:

```
Group By Key RDD =
(Sell, CompactBuffer(500, 800))
(Buy, CompactBuffer(1000, 600))
```

9. We apply the `reduceByKey()` function to the pair of RDDs to demonstrate the transformation. In this example, the function is, to sum up the total volume for the buy and sell signals. The Scala notation of (_+_) simply denotes adding two members at the time and producing a single result from it. Just like `reduce()`, we can apply any function (that is, inline for simple functions and named functions for more complex cases).

```
println("Reduce By Key RDD = ")
val reducedRDD = signaltypeRDD.reduceByKey(_+_)
reducedRDD.collect().foreach(println(_))
```

On running the previous code, you will get the following output:

```
Reduce By Key RDD =
(Sell,1300)
(Buy,1600)
```

How it works...

In this example we declared a list of items as being sold or purchased and their corresponding price (that is, typical commercial transaction). We then proceeded to calculate the sum using Scala shorthand notation (_+_). In the last step, we provided the total for each key group (that is, `Buy` or `Sell`). The key-value RDD is a powerful construct that can reduce coding while providing the functionality needed to group paired values into aggregated buckets. The `groupByKey()` and `reduceByKey()` functions mimic the same aggregation functionality, while `reduceByKey()` is more efficient due to less shuffling of the data while final results are being assembled.

See also

Documentation for `groupByKey()` and `reduceByKey()` operations under RDD is available
at http://spark.apache.org/docs/latest/api/scala/index.html#org.apache.spark.ap
i.java.JavaRDD.

Creating DataFrames from Scala data structures

In this recipe, we explore the DataFrame API, which provides a higher level of abstraction than RDDs for working with data. The API is similar to R and Python data frame facilities (pandas).

DataFrame simplifies coding and lets you use standard SQL to retrieve and manipulate data. Spark keeps additional information about DataFrames, which helps the API to manipulate the frames with ease. Every DataFrame will have a schema (either inferred from data or explicitly defined) which allows us to view the frame like an SQL table. The secret sauce of SparkSQL and DataFrame is that the catalyst optimizer will work behind the scenes to optimize access by rearranging calls in the pipeline.

How to do it...

1. Start a new project in IntelliJ or in an IDE of your choice. Make sure the necessary JAR files are included.

2. Set up the package location where the program will reside:

   ```
   package spark.ml.cookbook.chapter3
   ```

3. Set up the imports related to DataFrames and the required data structures and create the RDDs as needed for the example:

   ```
   import org.apache.spark.sql._
   ```

4. Import the packages for setting up the logging level for log4j. This step is optional, but we highly recommend it (change the level appropriately as you move through the development cycle).

   ```
   import org.apache.log4j.Logger
   import org.apache.log4j.Level
   ```

5. Set up the logging level to warning and error to cut down on output. See the previous step for package requirement.

   ```
   Logger.getLogger("org").setLevel(Level.ERROR)
   Logger.getLogger("akka").setLevel(Level.ERROR)
   ```

6. Set up the Spark context and application parameter so Spark can run.

```
val spark = SparkSession
  .builder
  .master("local[*]")
  .appName("myDataFrame")
  .config("Spark.sql.warehouse.dir", ".")
  .getOrCreate()
```

7. We set up the Scala data structures as two `List()` objects and a sequence (that is, `Seq()`). We then proceed to turn the `List` structures into RDDs for conversion to `DataFrames` for the next steps:

```
val signaltypeRDD =
spark.sparkContext.parallelize(List(("Buy",1000),("Sell",500),("Buy
",600),("Sell",800)))
val numList = List(1,2,3,4,5,6,7,8,9)
val numRDD = spark.sparkContext.parallelize(numList)
val myseq = Seq(
("Sammy","North",113,46.0),("Sumi","South",110,41.0),
("Sunny","East",111,51.0),("Safron","West",113,2.0 ))
```

8. We take a list which is turned into an RDD using the `parallelize()` method and use the `toDF()` method of the RDD to turn it into a DataFrame. The `show()` method allows us to view the DataFrame, which is similar to a SQL table.

```
val numDF = numRDD.toDF("mylist")
numDF.show
```

On running the previous code, you will get the following output.:

```
+------+
|mylist|
+------+
|     1|
|     2|
|     3|
|     4|
|     5|
|     6|
|     7|
|     8|
|     9|
+------+
```

9. In the following code snippet, we take a generic Scala **Seq** (**Sequence**) data structure and use `createDataFrame()` explicitly to create a DataFrame while naming the columns at the same time.

```
val df1 =
spark.createDataFrame(myseq).toDF("Name","Region","dept","Hours")
```

10. In the next two steps, we use the `show()` method to see the contents and then proceed to use `printscheme()` to show the inferred scheme based on types. In this example, the DataFrame correctly identified the integer and double in the Seq as the valid type for the two columns of numbers.

```
df1.show()
df1.printSchema()
```

On running the previous code, you will get the following output:

```
+-------+-------+----+------+
|   Name|Region|dept|Hours |
+-------+-------+----+------+
|  Sammy|  North| 113|  46.0|
|   Sumi|  South| 110|  41.0|
|  Sunny|   East| 111|  51.0|
| Safron|   West| 113|   2.0|
+-------+-------+----+------+

root
 |-- Name: string (nullable = true)
 |-- Region: string (nullable = true)
 |-- dept: integer (nullable = false)
 |-- Hours: double (nullable = false)
```

How it works...

In this recipe, we took two lists and a Seq data structure and converted them to DataFrame and used `df1.show()` and `df1.printSchema()` to display contents and schema for the table.

DataFrames can be created from both internal and external sources. Just like SQL tables, the DataFrames have schemas associated with them that can either be inferred or explicitly defined using Scala case classes or the `map()` function to explicitly convert while ingesting the data.

There's more...

To ensure completeness, we include the `import` statement that we used prior to Spark 2.0.0 to run the code (namely, Spark 1.5.2):

```
import org.apache.spark._
import org.apache.spark.rdd.RDD
import org.apache.spark.sql.SQLContext
import org.apache.spark.mllib.linalg
import org.apache.spark.util
import Array._
import org.apache.spark.sql._
import org.apache.spark.sql.types
import org.apache.spark.sql.DataFrame
import org.apache.spark.sql.Row;
import org.apache.spark.sql.types.{ StructType, StructField, StringType};
```

See also

Documentation for DataFrame is available at `https://spark.apache.org/docs/latest/sql-programming-guide.html`.

If you see any issues with implicit conversion, double check to make sure you have included the implicit import statement.

Example code for Spark 2.0:

```
import sqlContext.implicits
```

Operating on DataFrames programmatically without SQL

In this recipe, we explore how to manipulate DataFrame with code and method calls only (without SQL). The DataFrames have their own methods that allow you to perform SQL-like operations using a programmatic approach. We demonstrate some of these commands such as `select()`, `show()`, and `explain()` to get the point across that the DataFrame itself is capable of wrangling and manipulating the data without using SQL.

How to do it...

1. Start a new project in IntelliJ or in an IDE of your choice. Make sure the necessary JAR files are included.

2. Set up the package location where the program will reside

   ```
   package spark.ml.cookbook.chapter3
   ```

3. Set up the imports related to DataFrames and the required data structures and create the RDDs as needed for the example

   ```
   import org.apache.spark.sql._
   ```

4. Import the packages for setting up logging level for `log4j`. This step is optional, but we highly recommend it (change the level appropriately as you move through the development cycle).

   ```
   import org.apache.log4j.Logger
   import org.apache.log4j.Level
   ```

5. Set up the logging level to warning and error to cut down on output. See the previous step for package requirement.

   ```
   Logger.getLogger("org").setLevel(Level.ERROR)
   Logger.getLogger("akka").setLevel(Level.ERROR)
   ```

6. Set up the Spark context and application parameter so Spark can run.

   ```
   val spark = SparkSession
     .builder
     .master("local[*]")
     .appName("myDataFrame")
     .config("Spark.sql.warehouse.dir", ".")
     .getOrCreate()
   ```

7. We are creating an RDD from an external source, which is a comma-separated text file:

   ```
   val customersRDD =
   spark.sparkContext.textFile("../data/sparkml2/chapter3/customers13.
   txt") //Customer file
   ```

8. Here is a quick look at what the customer data file would look like

```
Customer data file
1101,susan,nyc,23
1204,adam,chicago,76
1123,joe,london,65
1109,tiffany,chicago,20
```

9. After creating the RDD for the corresponding customer data file, we proceed to explicitly parse and convert the data types using a map() function from the RDD. In this example, we want to make sure the last field (that is, age) is represented as an integer.

```
val custRDD = customersRDD.map {
  line => val cols = line.trim.split(",")
    (cols(0).toInt, cols(1), cols(2), cols(3).toInt)
}
```

10. In the third step, we convert the RDD to a DataFrame using a toDF() call.

```
val custDF = custRDD.toDF("custid","name","city","age")
```

11. Once we have the DataFrame ready, we want to display the contents quickly for visual verification and also print and verify the schema.

```
custDF.show()
custDF.printSchema()
```

On running the previous code, you will get the following output:

```
+------+-------+-------+---+
|custid|   name|   city|age|
+------+-------+-------+---+
|  1101|  susan|    nyc| 23|
|  1204|   adam|chicago| 76|
|  1123|    joe| london| 65|
|  1109|tiffany|chicago| 20|
+------+-------+-------+---+
root
|-- custid: integer (nullable = false)
|-- name: string (nullable = true)
|-- city: string (nullable = true)
|-- age: integer (nullable = false)
```

12. Having the DataFrame ready and inspected, we proceed to demonstrate DataFrame access and manipulation via `show()`, `select()`, `sort()`, `groupBy()`, and `explain()` APIs.

13. We use the `filter()` method to list customers that are more than 25 years old:

    ```
    custDF.filter("age > 25.0").show()
    ```

    On running the previous code, you will get the following output:

    ```
    +-------+----+-------+---+
    |custid|name|   city|age|
    +-------+----+-------+---+
    |  1204|adam|chicago| 76|
    |  1123| joe| london| 65|
    +-------+----+-------+---+
    ```

14. We use the `select()` method to display the names of customers.

```
custDF.select("name").show()
```

On running the previous code, you will get the following output.

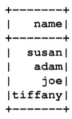

```
+-------+
|   name|
+-------+
|  susan|
|   adam|
|    joe|
|tiffany|
+-------+
```

15. We use `select()` to list multiple columns:

    ```
    custDF.select("name","city").show()
    ```

    On running the previous code, you will get the following output:

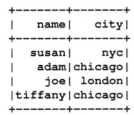

```
+-------+-------+
|   name|   city|
+-------+-------+
|  susan|    nyc|
|   adam|chicago|
|    joe| london|
|tiffany|chicago|
+-------+-------+
```

16. We use an alternative syntax to display and refer to fields within the DataFrame:

```
custDF.select(custDF("name"),custDF("city"),custDF("age")).show()
```

On running the previous code, you will get the following output:

```
+-------+-------+---+
|   name|   city|age|
+-------+-------+---+
|  susan|    nyc| 23|
|   adam|chicago| 76|
|    joe| london| 65|
|tiffany|chicago| 20|
+-------+-------+---+
```

17. Using `select()` and a predicate, to list customers' name and city where the age is less than 50:

```
custDF.select(custDF("name"),custDF("city"),custDF("age")
<50).show()
```

On running the previous code, you will get the following output:

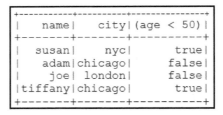

```
+-------+-------+----------+
|   name|   city|(age < 50)|
+-------+-------+----------+
|  susan|    nyc|      true|
|   adam|chicago|     false|
|    joe| london|     false|
|tiffany|chicago|      true|
+-------+-------+----------+
```

18. We use `sort()` and `groupBy()` to sort and group customers by their city of residence:

```
custDF.sort("city").groupBy("city").count().show()
```

On running the previous code, you will get the following output.

```
+-------+-----+
|   city|count|
+-------+-----+
|chicago|    2|
| london|    1|
|    nyc|    1|
+-------+-----+
```

19. We can also ask for a plan of execution: this command will be more relevant with upcoming recipes in which we use SQL to access and manipulate the DataFrame.

```
custDF.explain()
```

On running the previous code, you will get the following output:

```
== Physical Plan ==
TungstenProject [_1#10 AS custid#14,_2#11 AS name#15,_3#12 AS
city#16,_4#13 AS age#17]
  Scan PhysicalRDD[_1#10,_2#11,_3#12,_4#13]
```

How it works...

In this example, we loaded data from a text file into an RDD and then converted it to a DataFrame structure using the `.toDF()` API. We then proceeded to mimic SQL queries using built-in methods such as `select()`, `filter()`, `show()`, and `explain()` that help us to programmatically explore the data (no SQL). The `explain()` command shows the query plan which can be awfully useful to remove the bottleneck.

DataFrames provide multiple approaches to data wrangling.

For those comfortable with the DataFrame API and packages from R (https://cran.r-project.org) like dplyr or an older version, we have a programmatic API with an extensive set of methods that lets you do all your data wrangling via the API.

For those more comfortable with SQL, you can simply use SQL to retrieve and manipulate data as if you were using Squirrel or Toad to query the database.

There's more...

To ensure completeness, we include the `import` statements that we used prior to Spark 2.0.0 to run the code (namely, Spark 1.5.2):

```
import org.apache.spark._

import org.apache.spark.rdd.RDD
import org.apache.spark.sql.SQLContext
import org.apache.spark.mllib.linalg._
import org.apache.spark.util._
import Array._
import org.apache.spark.sql._
import org.apache.spark.sql.types._
```

```
import org.apache.spark.sql.DataFrame
import org.apache.spark.sql.Row;
import org.apache.spark.sql.types.{ StructType, StructField, StringType};
```

See also

Documentation for DataFrame is available
at `https://spark.apache.org/docs/latest/sql-programming-guide.html`.

If you see any issues with implicit conversion, double check to make sure you have
included the implicits `import` statement.

Example `import` statement for Spark 2.0:

```
import sqlContext.implicits._
```

Loading DataFrames and setup from an external source

In this recipe, we examine data manipulation using SQL. Spark's approach to provide, both
a pragmatic and SQL interface works very well in production settings in which we not only
require machine learning, but also access to existing data sources using SQL to ensure
compatibility and familiarity with existing SQL-based systems. DataFrame with SQL makes
for an elegant process toward integration in real-life settings.

How to do it...

1. Start a new project in IntelliJ or in an IDE of your choice. Make sure the necessary
   JAR files are included.

2. Set up the package location where the program will reside:

   ```
   package spark.ml.cookbook.chapter3
   ```

3. Set up the imports related to DataFrame and the required data structures and
   create the RDDs as needed for the example:

   ```
   import org.apache.spark.sql._
   ```

4. Import the packages for setting up the logging level for log4j. This step is optional, but we highly recommend it (change the level appropriately as you move through the development cycle).

```
import org.apache.log4j.Logger
import org.apache.log4j.Level
```

5. Set up the logging level to warning and Error to cut down on output. See the previous step for package requirement:

```
Logger.getLogger("org").setLevel(Level.ERROR)
Logger.getLogger("akka").setLevel(Level.ERROR)
```

6. Set up the Spark context and application parameter so Spark can run.

```
val spark = SparkSession
 .builder
 .master("local[*]")
 .appName("myDataFrame")
 .config("Spark.sql.warehouse.dir", ".")
 .getOrCreate()
```

7. We create the DataFrame corresponding to the customer file. In this step, we first create an RDD and then proceed to use the toDF() to convert the RDD to DataFrame and name the columns.

```
val customersRDD =
spark.sparkContext.textFile("../data/sparkml2/chapter3/customers13.
txt") //Customer file


val custRDD = customersRDD.map {
    line => val cols = line.trim.split(",")
        (cols(0).toInt, cols(1), cols(2), cols(3).toInt)
}
val custDF = custRDD.toDF("custid","name","city","age")
```

Customer data contents for reference:

```
custDF.show()
```

On running the preceding code, you will get the following output:

```
+-------+-------+-------+---+
|custid|   name|   city|age|
+-------+-------+-------+---+
|  1101|  susan|    nyc| 23|
|  1204|   adam|chicago| 76|
|  1123|    joe| london| 65|
|  1109|tiffany|chicago| 20|
+-------+-------+-------+---+
```

8. We create the DataFrame corresponding to the product file. In this step, we first create an RDD and then proceed to use the `toDF()` to convert the RDD to DataFrame and name the columns.

```
val productsRDD =
spark.sparkContext.textFile("../data/sparkml2/chapter3/products13.t
xt") //Product file
 val prodRDD = productsRDD.map {
     line => val cols = line.trim.split(",")
         (cols(0).toInt, cols(1), cols(2), cols(3).toDouble)
 }
```

9. We convert `prodRDD` to DataFrame:

```
val prodDF =
prodRDD.toDF("prodid","category","dept","priceAdvertised")
```

10. Using SQL select, we display the contents of the table.

Product data contents:

```
prodDF.show()
```

On running the previous code, you will get the following output:

```
+-------+--------+----+---------------+
|prodid|category|dept|priceAdvertised|
+-------+--------+----+---------------+
|    11|    home|   2|          23.55|
|    12|  garden|   5|           11.3|
|    23|    home|   6|          67.34|
|    89|  garden|   2|           3.05|
|   101|ligthing|   3|          21.21|
|    11|    home|   6|           21.0|
|    12|  garden|   5|           66.9|
+-------+--------+----+---------------+
```

11. We create the DataFrame corresponding to the `sales` file. In this step we first create an RDD and then proceed to use `toDF()` to convert the RDD to DataFrame and name the columns.

```
val salesRDD =
spark.sparkContext.textFile("../data/sparkml2/chapter3/sales13.txt"
) //Sales file
val saleRDD = salesRDD.map {
    line => val cols = line.trim.split(",")
        (cols(0).toInt, cols(1).toInt, cols(2).toDouble)
}
```

12. We convert the `saleRDD` to DataFrame:

```
val saleDF = saleRDD.toDF("prodid", "custid", "priceSold")
```

13. We use SQL select to display the table.

Sales data contents:

```
saleDF.show()
```

On running the previous code, you will get the following output:

```
+------+------+---------+
|prodid|custid|priceSold|
+------+------+---------+
|    11|  1204|    15.56|
|    12|  1204|     55.0|
|   101|  1109|    21.21|
|    11|  1109|     21.0|
|    89|  1123|     3.05|
|    89|  1204|      3.0|
|    23|  1101|    67.34|
|    23|  1101|    66.34|
+------+------+---------+
```

14. We print schemas for the customer, product, and sales DataFrames to verify schema after column definition and type conversion:

```
custDF.printSchema()
productDF.printSchema()
salesDF. printSchema()
```

On running the previous code, you will get the following output:

```
root
 |-- custid: integer (nullable = false)
 |-- name: string (nullable = true)
 |-- city: string (nullable = true)
 |-- age: integer (nullable = false)
root
 |-- prodid: integer (nullable = false)
 |-- category: string (nullable = true)
 |-- dept: string (nullable = true)
 |-- priceAdvertised: double (nullable = false)
root
 |-- prodid: integer (nullable = false)
 |-- custid: integer (nullable = false)
 |-- priceSold: double (nullable = false)
```

How it works...

In this example, we first loaded data into an RDD and then converted it into a DataFrame using the `toDF()` method. The DataFrame is very good at inferring types, but there are occasions that require manual intervention. We used the `map()` function after creating the RDD (lazy initialization paradigm applies) to massage the data either by type conversion or calling on more complicated user-defined functions (referenced in the `map()` method) to do the conversion or data wrangling. Finally, we proceeded to examine the schema for each of the three DataFrames using `show()` and `printSchema()`.

There's more...

To ensure completeness, we include the `import` statements that we used prior to Spark 2.0.0 to run the code (namely, Spark 1.5.2):

```
import org.apache.spark._
import org.apache.spark.rdd.RDD
import org.apache.spark.sql.SQLContext
import org.apache.spark.mllib.linalg._
import org.apache.spark.util._
import Array._
import org.apache.spark.sql._
import org.apache.spark.sql.types._
import org.apache.spark.sql.DataFrame
import org.apache.spark.sql.Row;
import org.apache.spark.sql.types.{ StructType, StructField, StringType};
```

See also

Documentation for DataFrame is available
at https://spark.apache.org/docs/latest/sql-programming-guide.html.

If you see any issues with implicit conversion, double check to make sure you have
included the implicits import statement.

Example import statement for Spark 1.5.2:

```
import sqlContext.implicits._
```

Using DataFrames with standard SQL language - SparkSQL

In this recipe, we demonstrate how to use DataFrame SQL capabilities to perform basic
CRUD operations, but there is nothing limiting you from using the SQL interface provided
by Spark to any level of sophistication (that is, DML) desired.

How to do it...

1. Start a new project in IntelliJ or in an IDE of your choice. Make sure the necessary
   JAR files are included.

2. Set up the package location where the program will reside

   ```
   package spark.ml.cookbook.chapter3
   ```

3. Set up the imports related to DataFrames and the required data structures and
   create the RDDs as needed for the example

   ```
   import org.apache.spark.sql._
   ```

4. Import the packages for setting up the logging level for log4j. This step is
   optional, but we highly recommend it (change the level appropriately as you
   move through the development cycle).

   ```
   import org.apache.log4j.Logger
   import org.apache.log4j.Level
   ```

5. Set up the logging level to warning and ERROR to cut down on output. See the previous step for package requirement.

```
Logger.getLogger("org").setLevel(Level.ERROR)
Logger.getLogger("akka").setLevel(Level.ERROR)
```

6. Set up the Spark context and application parameter so Spark can run.

```
val spark = SparkSession
.builder
.master("local[*]")
.appName("myDataFrame")
.config("Spark.sql.warehouse.dir", ".")
.getOrCreate()
```

7. We will be using the DataFrames created in the previous recipe to demonstrate the SQL capabilities of DataFrames. You can refer to the previous steps for details.

```
a. customerDF with columns: "custid","name","city","age"
b. productDF with Columns:
"prodid","category","dept","priceAdvertised"
c. saleDF with columns:    "prodid", "custid", "priceSold"

val customersRDD =
spark.sparkContext.textFile("../data/sparkml2/chapter3/customers13.
txt") //Customer file

val custRDD = customersRDD.map {
    line => val cols = line.trim.split(",")
      (cols(0).toInt, cols(1), cols(2), cols(3).toInt)
}
val custDF = custRDD.toDF("custid","name","city","age")
val productsRDD =
spark.sparkContext.textFile("../data/sparkml2/chapter3/products13.t
xt") //Product file

val prodRDD = productsRDD.map {
    line => val cols = line.trim.split(",")
      (cols(0).toInt, cols(1), cols(2), cols(3).toDouble)        }

val prodDF =
prodRDD.toDF("prodid","category","dept","priceAdvertised")

val salesRDD =
spark.sparkContext.textFile("../data/sparkml2/chapter3/sales13.txt"
) //Sales file
val saleRDD = salesRDD.map {
```

```
        line => val cols = line.trim.split(",")
            (cols(0).toInt, cols(1).toInt, cols(2).toDouble)
        }
    val saleDF = saleRDD.toDF("prodid", "custid", "priceSold")
```

8. Before we can use the DataFrame for queries via SQL, we have to register the DataFrame as a temp table so the SQL statements can refer to it without any Scala/Spark syntax. This step may cause confusion for many beginners as we are not creating any table (temp or permanent), but the call registerTempTable() (pre-Spark 2.0) and createOrReplaceTempView() (Spark 2.0+) creates a name in SQL land that the SQL statements can refer to without additional UDF or any domain-specific query language. In short, there is additional metadata that is kept by Spark in the background (registerTempTable() call), which facilitates querying in the execution phase.

9. Create the CustDf DataFrame as a name which SQL statements recognize as customers:

```
    custDF.createOrReplaceTempView("customers")
```

10. Create the prodDf DataFrame as a name which SQL statements recognize as product:

```
    prodDF.createOrReplaceTempView("products")
```

11. Create the saleDf DataFrame as a name which SQL statements recognize as sales:

```
    saleDF.createOrReplaceTempView("sales")
```

12. Now that everything is ready, let's demonstrate the power of DataFrames with standard SQL. For those who prefer not to work with SQL, the programmatic way is always at your fingertips.

13. In this example, we see how to select a column from the customers' table (it is not a SQL table underneath, but you can certainly abstract it as such).

```
    val query1DF = spark.sql ("select custid, name from customers")
    query1DF.show()
```

On running the previous code, you will get the following output.

```
+------+-------+
|custid|   name|
+------+-------+
|  1101|  susan|
|  1204|   adam|
|  1123|    joe|
|  1109|tiffany|
+------+-------+
```

14. Select multiple columns from the customer table:

```
val query2DF = spark.sql("select prodid, priceAdvertised from
products")
 query2DF.show()
```

On running the previous code, you will get the following output.

```
+------+---------------+
|prodid|priceAdvertised|
+------+---------------+
|    11|          23.55|
|    12|           11.3|
|    23|          67.34|
|    89|           3.05|
|   101|          21.21|
|    11|           21.0|
|    12|           66.9|
+------+---------------+
```

15. We print the schema for customer, product, and sales DataFrames to verify it after column definition and type conversion:

```
val query3DF = spark.sql("select sum(priceSold) as totalSold from
sales")
 query3DF.show()
```

On running the previous code, you will get the following output.

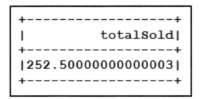

```
+------------------+
|         totalSold|
+------------------+
|252.50000000000003|
+------------------+
```

16. In this example, we join the sales and product tables and list all the customers that have purchased a product at more than 20% discount. This SQL joins the sales and product tables and then uses a simple formula to find products that are sold at a deep discount. To reiterate, the key aspect of DataFrame is that we use standard SQL without any special syntax.

```
val query4DF = spark.sql("select custid, priceSold, priceAdvertised
from sales s, products p where (s.priceSold/p.priceAdvertised <
.80) and p.prodid = s.prodid")
query4DF.show()
```

On running the previous code, you will get the following output.

```
|custid|priceSold|priceAdvertised|
+------+---------+---------------+
|  1204|    15.56|          23.55|
|  1204|    15.56|          21.0|
+------+---------+---------------+
```

We can always use the `explain()` method to examine the physical query plan that Spark SQL used to execute the query.

```
query4DF.explain()
```

On running the previous code, you will get the following output:

```
== Physical Plan ==
TungstenProject [custid#30,priceSold#31,priceAdvertised#25]
 Filter ((priceSold#31 / priceAdvertised#25) < 0.8)
 SortMergeJoin [prodid#29], [prodid#22]
 TungstenSort [prodid#29 ASC], false, 0
 TungstenExchange hashpartitioning(prodid#29)
 TungstenProject [_1#26 AS prodid#29,_2#27 AS custid#30,_3#28 AS
priceSold#31]
 Scan PhysicalRDD[_1#26,_2#27,_3#28]
 TungstenSort [prodid#22 ASC], false, 0
 TungstenExchange hashpartitioning(prodid#22)
 TungstenProject [_4#21 AS priceAdvertised#25,_1#18 AS prodid#22]
 Scan PhysicalRDD[_1#18,_2#19,_3#20,_4#21]
```

How it works...

The basic workflow for DataFrame using SQL is to first populate the DataFrame either through internal Scala data structures or via external data sources first, and then use the `createOrReplaceTempView()` call to register the DataFrame as a SQL-like artifact.

When you use DataFrames, you have the benefit of additional metadata that Spark stores (whether API or SQL approach) which can benefit you during the coding and execution.

While RDDs are still the workhorses of core Spark, the trend is toward the DataFrame approach which has successfully shown its capabilities in languages such as Python/Pandas or R.

There's more...

There has been a change for registration of a DataFrame as a table. Refer to this:

- For versions prior to Spark 2.0.0: `registerTempTable()`
- For Spark version 2.0.0 and previous: `createOrReplaceTempView()`

Pre-Spark 2.0.0 to register a DataFrame as a SQL table like artifact:

Before we can use the DataFrame for queries via SQL, we have to register the DataFrame as a temp table so the SQL statements can refer to it without any Scala/Spark syntax. This step may cause confusion for many beginners as we are not creating any table (temp or permanent), but the call `registerTempTable()` creates a name in SQL land that the SQL statements can refer to without additional UDF or without any domain-specific query language.

- Register the `CustDf` DataFrame as a name which SQL statements recognize as `customers`:

    ```
    custDF.registerTempTable("customers")
    ```

- Register the `prodDf` DataFrame as a name which SQL statements recognize as `product`:

    ```
    custDF.registerTempTable("customers")
    ```

- Register the `saleDf` DataFrame as a name which SQL statements recognize as `sales`:

```
custDF.registerTempTable("customers")
```

To ensure completeness, we include the `import` statements that we used prior to Spark 2.0.0 to run the code (namely, Spark 1.5.2):

```
import org.apache.spark._

import org.apache.spark.rdd.RDD
import org.apache.spark.sql.SQLContext
import org.apache.spark.mllib.linalg._
import org.apache.spark.util._
import Array._
import org.apache.spark.sql._
import org.apache.spark.sql.types._
import org.apache.spark.sql.DataFrame
import org.apache.spark.sql.Row;
import org.apache.spark.sql.types.{ StructType, StructField, StringType};
```

See also

Documentation for DataFrame is available at https://spark.apache.org/docs/latest/sql-programming-guide.html.

If you see any issues with implicit conversion, please double check to make sure you have included implicits `import` statement.

Example `import` statement for Spark 1.5.2

```
import sqlContext.implicits._
```

DataFrame is an extensive subsystem and deserves an entire book on its own. It makes complex data manipulation at scale available to SQL programmers.

Working with the Dataset API using a Scala Sequence

In this recipe, we examine the new Dataset and how it works with the *seq* Scala data structure. We often see a relationship between the LabelPoint data structure used with ML libraries and a Scala sequence (that is, seq data structure) that play nicely with dataset.

The Dataset is being positioned as a unifying API going forward. It is important to note that DataFrame is still available as an alias described as `Dataset[Row]`. We have covered the SQL examples extensively via DataFrame recipes, so we concentrate our efforts on other variations for dataset.

How to do it...

1. Start a new project in IntelliJ or in an IDE of your choice. Make sure the necessary JAR files are included.

2. Set up the package location where the program will reside

   ```
   package spark.ml.cookbook.chapter3
   ```

3. Import the necessary packages for a Spark session to get access to the cluster and `Log4j.Logger` to reduce the amount of output produced by Spark.

   ```
   import org.apache.log4j.{Level, Logger}
   import org.apache.spark.sql.SparkSession
   ```

4. Define a Scala `case class` to model data for processing, and the `Car` class will represent electric and hybrid cars.

   ```
   case class Car(make: String, model: String, price: Double,
   style: String, kind: String)
   ```

5. Let's create a Scala sequence and populate it with electric and hybrid cars.

   ```
   val carData =
   Seq(
   Car("Tesla", "Model S", 71000.0, "sedan","electric"),
   Car("Audi", "A3 E-Tron", 37900.0, "luxury","hybrid"),
   Car("BMW", "330e", 43700.0, "sedan","hybrid"),
   Car("BMW", "i3", 43300.0, "sedan","electric"),
   Car("BMW", "i8", 137000.0, "coupe","hybrid"),
   Car("BMW", "X5 xdrive40e", 64000.0, "suv","hybrid"),
   ```

```
Car("Chevy", "Spark EV", 26000.0, "coupe","electric"),
Car("Chevy", "Volt", 34000.0, "sedan","electric"),
Car("Fiat", "500e", 32600.0, "coupe","electric"),
Car("Ford", "C-Max Energi", 32600.0, "wagon/van","hybrid"),
Car("Ford", "Focus Electric", 29200.0, "sedan","electric"),
Car("Ford", "Fusion Energi", 33900.0, "sedan","electric"),
Car("Hyundai", "Sonata", 35400.0, "sedan","hybrid"),
Car("Kia", "Soul EV", 34500.0, "sedan","electric"),
Car("Mercedes", "B-Class", 42400.0, "sedan","electric"),
Car("Mercedes", "C350", 46400.0, "sedan","hybrid"),
Car("Mercedes", "GLE500e", 67000.0, "suv","hybrid"),
Car("Mitsubishi", "i-MiEV", 23800.0, "sedan","electric"),
Car("Nissan", "LEAF", 29000.0, "sedan","electric"),
Car("Porsche", "Cayenne", 78000.0, "suv","hybrid"),
Car("Porsche", "Panamera S", 93000.0, "sedan","hybrid"),
Car("Tesla", "Model X", 80000.0, "suv","electric"),
Car("Tesla", "Model 3", 35000.0, "sedan","electric"),
Car("Volvo", "XC90 T8", 69000.0, "suv","hybrid"),
Car("Cadillac", "ELR", 76000.0, "coupe","hybrid")
)
```

6. Configure output level to ERROR to reduce Spark's logging output.

```
Logger.getLogger("org").setLevel(Level.ERROR)
Logger.getLogger("akka").setLevel(Level.ERROR)
```

7. Create a SparkSession yielding access to the Spark cluster, including the underlying session object attributes and functions.

```
val spark = SparkSession
.builder
.master("local[*]")
.appName("mydatasetseq")
.config("Spark.sql.warehouse.dir", ".")
.getOrCreate()
```

8. Import Spark implicits, therefore adding in behavior with only an import.

```
import spark.implicits._
```

9. Next, we will create a Dataset from the car data sequence utilizing the Spark session's createDataset() method.

```
val cars = spark.createDataset(MyDatasetData.carData)
// carData is put in a separate scala object MyDatasetData
```

10. Let's print out the results as confirmation that our method invocation transformed the sequence into a Spark Dataset by invoking the show method.

```
infecars.show(false)
+----------+--------------+--------+---------+--------+
|make      |model         |price   |style    |kind    |

+----------+--------------+--------+---------+--------+
|Tesla     |Model S       |71000.0 |sedan    |electric|
|Audi      |A3 E-Tron     |37900.0 |luxury   |hybrid  |
|BMW       |330e          |43700.0 |sedan    |hybrid  |
|BMW       |i3            |43300.0 |sedan    |electric|
|BMW       |i8            |137000.0|coupe    |hybrid  |
|BMW       |X5 xdrive40e  |64000.0 |suv      |hybrid  |
|Chevy     |Spark EV      |26000.0 |coupe    |electric|
|Chevy     |Volt          |34000.0 |sedan    |electric|
|Fiat      |500e          |32600.0 |coupe    |electric|
|Ford      |C-Max Energi  |32600.0 |wagon/van|hybrid  |
|Ford      |Focus Electric|29200.0 |sedan    |electric|
|Ford      |Fusion Energi |33900.0 |sedan    |electric|
|Hyundai   |Sonata        |35400.0 |sedan    |hybrid  |
|Kia       |Soul EV       |34500.0 |sedan    |electric|
|Mercedes  |B-Class       |42400.0 |sedan    |electric|
|Mercedes  |C350          |46400.0 |sedan    |hybrid  |
|Mercedes  |GLE500e       |67000.0 |suv      |hybrid  |
|Mitsubishi|i-MiEV        |23800.0 |sedan    |electric|
|Nissan    |LEAF          |29000.0 |sedan    |electric|
|Porsche   |Cayenne       |78000.0 |suv      |hybrid  |
+----------+--------------+--------+---------+--------+
only showing top 20 rows
```

11. Print out the Dataset's implied column names. We can now use class attribute names as column names.

```
cars.columns.foreach(println)
make
model
price
style
kind
```

12. Let's show the automatically generated schema, and validate inferred data types.

```
println(cars.schema)
StructType(StructField(make,StringType,true),
StructField(model,StringType,true),
StructField(price,DoubleType,false),
StructField(style,StringType,true),
StructField(kind,StringType,true))
```

13. Finally, we will filter the Dataset on price referring to the `Car` class attribute price as a column and show results.

```
cars.filter(cars("price") > 50000.00).show()
```

```
+--------+------------+--------+-----+--------+
|    make|       model|   price|style|    kind|
+--------+------------+--------+-----+--------+
|   Tesla|     Model S| 71000.0|sedan|electric|
|     BMW|          i8|137000.0|coupe|  hybrid|
|     BMW|X5 xdrive40e| 64000.0|  suv|  hybrid|
|Mercedes|     GLE500e| 67000.0|  suv|  hybrid|
| Porsche|     Cayenne| 78000.0|  suv|  hybrid|
| Porsche|  Panamera S| 93000.0|sedan|  hybrid|
|   Tesla|     Model X| 80000.0|  suv|electric|
|   Volvo|     XC90 T8| 69000.0|  suv|  hybrid|
|Cadillac|         ELR| 76000.0|coupe|  hybrid|
+--------+------------+--------+-----+--------+
```

14. We close the program by stopping the Spark session.

```
spark.stop()
```

How it works...

In this recipe, we introduced Spark's Dataset feature which first appeared in Spark 1.6 and which was further refined in subsequent releases. First, we created an instance of a Dataset from a Scala sequence with the help of the `createDataset()` method belonging to the Spark session. The next step was to print out meta information about the generated Datatset to establish that the creation transpired as expected. Finally, snippets of Spark SQL were used to filter the Dataset by the price column for any price greater than $50, 000.00 and show the final results of execution.

There's more...

Dataset has a view called `DataFrame`, which is a Dataset of `rows` which is untyped. The Dataset still retains all the transformation abilities of RDD such as `filter()`, `map()`, `flatMap()`, and so on. This is one of the reasons we find Datasets easy to use if we have programmed in Spark using RDDs.

See also

- Documentation for Dataset can be found at `http://spark.apache.org/docs/latest/api/scala/index.html#org.apache.spark.sql.Dataset`.
- KeyValue grouped dataset can be found at `http://spark.apache.org/docs/latest/api/scala/index.html#org.apache.spark.sql.KeyValueGroupedDataset`
- Relational grouped dataset can be found at `http://spark.apache.org/docs/latest/api/scala/index.html#org.apache.spark.sql.RelationalGroupedDataset`

Creating and using Datasets from RDDs and back again

In this recipe, we explore how to use RDD and interact with Dataset to build a multi-stage machine learning pipeline. Even though the Dataset (conceptually thought of as RDD with strong type-safety) is the way forward, you still have to be able to interact with other machine learning algorithms or codes that return/operate on RDD for either legacy or coding reasons. In this recipe, we also explore how to create and convert from Dataset to RDD and back.

How to do it...

1. Start a new project in IntelliJ or in an IDE of your choice. Make sure the necessary JAR files are included.

2. Set up the package location where the program will reside:

   ```
   package spark.ml.cookbook.chapter3
   ```

3. Import the necessary packages for Spark session to get access to the cluster and `Log4j.Logger` to reduce the amount of output produced by Spark.

   ```
   import org.apache.log4j.{Level, Logger}
   import org.apache.spark.sql.SparkSession
   ```

4. Define a Scala case class to model data for processing.

```scala
case class Car(make: String, model: String, price: Double,
style: String, kind: String)
```

5. Let's create a Scala sequence and populate it with electric and hybrid cars.

```scala
val carData =
Seq(
Car("Tesla", "Model S", 71000.0, "sedan","electric"),
Car("Audi", "A3 E-Tron", 37900.0, "luxury","hybrid"),
Car("BMW", "330e", 43700.0, "sedan","hybrid"),
Car("BMW", "i3", 43300.0, "sedan","electric"),
Car("BMW", "i8", 137000.0, "coupe","hybrid"),
Car("BMW", "X5 xdrive40e", 64000.0, "suv","hybrid"),
Car("Chevy", "Spark EV", 26000.0, "coupe","electric"),
Car("Chevy", "Volt", 34000.0, "sedan","electric"),
Car("Fiat", "500e", 32600.0, "coupe","electric"),
Car("Ford", "C-Max Energi", 32600.0, "wagon/van","hybrid"),
Car("Ford", "Focus Electric", 29200.0, "sedan","electric"),
Car("Ford", "Fusion Energi", 33900.0, "sedan","electric"),
Car("Hyundai", "Sonata", 35400.0, "sedan","hybrid"),
Car("Kia", "Soul EV", 34500.0, "sedan","electric"),
Car("Mercedes", "B-Class", 42400.0, "sedan","electric"),
Car("Mercedes", "C350", 46400.0, "sedan","hybrid"),
Car("Mercedes", "GLE500e", 67000.0, "suv","hybrid"),
Car("Mitsubishi", "i-MiEV", 23800.0, "sedan","electric"),
Car("Nissan", "LEAF", 29000.0, "sedan","electric"),
Car("Porsche", "Cayenne", 78000.0, "suv","hybrid"),
Car("Porsche", "Panamera S", 93000.0, "sedan","hybrid"),
Car("Tesla", "Model X", 80000.0, "suv","electric"),
Car("Tesla", "Model 3", 35000.0, "sedan","electric"),
Car("Volvo", "XC90 T8", 69000.0, "suv","hybrid"),
Car("Cadillac", "ELR", 76000.0, "coupe","hybrid")
)
```

6. Set output level to ERROR to reduce Spark's logging output.

```scala
Logger.getLogger("org").setLevel(Level.ERROR)
Logger.getLogger("akka").setLevel(Level.ERROR)
```

7. Initialize a Spark session specifying configurations with the builder pattern, thus making an entry point available for the Spark cluster.

```
val spark = SparkSession
.builder
.master("local[*]")
.appName("mydatasetrdd")
.config("Spark.sql.warehouse.dir", ".")
.getOrCreate()
```

8. Next, we retrieve a reference to the Spark context from the Spark session, because we will need it later to generate an RDD.

```
val sc = spark.sparkContext
```

9. Import Spark implicits, therefore adding in behavior with only an import.

```
import spark.implicits._
```

10. Let's make an RDD from the car data sequence.

```
val rdd = spark.makeRDD(MyDatasetData.carData)
```

11. Next, we will create a Dataset from the RDD containing the car data by making use of Spark's session createDataset() method.

```
val cars = spark.createDataset(rdd)
```

12. Let's print out the Dataset to validate that creation happened as we would expect via the show method.

```
cars.show(false)
```

On running the previous code, you will get the following output.

```
+----------+---------------+--------+---------+--------+
|make      |model          |price   |style    |kind    |
+----------+---------------+--------+---------+--------+
|Tesla     |Model S        |71000.0 |sedan    |electric|
|Audi      |A3 E-Tron      |37900.0 |luxury   |hybrid  |
|BMW       |330e           |43700.0 |sedan    |hybrid  |
|BMW       |i3             |43300.0 |sedan    |electric|
|BMW       |i8             |137000.0|coupe    |hybrid  |
|BMW       |X5 xdrive40e   |64000.0 |suv      |hybrid  |
|Chevy     |Spark EV       |26000.0 |coupe    |electric|
|Chevy     |Volt           |34000.0 |sedan    |electric|
|Fiat      |500e           |32600.0 |coupe    |electric|
|Ford      |C-Max Energi   |32600.0 |wagon/van|hybrid  |
|Ford      |Focus Electric |29200.0 |sedan    |electric|
|Ford      |Fusion Energi  |33900.0 |sedan    |electric|
|Hyundai   |Sonata         |35400.0 |sedan    |hybrid  |
|Kia       |Soul EV        |34500.0 |sedan    |electric|
|Mercedes  |B-Class        |42400.0 |sedan    |electric|
|Mercedes  |C350           |46400.0 |sedan    |hybrid  |
|Mercedes  |GLE500e        |67000.0 |suv      |hybrid  |
|Mitsubishi|i-MiEV         |23800.0 |sedan    |electric|
|Nissan    |LEAF           |29000.0 |sedan    |electric|
|Porsche   |Cayenne        |78000.0 |suv      |hybrid  |
+----------+---------------+--------+---------+--------+
only showing top 20 rows
```

13. Next, we will print out the implied column names.

```
cars.columns.foreach(println)
make
model
price
style
kind
```

14. Let's show the automatically generated schema, and validate that the inferred data types are correct.

```
println(cars.schema)
StructType(StructField(make,StringType,true),
StructField(model,StringType,true),
StructField(price,DoubleType,false),
StructField(style,StringType,true),
StructField(kind,StringType,true))
```

15. Now, let's group the Dataset by make, and count the number of makes in our dataset.

```
cars.groupBy("make").count().show()
```

On running the previous code, you will get the following output.

```
+----------+-----+
|      make|count|
+----------+-----+
|Mitsubishi|    1|
|       Kia|    1|
|     Volvo|    1|
|   Hyundai|    1|
|      Audi|    1|
|  Cadillac|    1|
|  Mercedes|    3|
|     Tesla|    3|
|       BMW|    4|
|     Chevy|    2|
|   Porsche|    2|
|    Nissan|    1|
|      Fiat|    1|
|      Ford|    3|
+----------+-----+
```

16. The next step will use Spark's SQL on the Dataset, filtering by make for the value of Tesla, and transforming the resulting Dataset back into an RDD.

```
val carRDD = cars.where("make = 'Tesla'").rdd
Car(Tesla,Model X,80000.0,suv,electric)
Car(Tesla,Model 3,35000.0,sedan,electric)
Car(Tesla,Model S,71000.0,sedan,electric)
```

17. Finally, display the contents of the RDD, taking advantage of the `foreach()` method.

```
carRDD.foreach(println)
Car(Tesla,Model X,80000.0,suv,electric)
Car(Tesla,Model 3,35000.0,sedan,electric)
Car(Tesla,Model S,71000.0,sedan,electric)
```

18. We close the program by stopping the Spark session.

```
spark.stop()
```

How it works...

In this section, we transformed an RDD into a Dataset and finally transformed it back to an RDD. We began with a Scala sequence which was changed into an RDD. After the creation of the RDD, invocation of Spark's session `createDataset()` method occurred, passing the RDD as an argument while receiving a Dataset as the result.

Next, the Dataset was grouped by the make column, counting the existence of various makes of cars. The next step involved filtering the Dataset for makes of Tesla and transforming the results back to an RDD. Finally, we displayed the resulting RDD by way of the RDD `foreach()` method.

There's more...

The Dataset source file in Spark is only about 2500+ lines of Scala code. It is a very nice piece of code which can be leveraged for specialization under Apache license. We list the following URL and encourage you to at least scan the file and understand how buffering comes into play when using Dataset.

Source code for Datasets hosted on GitHub is available at `https://github.com/apache/spark/blob/master/sql/core/src/main/scala/org/apache/spark/sql/Dataset.scala`.

See also

- Documentation for Dataset can be found at `http://spark.apache.org/docs/latest/api/scala/index.html#org.apache.spark.sql.Dataset`
- KeyValue grouped Dataset can be found at `http://spark.apache.org/docs/latest/api/scala/index.html#org.apache.spark.sql.KeyValueGroupedDataset`
- Relational grouped Dataset can be found at `http://spark.apache.org/docs/latest/api/scala/index.html#org.apache.spark.sql.RelationalGroupedDataset`

Working with JSON using the Dataset API and SQL together

In this recipe, we explore how to use JSON with Dataset. The JSON format has rapidly become the de-facto standard for data interoperability in the last 5 years.

We explore how Dataset uses JSON and executes API commands like `select()`. We then progress by creating a view (that is, `createOrReplaceTempView()`) and then execute a SQL query to demonstrate how to query against a JSON file using API and SQL with ease.

How to do it...

1. Start a new project in IntelliJ or in an IDE of your choice. Make sure the necessary JAR files are included.

2. We will use a JSON data file named `cars.json` which has been created for this example:

   ```
   {"make": "Telsa", "model": "Model S", "price": 71000.00, "style":
   "sedan", "kind": "electric"}
   {"make": "Audi", "model": "A3 E-Tron", "price": 37900.00, "style":
   "luxury", "kind": "hybrid"}
   {"make": "BMW", "model": "330e", "price": 43700.00, "style":
   "sedan", "kind": "hybrid"}
   ```

3. Set up the package location where the program will reside

   ```
   package spark.ml.cookbook.chapter3
   ```

4. Import the necessary packages for the Spark session to gain access to the cluster and `Log4j.Logger` to reduce the amount of output produced by Spark.

   ```
   import org.apache.log4j.{Level, Logger}
   import org.apache.spark.sql.SparkSession
   ```

5. Define a Scala `case class` to model data for processing.

   ```
   case class Car(make: String, model: String, price: Double,
   style: String, kind: String)
   ```

6. Set output level to ERROR to reduce Spark's logging output.

   ```
   Logger.getLogger("org").setLevel(Level.ERROR)
   Logger.getLogger("akka").setLevel(Level.ERROR)
   ```

7. Initialize a Spark session creating an entry point for access to the Spark cluster.

   ```
   val spark = SparkSession
   .builder
   .master("local[*]")
   .appName("mydatasmydatasetjsonetrdd")
   .config("Spark.sql.warehouse.dir", ".")
   .getOrCreate()
   ```

8. Import Spark implicits, therefore adding in behavior with only an import.

```
import spark.implicits._
```

9. Now, we will load the JSON data file into memory, specifying the class type as Car.

```
val cars =
spark.read.json("../data/sparkml2/chapter3/cars.json").as[Car]
```

10. Let's print out the data from our generated Dataset of type Car.

```
cars.show(false)
```

```
+--------+---------+--------------+--------+---------+
|kind    |make     |model         |price   |style    |
+--------+---------+--------------+--------+---------+
|electric|Telsa    |Model S       |71000.0 |sedan    |
|hybrid  |Audi     |A3 E-Tron     |37900.0 |luxury   |
|hybrid  |BMW      |330e          |43700.0 |sedan    |
|electric|BMW      |i3            |43300.0 |sedan    |
|hybrid  |BMW      |i8            |137000.0|coupe    |
|hybrid  |BMW      |X5 xdrive40e  |64000.0 |suv      |
|electric|Chevy    |Spark EV      |26000.0 |coupe    |
|electric|Chevy    |Volt          |34000.0 |sedan    |
|electric|Fiat     |500e          |32600.0 |coupe    |
|hybrid  |Ford     |C-Max Energi  |32600.0 |wagon/van|
|electric|Ford     |Focus Electric|29200.0 |sedan    |
|electric|Ford     |Fusion Energi |33900.0 |sedan    |
|hybrid  |Hyundai  |Sonata        |35400.0 |sedan    |
|electric|Kia      |Soul EV       |34500.0 |sedan    |
|electric|Mercedes |B-Class       |42400.0 |sedan    |
|hybrid  |Mercedes |C350          |46400.0 |sedan    |
|hybrid  |Mercedes |GLE500e       |67000.0 |suv      |
|electric|Mitsubishi|i-MiEV       |23800.0 |sedan    |
|electric|Nissan   |LEAF          |29000.0 |sedan    |
|hybrid  |Porsche  |Cayenne       |78000.0 |suv      |
+--------+---------+--------------+--------+---------+
only showing top 20 rows
```

11. Next, we will display column names of the Dataset to verify that the cars' JSON attribute names were processed correctly.

```
cars.columns.foreach(println)
make
model
price
style
kind
```

12. Let's see the automatically generated schema and validate the inferred data types.

```
println(cars.schema)
StructType(StructField(make,StringType,true),
StructField(model,StringType,true),
StructField(price,DoubleType,false),
StructField(style,StringType,true),
StructField(kind,StringType,true))
```

13. In this step, we will select the Dataset's `make` column, removing duplicates by applying the `distinct` method and showing the results.

```
cars.select("make").distinct().show()
```

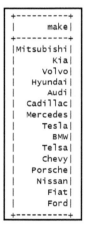

14. Next, create a view on the cars Dataset so we can execute a literal Spark SQL query string against the dataset.

```
cars.createOrReplaceTempView("cars")
```

15. Finally, we execute a Spark SQL query filtering the Dataset for electric cars, and returning only three of the defined columns.

```
spark.sql("select make, model, kind from cars where kind =
'electric'").show()
```

```
+----------+---------------+--------+
|      make|          model|    kind|
+----------+---------------+--------+
|     Telsa|        Model S|electric|
|       BMW|             i3|electric|
|     Chevy|       Spark EV|electric|
|     Chevy|           Volt|electric|
|      Fiat|           500e|electric|
|      Ford| Focus Electric|electric|
|      Ford|  Fusion Energi|electric|
|       Kia|        Soul EV|electric|
|  Mercedes|        B-Class|electric|
|Mitsubishi|          i-MiEV|electric|
|    Nissan|           LEAF|electric|
|     Tesla|        Model X|electric|
|     Tesla|        Model 3|electric|
+----------+---------------+--------+
```

16. We close the program by stopping the Spark session.

```
spark.stop()
```

How it works...

It is extremely straightforward to read a **JavaScript Object Notation (JSON)** data file and to transform it into a Dataset with Spark. JSON has become a widely used data format over the past several years and Spark's support for the format is substantial.

In the first part, we demonstrated loading JSON into a Dataset by means of built-in JSON parsing functionality in Spark's session. You should take note of Spark's built-in functionality that transforms the JSON data into the car case class.

In the second part, we demonstrated Spark SQL being applied on the Dataset to wrangle the said data into a desirable state. We utilized the Dataset's select method to retrieve the make column and apply the distinct method for the removal of duplicates. Next, we set up a view on the cars Dataset, so we can apply SQL queries against it. Finally, we used the session's SQL method to execute a literal SQL query string against the Dataset, retrieving any items which are of kind electric.

There's more...

To fully understand and master the Dataset API, be sure to understand the concept of Row and Encoder.

Datasets follow the *lazy execution* paradigm, meaning that execution only occurs by invoking actions in Spark. When we execute an action, the Catalyst query optimizer produces a logical plan and generates a physical plan for optimized execution in a parallel distributed manner. See the figure in the introduction for all the detailed steps.

Documentation for Row is available

at http://spark.apache.org/docs/latest/api/scala/index.html#org.apache.spark.sq l.Dataset

Documentation for Encoder is available

at http://spark.apache.org/docs/latest/api/scala/index.html#org.apache.spark.sq l.Encoder

See also

- Documentation for Dataset is available
  at http://spark.apache.org/docs/latest/api/scala/index.html#org.apache. spark.sql.Dataset
- Documentation for KeyValue grouped Dataset is available
  at http://spark.apache.org/docs/latest/api/scala/index.html#org.apache. spark.sql.KeyValueGroupedDataset
- Documentation for relational grouped
  Dataset http://spark.apache.org/docs/latest/api/scala/index.html#org.ap ache.spark.sql.RelationalGroupedDataset

Again, be sure to download and explore the Dataset source file, which is about 2500+ lines from GitHub. Exploring the Spark source code is the best way to learn advanced programming in Scala, Scala Annotations, and Spark 2.0 itself.

Noteworthy for Pre-Spark 2.0 users:

- SparkSession is the single entry point into the system. SQLContext and HiveContext are replaced by SparkSession.
- For Java users, be sure to replace DataFrame with Dataset<Row>.
- Use the new catalog interface via SparkSession to execute cacheTable(), dropTempView(), createExternalTable(), and ListTable(), and so on.

- DataFrame and DataSet API
  - `unionALL()` is deprecated and you should now use `union()` instead.
  - `explode()` should be replaced by `functions.explode()` plus `select()` or `flatMap()`
  - `registerTempTable` has been deprecated and replaced by `createOrReplaceTempView()`
- The `Dataset()` API source code (that is, `Dataset.scala`) can be found via GitHub at https://github.com/apache/spark/blob/master/sql/core/src/main/scala/org/apache/spark/sql/Dataset.scala

Functional programming with the Dataset API using domain objects

In this recipe, we explore how functional programming works with Dataset. We use the Dataset and functional programming to separate the cars (domain object) by their models.

How to do it...

1. Start a new project in IntelliJ or in an IDE of your choice. Make sure the necessary JAR files are included.

2. Use package instruction to provide the right path

   ```
   package spark.ml.cookbook.chapter3
   ```

3. Import the necessary packages for Spark context to get access to the cluster and `Log4j.Logger` to reduce the amount of output produced by Spark.

   ```
   import org.apache.log4j.{Level, Logger}
   import org.apache.spark.sql.{Dataset, SparkSession}
   import spark.ml.cookbook.{Car, mydatasetdata}
   import scala.collection.mutable
   import scala.collection.mutable.ListBuffer
   import org.apache.log4j.{Level, Logger}
   import org.apache.spark.sql.SparkSession
   ```

4. Define a Scala case to contain our data for processing, and our car class will represent electric and hybrid cars.

```scala
case class Car(make: String, model: String, price: Double,
style: String, kind: String)
```

5. Let's create a `Seq` populated with electric and hybrid cars.

```scala
val carData =
Seq(
Car("Tesla", "Model S", 71000.0, "sedan","electric"),
Car("Audi", "A3 E-Tron", 37900.0, "luxury","hybrid"),
Car("BMW", "330e", 43700.0, "sedan","hybrid"),
Car("BMW", "i3", 43300.0, "sedan","electric"),
Car("BMW", "i8", 137000.0, "coupe","hybrid"),
Car("BMW", "X5 xdrive40e", 64000.0, "suv","hybrid"),
Car("Chevy", "Spark EV", 26000.0, "coupe","electric"),
Car("Chevy", "Volt", 34000.0, "sedan","electric"),
Car("Fiat", "500e", 32600.0, "coupe","electric"),
Car("Ford", "C-Max Energi", 32600.0, "wagon/van","hybrid"),
Car("Ford", "Focus Electric", 29200.0, "sedan","electric"),
Car("Ford", "Fusion Energi", 33900.0, "sedan","electric"),
Car("Hyundai", "Sonata", 35400.0, "sedan","hybrid"),
Car("Kia", "Soul EV", 34500.0, "sedan","electric"),
Car("Mercedes", "B-Class", 42400.0, "sedan","electric"),
Car("Mercedes", "C350", 46400.0, "sedan","hybrid"),
Car("Mercedes", "GLE500e", 67000.0, "suv","hybrid"),
Car("Mitsubishi", "i-MiEV", 23800.0, "sedan","electric"),
Car("Nissan", "LEAF", 29000.0, "sedan","electric"),
Car("Porsche", "Cayenne", 78000.0, "suv","hybrid"),
Car("Porsche", "Panamera S", 93000.0, "sedan","hybrid"),
Car("Tesla", "Model X", 80000.0, "suv","electric"),
Car("Tesla", "Model 3", 35000.0, "sedan","electric"),
Car("Volvo", "XC90 T8", 69000.0, "suv","hybrid"),
Car("Cadillac", "ELR", 76000.0, "coupe","hybrid")
)
```

6. Set output level to ERROR to reduce Spark's output.

```scala
Logger.getLogger("org").setLevel(Level.ERROR)
Logger.getLogger("akka").setLevel(Level.ERROR)
```

7. Create a SparkSession yielding access to the Spark cluster and underlying session object attributes such as the SparkContext and SparkSQLContext.

```
val spark = SparkSession
.builder
.master("local[*]")
.appName("mydatasetseq")
.config("spark.sql.warehouse.dir", ".")
.getOrCreate()
```

8. Import spark implicits, therefore adding in behavior with only an import.

```
import spark.implicits._
```

9. Now we will create a Dataset from the car data Seq utilizing the SparkSessions's `createDataset()` function.

```
val cars = spark.createDataset(MyDatasetData.carData)
```

10. Display the Dataset to understand how to transform data in subsequent steps.

```
cars.show(false)
```

On running the previous code, you will get the following output.

```
+----------+--------------+--------+---------+--------+
|make      |model         |price   |style    |kind    |
+----------+--------------+--------+---------+--------+
|Tesla     |Model S       |71000.0 |sedan    |electric|
|Audi      |A3 E-Tron     |37900.0 |luxury   |hybrid  |
|BMW       |330e          |43700.0 |sedan    |hybrid  |
|BMW       |i3            |43300.0 |sedan    |electric|
|BMW       |i8            |137000.0|coupe    |hybrid  |
|BMW       |X5 xdrive40e  |64000.0 |suv      |hybrid  |
|Chevy     |Spark EV      |26000.0 |coupe    |electric|
|Chevy     |Volt          |34000.0 |sedan    |electric|
|Fiat      |500e          |32600.0 |coupe    |electric|
|Ford      |C-Max Energi  |32600.0 |wagon/van|hybrid  |
|Ford      |Focus Electric|29200.0 |sedan    |electric|
|Ford      |Fusion Energi |33900.0 |sedan    |electric|
|Hyundai   |Sonata        |35400.0 |sedan    |hybrid  |
|Kia       |Soul EV       |34500.0 |sedan    |electric|
|Mercedes  |B-Class       |42400.0 |sedan    |electric|
|Mercedes  |c350          |46400.0 |sedan    |hybrid  |
|Mercedes  |GLE500e       |67000.0 |suv      |hybrid  |
|Mitsubishi|i-MiEV        |23800.0 |sedan    |electric|
|Nissan    |LEAF          |29000.0 |sedan    |electric|
|Porsche   |Cayenne       |78000.0 |suv      |hybrid  |
+----------+--------------+--------+---------+--------+
only showing top 20 rows
```

11. Now we construct a functional sequence of steps to transform the original Dataset into data grouped by make with all various models attached.

```scala
val modelData = cars.groupByKey(_.make).mapGroups({
case (make, car) => {
val carModel = new ListBuffer[String]()
            car.map(_.model).foreach({
                c =>  carModel += c
        })
        (make, carModel)
      }
    })
```

12. Let's display results from our previous sequence of functional logic for validation.

```scala
modelData.show(false)
```

On running the previous code, you will get the following output.

```
+----------+----------------------------------------------+
|_1        |_2                                            |
+----------+----------------------------------------------+
|Mitsubishi|[i-MiEV]                                      |
|Kia       |[Soul EV]                                     |
|Volvo     |[XC90 T8]                                     |
|Hyundai   |[Sonata]                                      |
|Audi      |[A3 E-Tron]                                   |
|Cadillac  |[ELR]                                         |
|Mercedes  |[B-class, C350, GLE500e]                      |
|Tesla     |[Model S, Model X, Model 3]                   |
|BMW       |[330e, i3, i8, X5 xdrive40e]                  |
|Chevy     |[Spark EV, Volt]                              |
|Porsche   |[Cayenne, Panamera S]                         |
|Nissan    |[LEAF]                                        |
|Fiat      |[500e]                                        |
|Ford      |[C-Max Energi, Focus Electric, Fusion Energi]|
+----------+----------------------------------------------+
```

13. We close the program by stopping the Spark session.

```scala
spark.stop()
```

How it works...

In this example, we use a Scala sequence data structure to hold the original data, which is a series of cars and their attributes. Using `createDataset()`, we create a DataSet and populate it. We then proceed to use the 'make' attribute with `groupBy` and `mapGroups()` to list cars by their models using a functional paradigm with DataSet. Using this form of functional programming with domain objects was not impossible before DataSet (for example, the case class with RDD or UDF with DataFrame), but the DataSet construct makes this easy and intrinsic.

There's more...

Be sure to include the `implicits` statement in all your DataSet coding:

```
import spark.implicits._
```

See also

The documentation for Datasets can be accessed at `http://spark.apache.org/docs/latest/api/scala/index.html#org.apache.spark.sql.Dataset`.

12
Common Recipes for Implementing a Robust Machine Learning System

In this chapter, we will cover:

- Spark's basic statistical API to help you build your own algorithms
- ML pipelines for real-life machine learning applications
- Normalizing data with Spark
- Splitting data for training and testing
- Common operations with the new Dataset API
- Creating and using RDD versus DataFrame versus Dataset from a text file in Spark 2.0
- LabeledPoint data structure for Spark ML
- Getting access to Spark cluster in Spark 2.0+
- Getting access to Spark cluster pre-Spark 2.0
- Getting access to SparkContext vis-a-vis SparkSession object in Spark 2.0
- New model export and PMML markup in Spark 2.0
- Regression model evaluation using Spark 2.0
- Binary classification model evaluation using Spark 2.0
- Multilabel classification model evaluation using Spark 2.0
- Multiclass classification model evaluation using Spark 2.0
- Using the Scala Breeze library to do graphics in Spark 2.0

Introduction

In every line of business, ranging from running a small business to creating and managing a mission-critical application, there are a number of tasks that are common and need to be included as a part of almost every workflow that is required during the course of executing the functions. This is true even for building robust machine learning systems. In Spark machine learning, some of these tasks range from splitting the data for model development (train, test, validate) to normalizing input feature vector data to creating ML pipelines via the Spark API. We provide a set of recipes in this chapter to enable the reader to think about what is actually required to implement an end-to-end machine learning system.

This chapter attempts to demonstrate a number of common tasks which are present in any robust Spark machine learning system implementation. To avoid redundant references these common tasks in every recipe covered in this book, we have factored out such common tasks as short recipes in this chapter, which can be leveraged as needed while reading the other chapters. These recipes can either stand alone or be included as pipeline subtasks in a larger system. Please note that these common recipes are emphasized in the larger context of machine learning algorithms in later chapters, while also including them as independent recipes in this chapter for completeness.

Spark's basic statistical API to help you build your own algorithms

In this recipe, we cover Spark's multivariate statistical summary (that is, *Statistics.colStats*) such as correlation, stratified sampling, hypothesis testing, random data generation, kernel density estimators, and much more, which can be applied to extremely large datasets while taking advantage of both parallelism and resiliency via RDDs.

How to do it...

1. Start a new project in IntelliJ or in an IDE of your choice. Make sure that the necessary JAR files are included.

2. Set up the package location where the program will reside:

```
package spark.ml.cookbook.chapter4
```

3. Import the necessary packages for the Spark session to gain access to the cluster and `log4j.Logger` to reduce the amount of output produced by Spark:

```
import org.apache.spark.mllib.linalg.Vectors
import org.apache.spark.mllib.stat.Statistics
import org.apache.spark.sql.SparkSession
import org.apache.log4j.Logger
import org.apache.log4j.Level
```

4. Set the output level to ERROR to reduce Spark's logging output:

```
Logger.getLogger("org").setLevel(Level.ERROR)
Logger.getLogger("akka").setLevel(Level.ERROR)
```

5. Initialize a Spark session specifying configurations with the builder pattern, thus making an entry point available for the Spark cluster:

```
val spark = SparkSession
.builder
.master("local[*]")
.appName("Summary Statistics")
.config("spark.sql.warehouse.dir", ".")
.getOrCreate()
```

6. Let's retrieve the Spark session underlying the SparkContext to use when generating RDDs:

```
val sc = spark.sparkContext
```

7. Now we create a RDD with the handcrafted data to illustrate usage of summary statistics:

```
val rdd = sc.parallelize(
  Seq(
    Vectors.dense(0, 1, 0),
    Vectors.dense(1.0, 10.0, 100.0),
    Vectors.dense(3.0, 30.0, 300.0),
    Vectors.dense(5.0, 50.0, 500.0),
    Vectors.dense(7.0, 70.0, 700.0),
    Vectors.dense(9.0, 90.0, 900.0),
    Vectors.dense(11.0, 110.0, 1100.0)
  )
)
```

8. We use Spark's statistics objects by invoking the method `colStats()` and passing the RDD as an argument:

```
val summary = Statistics.colStats(rdd)
```

The `colStats()` method will return a `MultivariateStatisticalSummary`, which contains the computed summary statistics:

```
println("mean:" + summary.mean)
println("variance:" +summary.variance)
println("none zero" + summary.numNonzeros)
println("min:" + summary.min)
println("max:" + summary.max)
println("count:" + summary.count)
mean:[5.142857142857142,51.57142857142857,514.2857142857142]
variance:[16.80952380952381,1663.952380952381,168095.2380952381]
none zero[6.0,7.0,6.0]
min:[0.0,1.0,0.0]
max:[11.0,110.0,1100.0]
count:7
```

9. We close the program by stopping the Spark session:

```
spark.stop()
```

How it works...

We created an RDD from dense vector data followed by the generation of summary statistics on it using the statistics object. Once the `colStats()` method returned, we retrieved summary statistics such as the mean, variance, minimum, maximum, and so on.

There's more...

It cannot be emphasized enough how efficient the statistical API is on large datasets. These APIs will provide you with basic elements to implement any statistical learning algorithm from scratch. Based on our research and experience with half versus full matrix factorization, we encourage you to first read the source code and make sure that there isn't an equivalent functionality already implemented in Spark before implementing your own.

While we only demonstrate a basic statistics summary here, Spark comes equipped out of the box with:

- Correlation: `Statistics.corr(seriesX, seriesY, "type of correlation")`:
  - Pearson (default)
  - Spearman
- Stratified sampling - RDD API:
  - With a replacement RDD
  - Without a replacement - requires an additional pass
- Hypothesis testing:
  - Vector - `Statistics.chiSqTest( vector )`
  - Matrix - `Statistics.chiSqTest( dense matrix )`
- **Kolmogorov-Smirnov (KS)** test for equality - one or two-sided:
  - `Statistics.kolmogorovSmirnovTest(RDD, "norm", 0, 1)`
- Random data generator - `normalRDD()`:
  - Normal - can specify a parameter
  - Lots of option plus `map()`s to generate any distribution
- Kernel density estimator - `KernelDensity().estimate( data )`

A quick reference to the *Goodness of fit* concept in statistics can be found at `https://en.wikipedia.org/wiki/Goodness_of_fit` link.

See also

Documentation for more multivariate statistical summary:

- `https://spark.apache.org/docs/latest/api/scala/index.html#org.apache.spark.mllib.stat.MultivariateStatisticalSummary`

ML pipelines for real-life machine learning applications

This is the first of two recipes which cover the ML pipeline in Spark 2.0. For a more advanced treatment of ML pipelines with additional details such as API calls and parameter extraction, see later chapters in this book.

In this recipe, we attempt to have a single pipeline that can tokenize text, use HashingTF (an old trick) to map term frequencies, run a regression to fit a model, and then predict which group a new term belongs to (for example, news filtering, gesture classification, and so on).

How to do it...

1. Start a new project in IntelliJ or in an IDE of your choice. Make sure that the necessary JAR files are included.

2. Set up the package location where the program will reside:

   ```
   package spark.ml.cookbook.chapter4
   ```

3. Import the necessary packages for the Spark session to gain access to the cluster and `log4j.Logger` to reduce the amount of output produced by Spark:

   ```
   import org.apache.spark.ml.Pipeline
   import org.apache.spark.ml.classification.LogisticRegression
   import org.apache.spark.ml.feature.{HashingTF, Tokenizer}
   import org.apache.spark.sql.SparkSession
   import org.apache.log4j.{Level, Logger}
   ```

4. Set the output level to ERROR to reduce Spark's logging output:

   ```
   Logger.getLogger("org").setLevel(Level.ERROR)
   Logger.getLogger("akka").setLevel(Level.ERROR)
   ```

5. Initialize a Spark session specifying configurations with the builder pattern, thus making an entry point available for the Spark cluster:

   ```
   val spark = SparkSession
   .builder
   .master("local[*]")
   .appName("My Pipeline")
   .config("spark.sql.warehouse.dir", ".")
   .getOrCreate()
   ```

6. Let's create a training set DataFrame with several random text documents:

```
val trainset = spark.createDataFrame(Seq(
  (1L, 1, "spark rocks"),
  (2L, 0, "flink is the best"),
  (3L, 1, "Spark rules"),
  (4L, 0, "mapreduce forever"),
  (5L, 0, "Kafka is great")
)).toDF("id", "label", "words")
```

7. Create a tokenizer to parse the text documents into individual terms:

```
val tokenizer = new Tokenizer()
  .setInputCol("words")
  .setOutputCol("tokens")
```

8. Create a HashingTF for transforming terms into feature vectors:

```
val hashingTF = new HashingTF()
  .setNumFeatures(1000)
  .setInputCol(tokenizer.getOutputCol)
  .setOutputCol("features")
```

9. Create a logistic regression class to generate a model to predict which group a new text document belongs to:

```
val lr = new LogisticRegression()
  .setMaxIter(15)
  .setRegParam(0.01)
```

10. Next, we construct a data pipeline with an array of three stages:

```
val pipeline = new Pipeline()
  .setStages(Array(tokenizer, hashingTF, lr))
```

11. Now, we train the model so we can make predictions later:

```
val model = pipeline.fit(trainset)
```

12. Let's create a test dataset to validate our trained model:

```
val testSet = spark.createDataFrame(Seq(
  (10L, 1, "use spark please"),
  (11L, 2, "Kafka")
)).toDF("id", "label", "words")
```

13. Finally, we transform the test set using the trained model, generating predictions:

```
model.transform(testSet).select("probability",
"prediction").show(false)
```

```
+-------------------------------------------+----------+
|probability                                |prediction|
+-------------------------------------------+----------+
|[0.1188495343876135,0.8811504656123865]    |1.0       |
|[0.6377057793949985,0.36229422060500155]   |0.0       |
+-------------------------------------------+----------+
```

14. We close the program by stopping the Spark session:

```
spark.stop()
```

How it works...

In this section, we investigated constructing a simple machine learning pipeline with Spark. We began with creating a DataFrame comprised of two groups of text documents and then proceeded to set up a pipeline.

First, we created a tokenizer to parse text documents into terms followed by the creation of the HashingTF to convert the terms into features. Then, we created a logistic regression object to predict which group a new text document belongs to.

Second, we constructed the pipeline by passing an array of arguments to it, specifying three stages of execution. You will notice each subsequent stage provides the result as a specified column while using the previous stage's output column as the input.

Finally, we trained the model by invoking fit() on the pipeline object and defining a set of test data for verification. Next, we transformed the test set with the model, producing which of the defined two groups the text documents in the test set belong to.

There's more...

The pipeline in Spark ML was inspired by scikit-learn in Python, which is referenced here for completeness:

```
http://scikit-learn.org/stable/
```

ML pipelines make it easy to combine multiple algorithms used to implement a production task in Spark. It would be unusual to see a use case in a real-life situation that is made of a single algorithm. Often a number of cooperating ML algorithms work together to achieve a complex use case. For example, in LDA-based systems (for example, news briefings) or human emotion detection, there are a number of steps before and after the core system to be implemented as a single pipe to produce any meaningful and production-worthy system. See the following link for a real-life use case requiring a pipeline to implement a robust system:

`https://www.thinkmind.org/index.php?view=article&articleid=achi_2013_15_50_2024` `1`

See also

Documentation for more multivariate statistical summary:

- Pipeline docs are available at `https://spark.apache.org/docs/latest/api/` `scala/index.html#org.apache.spark.ml.Pipeline`
- Pipeline model that is useful when we load and save the `.load()`, `.save()` methods: `https://spark.apache.org/docs/latest/api/scala/index.` `html#org.apache.spark.ml.PipelineModel`
- Pipeline stage information is available at `https://spark.apache.org/docs/` `latest/api/scala/index.html#org.apache.spark.ml.PipelineStage`
- HashingTF, a nice old trick to map a sequence to their term frequency in text analytics is available at `https://spark.apache.org/docs/latest/api/scala/` `index.html#org.apache.spark.mllib.feature.HashingTF`

Normalizing data with Spark

In this recipe, we demonstrate normalizing (scaling) the data prior to importing the data into an ML algorithm. There are a good number of ML algorithms such as **Support Vector Machine (SVM)** that work better with scaled input vectors rather than with the raw values.

How to do it...

1. Go to the UCI Machine Learning Repository and download the `http://archive.ics.uci.edu/ml/machine-learning-databases/wine/wine.data` file.

2. Start a new project in IntelliJ or in an IDE of your choice. Make sure that the necessary JAR files are included.

3. Set up the package location where the program will reside:

   ```
   package spark.ml.cookbook.chapter4
   ```

4. Import the necessary packages for the Spark session to gain access to the cluster and `log4j.Logger` to reduce the amount of output produced by Spark:

   ```
   import org.apache.spark.sql.SparkSession
   import org.apache.spark.ml.linalg.{Vector, Vectors}
   import org.apache.spark.ml.feature.MinMaxScaler
   ```

5. Define a method to parse wine data into a tuple:

   ```
   def parseWine(str: String): (Int, Vector) = {
   val columns = str.split(",")
   (columns(0).toInt, Vectors.dense(columns(1).toFloat,
   columns(2).toFloat, columns(3).toFloat))
     }
   ```

6. Set the output level to ERROR to reduce Spark's logging output:

   ```
   Logger.getLogger("org").setLevel(Level.ERROR)
   Logger.getLogger("akka").setLevel(Level.ERROR)
   ```

7. Initialize a Spark session specifying configurations with the builder pattern, thus making an entry point available for the Spark cluster:

   ```
   val spark = SparkSession
   .builder
   .master("local[*]")
   .appName("My Normalize")
   .getOrCreate()
   ```

8. Import `spark.implicits`, therefore adding in behavior with only an `import`:

```
import spark.implicits._
```

9. Let's load the wine data into memory, taking only the first four columns and converting the latter three into a new feature vector:

```
val data =
Spark.read.text("../data/sparkml2/chapter4/wine.data").as[String].m
ap(parseWine)
```

10. Next, we generate a DataFrame with two columns:

```
val df = data.toDF("id", "feature")
```

11. Now, we will print out the DataFrame schema and display data contained within the DataFrame:

```
df.printSchema()
df.show(false)
```

```
root
 |-- id: integer (nullable = true)
 |-- feature: vector (nullable = true)

+---+-------------------------------------------------------------+
|id |feature                                                      |
+---+-------------------------------------------------------------+
|1  |[14.229999542236328,1.7100000381469727,2.430000066757202]    |
|1  |[13.199999809265137,1.7799999713897705,2.140000104904175]    |
|1  |[13.15999984741211,2.359999895095825,2.6700000762939453]     |
|1  |[14.369999885559082,1.9500000476837158,2.5]                  |
|1  |[13.239999771118164,2.5899999141693115,2.869999885559082]    |
|1  |[14.199999809265137,1.7599999904632568,2.450000047683716]    |
|1  |[14.390000343322754,1.8700000047683716,2.450000047683716]    |
|1  |[14.0600004196167,2.1500000953674316,2.609999895095825]      |
|1  |[14.829999923706055,1.6399999856948853,2.1700000762939453]   |
|1  |[13.859999656677246,1.350000023841858,2.2699999809265137]    |
|1  |[14.100000381469727,2.1600000858306885,2.299999952316284]    |
|1  |[14.119999885559082,1.4800000190734863,2.319999933242798]    |
|1  |[13.75,1.7300000190734863,2.4100000858306885]                |
|1  |[14.75,1.7300000190734863,2.390000104904175]                 |
|1  |[14.380000114440918,1.8700000047683716,2.380000114440918]    |
|1  |[13.630000114440918,1.809999942779541,2.700000047683716]     |
|1  |[14.300000190734863,1.9199999570846558,2.7200000286102295]   |
|1  |[13.829999923706055,1.5700000524520874,2.619999885559082]    |
|1  |[14.1899995803833,1.590000033378601,2.4800000190734863]      |
|1  |[13.640000343322754,3.0999999046325684,2.559999942779541]    |
+---+-------------------------------------------------------------+
only showing top 20 rows
```

12. Finally, we generate the scaling model and transform the feature into a common range between a negative and positive one displaying the results:

```
val scale = new MinMaxScaler()
        .setInputCol("feature")
        .setOutputCol("scaled")
        .setMax(1)
        .setMin(-1)
scale.fit(df).transform(df).select("scaled").show(false)
```

```
+-----------------------------------------------------------------+
|scaled                                                           |
+-----------------------------------------------------------------+
|[0.6842103413928011,-0.6166007929349322,0.1443850799183537]     |
|[0.14210524598647445,-0.5889328361222417,-0.165775306299344]    |
|[0.1210526355415828,-0.3596838626296277,0.40106958144216076]    |
|[0.7578947289168343,-0.5217391324834041,0.21925131848980062]    |
|[0.1631578564313660,-0.2687747674370553,0.6149731202177233]     |
|[0.6684210090425888,-0.5968379666401532,0.1657754337959101]     |
|[0.7684212851061929,-0.5533597016733449,0.1657754337959101]     |
|[0.5947371234523811,-0.44268773306769926,0.3368982648163601]    |
|[1.0,-0.6442687968659172,-0.13368977548300953]                  |
|[0.4894735692940979,-0.7588932836122242,-0.02673800609522836]   |
|[0.6157897338972727,-0.43873516780874344,0.005347524721106112]  |
|[0.6263157881528056,-0.7075098881275044,0.02673787859866228]    |
|[0.4315790160541024,-0.6086956624170206,0.12299472604079753]    |
|[0.9578947791102168,-0.6086956624170206,0.10160437216324114]    |
|[0.7631580070115136,-0.5533597016733449,0.09090919522446317]    |
|[0.3684211847194278,-0.5770751403453742,0.4331551122584951]     |
|[0.7210527861217304,-0.533596875378566,0.4545454661360515]      |
|[0.4736842369438856,-0.6719367536786077,0.34759344175513807]    |
|[0.6631577309479095,-0.6640316231606962,0.19786069461224445]    |
|[0.3736844628141069,-0.06719375075713208,0.2834223801224693]    |
+-----------------------------------------------------------------+
only showing top 20 rows
```

13. We close the program by stopping the Spark session:

```
spark.stop()
```

How it works...

In this example, we explored feature scaling which is a critical step in most machine learning algorithms such as **classifiers**. We started out by loading the wine data files, extracted an identifier, and used the next three columns to create a feature vector.

Then, we created a `MinMaxScaler` object, configuring a minimum and maximum range to scale our values into. We invoked the scaling model by executing the `fit()` method on the scaler class, and then we used the model to scale the values in our DataFrame.

Finally, we displayed the resulting DataFrame and we noticed feature vector values ranges are between negative 1 and positive 1.

There's more...

The roots of normalizing and scaling can be better understood by examining the concept of **unit vectors** in introductory linear algebra. Please see the following links for some common references for unit vectors:

- You can refer to unit vectors at `https://en.wikipedia.org/wiki/Unit_vector`
- For scalar, you can refer to `https://en.wikipedia.org/wiki/Scalar_(mathematics)`

In the case of input sensitive algorithms, such as SVM, it is recommended that the algorithm is trained on scaled values (for example, range from 0 to 1) of the features rather than the absolute values as represented by the original vector.

See also

Documentation for `MinMaxScaler` is available at `https://spark.apache.org/docs/latest/api/scala/index.html#org.apache.spark.ml.feature.MinMaxScaler`

We want to emphasize that `MinMaxScaler` is an extensive API that extends the `Estimator` (a concept from the ML pipeline) and when used correctly can lead to achieving coding efficiency and high accuracy results.

Splitting data for training and testing

In this recipe, you will learn to use Spark's API to split your available input data into different datasets that can be used for training and validation phases. It is common to use an 80/20 split, but other variations of splitting the data can be considered as well based on your preference.

How to do it...

1. Go to the UCI Machine Learning Repository and download the `http://archive.ics.uci.edu/ml/machine-learning-databases/00359/NewsAggregatorDataset.zip` file.

2. Start a new project in IntelliJ or in an IDE of your choice. Make sure that the necessary JAR files are included.

3. Set up the package location where the program will reside:

```
package spark.ml.cookbook.chapter4
```

4. Import the necessary packages for the Spark session to gain access to the cluster and `log4j.Logger` to reduce the amount of output produced by Spark:

```
import org.apache.spark.sql.SparkSession
import org.apache.log4j.{ Level, Logger}
```

5. Set the output level to ERROR to reduce Spark's logging output:

```
Logger.getLogger("org").setLevel(Level.ERROR)
Logger.getLogger("akka").setLevel(Level.ERROR)
```

6. Initialize a Spark session specifying configurations with the builder pattern, thus making an entry point available for the Spark cluster:

```
val spark = SparkSession
.builder
.master("local[*]")
.appName("Data Splitting")
.getOrCreate()
```

7. We begin with loading a data file by way of the Spark session's `csv()` method to parse and load data into a dataset:

```
val data =
spark.read.csv("../data/sparkml2/chapter4/newsCorpora.csv")
```

8. Now, we count how many items the CSV loader parsed and loaded into memory. We will need this value later to reconcile data splitting.

```
val rowCount = data.count()
println("rowCount=" + rowCount)
```

9. Next, we utilize the dataset's `randomSplit` method to split the data into two buckets with allocations of 80% and 20% of data each:

```
val splitData = data.randomSplit(Array(0.8, 0.2))
```

10. The `randomSplit` method returns an array with two sets of data, the first set with 80% of data being the training set and the next with 20% being the testing set:

```
val trainingSet = splitData(0)
val testSet = splitData(1)
```

11. Let's generate counts for both training and testing sets:

```
val trainingSetCount = trainingSet.count()
val testSetCount = testSet.count()
```

12. Now we reconcile the values, and notice that the original row count is `415606` and the final summation of the training and testing sets equals `415606`:

```
println("trainingSetCount=" + trainingSetCount)
println("testSetCount=" + testSetCount)
println("setRowCount=" + (trainingSetCount+testSetCount))
rowCount=415606
trainingSetCount=332265
testSetCount=83341
setRowCount=415606
```

13. We close the program by stopping the Spark session:

```
spark.stop()
```

How it works...

We began by loading the data file `newsCorpora.csv` and then by way of the `randomSplit()` method attached to the dataset object, we split the dataset.

There's more...

To validate the result, we must set up a Delphi technique in which the test data is absolutely unknown to the model. See Kaggle competitions for details at `https://www.kaggle.com/competitions`.

Three types of datasets are needed for a robust ML system:

- **Training dataset**: This is used to fit a model to sample
- **Validation dataset**: This is used to estimate the delta or prediction error for the fitted model (trained by training set)
- **Test dataset**: This is used to assess the model generalization error once a final model is selected

See also

Documentation for `randomSplit()` is available at `https://spark.apache.org/docs/latest/api/scala/index.html#org.apache.spark.api.java.JavaRDD@randomSplit(weights:Array%5BDouble%5D):Array%5Borg.apache.spark.api.java.JavaRDD%5BT%5D%5D`.

The `randomSplit()` is a method call within an RDD. While the number of RDD method calls can be overwhelming, mastering this Spark concept and API is a must.

API signature is as follows:

```
def randomSplit(weights: Array[Double]): Array[JavaRDD[T]]
```

Randomly splits this RDD with the provided weights.

Common operations with the new Dataset API

In this recipe, we cover the Dataset API, which is the way forward for data wrangling in Spark 2.0 and beyond. In this chapter ,we cover some of the common, repetitive operations that are required to work with these new API sets. Additionally, we demonstrate the query plan generated by the Spark SQL Catalyst optimizer.

How to do it...

1. Start a new project in IntelliJ or in an IDE of your choice. Make sure that the necessary JAR files are included.

2. We will use a JSON data file named `cars.json`, which has been created for this example:

   ```
   name,city
   Bears,Chicago
   Packers,Green Bay
   Lions,Detroit
   Vikings,Minnesota
   ```

3. Set up the package location where the program will reside:

   ```
   package spark.ml.cookbook.chapter4
   ```

4. Import the necessary packages for the Spark session to get access to the cluster and `log4j.Logger` to reduce the amount of output produced by Spark:

   ```
   import org.apache.spark.ml.Pipeline
   import org.apache.spark.ml.classification.LogisticRegression
   import org.apache.spark.ml.feature.{HashingTF, Tokenizer}
   import org.apache.spark.sql.SparkSession
   import org.apache.log4j.{Level, Logger}
   ```

5. Define a Scala `case class` to model the data:

   ```
   case class Team(name: String, city: String)
   ```

6. Set the output level to ERROR to reduce Spark's logging output:

   ```
   Logger.getLogger("org").setLevel(Level.ERROR)
   Logger.getLogger("akka").setLevel(Level.ERROR)
   ```

7. Initialize a Spark session specifying configurations with the builder pattern, thus making an entry point available for the Spark cluster:

   ```
   val spark = SparkSession
   .builder
   .master("local[*]")
   .appName("My Dataset")
   .config("spark.sql.warehouse.dir", ".")
   .getOrCreate()
   ```

8. Import `spark.implicits`, therefore adding in behavior with only an `import`:

    ```
    import spark.implicits._
    ```

9. Let's create a dataset from a Scala list and print out the results:

    ```
    val champs = spark.createDataset(List(Team("Broncos", "Denver"),
    Team("Patriots", "New England")))
    champs.show(false)
    ```

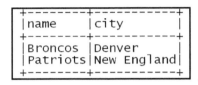

10. Next, we will load a CSV into memory and transform it into a dataset of type `Team`:

    ```
    val teams = spark.read
      .option("Header", "true")
      .csv("../data/sparkml2/chapter4/teams.csv")
      .as[Team]

    teams.show(false)
    ```

11. Now we demonstrate a transversal of the teams dataset by use of the `map` function, yielding a new dataset of city names:

    ```
    val cities = teams.map(t => t.city)
    cities.show(false)
    ```

```
+---------+
|value    |
+---------+
|Chicago  |
|Green Bay|
|Detroit  |
|Minnesota|
+---------+
```

12. Display the execution plan for retrieving city names:

```
cities.explain()
== Physical Plan ==
*SerializeFromObject [staticinvoke(class
org.apache.spark.unsafe.types.UTF8String, StringType, fromString,
input[0, java.lang.String, true], true) AS value#26]
+- *MapElements <function1>, obj#25: java.lang.String
+- *DeserializeToObject newInstance(class Team), obj#24: Team
+- *Scan csv [name#9,city#10] Format: CSV, InputPaths:
file:teams.csv, PartitionFilters: [], PushedFilters: [],
ReadSchema: struct<name:string,city:string>
```

13. Finally, we save the `teams` dataset to a JSON file:

```
teams.write
.mode(SaveMode.Overwrite)
.json("../data/sparkml2/chapter4/teams.json"){"name":"Bears","city"
:"Chicago"}
{"name":"Packers","city":"Green Bay"}
{"name":"Lions","city":"Detroit"}
{"name":"Vikings","city":"Minnesota"}
```

14. We close the program by stopping the Spark session:

```
spark.stop()
```

How it works...

First, we created a dataset from a Scala list and displayed the output to validate the creation of the dataset as expected. Second, we loaded a **comma-separated value (CSV)** file into memory, transforming it into a dataset of type `Team`. Third, we executed the `map()` function over our dataset to build a list of team city names and printed out the execution plan used to generate the dataset. Finally, we persisted the `teams` dataset we previously loaded into a JSON formatted file for future use.

There's more...

Please take a note of some interesting points on datasets:

- Datasets use *lazy* evaluation
- Datasets take advantage of the Spark SQL Catalyst optimizer
- Datasets take advantage of the tungsten off-heap memory management
- There are plenty of systems that will remain pre-Spark 2.0 for the next 2 year so you must still learn and master RDDs and DataFrame for practical reasons.

See also

Documentation for Dataset is available at `https://spark.apache.org/docs/latest/api/scala/index.html#org.apache.spark.sql.Dataset`.

Creating and using RDD versus DataFrame versus Dataset from a text file in Spark 2.0

In this recipe, we explore the subtle differences in creating RDD, DataFrame, and Dataset from a text file and their relationship to each other via a short sample code:

```
Dataset: spark.read.textFile()
RDD: spark.sparkContext.textFile()
DataFrame: spark.read.text()
```

 Assume `spark` is the session name

How to do it...

1. Start a new project in IntelliJ or in an IDE of your choice. Make sure the necessary JAR files are included.
2. Set up the package location where the program will reside:

```
package spark.ml.cookbook.chapter4
```

3. Import the necessary packages for the Spark session to gain access to the cluster and `log4j.Logger` to reduce the amount of output produced by Spark:

```
import org.apache.log4j.{Level, Logger}
import org.apache.spark.sql.SparkSession
```

4. We also define a `case class` to host the data used:

```
case class Beatle(id: Long, name: String)
```

5. Set the output level to ERROR to reduce Spark's logging output:

```
Logger.getLogger("org").setLevel(Level.ERROR)
```

6. Initialize a Spark session specifying configurations with the builder pattern, thus making an entry point available for the Spark cluster:

```
val spark = SparkSession
.builder
.master("local[*]")
.appName("DatasetvsRDD")
.config("spark.sql.warehouse.dir", ".")
.getOrCreate()
```

7. In the following block, we let Spark *create a dataset* object from a text file.

The text file contains very simple data (each line contains an ID and name separated by a comma):

```
import spark.implicits._

val ds =
spark.read.textFile("../data/sparkml2/chapter4/beatles.txt").map(li
ne => {
val tokens = line.split(",")
Beatle(tokens(0).toLong, tokens(1))
}).as[Beatle]
```

We read the file in and parse the data in the file. The dataset object is created by Spark. We confirm the type in the console and then display the data:

```
println("Dataset Type: " + ds.getClass)
ds.show()
```

From the console output:

```
Dataset Type: class org.apache.spark.sql.Dataset
```

```
+---+------+
| id|  name|
+---+------+
|  1|  John|
|  2|  Paul|
|  3|George|
|  4| Ringo|
+---+------+
```

8. Now we create an RDD with the same data file, in a very similar way as the preceding step:

```scala
val rdd =
spark.sparkContext.textFile("../data/sparkml2/chapter4/beatles.txt"
).map(line => {
val tokens = line.split(",")
Beatle(tokens(0).toLong, tokens(1))
 })
```

We then confirm that it is an RDD and display the data in the console:

```scala
println("RDD Type: " + rdd.getClass)
rdd.collect().foreach(println)
```

Note that the method is very similar but different.

From the console output:

```
RDD Type: class org.apache.spark.rdd.MapPartitionsRDD
Beatle(1,John)
Beatle(2,Paul)
Beatle(3,George)
Beatle(4,Ringo)
```

9. DataFrame is another common data structure utilized by Spark communities. We show a similar way to create a DataFrame using the similar method based on the same data file:

```
val df =
spark.read.text("../data/sparkml2/chapter4/beatles.txt").map(
  row => { // Dataset[Row]
val tokens = row.getString(0).split(",")
  Beatle(tokens(0).toLong, tokens(1))
  }).toDF("bid", "bname")
```

We then confirm that it is a DataFrame.

```
println("DataFrame Type: " + df.getClass)
df.show()
```

Note that `DataFrame = Dataset[Row]`, so the type is Dataset.

From the console output:

```
DataFrame Type: class org.apache.spark.sql.Dataset
```

```
+---+------+
|bid| bname|
+---+------+
|  1|  John|
|  2|  Paul|
|  3|George|
|  4| Ringo|
+---+------+
```

10. We close the program by stopping the Spark session:

```
spark.stop()
```

How it works...

We create an RDD, DataFrame, and Dataset object using a similar method from the same text file and confirm the type using the `getClass` method:

```
Dataset: spark.read.textFile
RDD: spark.sparkContext.textFile
DataFrame: spark.read.text
```

Please note that they are very similar and sometimes confusing. Spark 2.0 has transformed DataFrame into an alias for `Dataset[Row]`, making it truly a dataset. We showed the preceding methods to let the user pick an example to create their own datatype flavor.

There's more...

Documentation for datatypes is available at `http://spark.apache.org/docs/latest/sql-programming-guide.html`.

If you are unsure as to what kind of data structure you have at hand (sometimes the difference is not obvious), use the `getClass` method to verify.

Spark 2.0 has transformed DataFrame into an alias for `Dataset[Row]`. While RDD and Dataram remain fully viable for near future, it is best to learn and code new projects using the dataset.

See also

Documentation for RDD and Dataset is available at the following websites:

- `http://spark.apache.org/docs/latest/api/scala/index.html#org.apache.spark.rdd.RDD`
- `http://spark.apache.org/docs/latest/api/scala/index.html#org.apache.spark.sql.Dataset`

LabeledPoint data structure for Spark ML

LabeledPoint is a data structure that has been around since the early days for packaging a feature vector along with a label so it can be used in unsupervised learning algorithms. We demonstrate a short recipe that uses LabeledPoint, the **Seq** data structure, and DataFrame to run a logistic regression for binary classification of the data.

How to do it...

1. Start a new project in IntelliJ or in an IDE of your choice. Make sure that the necessary JAR files are included.

2. Set up the package location where the program will reside:

```
package spark.ml.cookbook.chapter4
```

3. Import the necessary packages for SparkContext to get access to the cluster:

```
import org.apache.spark.ml.feature.LabeledPoint
import org.apache.spark.ml.linalg.Vectors
import org.apache.spark.ml.classification.LogisticRegression
import org.apache.spark.sql._
```

4. Create Spark's configuration and SparkContext so we can have access to the cluster:

```
val spark = SparkSession
.builder
.master("local[*]")
.appName("myLabeledPoint")
.config("spark.sql.warehouse.dir", ".")
.getOrCreate()
```

5. We create the LabeledPoint, using the `SparseVector` and `DenseVector`. In the following code blocks, the first four LabeledPoints are created by the `DenseVector`, the last two LabeledPoints are created by the `SparseVector`:

```
val myLabeledPoints = spark.createDataFrame(Seq(
LabeledPoint(1.0, Vectors.dense(0.0, 1.1, 0.1)),
LabeledPoint(0.0, Vectors.dense(2.0, 1.0, -1.0)),
LabeledPoint(0.0, Vectors.dense(2.0, 1.3, 1.0)),
LabeledPoint(1.0, Vectors.dense(0.0, 1.2, -0.5)),

LabeledPoint(0.0, Vectors.sparse(3, Array(0,2), Array(1.0,3.0))),
LabeledPoint(1.0, Vectors.sparse(3, Array(1,2), Array(1.2,-0.4)))

))
```

The DataFrame objects are created from the preceding LabeledPoint.

6. We verify the raw data count and process data count.

7. You can operate a `show()` function call to the DataFrame created:

```
myLabeledPoints.show()
```

8. You will see the following in the console:

```
+-----+--------------------+
|label|            features|
+-----+--------------------+
|  1.0|      [0.0,1.1,0.1]|
|  0.0|      [2.0,1.0,-1.0]|
|  0.0|      [2.0,1.3,1.0]|
|  1.0|      [0.0,1.2,-0.5]|
|  0.0| (3,[0,2],[1.0,3.0])|
|  1.0|(3,[1,2],[1.2,-0.4])|
+-----+--------------------+
```

9. We create a simple LogisticRegression model from the data structure we just created:

```
val lr = new LogisticRegression()

lr.setMaxIter(5)
.setRegParam(0.01)
val model = lr.fit(myLabeledPoints)

println("Model was fit using parameters: " +
model.parent.extractParamMap())
```

In the console, it will show the following `model` parameters:

```
Model was fit using parameters: {
  logreg_6aebbb683272-elasticNetParam: 0.0,
  logreg_6aebbb683272-featuresCol: features,
  logreg_6aebbb683272-fitIntercept: true,
  logreg_6aebbb683272-labelCol: label,
  logreg_6aebbb683272-maxIter: 5,
  logreg_6aebbb683272-predictionCol: prediction,
  logreg_6aebbb683272-probabilityCol: probability,
  logreg_6aebbb683272-rawPredictionCol: rawPrediction,
  logreg_6aebbb683272-regParam: 0.01,
  logreg_6aebbb683272-standardization: true,
  logreg_6aebbb683272-threshold: 0.5,
  logreg_6aebbb683272-tol: 1.0E-6
}
```

10. We then close the program by stopping the Spark session:

```
spark.stop()
```

How it works...

We used a LabeledPoint data structure to model features and drive training of a logistics regression model. We began by defining a group of LabeledPoints, which are used to create a DataFrame for further processing. Then, we created a logistic regression object and passed LabeledPoint DataFrame as an argument to it so we could train our model. Spark ML APIs are designed to work well with the LabeledPoint format and require minimal intervention.

There's more...

A LabeledPoint is a popular structure used to package data as a `Vector` + a `Label` which can be purposed for supervised machine learning algorithms. A typical layout of the LabeledPoint is given here:

```
Seq(
LabeledPoint (Label, Vector(data, data, data))
......
LabeledPoint (Label, Vector(data, data, data))
)
```

Please note that not only dense but also sparse vectors can be used with LabeledPoint, which will make a huge difference in efficiency especially if you have a large and sparse dataset housed in the driver during testing and development.

See also

- LabeledPoint API documentation is available
  at `https://spark.apache.org/docs/latest/api/scala/index.html#org.apache.spark.ml.feature.LabeledPoint`
- DenseVector API documentation is available
  at `https://spark.apache.org/docs/latest/api/scala/index.html#org.apache.spark.ml.linalg.DenseVector`
- SparseVector API documentation is available
  at `https://spark.apache.org/docs/latest/api/scala/index.html#org.apache.spark.ml.linalg.SparseVector`

Getting access to Spark cluster in Spark 2.0

In this recipe, we demonstrate how to get access to a Spark cluster using a single point access named SparkSession. Spark 2.0 abstracts multiple contexts (such as SQLContext, HiveContext) into a single entry point, SparkSession, which allows you to get access to all Spark subsystems in a unified way.

How to do it...

1. Start a new project in IntelliJ or in an IDE of your choice. Make sure that the necessary JAR files are included.
2. Set up the package location where the program will reside:

```
package spark.ml.cookbook.chapter4
```

3. Import the necessary packages for SparkContext to get access to the cluster.
4. In Spark 2.x, SparkSession is more commonly used instead.

```
import org.apache.spark.sql.SparkSession
```

5. Create Spark's configuration and SparkSession so we can have access to the cluster:

```
val spark = SparkSession
.builder
.master("local[*]") // if use cluster master("spark://master:7077")
.appName("myAccesSparkCluster20")
.config("spark.sql.warehouse.dir", ".")
.getOrCreate()
```

The preceding code utilizes the master() function to set the cluster type to local. A comment is provided to show how to run the local cluster running on a specific port.

The -D option value will be overridden by the cluster master parameter set in the code if both exist.

In a SparkSession object, we typically use the master() function, while pre-Spark 2.0, in the SparkConf object, uses the setMaster() function.

The following are the three sample ways to connect to a cluster in different modes:

1. Running in `local` mode:

   ```
   master("local")
   ```

2. Running in cluster mode:

   ```
   master("spark://yourmasterhostIP:port")
   ```

3. Passing the master value in:

   ```
   -Dspark.master=local
   ```

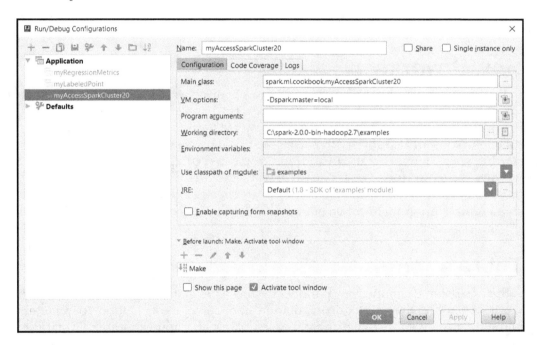

4. We read a CSV file in and parse the CSV file into Spark using the following code:

   ```
   val df = spark.read
           .option("header","True")
           .csv("../data/sparkml2/chapter4/mySampleCSV.csv")
   ```

5. We show the DataFrame in the console:

   ```
   df.show()
   ```

6. And you will see the following in the console:

```
+----+----+----+----------+
|col1|col2|col3|      col4|
+----+----+----+----------+
|   1|  16| 4.0|1217897793|
|   1|  24| 1.5|1217895807|
|   1|  32| 4.0|1217896246|
|   1|  47| 4.0|1217896556|
|   1|  50| 4.0|1217896523|
+----+----+----+----------+
```

7. We then close the program by stopping the Spark session:

```
spark.stop()
```

How it works...

In this example, we show how to connect to a Spark cluster using local and remote options for an application. First, we create a `SparkSession` object which will grant us access to a Spark cluster by specifying whether the cluster is local or remote using the `master()` function. You can also specify the master location by passing a JVM argument when starting your client program. In addition, you can configure an application name and a working data directory. Next, you invoked the `getOrCreate()` method to create a new `SparkSession` or hand you a reference to an already existing session. Finally, we execute a small sample program to prove our `SparkSession` object creation is valid.

There's more...

A Spark session has numerous parameters and APIs that can be set and exercised, but it is worth consulting the Spark documentation since some of the methods/parameters are marked with the status **Experimental** or left blank - for non-experimental statuses (15 minimum as of our last examination).

Another change to be aware of is to use `spark.sql.warehouse.dir` for the location of the tables. Spark 2.0 uses `spark.sql.warehouse.dir` to set warehouse locations to store tables rather than `hive.metastore.warehouse.dir`. The default value for `spark.sql.warehouse.dir` is `System.getProperty("user.dir")`.

Also see `spark-defaults.conf` for more details.

Also noteworthy are the following:

- Some of our favorite and interesting APIs from the Spark 2.0 documentation:

  Def **version**: String

The version of Spark on which this application is running:

- Def **sql**(sqlText: String): DataFrame

  Executes a SQL query using Spark, returning the result as a DataFrame - **Preferred Spark 2.0**

- Val **sqlContext**: SQLContext

  A wrapped version of this session in the form of a SQLContext, for backward compatibility.

- lazy val **conf**: RuntimeConfig

  Runtime configuration interface for Spark.

- lazy val **catalog**: Catalog

  Interface through which the user may create, drop, alter, or query underlying databases, tables, functions, and so on.

- **Def newSession(): SparkSession**

  Starts a new session with isolated SQL configurations and temporary tables; registered functions are isolated, but share the underlying SparkContext and cached data.

- Def **udf**: UDFRegistration

  A collection of methods for registering user-defined functions (UDF).

We can create both DataFrame and Dataset directly via the Spark session. It works, but is marked as experimental in Spark 2.0.0.

If you are going to do any SQL related work, SparkSession is now the entry point to Spark SQL. SparkSession is the first object that you have to create in order to create Spark SQL applications.

See also

Documentation for `SparkSession` API documents is available
at `https://spark.apache.org/docs/latest/api/scala/index.html#org.apache.spark.sql.SparkSession`.

Getting access to Spark cluster pre-Spark 2.0

This is a *pre-Spark 2.0 recipe*, but it will be helpful for developers who want to quickly compare and contrast the cluster access for porting pre-Spark 2.0 programs to Spark 2.0's new paradigm.

How to do it...

1. Start a new project in IntelliJ or in an IDE of your choice. Make sure that the necessary JAR files are included.

2. Set up the package location where the program will reside:

   ```
   package spark.ml.cookbook.chapter4
   ```

3. Import the necessary packages for SparkContext to get access to the cluster:

   ```
   import org.apache.spark.{SparkConf, SparkContext}
   ```

4. Create Spark's configuration and SparkContext so we can have access to the cluster:

   ```
   val conf = new SparkConf()
   .setAppName("MyAccessSparkClusterPre20")
   .setMaster("local[4]") // if cluster
   setMaster("spark://MasterHostIP:7077")
   .set("spark.sql.warehouse.dir", ".")

   val sc = new SparkContext(conf)
   ```

The preceding code utilizes the `setMaster()` function to set the cluster master location. As you can see, we are running the code in `local` mode.

The −D option value will be overridden by the cluster master parameter set in the code if both exist).

The following are the three sample ways to connect to the cluster in different modes:

1. Running in local mode:

   ```
   setMaster("local")
   ```

2. Running in cluster mode:

   ```
   setMaster("spark://yourmasterhostIP:port")
   ```

3. Passing the master value in:

   ```
   -Dspark.master=local
   ```

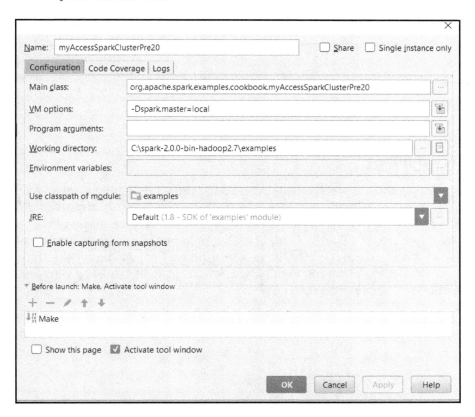

4. We use the preceding SparkContext to read a CSV file in and parse the CSV file into Spark using the following code:

```
val file = sc.textFile("../data/sparkml2/chapter4/mySampleCSV.csv")
val headerAndData = file.map(line => line.split(",").map(_.trim))
val header = headerAndData.first
val data = headerAndData.filter(_(0) != header(0))
val maps = data.map(splits => header.zip(splits).toMap)
```

5. We take the sample result and print them in the console:

```
val result = maps.take(4)
result.foreach(println)
```

6. And you will see the following in the console:

```
Map(col1 -> 1, col2 -> 16, col3 -> 4.0, col4 -> 1217897793)
Map(col1 -> 1, col2 -> 24, col3 -> 1.5, col4 -> 1217895807)
Map(col1 -> 1, col2 -> 32, col3 -> 4.0, col4 -> 1217896246)
Map(col1 -> 1, col2 -> 47, col3 -> 4.0, col4 -> 1217896556)
```

7. We then close the program by stopping the SparkContext:

```
sc.stop()
```

How it works...

In this example, we show how to connect to a Spark cluster using the local and remote modes prior to Spark 2.0. First, we create a `SparkConf` object and configure all the required parameters. We will specify the master location, application name, and working data directory. Next, we create a SparkContext passing the `SparkConf` as an argument to access a Spark cluster. Also, you can specify the master location my passing a JVM argument when starting your client program. Finally, we execute a small sample program to prove our SparkContext is functioning correctly.

There's more...

Prior to Spark 2.0, getting access to a Spark cluster was done via **SparkContext**.

The access to the subsystems such as SQL was per-specific names context (for example, SQLContext).

Spark 2.0 changed how we gain access to a cluster by creating a single unified access point (namely, SparkSession).

See also

Documentation for SparkContext is available
at https://spark.apache.org/docs/latest/api/scala/index.html#org.apache.spark.S
parkContext.

Getting access to SparkContext vis-a-vis SparkSession object in Spark 2.0

In this recipe, we demonstrate how to get hold of SparkContext using a SparkSession object in Spark 2.0. This recipe will demonstrate the creation, usage, and back and forth conversion of RDD to Dataset. The reason this is important is that even though we prefer Dataset going forward, we must still be able to use and augment the legacy (pre-Spark 2.0) code mostly utilizing RDD.

How to do it...

1. Start a new project in IntelliJ or in an IDE of your choice. Make sure the necessary JAR files are included.
2. Set up the package location where the program will reside:

```
package spark.ml.cookbook.chapter4
```

3. Import the necessary packages for the Spark session to gain access to the cluster and `log4j.Logger` to reduce the amount of output produced by Spark:

```
import org.apache.log4j.{Level, Logger}
import org.apache.spark.sql.SparkSession
import scala.util.Random
```

4. Set the output level to ERROR to reduce Spark's logging output:

```
Logger.getLogger("org").setLevel(Level.ERROR)
```

5. Initialize a Spark session specifying configurations with the builder pattern, thus making an entry point available for the Spark cluster:

```
val session = SparkSession
.builder
.master("local[*]")
.appName("SessionContextRDD")
.config("spark.sql.warehouse.dir", ".")
.getOrCreate()
```

6. We first show how to use `sparkContext` to create RDD. The following code samples were very common in Spark 1.x:

```
import session.implicits._

// SparkContext
val context = session.sparkContext
```

We get the `SparkContext` object:

```
println("SparkContext")

val rdd1 = context.makeRDD(Random.shuffle(1 to 10).toList)
rdd1.collect().foreach(println)
println("-" * 45)

val rdd2 = context.parallelize(Random.shuffle(20 to 30).toList)
rdd2.collect().foreach(println)
println("\n End of SparkContext> " + ("-" * 45))
```

We first create `rdd1` from the `makeRDD` method and display the RDD in the console:

```
SparkContext
4
6
1
10
5
2
7
3
9
8
```

We then use the `parallelize` method to generate `rdd2`, and display the data in the RDD in the console.

From the console output:

```
25
28
30
29
20
22
27
23
24
26
21
 End of SparkContext
```

7. Now we show the way to use the `session` object to create the dataset:

```
val dataset1 = session.range(40, 50)
 dataset1.show()

val dataset2 = session.createDataset(Random.shuffle(60 to
70).toList)
 dataset2.show()
```

We generated `dataset1` and `dataset2` using different methods.

From the console output:

For dataset1:

```
+---+
| id|
+---+
|  40|
|  41|
|  42|
|  43|
|  44|
|  45|
|  46|
|  47|
|  48|
|  49|
+---+
```

For dataset2:

```
+-----+
|value|
+-----+
|   61|
|   68|
|   62|
|   67|
|   70|
|   64|
|   69|
|   65|
|   60|
|   66|
|   63|
+-----+
```

8. We show the way to retrieve the underlying RDD from the dataset:

```
// retrieve underlying RDD from Dataset
val rdd3 = dataset2.rdd
rdd3.collect().foreach(println)
```

From the console output:

```
61
68
62
67
70
64
69
```

```
65
60
66
63
```

9. The following block shows a way to convert RDD to Dataset object:

```
// convert rdd to Dataset
val rdd4 = context.makeRDD(Random.shuffle(80 to 90).toList)
val dataset3 = session.createDataset(rdd4)
dataset3.show()
```

From the console output:

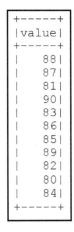

10. We close the program by stopping the Spark session:

```
session.stop()
```

How it works...

We created RDD using the SparkContext; this was widely used in Spark 1.x. We also demonstrated a way to create Dataset in Spark 2.0 using the Session object. The conversion back and forth is necessary to deal with pre-Spark 2.0 code in production today.

The technical message from this recipe is that while DataSet is the preferred method of data wrangling going forward, we can always use the API to go back and forth to RDD and vice versa.

There's more...

More about the datatypes can be found at `http://spark.apache.org/docs/latest/sql-programming-guide.html`.

See also

Documentation for SparkContext and SparkSession is available at the following websites:

- `http://spark.apache.org/docs/latest/api/scala/index.html#org.apache.spark.SparkContext`
- `http://spark.apache.org/docs/latest/api/scala/index.html#org.apache.spark.sql.SparkSession`

New model export and PMML markup in Spark 2.0

In this recipe, we explore the model export facility available in Spark 2.0 to use **Predictive Model Markup Language** (**PMML**). This standard XML-based language allows you to export and run your models on other systems (some limitations apply). You can explore the *There's more...* section for more information.

How to do it...

1. Start a new project in IntelliJ or in an IDE of your choice. Make sure that the necessary JAR files are included.
2. Set up the package location where the program will reside:

```
package spark.ml.cookbook.chapter4
```

3. Import the necessary packages for SparkContext to get access to the cluster:

```
import org.apache.spark.mllib.linalg.Vectors
import org.apache.spark.sql.SparkSession
import org.apache.spark.mllib.clustering.KMeans
```

4. Create Spark's configuration and SparkContext:

```
val spark = SparkSession
.builder
.master("local[*]")    // if use cluster
master("spark://master:7077")
.appName("myPMMLExport")
.config("spark.sql.warehouse.dir", ".")
.getOrCreate()
```

5. We read the data from a text file; the data file contains a sample dataset for a KMeans model:

```
val data =
spark.sparkContext.textFile("../data/sparkml2/chapter4/my_kmeans_da
ta_sample.txt")

val parsedData = data.map(s => Vectors.dense(s.split('
').map(_.toDouble))).cache()
```

6. We set up the parameters for the KMeans model, and train the model using the preceding datasets and parameters:

```
val numClusters = 2
val numIterations = 10
val model = KMeans.train(parsedData, numClusters, numIterations)
```

7. We have effectively created a simple KMeans model (by setting the number of clusters to 2) from the data structure we just created.

```
println("MyKMeans PMML Model:\n" + model.toPMML)
```

In the console, it will show the following model:

```
MyKMeans PMML Model:
<?xml version="1.0" encoding="UTF-8" standalone="yes"?>
<PMML version="4.2" xmlns="http://www.dmg.org/PMML-4_2">
    <Header description="k-means clustering">
        <Application name="Apache Spark MLlib" version="2.0.0"/>
        <Timestamp>2016-11-06T13:34:57</Timestamp>
    </Header>
    <DataDictionary numberOfFields="3">
        <DataField name="field_0" optype="continuous"
dataType="double"/>
        <DataField name="field_1" optype="continuous"
dataType="double"/>
        <DataField name="field_2" optype="continuous"
dataType="double"/>
    </DataDictionary>
    <ClusteringModel modelName="k-means" functionName="clustering"
modelClass="centerBased" numberOfClusters="2">
        <MiningSchema>
            <MiningField name="field_0" usageType="active"/>
            <MiningField name="field_1" usageType="active"/>
            <MiningField name="field_2" usageType="active"/>
        </MiningSchema>
        <ComparisonMeasure kind="distance">
            <squaredEuclidean/>
        </ComparisonMeasure>
        <ClusteringField field="field_0"
compareFunction="absDiff"/>
        <ClusteringField field="field_1"
compareFunction="absDiff"/>
        <ClusteringField field="field_2"
compareFunction="absDiff"/>
        <Cluster name="cluster_0">
            <Array n="3" type="real">9.06 9.179999999999998
9.12</Array>
        </Cluster>
        <Cluster name="cluster_1">
            <Array n="3" type="real">0.1166666666666665
0.1166666666666665 0.13333333333333333</Array>
        </Cluster>
    </ClusteringModel>
</PMML>
```

8. We then export the PMML to an XML file in the data directory:

```
model.toPMML("../data/sparkml2/chapter4/myKMeansSamplePMML.xml")
```

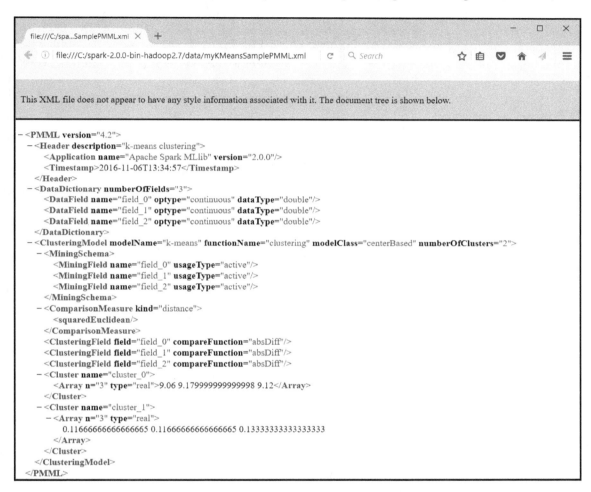

9. We then close the program by stopping the Spark session:

```
spark.stop()
```

How it works...

After you spend the time to train a model, the next step will be to persist the model for future use. In this recipe, we began by training a KMeans model to generate model info for persistence in later steps. Once we have the trained model, we invoke the `toPMML()` method on the model converting it into PMML for storage. The invocation of the method generates an XML document, then the XML document text can easily be persisted to a file.

There's more...

PMML is a standard developed by the **Data Mining Group** (**DMG**). The standard enables inter-platform interoperability by letting you build on one system and then deploy to another system in production. The PMML standard has gained momentum and has been adopted by most vendors. At its core, the standard is based on an XML document with the following:

- Header with general information
- Dictionary describing field level definitions used by the third component (the model)
- Model structure and parameters

As of this writing, the Spark 2.0 Machine Library support for PMML exporting is currently limited to:

- Linear Regression
- Logistic Regression
- Ridge Regression
- Lasso
- SVM
- KMeans

You can export the model to the following file types in Spark:

- Local filesystem:

```
Model_a.toPMML("/xyz/model-name.xml")
```

- Distributed filesystem:

```
Model_a.toPMML(SparkContext, "/xyz/model-name")
```

- Output stream--acting as a pipe:

```
Model_a.toPMML(System.out)
```

See also

Documentation for PMMLExportable API documents at http://spark.apache.org/docs/latest/api/scala/index.html#org.apache.spark.mllib.pmml.PMMLExportable.

Regression model evaluation using Spark 2.0

In this recipe, we explore how to evaluate a regression model (a regression decision tree in this example). Spark provides the **RegressionMetrics** facility which has basic statistical facilities such as **Mean Squared Error** (**MSE**), R-Squared, and so on, right out of the box.

The objective in this recipe is to understand the evaluation metrics provided by Spark out of the box.

How to do it...

1. Start a new project in IntelliJ or in an IDE of your choice. Make sure that the necessary JAR files are included.

2. Set up the package location where the program will reside:

```
package spark.ml.cookbook.chapter4
```

3. Import the necessary packages for SparkContext to get access to the cluster:

```
import org.apache.spark.mllib.evaluation.RegressionMetrics
import org.apache.spark.mllib.linalg.Vectors
import org.apache.spark.mllib.regression.LabeledPoint
import org.apache.spark.mllib.tree.DecisionTree
import org.apache.spark.sql.SparkSession
```

4. Create Spark's configuration and SparkContext:

```
val spark = SparkSession
.builder
.master("local[*]")
.appName("myRegressionMetrics")
.config("spark.sql.warehouse.dir", ".")
.getOrCreate()
```

5. We utilize the Wisconsin breast cancer dataset as an example dataset for the regression model.

The **Wisconsin breast cancer** dataset was obtained from the University of Wisconsin Hospital from Dr. William H Wolberg. The dataset was gained periodically as Dr.Wolberg reported his clinical cases.

```
val rawData =
spark.sparkContext.textFile("../data/sparkml2/chapter4/breast-cancer-wisconsin.data")
val data = rawData.map(_.trim)
    .filter(text => !(text.isEmpty || text.indexOf("?") > -1))
    .map { line =>
      val values = line.split(',').map(_.toDouble)
      val slicedValues = values.slice(1, values.size)
      val featureVector = Vectors.dense(slicedValues.init)
      val label = values.last / 2 -1
      LabeledPoint(label, featureVector)

    }
```

We load the data into Spark and filter the missing values in the data.

6. We split the dataset in the ratio of 70:30 to create two datasets, one used for training the model, and the other for testing the model:

```
val splits = data.randomSplit(Array(0.7, 0.3))
val (trainingData, testData) = (splits(0), splits(1))
```

7. We set up the parameters and using the `DecisionTree` model, after the training dataset, we use the test dataset to do the prediction:

```
val categoricalFeaturesInfo = Map[Int, Int]()
val impurity = "variance"
val maxDepth = 5
val maxBins = 32

val model = DecisionTree.trainRegressor(trainingData,
categoricalFeaturesInfo, impurity,
maxDepth, maxBins)
val predictionsAndLabels = testData.map(example =>
(model.predict(example.features), example.label)
)
```

8. We instantiate the `RegressionMetrics` object and start the evaluation:

```
val metrics = new RegressionMetrics(predictionsAndLabels)
```

9. We print out the statistics value in the console:

```
// Squared error
println(s"MSE = ${metrics.meanSquaredError}")
 println(s"RMSE = ${metrics.rootMeanSquaredError}")

 // R-squared
println(s"R-squared = ${metrics.r2}")

 // Mean absolute error
println(s"MAE = ${metrics.meanAbsoluteError}")

 // Explained variance
println(s"Explained variance = ${metrics.explainedVariance}")
```

From the console output:

```
MSE = 0.06071332254584681
RMSE = 0.2464007356844675
R-squared = 0.7444017305996473
MAE = 0.0691747572815534
Explained variance = 0.22591111058744653
```

10. We then close the program by stopping the Spark session:

```
spark.stop()
```

How it works...

In this recipe, we explored the generation of regression metrics to help us evaluate our regression model. We began to load a breast cancer data file and then split it in a 70/30 ratio to create training and test datasets. Next, we trained a `DecisionTree` regression model and utilized it to make predictions on our test set. Finally, we took the predictions and generated regression metrics which gave us the squared error, R-squared, mean absolute error, and explained variance.

There's more...

We can use `RegressionMetrics()` to produce the following statistical measures:

- MSE
- RMSE
- R-squared
- MAE
- Explained variance

Documentation on regression validation is available
at `https://en.wikipedia.org/wiki/Regression_validation`.

R-Squared/coefficient of determination is available
at `https://en.wikipedia.org/wiki/Coefficient_of_determination`.

See also

- The Wisconsin breast cancer dataset could be downloaded
  at `ftp://ftp.cs.wisc.edu/math-prog/cpo-dataset/machine-learn/cancer/cancer1/datacum`
- Regression metrics documents are available at `http://spark.apache.org/docs/latest/api/scala/index.html#org.apache.spark.mllib.evaluation.RegressionMetrics`

Binary classification model evaluation using Spark 2.0

In this recipe, we demonstrate the use of the `BinaryClassificationMetrics` facility in Spark 2.0 and its application to evaluating a model that has a binary outcome (for example, a logistic regression).

The purpose here is not to showcase the regression itself, but to demonstrate how to go about evaluating it using common metrics such as **receiver operating characteristic (ROC)**, Area Under ROC Curve, thresholds, and so on.

How to do it...

1. Start a new project in IntelliJ or in an IDE of your choice. Make sure that the necessary JAR files are included.

2. Set up the package location where the program will reside:

```
package spark.ml.cookbook.chapter4
```

3. Import the necessary packages for SparkContext to get access to the cluster:

```
import org.apache.spark.sql.SparkSession
import org.apache.spark.mllib.classification.LogisticRegressionWithLBFGS
import org.apache.spark.mllib.evaluation.BinaryClassificationMetrics
import org.apache.spark.mllib.regression.LabeledPoint
import org.apache.spark.mllib.util.MLUtils
```

4. Create Spark's configuration and SparkContext:

```
val spark = SparkSession
.builder
.master("local[*]")
.appName("myBinaryClassification")
.config("spark.sql.warehouse.dir", ".")
.getOrCreate()
```

5. We download the dataset, originally from the UCI, and modify it to fit the need for the code:

```
// Load training data in LIBSVM format
//https://www.csie.ntu.edu.tw/~cjlin/libsvmtools/datasets/binary.html
val data = MLUtils.loadLibSVMFile(spark.sparkContext,
"../data/sparkml2/chapter4/myBinaryClassificationData.txt")
```

The dataset is a modified dataset. The original adult dataset has 14 features, among which six are continuous and eight are categorical. In this dataset, continuous features are discretized into quantiles, and each quantile is represented by a binary feature. We modified the data to fit the purpose of the code. Details of the dataset feature can be found at the `http://archive.ics.uci.edu/ml/index.php` UCI site.

6. We split the dataset into training and test parts in a ratio of 60:40 random split, then get the model:

```
val Array(training, test) = data.randomSplit(Array(0.6, 0.4), seed
= 11L)
 training.cache()

 // Run training algorithm to build the model
val model = new LogisticRegressionWithLBFGS()
 .setNumClasses(2)
 .run(training)
```

7. We create the prediction using the model created by the training dataset:

```
val predictionAndLabels = test.map { case LabeledPoint(label,
features) =>
 val prediction = model.predict(features)
 (prediction, label)
 }
```

8. We create the `BinaryClassificationMetrics` object from the predication, and start the evaluation on the metrics:

```
val metrics = new BinaryClassificationMetrics(predictionAndLabels)
```

9. We print out the precision by `Threashold` in the console:

```
val precision = metrics.precisionByThreshold
precision.foreach { case (t, p) =>
println(s"Threshold: $t, Precision: $p")
}
```

From the console output:

```
Threshold: 2.9751613212299755E-210, Precision: 0.5405405405405406
Threshold: 1.0, Precision: 0.4838709677419355
Threshold: 1.5283665404870175E-268, Precision: 0.5263157894736842
Threshold: 4.889258814400478E-95, Precision: 0.5
```

10. We print out the `recallByThreshold` in the console:

```
val recall = metrics.recallByThreshold
recall.foreach { case (t, r) =>
println(s"Threshold: $t, Recall: $r")
}
```

From the console output:

```
Threshold: 1.0779893231660571E-300, Recall: 0.6363636363636364
Threshold: 6.830452412352692E-181, Recall: 0.5151515151515151
Threshold: 0.0, Recall: 1.0
Threshold: 1.1547199216963482E-194, Recall: 0.5757575757575758
```

11. We print out the `fmeasureByThreshold` in the console:

```
val f1Score = metrics.fMeasureByThreshold
f1Score.foreach { case (t, f) =>
println(s"Threshold: $t, F-score: $f, Beta = 1")
}
```

From the console output:

```
Threshold: 1.0, F-score: 0.46874999999999994, Beta = 1
Threshold: 4.889258814400478E-95, F-score: 0.49230769230769234,
Beta = 1
Threshold: 2.2097791212639423E-117, F-score: 0.48484848484848486,
Beta = 1

val beta = 0.5
val fScore = metrics.fMeasureByThreshold(beta)
f1Score.foreach { case (t, f) =>
  println(s"Threshold: $t, F-score: $f, Beta = 0.5")
}
```

From the console output:

```
Threshold: 2.9751613212299755E-210, F-score: 0.5714285714285714,
Beta = 0.5
Threshold: 1.0, F-score: 0.46874999999999994, Beta = 0.5
Threshold: 1.5283665404870175E-268, F-score: 0.5633802816901409,
Beta = 0.5
Threshold: 4.889258814400478E-95, F-score: 0.49230769230769234,
Beta = 0.5
```

12. We print out the `Area Under Precision Recall Curve` in the console:

```
val auPRC = metrics.areaUnderPR
println("Area under precision-recall curve = " + auPRC)
```

From the console output:

```
Area under precision-recall curve = 0.5768388996048239
```

13. We print out the Area Under ROC curve in the console:

```
val thresholds = precision.map(_._1)

val roc = metrics.roc

val auROC = metrics.areaUnderROC
println("Area under ROC = " + auROC)
```

From the console output:

```
Area under ROC = 0.6983957219251337
```

14. We then close the program by stopping the Spark session:

```
spark.stop()
```

How it works...

In this recipe, we investigated the evaluation of metrics for binary classification. First, we loaded the data, which is in the `libsvm` format, and split it in the ratio of 60:40, resulting in the creation of a training and a test set of data. Next, we trained a logistic regression model followed by generating predictions from our test set.

Once we had our predictions, we created a binary classification metrics object. Finally, we retrieved the true positive rate, positive predictive value, receiver operating curve, the area under receiver operating curve, the area under precision recall curve, and F-measure to evaluate our model for fitness.

There's more...

Spark provides the following metrics to facilitate evaluation:

- TPR - True Positive Rate
- PPV - Positive Predictive Value
- F - F-Measure
- ROC - Receiver Operating Curve
- AUROC - Area Under Receiver Operating Curve
- AUORC - Area Under Precision-Recall Curve

The following links should provide a good introductory material for the metrics:

- https://en.wikipedia.org/wiki/Receiver_operating_characteristic
- https://en.wikipedia.org/wiki/Sensitivity_and_specificity
- https://en.wikipedia.org/wiki/F1_score

See also

Documentation for the original dataset information is available at the following links:

- https://www.csie.ntu.edu.tw/~cjlin/libsvmtools/datasets/binary.html
- http://archive.ics.uci.edu/ml/datasets.html

Documentation for binary classification metrics is available at http://spark.apache.org/docs/latest/api/scala/index.html#org.apache.spark.ml lib.evaluation.BinaryClassificationMetrics.

Multiclass classification model evaluation using Spark 2.0

In this recipe, we explore `MulticlassMetrics`, which allows you to evaluate a model that classifies the output to more than two labels (for example, red, blue, green, purple, do-not-know). It highlights the use of a confusion matrix (`confusionMatrix`) and model accuracy.

How to do it...

1. Start a new project in IntelliJ or in an IDE of your choice. Make sure that the necessary JAR files are included.

2. Set up the package location where the program will reside:

   ```
   package spark.ml.cookbook.chapter4
   ```

3. Import the necessary packages for SparkContext to get access to the cluster:

   ```
   import org.apache.spark.sql.SparkSession
   import
   org.apache.spark.mllib.classification.LogisticRegressionWithLBFGS
   import org.apache.spark.mllib.evaluation.MulticlassMetrics
   import org.apache.spark.mllib.regression.LabeledPoint
   import org.apache.spark.mllib.util.MLUtils
   ```

4. Create Spark's configuration and SparkContext:

   ```
   val spark = SparkSession
   .builder
   .master("local[*]")
   .appName("myMulticlass")
   .config("spark.sql.warehouse.dir", ".")
   .getOrCreate()
   ```

5. We download the dataset, originally from the UCI, and modify it to fit the need of the code:

   ```
   // Load training data in LIBSVM format
   //https://www.csie.ntu.edu.tw/~cjlin/libsvmtools/datasets/multiclas
   s.html
   val data = MLUtils.loadLibSVMFile(spark.sparkContext,
   "../data/sparkml2/chapter4/myMulticlassIrisData.txt")
   ```

The dataset is a modified dataset. The original Iris Plant dataset has four features. We modified the data to fit the purpose of the code. Details of the dataset features can be found at the UCI site.

6. We split the dataset into training and test parts in a ratio of 60% versus 40% random split, then get the model:

```
val Array(training, test) = data.randomSplit(Array(0.6, 0.4), seed
= 11L)
 training.cache()

 // Run training algorithm to build the model
val model = new LogisticRegressionWithLBFGS()
 .setNumClasses(3)
 .run(training)
```

7. We compute the raw score on the test dataset:

```
val predictionAndLabels = test.map { case LabeledPoint(label,
features) =>
 val prediction = model.predict(features)
 (prediction, label)
 }
```

8. We create the `MulticlassMetrics` object from the predication, and start the evaluation on the metrics:

```
val metrics = new MulticlassMetrics(predictionAndLabels)
```

9. We print out the confusion matrix in the console:

```
println("Confusion matrix:")
println(metrics.confusionMatrix)
```

From the console output:

```
Confusion matrix:
18.0 0.0 0.0
0.0 15.0 8.0
0.0 0.0 22.0
```

10. We print out the overall statistics in the console:

```
val accuracy = metrics.accuracy
println("Summary Statistics")
println(s"Accuracy = $accuracy")
```

From the console output:

```
Summary Statistics
Accuracy = 0.873015873015873
```

11. We print out the precision by label value in the console:

```
val labels = metrics.labels
labels.foreach { l =>
 println(s"Precision($l) = " + metrics.precision(l))
 }
```

From the console output:

```
Precision(0.0) = 1.0
Precision(1.0) = 1.0
Precision(2.0) = 0.7333333333333333
```

12. We print out the recall by label in the console:

```
labels.foreach { l =>
println(s"Recall($l) = " + metrics.recall(l))
 }
```

From the console output:

```
Recall(0.0) = 1.0
Recall(1.0) = 0.6521739130434783
Recall(2.0) = 1.0
```

13. We print out the false positive rate by label in the console:

```
labels.foreach { l =>
 println(s"FPR($l) = " + metrics.falsePositiveRate(l))
 }
```

From the console output:

```
FPR(0.0) = 0.0
FPR(1.0) = 0.0
FPR(2.0) = 0.1951219512195122
```

14. We print out the F-measure by label in the console:

```
labels.foreach { l =>
 println(s"F1-Score($l) = " + metrics.fMeasure(l))
 }
```

From the console output:

```
F1-Score(0.0) = 1.0
F1-Score(1.0) = 0.7894736842105263
F1-Score(2.0) = 0.846153846153846
```

15. We print out the weighted statistics value in the console:

```
println(s"Weighted precision: ${metrics.weightedPrecision}")
 println(s"Weighted recall: ${metrics.weightedRecall}")
 println(s"Weighted F1 score: ${metrics.weightedFMeasure}")
 println(s"Weighted false positive rate:
 ${metrics.weightedFalsePositiveRate}")
```

From the console output:

```
Weighted precision: 0.9068783068783068
Weighted recall: 0.873015873015873
Weighted F1 score: 0.8694171325750273
Weighted false positive rate: 0.06813782423538521
```

16. We then close the program by stopping the Spark session:

```
spark.stop()
```

How it works...

In this recipe, we explored generating evaluation metrics for a multi-classification model. First, we loaded the Iris data into memory and split it in a ratio of 60:40. Second, we trained a logistic regression model with the number of classifications set to three. Third, we made predictions with the test dataset and utilized `MultiClassMetric` to generate evaluation measurements. Finally, we evaluated metrics such as the model accuracy, weighted precision, weighted recall, weighted F1 score, weighted false positive rate, and so on.

There's more...

While the scope of the book does not allow for a complete treatment of the confusion matrix, a short explanation and a link are provided as a quick reference.

The confusion matrix is just a fancy name for an error matrix. It is mostly used in unsupervised learning to visualize the performance. It is a layout that captures actual versus predicted outcomes with an identical set of labels in two dimensions:

Confusion Matrix

	Predicted		
	Label1	*Label2*	*Label3*
	18.0	*0.0*	*0.0*
Actual	*0.0*	*15.0*	*8.0*
	0.0	*0.0*	*22.0*

To get a quick introduction to the confusion matrix in unsupervised and supervised statistical learning systems, see `https://en.wikipedia.org/wiki/Confusion_matrix`.

See also

Documentation for original dataset information is available at the following websites:

- `https://www.csie.ntu.edu.tw/~cjlin/libsvmtools/datasets/multiclass.html`
- `http://archive.ics.uci.edu/ml/datasets/Iris`

Documentation for multiclass classification metrics is available at:

- `http://spark.apache.org/docs/latest/api/scala/index.html#org.apache.spark.mllib.evaluation.MulticlassMetrics`

Multilabel classification model evaluation using Spark 2.0

In this recipe, we explore multilabel classification `MultilabelMetrics` in Spark 2.0 which should not be mixed up with the previous recipe dealing with multiclass classification `MulticlassMetrics`. The key to exploring this recipe is to concentrate on evaluation metrics such as Hamming loss, accuracy, f1-measure, and so on, and what they measure.

How to do it...

1. Start a new project in IntelliJ or in an IDE of your choice. Make sure that the necessary JAR files are included.

2. Set up the package location where the program will reside:

   ```
   package spark.ml.cookbook.chapter4
   ```

3. Import the necessary packages for SparkContext to get access to the cluster:

   ```
   import org.apache.spark.sql.SparkSession
   import org.apache.spark.mllib.evaluation.MultilabelMetrics
   import org.apache.spark.rdd.RDD
   ```

4. Create Spark's configuration and SparkContext:

   ```
   val spark = SparkSession
   .builder
   .master("local[*]")
   .appName("myMultilabel")
   .config("spark.sql.warehouse.dir", ".")
   .getOrCreate()
   ```

5. We create the dataset for the evaluation model:

   ```
   val data: RDD[(Array[Double], Array[Double])] =
   spark.sparkContext.parallelize(
   Seq((Array(0.0, 1.0), Array(0.1, 2.0)),
        (Array(0.0, 2.0), Array(0.1, 1.0)),
        (Array.empty[Double], Array(0.0)),
        (Array(2.0), Array(2.0)),
        (Array(2.0, 0.0), Array(2.0, 0.0)),
        (Array(0.0, 1.0, 2.0), Array(0.0, 1.0)),
        (Array(1.0), Array(1.0, 2.0))), 2)
   ```

6. We create the `MultilabelMetrics` object from the predication, and start the evaluation on the metrics:

   ```
   val metrics = new MultilabelMetrics(data)
   ```

7. We print out the overall statistics summary in the console:

```
println(s"Recall = ${metrics.recall}")
println(s"Precision = ${metrics.precision}")
println(s"F1 measure = ${metrics.f1Measure}")
println(s"Accuracy = ${metrics.accuracy}")
```

From the console output:

```
Recall = 0.5
Precision = 0.5238095238095238
F1 measure = 0.4952380952380952
Accuracy = 0.4523809523809524
```

8. We print out the individual label value in the console:

```
metrics.labels.foreach(label =>
 println(s"Class $label precision = ${metrics.precision(label)}"))
 metrics.labels.foreach(label => println(s"Class $label recall =
${metrics.recall(label)}"))
 metrics.labels.foreach(label => println(s"Class $label F1-score =
${metrics.f1Measure(label)}"))
```

From the console output:

```
Class 0.0 precision = 0.5
Class 1.0 precision = 0.6666666666666666
Class 2.0 precision = 0.5
Class 0.0 recall = 0.6666666666666666
Class 1.0 recall = 0.6666666666666666
Class 2.0 recall = 0.5
Class 0.0 F1-score = 0.5714285714285715
Class 1.0 F1-score = 0.6666666666666666
Class 2.0 F1-score = 0.5
```

9. We print out the micro-statistics value in the console:

```
println(s"Micro recall = ${metrics.microRecall}")
println(s"Micro precision = ${metrics.microPrecision}")
println(s"Micro F1 measure = ${metrics.microF1Measure}")
From the console output:
Micro recall = 0.5
Micro precision = 0.5454545454545454
Micro F1 measure = 0.5217391304347826
```

10. We print out the Hamming loss and subset accuracy from the metrics in the console:

```
println(s"Hamming loss = ${metrics.hammingLoss}")
println(s"Subset accuracy = ${metrics.subsetAccuracy}")
From the console output:
Hamming loss = 0.39285714285714285
Subset accuracy = 0.2857142857142857
```

11. We then close the program by stopping the Spark session.

```
spark.stop()
```

How it works...

In this recipe, we investigated generating evaluation metrics for the multilabel classification model. We began with manually creating a dataset for the model evaluation. Next, we passed our dataset as an argument to the `MultilabelMetrics` and generated evaluation metrics. Finally, we printed out various metrics such as micro recall, micro precision, micro f1-measure, Hamming loss, subset accuracy, and so on.

There's more...

Note that the multilabel and multiclass classifications sound similar, but they are two different things.

All multilabel `MultilabelMetrics()` method is trying to accomplish is to map a number of inputs (x) to a binary vector (y) rather than numerical values in a typical classification system.

The important metrics associated with the multilabel classification are (see the preceding code):

- Accuracy
- Hamming loss
- Precision
- Recall
- F1

A full explanation of each parameter is out of scope, but the following link provides a short treatment for the multilabel metrics:

```
https://en.wikipedia.org/wiki/Multi-label_classification
```

See also

Documentation for multilabel classification metrics:

- `http://spark.apache.org/docs/latest/api/scala/index.html#org.apache.sp ark.mllib.evaluation.MultilabelMetrics`

Using the Scala Breeze library to do graphics in Spark 2.0

In this recipe, we will use the functions `scatter()` and `plot()` from the Scala Breeze linear algebra library (part of) to draw a scatter plot from a two-dimensional data. Once the results are computed on the Spark cluster, either the actionable data can be used in the driver for drawing or a JPEG or GIF can be generated in the backend and pushed forward for efficiency and speed (popular with GPU-based analytical databases such as MapD)

How to do it...

1. First, we need to download the necessary ScalaNLP library. Download the JAR from the Maven repository available
   at `https://repo1.maven.org/maven2/org/scalanlp/breeze-viz_2.11/0.12/bre eze-viz_2.11-0.12.jar`.

2. Place the JAR in the `C:\spark-2.0.0-bin-hadoop2.7\examples\jars` directory on a Windows machine:

3. In macOS, please put the JAR in its correct path. For our setting examples, the path is `/Users/USERNAME/spark/spark-2.0.0-bin-hadoop2.7/examples/jars/`.

4. The following is the sample screenshot showing the JARs:

5. Start a new project in IntelliJ or in an IDE of your choice. Make sure the necessary JAR files are included.

6. Set up the package location where the program will reside:

```
package spark.ml.cookbook.chapter4
```

7. Import the necessary packages for the Spark session to gain access to the cluster and `log4j.Logger` to reduce the amount of output produced by Spark:

```
import org.apache.log4j.{Level, Logger}
import org.apache.spark.sql.SparkSession
import breeze.plot._

import scala.util.Random
```

8. Set the output level to ERROR to reduce Spark's logging output:

```
Logger.getLogger("org").setLevel(Level.ERROR)
```

9. Initialize a Spark session by specifying configurations with the builder pattern, thus making an entry point available for the Spark cluster:

```
val spark = SparkSession
.builder
.master("local[*]")
.appName("myBreezeChart")
.config("spark.sql.warehouse.dir", ".")
.getOrCreate()
```

10. Now we create the figure object, and set the parameter for the figure:

```
import spark.implicits._

val fig = Figure()
val chart = fig.subplot(0)

chart.title = "My Breeze-Viz Chart"
chart.xlim(21,100)
chart.ylim(0,100000)
```

11. We create a dataset from random numbers, and display the dataset.

12. The dataset will be used later.

```
val ages = spark.createDataset(Random.shuffle(21 to
100).toList.take(45)).as[Int]

ages.show(false)
```

From the console output:

```
+-----+
|value|
+-----+
|85   |
|51   |
|82   |
|78   |
|45   |
|42   |
|35   |
|94   |
|72   |
|22   |
|44   |
|33   |
|48   |
|29   |
|47   |
|59   |
|91   |
|21   |
|28   |
|64   |
+-----+
only showing top 20 rows
```

13. We collect the dataset, and set up the x and y axis.
14. For the photo part, we convert the datatype to double, and derive the value to $y2$.
15. We use the Breeze library's scatter method to put the data into the chart, and plot the diagonal line with the plot method from Breeze:

```
val x = ages.collect()
val y = Random.shuffle(20000 to 100000).toList.take(45)

val x2 = ages.collect().map(xx => xx.toDouble)
val y2 = x2.map(xx => (1000 * xx) + (xx * 2))

chart += scatter(x, y, _ => 0.5)
chart += plot(x2, y2)

chart.xlabel = "Age"
chart.ylabel = "Income"

fig.refresh()
```

16. We set the label for both the x axis and y axis and refresh the figure object.
17. The following is the generated Breeze chart:

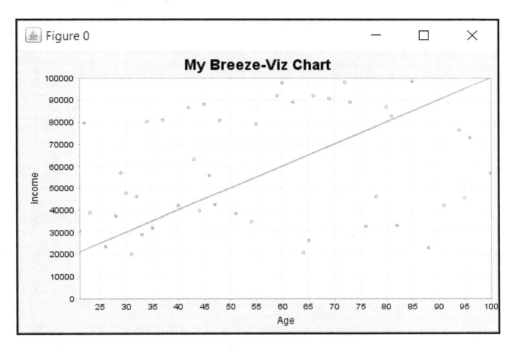

18. We close the program by stopping the Spark session:

```
spark.stop()
```

How it works...

In this recipe, we created a dataset in Spark from random numbers. We then created a Breeze figure and set up the basic parameters. We derived x, y data from the created dataset.

We used Breeze's `scatter()` and `plot()` functions to do graphics using the Breeze library.

There's more...

One can use Breeze as an alternative to more complicated and powerful charting libraries such as JFreeChart, demonstrated in the previous chapter. The ScalaNLP project tends to be optimized with Scala goodies such as implicit conversions that make the coding relatively easier.

The Breeze graphics JAR file can be downloaded at `http://central.maven.org/maven2/org/scalanlp/breeze-viz_2.11/0.12/breeze-viz_2.11-0.12.jar`.

More about Breeze graphics can be found at `https://github.com/scalanlp/breeze/wiki/Quickstart`.

The API document (please note, the API documentation is not necessarily up-to-date) can be found at `http://www.scalanlp.org/api/breeze/#package`.

> Note that once you are in the root package, you need click on **Breeze** to see the details.

See also

For more information on Breeze, see the original material on GitHub at `https://github.com/scalanlp/breeze`.

> Note that once you are in the root package, you need to click on **Breeze** to see the details.

For more information regarding the Breeze API documentation, please download the `https://repo1.maven.org/maven2/org/scalanlp/breeze-viz_2.11/0.12/breeze-viz_2.11-0.12-javadoc.jar` JAR.

13
Recommendation Engine that Scales with Spark

In this chapter, we will cover:

- Setting up the required data for a scalable recommendation engine in Spark 2.0
- Exploring the movies data details for the recommendation system in Spark 2.0
- Exploring the rating data details for the recommendation system in Spark 2.0
- Building a scalable recommendation engine using collaborative filtering in Spark 2.0

Introduction

In the previous chapters, we used short recipes and extremely simplified code to demonstrate basic building blocks and concepts governing the Spark machine library. In this chapter, we present a more developed application that addresses specific machine learning library domains using Spark's API and facilities. The number of recipes is less in this chapter; however, we get into a more ML application setting.

In this chapter, we explore the recommendation system and its implementation using a matrix factorization technique that draws on latent factor models called **alternating least square (ALS)**. In a nutshell, when we try to factorize a large matrix of user-item ratings into two lower ranked, skinnier matrices, we often face a non-linear or non-convex optimization problem that is very difficult to solve. It happens that we are very good at solving convex optimization problems by fixing one leg and partially solving the other and then going back and forth (hence alternating); we can solve this factorization (hence discovering a set of latent factors) much better using known optimization techniques in parallel.

We use a popular dataset (movie lens dataset) to implement the recommendation engine, but unlike in other chapters, we use two recipes to explore the data and also show how you can introduce graphical elements such as the JFreeChart popular library to your Spark machine learning toolkit.

The following figure shows the flow of the concepts and recipes in this chapter to demonstrate an ALS recommendation application:

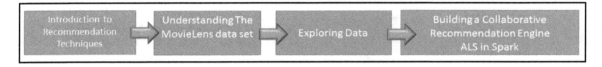

Recommendation engines have been around for a long time and were used in early e-commerce systems of the 1990s, using techniques ranging from hardcoded product association to content-based recommendations driven by profiling. The modern systems use **collaboration filtering** (**CF**) to address the shortcomings of the early systems and also to address the scale and latency (for example, 100 ms max and less) that is necessary to compete in modern commerce systems (for example, Amazon, Netflix, eBay, News, and so on).

The modern systems use CF based on historical interactions and records (page view, purchases, rating, and so on). These systems address two major issues, mainly scalability and sparseness (that is, we do not have all the ratings for all movies or songs). Most systems use a variation of Alternating Least Square with Weighted Lambda Regularization that can be parallelized on most major platforms (for example, Spark). Having said that, a practical system implemented for commercial purposes uses many augmentations to deal with bias (that is, not all movies and users are equal) and temporal issues (that is, users' choice will change and the inventory of items will change) that are present in today's ecosystem. Having worked on a smart and leading edge e-commerce system, building a competitive recommender is not a purist approach, but a practical one that uses multiple techniques, arriving at the affinity matrix/heat map as the context utilizing all three techniques (collaborative filtering, content-based filtering, and similarity) at the minimum.

The reader is encouraged to look up white papers and material that refer to the problem of cold start in recommendation systems.

To set the context, the following figure provides a high-level taxonomy of methods that are available to build recommendation systems. We briefly cover some of the pros and cons of each system but concentrate on matrix factorization (latent factor model) that is available in Spark.

While both **single value decomposition (SVD)** and **alternative least squares (ALS)** are available, we concentrate on ALS implementation with MovieLens data due to the shortcomings of SVD in handling missing data among other things.

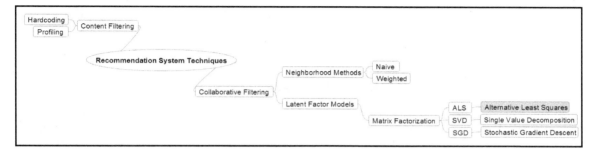

The recommendation engine techniques in use are explained in the following section.

Content filtering

Content filtering is one of the original techniques for recommendation engines. It relies on user profiles to make recommendations. This approach relies mostly on pre-existing profiles for users (type, demographics, income, geo-location, ZIP code) and inventory (characteristics of a product, movie, or a song) to infer attribution which then can be filtered and acted upon. The main issue is that the pre-existing knowledge is often incomplete and expensive to source. This technique is more than a decade old and is still being practiced.

Collaborative filtering

Collaborative filtering is the workhorse of modern recommendation systems and relies on user interaction in the ecosystem rather than profiles to make recommendations.

This technique relies on past user behavior and product ratings and does not assume any pre-existing knowledge. In short, users rate the inventory items and the assumption is that customer taste will remain relatively constant over time, which can be exploited to provide recommendations. Having said that, an intelligent system will augment and reorder recommendations with any available context (for example, the user is a female who has logged in from China).

The main issue with this class of techniques is cold start, but its advantages of being domain free, with more accuracy and easy scalability, has made it a winner in the age of big data.

Neighborhood method

This technique is mostly implemented as **weighted local neighborhood**. In its core, it is a similarity technique and relies heavily on assumptions about items and users. While it is easy to understand and implement the technique, the algorithm suffers from a lack of scalability and accuracy.

Latent factor models techniques

This technique attempts to explain users' ratings of inventory items (for example, products on Amazon) by inferring a secondary set of latent factors which are inferred from ratings. The power comes from the fact that you do not need to know the factors ahead of time (similar to PCA techniques), but they are simply inferred from the ratings themselves. We derive the latent factors using matrix factorization techniques which are popular due to the extreme scalability, accuracy of predictions, and flexibility (they allow for bias and the temporal nature of the user and inventory).

- **Singular Value Decomposition (SVD)**: SVD has been available in Spark from the early days, but we recommend not to use it as a core technique due to the problem of its ability to deal with sparseness of data in real life (for example, a user will not usually rate everything), overfitting, and order (do we really need to produce the bottom 1,000 recommendations?).
- **Stochastic Gradient Decent (SGD)**: SGD is easy to implement and has faster running times due to its approach of looking at one movie and one user/item vector at a time (pick a movie and update the profile a little bit for that user versus a batch approach). We can implement this using the matrix facility and SGD in Spark as needed.
- **Alternating Least Square (ALS)**: Please see ALS before you take on this journey. Available in Spark, ALS can take advantage of parallelization from the start. Spark implements full matrix factorization under the hood, contrary to the common belief that Spark uses half factorization. We encourage the reader to refer to the source code to verify this for themselves. Spark provides API for both **explicit** (rating available) and **implicit** (an indirect inference needed--for example, the length of time a track is played rather than a rating). We discuss the bias and temporal issues in the recipe itself, by introducing mathematics and intuition to make our point.

Setting up the required data for a scalable recommendation engine in Spark 2.0

In this recipe, we examine downloading the MovieLens public dataset and take a first exploratory view of the data. We will use the explicit data based on customer ratings from the MovieLens dataset. The MovieLens dataset contains 1,000,000 ratings of 4,000 movies from 6,000 users.

You will need one of the following command line tools to retrieve the specified data: `curl` (recommended for Mac) or `wget` (recommended for Windows or Linux).

How to do it...

1. You can start with downloading the dataset using either of the following commands:

   ```
   wget http://files.grouplens.org/datasets/movielens/ml-1m.zip
   ```

   You can also use the following command:

   ```
   curl http://files.grouplens.org/datasets/movielens/ml-1m.zip -o
   ml-1m.zip
   ```

2. Now you need to decompress the ZIP:

   ```
   unzip ml-1m.zip
   creating: ml-1m/
   inflating: ml-1m/movies.dat
   inflating: ml-1m/ratings.dat
   inflating: ml-1m/README
   inflating: ml-1m/users.dat
   ```

   The command will create a directory named `ml-1m` with data files decompressed inside.

3. Change into the directory `m1-1m`:

   ```
   cd m1-1m
   ```

4. Now we begin our first steps of data exploration by verifying how the data in `movies.dat` is formatted:

```
head -5 movies.dat
1::Toy Story (1995)::Animation|Children's|Comedy
2::Jumanji (1995)::Adventure|Children's|Fantasy
3::Grumpier Old Men (1995)::Comedy|Romance
4::Waiting to Exhale (1995)::Comedy|Drama
5::Father of the Bride Part II (1995)::Comedy
```

5. Now we take a look at the ratings data to know how it is formatted:

```
head -5 ratings.dat
1::1193::5::978300760
1::661::3::978302109
1::914::3::978301968
1::3408::4::978300275
1::2355::5::978824291
```

How it works...

The MovieLens dataset is an excellent alternative to the original Netflix KDD cup dataset. This dataset comes in multiple sets ranging from small (100 K set) to large (1 M and 20 M set). For those users interested in tweaking the source code to add their own augmentation (for example, the change regularization technique), the range of the dataset makes it easy to study the scaling effect and look at the performance curve versus Spark utilization per executive, as the data scales from 100 K to 20 M.

The URL to download is `http://grouplens.org/datasets/movielens/`.

There's more...

Take a closer look at where we downloaded the data from because more datasets are available for use at `http://files.grouplens.org/datasets/`.

The following figure depicts the size and extent of the data. For this chapter, we use the small set so it can easily run on a small laptop with limited resources.

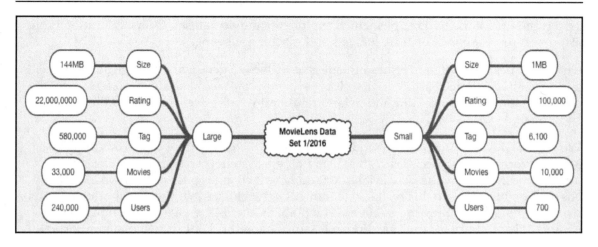

Source: MovieLens

See also

Please read through the README file contained within the directory that you unzipped the data to. The README file contains information about data file formats and data descriptions.

There is also a MovieLens genome tag set that can be used for reference.

- Computed tag-movie 11 million
- Relevance scores from a pool of 1,100 tags
- Applied to 10,000 movies

For those interested in exploring the original Netflix dataset, please see the `http://academictorrents.com/details/9b13183dc4d60676b773c9e2cd6de5e5542cee9a` URL.

Exploring the movies data details for the recommendation system in Spark 2.0

In this recipe, we will begin to explore the movie data file by parsing data into a Scala `case` class and generating a simple metric. The key here is to acquire an understanding of our data, so in the later stages, if nebulous results arise, we will have some insight to make an informed conclusion about the correctness of our results.

This is the first of the two recipes which explore the movie dataset. Data exploration is an important first step in statistical analysis and machine learning.

One of the best ways to understand the data quickly is to generate a data visualization of it, and we will use JFreeChart to do that. It is very important to make sure you feel comfortable with the data and understand firsthand what is in each file, and the story it tries to tell.

We must always explore, understand, and visualize the data before we do anything else. Most performances and misses with ML and others systems can be traced to a lack of understanding of how the data is laid out and how it changes over time. If we look at the chart given in step 14 in this recipe, one immediately realizes that the distribution of movies over the years is not uniform, but skewed with high kurtosis. While we are not going to explore this property for optimization and sampling in this book, it makes an important point about the nature of the movie data.

How to do it...

1. Start a new project in IntelliJ or in an IDE of your choice. Make sure the necessary JAR files are included.

2. JFreeChart JAR can be downloaded from the `https://sourceforge.net/ projects/jfreechart/files/` site.

3. Please make sure that the JFreeChart library and its dependencies (JCommon) are on the classpath for the chapter.

4. We define the package information for the Scala program:

```
package spark.ml.cookbook.chapter7
```

5. Import the necessary packages:

```
import java.text.DecimalFormat
import org.apache.log4j.{Level, Logger}
import org.apache.spark.sql.SparkSession
import org.jfree.chart.{ChartFactory, ChartFrame, JFreeChart}
import org.jfree.chart.axis.NumberAxis
import org.jfree.chart.plot.PlotOrientation
import org.jfree.data.xy.{XYSeries, XYSeriesCollection}
```

6. We now define a Scala `case class` to model movie data:

```
case class MovieData(movieId: Int, title: String, year: Int, genre:
Seq[String])
```

7. Let's define a function to display a JFreeChart within a window that will be invoked later. There are many options for charts and plots in this package that can be explored:

```
def show(chart: JFreeChart) {
 val frame = new ChartFrame("plot", chart)
 frame.pack()
 frame.setVisible(true)
 }
```

8. In this step, we define a function for parsing a single line of data from the `movie.dat` file into our movie `case class`:

```
def parseMovie(str: String): MovieData = {
 val columns = str.split("::")
 assert(columns.size == 3)

 val titleYearStriped = """\(|\)""".r.replaceAllIn(columns(1), " ")
 val titleYearData = titleYearStriped.split(" ")

 MovieData(columns(0).toInt,
 titleYearData.take(titleYearData.size - 1).mkString(" "),
 titleYearData.last.toInt,
 columns(2).split("|"))
 }
```

9. We are ready to start building our `main` function, so let's start with defining the location of our `movie.dat` file:

```
val movieFile = "../data/sparkml2/chapter7/movies.dat"
```

10. Create Spark's session object and setup configuration:

```
val spark = SparkSession
 .builder
.master("local[*]")
 .appName("MovieData App")
 .config("spark.sql.warehouse.dir", ".")
 .config("spark.executor.memory", "2g")
 .getOrCreate()
```

11. The interleaving of log messages leads to hard-to-read output; therefore, set the logging level to ERROR:

```
Logger.getLogger("org").setLevel(Level.ERROR)
```

12. Create a dataset of all the movies from the data file:

```
import spark.implicits._
val movies = spark.read.textFile(movieFile).map(parseMovie)
```

13. Group all the movies by year, released using Spark SQL:

```
movies.createOrReplaceTempView("movies")
val moviesByYear = spark.sql("select year, count(year) as count
from movies group by year order by year")
```

14. We now display a histogram chart with the movies grouped by the year of release:

```
val histogramDataset = new XYSeriesCollection()
val xy = new XYSeries("")
moviesByYear.collect().foreach({
row => xy.add(row.getAs[Int]("year"), row.getAs[Long]("count"))
})

histogramDataset.addSeries(xy)

val chart = ChartFactory.createHistogram(
"", "Year", "Movies Per Year", histogramDataset,
PlotOrientation.VERTICAL, false, false, false)
val chartPlot = chart.getXYPlot()

val xAxis = chartPlot.getDomainAxis().asInstanceOf[NumberAxis]
xAxis.setNumberFormatOverride(new DecimalFormat("####"))

show(chart)
```

15. See the chart produced to get a good feel for the movie dataset. There are at least two to four other ways that data can be visualized, which can be explored by the reader.

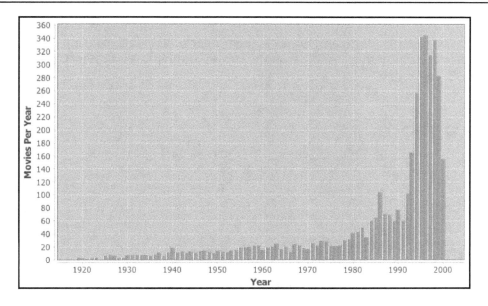

16. We close the program by stopping the Spark session:

```
spark.stop()
```

How it works...

When the program started to execute, we initialized a SparkContext in our driver program to start the task of processing the data. This implies that the data must fit in the driver's memory (user's station), which is not a server requirement in this case. Alternative methods of divide and conquer must be devised to deal with extreme datasets (partial retrieval and the assembly at destination).

We continued by loading and parsing the data file into a dataset with the data type of the movies. The movie dataset was then grouped by year, yielding a map of movies keyed by year, with buckets of associated movies attached.

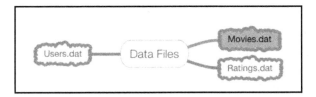

Next, we extracted the year with the count of the number of movies associated with the specific year to generate our histogram. We then collected the data, causing the entire resulting data collection to materialize on the driver, and passed it to JFreeChart to build the data visualization.

There's more...

You need to be cognizant of our use of Spark SQL because of its flexibility. More information is available

at `http://spark.apache.org/docs/latest/sql-programming-guide.html#running-sql-queries-programmatically`.

See also

For more on using JFreechart, refer to the JFreeChart API documentation at `http://www.jfree.org/jfreechart/api.html`.

You can find a good tutorial on JFreeChart at the `http://www.tutorialspoint.com/jfreechart/` link.

The link for the JFreeChart itself is `http://www.jfree.org/index.html`.

Exploring the ratings data details for the recommendation system in Spark 2.0

In this recipe, we explore the data from the user/rating perspective to understand the nature and property of our data file. We will start to explore the ratings data file by parsing data into a Scala case class and generating visualization for insight. The ratings data will be used a little later to generate features for our recommendation engine. Again, we stress that the first step in any data science/machine learning exercise should be the visualization and exploration of the data.

Once again, the best way of understanding data quickly is to generate a data visualization of it, and we will use a JFreeChart scatterplot to do this. A quick look at the chart of *users by ratings* produced by the JFreeChart plot shows a resemblance to a multinomial distribution with outliers and an increasing sparsity when ratings are increased in magnitude.

How to do it...

1. Start a new project in IntelliJ or in an IDE of your choice. Make sure the necessary JAR files are included.

2. We define the package information for the Scala program:

```
package spark.ml.cookbook.chapter7
```

3. Import the necessary packages:

```
import java.text.DecimalFormat
import org.apache.log4j.{Level, Logger}
import org.apache.spark.sql.SparkSession
import org.jfree.chart.{ChartFactory, ChartFrame, JFreeChart}
import org.jfree.chart.axis.NumberAxis
import org.jfree.chart.plot.PlotOrientation
import org.jfree.data.xy.{XYSeries, XYSeriesCollection}
```

4. We now define a Scala `case class` to model the ratings data:

```
case class Rating(userId: Int, movieId: Int, rating: Float,
timestamp: Long)
```

5. Let's define a function to display a JFreeChart within a window:

```
def show(chart: JFreeChart) {
val frame = new ChartFrame("plot", chart)
frame.pack()
frame.setVisible(true)
}
```

6. In this step, we define a function for parsing a single line of data from the `ratings.dat` file into the rating `case class`:

```
def parseRating(str: String): Rating = {
val columns = str.split("::")
assert(columns.size == 4)
Rating(columns(0).toInt, columns(1).toInt, columns(2).toFloat,
columns(3).toLong)
}
```

7. We are ready to begin building our `main` function, so let's start with the location of our `ratings.dat` file:

```
val ratingsFile = "../data/sparkml2/chapter7/ratings.dat"
```

8. Create Spark's configuration, SparkSession. In this example, we show for the first time how to set the Spark executor memory (for example, 2 gig) on a small laptop. You must increase this allocation if you want to use the large dataset (the 144 MB set):

```
val spark = SparkSession
 .builder
.master("local[*]")
 .appName("MovieRating App")
 .config("spark.sql.warehouse.dir", ".")
 .config("spark.executor.memory", "2g")
 .getOrCreate()
```

9. The interleaving of log messages leads to hard to-read output; therefore, set the logging level to ERROR:

```
Logger.getLogger("org").setLevel(Level.ERROR)
```

10. Create a dataset of all the ratings from the data file:

```
import spark.implicits._
 val ratings = spark.read.textFile(ratingsFile).map(parseRating)
```

11. Now we convert the ratings dataset into a memory table view, where we can execute the Spark SQL query:

```
ratings.createOrReplaceTempView("ratings")
```

12. We now produce a list of all user ratings grouped by user, with their totals:

```
val resultDF = spark.sql("select ratings.userId, count(*) as count
from ratings group by ratings.userId")
resultDF.show(25, false);
```

From the console output:

```
From the Console output;
+------+-----+
|userId|count|
+------+-----+
|148   |624  |
|463   |123  |
|471   |105  |
|496   |119  |
|833   |21   |
|1088  |1176 |
|1238  |45   |
|1342  |92   |
|1580  |37   |
|1591  |314  |
|1645  |522  |
|1829  |30   |
|1959  |61   |
|2122  |208  |
|2142  |77   |
|2366  |41   |
|2659  |161  |
|2866  |205  |
|3175  |87   |
|3749  |118  |
|3794  |44   |
|3918  |26   |
|3997  |315  |
|4101  |95   |
|4519  |42   |
+------+-----+
only showing top 25 rows
```

13. Display a scatterplot chart with ratings per user. We choose a scatterplot to demonstrate a different way to look at the data from the previous recipe. We encourage readers to explore standardization techniques (for example, remove mean) or a volatility varying regime (for example, GARCH) to explore the autoregressive conditional heteroscedasticity property of this dataset (which is beyond the scope of this book). The reader is advised to consult any advanced time series book to develop an understanding of time varying volatility of the time series and how to correct this before usage.

```scala
val scatterPlotDataset = new XYSeriesCollection()
 val xy = new XYSeries("")

resultDF.collect().foreach({r => xy.add(
r.getAs[Integer]("userId"), r.getAs[Integer]("count")) })

scatterPlotDataset.addSeries(xy)

val chart = ChartFactory.createScatterPlot(
"", "User", "Ratings Per User", scatterPlotDataset,
```

```
    PlotOrientation.VERTICAL, false, false, false)
  val chartPlot = chart.getXYPlot()

  val xAxis = chartPlot.getDomainAxis().asInstanceOf[NumberAxis]
  xAxis.setNumberFormatOverride(new DecimalFormat("####"))
```

14. Display the chart:

```
show(chart)
```

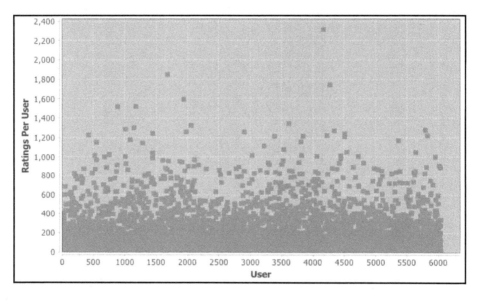

15. We close the program by stopping the Spark session:

```
spark.stop()
```

How it works...

We began by loading and parsing the data file into a dataset with the data type ratings, and finally converted it to a DataFrame. The DataFrame was then used to execute a Spark SQL query that grouped all the ratings by user with their totals.

A full understanding of the API and its concepts (lazy instantiation, staging, pipelining, and caching) is critical for every Spark developer.

Finally, we passed the result set of data to the JFreeChart scatterplot component to display our chart.

There's more...

A Spark DataFrame is a distributed collection of data organized into named columns. All DataFrame operations are also automatically parallelized and distributed on clusters. Also, DataFrames are lazily evaluated like RDDs.

See also

Documentation on DataFrames can be found at `http://spark.apache.org/docs/latest/sql-programming-guide.html`.

A good tutorial on JFreeChart can be found at the `http://www.tutorialspoint.com/jfreechart/` linking.

JFreeChart can be downloaded from the `http://www.jfree.org/index.html` URL.

Building a scalable recommendation engine using collaborative filtering in Spark 2.0

In this recipe, we will be demonstrating a recommendation system that utilizes a technique known as collaborative filtering. At the core, collaborative filtering analyzes the relationship between users themselves and the dependencies between the inventory (for example, movies, books, news articles, or songs) to identify user-to-item relationships based on a set of secondary factors called **latent factors** (for example, female/male, happy/sad, active/passive). The key here is that you do not need to know the latent factors in advance.

The recommendation will be produced via the ALS algorithm which is a collaborative filtering technique. At a high level, collaborative filtering entails making predictions of what a user may be interested in based on collecting previously known preferences, combined with the preferences of many other users. We will be using the ratings data from the MovieLens dataset and will convert it into input features for the recommendation algorithm.

How to do it...

1. Start a new project in IntelliJ or in an IDE of your choice. Make sure the necessary JAR files are included.

2. We define the package information for the Scala program:

```
package spark.ml.cookbook.chapter7
```

3. Import the necessary packages:

```
import org.apache.log4j.{Level, Logger}
 import org.apache.spark.sql.SparkSession
 import org.apache.spark.ml.recommendation.ALS
```

4. We now define two Scala case classes, to model movie and ratings data:

```
case class Movie(movieId: Int, title: String, year: Int, genre:
Seq[String])
 case class FullRating(userId: Int, movieId: Int, rating: Float,
timestamp: Long)
```

5. In this step, we define functions for parsing a single line of data from the ratings.dat file into the ratings case class, and for parsing a single line of data from the movies.dat file into the movie case class:

```
def parseMovie(str: String): Movie = {
val columns = str.split("::")
assert(columns.size == 3)

val titleYearStriped = """\(|\)""".r.replaceAllIn(columns(1), " ")
val titleYearData = titleYearStriped.split(" ")

Movie(columns(0).toInt,
    titleYearData.take(titleYearData.size - 1).mkString(" "),
    titleYearData.last.toInt,
    columns(2).split("|"))
 }
```

```
def parseFullRating(str: String): FullRating = {
val columns = str.split("::")
assert(columns.size == 4)
FullRating(columns(0).toInt, columns(1).toInt, columns(2).toFloat,
columns(3).toLong)
  }
```

6. We are ready to begin building our `main` function, so let's start with the locations of the `movie.dat` and `ratings.dat` file:

```
val movieFile = "../data/sparkml2/chapter7/movies.dat"
val ratingsFile = "../data/sparkml2/chapter7/ratings.dat"
```

7. Create a SparkSession object and its related configuration:

```
val spark = SparkSession
 .builder
.master("local[*]")
 .appName("MovieLens App")
 .config("spark.sql.warehouse.dir", ".")
 .config("spark.executor.memory", "2g")
 .getOrCreate()
```

8. The interleaving of log messages leads to hard-to-read output; therefore, set the logging level to ERROR:

```
Logger.getLogger("org").setLevel(Level.ERROR)
```

9. Create a dataset of all the ratings and register it as a temporary view in memory so it can be queried with SQL:

```
val ratings = spark.read.textFile(ratingsFile).map(parseFullRating)

val movies =
spark.read.textFile(movieFile).map(parseMovie).cache()
 movies.createOrReplaceTempView("movies")
```

10. Execute the SQL query against the view:

```
val rs = spark.sql("select movies.title from movies")
rs.show(25)
```

From the console output:

```
From the Console output:
+--------------------+
|               title|
+--------------------+
|         Toy Story  |
|           Jumanji  |
|   Grumpier Old Men |
|  Waiting to Exhale |
| Father of the Bri...|
|               Heat |
|            Sabrina |
|       Tom and Huck |
|       Sudden Death |
|          GoldenEye |
| American Presiden...|
| Dracula: Dead and...|
|              Balto |
|              Nixon |
|    Cutthroat Island|
|             Casino |
| Sense and Sensibi...|
|         Four Rooms |
| Ace Ventura: When...|
|        Money Train |
|         Get Shorty |
|            Copycat |
|          Assassins |
|             Powder |
|   Leaving Las Vegas|
+--------------------+
only showing top 25 rows
```

11. We categorize the ratings data into training and test datasets. The training data will be used to train the alternate least squares recommendation machine learning algorithm, and the test data will be used later to evaluate the accuracy between the predictions and the test data:

```scala
val splits = ratings.randomSplit(Array(0.8, 0.2), 0L)
val training = splits(0).cache()
val test = splits(1).cache()

val numTraining = training.count()
val numTest = test.count()
println(s"Training: $numTraining, test: $numTest.")
```

12. Now create a fictitious user with a user ID of zero, generating a dataset of several ratings. This user will allow us later to better understand the predictions computed by the ALS algorithm:

```
val testWithOurUser = spark.createDataset(Seq(
  FullRating(0, 260, 0f, 0), // Star Wars: Episode IV - A New Hope
  FullRating(0, 261, 0f, 0), // Little Women
  FullRating(0, 924, 0f, 0), // 2001: A Space Odyssey
  FullRating(0, 1200, 0f, 0), // Aliens
  FullRating(0, 1307, 0f, 0) // When Harry Met Sally...
)).as[FullRating]

val trainWithOurUser = spark.createDataset(Seq(
  FullRating(0, 76, 3f, 0), // Screamers
  FullRating(0, 165, 4f, 0), // Die Hard: With a Vengeance
  FullRating(0, 145, 2f, 0), // Bad Boys
  FullRating(0, 316, 5f, 0), // Stargate
  FullRating(0, 1371, 5f, 0), // Star Trek: The Motion Picture
  FullRating(0, 3578, 4f, 0), // Gladiator
  FullRating(0, 3528, 1f, 0) // Prince of Tides
)).as[FullRating]
```

13. Append `testWithOurUser` to the original training set utilizing the dataset union method. Also, use the `unpersist` method on the original training set and the test set of free resources:

```
val testSet = test.union(testWithOurUser)
test.unpersist()
val trainSet = training.union(trainWithOurUser)
training.unpersist()
```

14. Create the ALS object and set up the parameters.

    Use the train dataset to get the model.

```
val als = new ALS()
 .setUserCol("userId")
 .setItemCol("movieId")
 .setRank(10)
 .setMaxIter(10)
 .setRegParam(0.1)
 .setNumBlocks(10)
val model = als.fit(trainSet.toDF)
```

15. We let the model work on the test dataset:

```
val predictions = model.transform(testSet.toDF())
predictions.cache()
predictions.show(10, false)
```

From the console output:

```
From the console output:

+------+-------+------+---------+----------+
|userId|movieId|rating|timestamp|prediction|
+------+-------+------+---------+----------+
|53    |148    |5.0   |977987826|3.360202  |
|3184  |148    |4.0   |968708953|3.1396782 |
|1242  |148    |3.0   |974909976|2.4897025 |

|3829  |148    |2.0   |965940170|2.3191774 |
|2456  |148    |2.0   |974178993|2.7297301 |
|4858  |463    |3.0   |963746396|2.4874766 |
|3032  |463    |4.0   |970356224|4.275539  |
|2210  |463    |3.0   |974601869|2.8614724 |
|4510  |463    |2.0   |966800044|2.205242  |
|3562  |463    |2.0   |966790403|2.9360452 |
+------+-------+------+---------+----------+
only showing top 10 rows
```

16. Build an in-memory table which has all the predictions for the Spark SQL query:

```
val allPredictions = predictions.join(movies, movies("movieId") ===
predictions("movieId"), "left")
```

17. Retrieve the ratings and predictions from the table and display the first 20 rows in the console:

```
allPredictions.select("userId", "rating", "prediction",
"title") show(false)
```

From the console output:

```
From the Console output:

+------+------+----------+-----------------------------+
|userId|rating|prediction|title                        |
+------+------+----------+-----------------------------+
|53    |5.0   |3.360202  |Awfully Big Adventure, An    |
|3184  |4.0   |3.1396782 |Awfully Big Adventure, An    |
|1242  |3.0   |2.4897025 |Awfully Big Adventure, An    |
|3829  |2.0   |2.3191774 |Awfully Big Adventure, An    |
|2456  |2.0   |2.7297301 |Awfully Big Adventure, An    |
|4858  |3.0   |2.4874766 |Guilty as Sin                |
|3032  |4.0   |4.275539  |Guilty as Sin                |
|2210  |3.0   |2.8614724 |Guilty as Sin                |
|4510  |2.0   |2.205242  |Guilty as Sin                |
|3562  |2.0   |2.9360452 |Guilty as Sin                |
|746   |1.0   |2.1229248 |Guilty as Sin                |
|5511  |2.0   |3.4050038 |Guilty as Sin                |
|331   |4.0   |2.572236  |Guilty as Sin                |
|3829  |2.0   |2.0906088 |Guilty as Sin                |
|5831  |4.0   |2.9544487 |Guilty as Sin                |
|392   |4.0   |3.579655  |Hudsucker Proxy, The         |
|1265  |4.0   |3.574471  |Hudsucker Proxy, The         |
|4957  |3.0   |3.473529  |Hudsucker Proxy, The         |
|78    |4.0   |3.5066679 |Hudsucker Proxy, The         |
|1199  |3.0   |2.7609487 |Hudsucker Proxy, The         |
+------+------+----------+-----------------------------+
only showing top 20 rows
```

18. Now get a specific user's movie prediction:

```
allPredictions.select("userId", "rating", "prediction",
"title").where("userId=0").show(false)
```

From the console output:

```
From the Console output:
+------+------+----------+--------------------------------+
|userId|rating|prediction|title                           |
+------+------+----------+--------------------------------+
|0     |0.0   |2.624456  |When Harry Met Sally...         |
|0     |0.0   |4.1649804 |2001: A Space Odyssey           |
|0     |0.0   |3.994494  |Aliens                          |
|0     |0.0   |2.2429814 |Little Women                    |
|0     |0.0   |4.5856667 |Star Wars: Episode IV - A New Hope |
+------+------+----------+--------------------------------+
```

19. We close the program by stopping the Spark session:

```
spark.stop()
```

How it works...

Due to the complex nature of the program, we provide a conceptual explanation and then proceed to explain the details of the program.

The following figure depicts a conceptual view of ALS and how it factorizes the user/movie/rating matrix, which is a high-ranking order matrix to a lower order tall and skinny matrix, and a vector of latent factors: f(users) and f(movies).

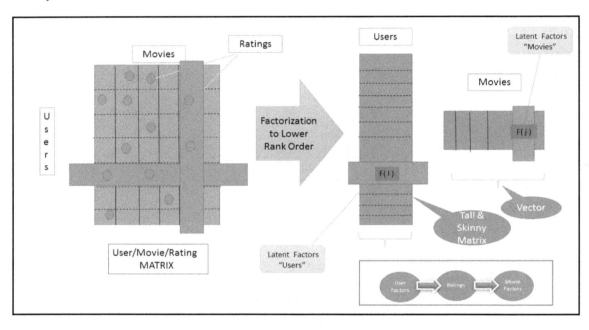

Another way to think about it is that these factors can be used to place the movie in an n dimensional space that will be matched to a given recommendation for a given user. It is always desirable to view machine learning as a search query in a dimensional variable space. The point to remember is that the latent factor (learned geometry space) is not pre-defined and can be as low as 10 to 100 or 1,000 depending on what is being searched or factorized. Our recommendation, then, can be viewed as placing a probability mass within the n-dimensional space. The following figure provides an extremely simplified view of a possible two-factor model (two-dimensional) to demonstrate the point:

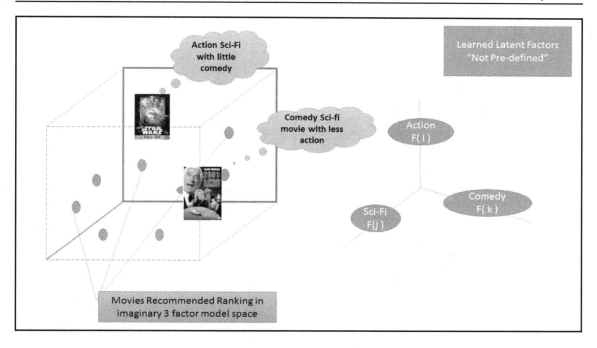

While the implementation of ALS can vary a bit from system to system, at its core it is an iterative full-factorization method (in Spark) with weighed regularization. Spark's documentation and tutorials provide an insight into the actual math and the nature of the algorithm. It depicts the algorithm as follows:

Iterate:

$$f[i] = \arg \min_{w \in \mathbb{R}^d} \sum_{j \in \mathrm{Nbrs}(i)} \left(r_{ij} - w^T f[j]\right)^2 + \lambda \|w\|_2^2$$

Source: Apache Spark Documentation 1.6.1

The best way to understand this formula/algorithm is to think of it as an iterating apparatus which is trying to discover the latent factors by alternating between inputs (that is, fix one of the inputs and then approximate/optimize the other--and then back and forth), while trying to minimize the least square error (MSE) with respect to a regularization penalty of weighted lambda. A more detailed explanation is provided in the next section.

The program flow is as follows:

- The example started, by loading the ratings and movie data from the MovieLens dataset. The loaded data was then transformed into Scala case classes for further processing. The next step was to partition the ratings data into a training set and test set. The training set data was used to train the machine learning algorithm. Training is the process in machine learning used to build a model so it can provide the appropriate results needed. The test data will be used to validate the results in the final step.

- The fictitious users, or user ID zero, step configured a single user not included in the original dataset to help lend insight to the results by creating a dataset on the fly with random information, and finally appending it to the training set. The ALS algorithm was invoked by passing the training set data to it, comprised of the user ID, movie ID, and rating, subsequently yielding a matrix factorization model from Spark. The prediction generation was performed for the user ID zero and test dataset.

- The final results were displayed by combining rating information with the movie data so the results could be understood and displayed in the original rating next to the estimated rating. The final step was to compute the root mean squared error of the generated rating, with the existing rating contained within the test dataset. The RMSE will tell us how accurate the train model is.

There's more...

People often struggle with ALS even though at its core it is a simple linear algebra operation with an added regularization penalty. What makes ALS powerful is its ability to be parallelized and to deal with scale (for example, Spotify).

ALS in layman's language involves the following:

- With ALS, you basically want to factorize a large matrix of ratings X (100 million plus users is not a stretch at all) and user product ratings into two matrices of A and B, with lower ranks (see any introductory linear algebra book). The problem is that it often becomes a very hard non-linear optimization problem to solve. To remedy with ALS, you introduce a simple solution (**A** for **Alternating**) in which you fix one of the matrices and partially solve the other leg (the other matrix) using the least square methods for optimization (**LS** stands for **Least Square**). Once this step is complete, you then alternate, but this time you fix the second leg (matrix) and solve the first.

- To control overfitting, we introduce a regularization leg to the original equation. This step is usually a weighted regularization and is controlled by a parameter lambda that controls the amount of penalty or flattening.
- In short, what makes this interesting is the fact that this method matrix factorization lends itself very well to parallel operations, which is Spark's speciality at its core.

For a deep understanding of the ALS algorithm, we cite two original papers that are considered to be classics in this area:

From the ACM Digital Library using `http://dl.acm.org/citation.cfm?id=1608614` link.

From the IEEE Digital
Library `http://ieeexplore.ieee.org/xpl/login.jsp?tp=&arnumber=5197422&url=http%3A%2F%2Fieeexplore.ieee.org%2Fxpls%2Fabs_all.jsp%3Farnumber%3D5197422`.

The following figure shows ALS from a more mathematical view, from the original paper cited previously:

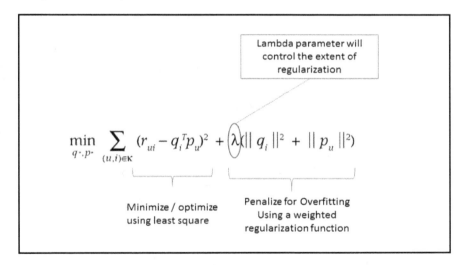

Use the RankingMetrics metrics class to evaluate the model performance. Parameters are similar to classes used for evaluation (binary and multinomial) of the regression models:

- Recall
- Precision
- fMeasure

The RankingMetrics class provided by MLlib can be used for evaluating models and quantifying model effectiveness.

The RankingMetrics API documentation can be found at `http://spark.apache.org/docs/latest/api/scala/index.html#org.apache.spark.mllib.evaluation.RankingMetrics`.

See also

Spark 2.0 ML documentation to explore the ALS API:

- `https://spark.apache.org/docs/latest/mllib-collaborative-filtering.html`
- `https://spark.apache.org/docs/latest/api/scala/index.html#org.apache.spark.ml.recommendation.ALS`
- `https://spark.apache.org/docs/latest/api/scala/index.html#org.apache.spark.ml.recommendation.ALSModel`

Spark 2.0 MLlib documentation is available
at `https://spark.apache.org/docs/latest/api/scala/index.html#org.apache.spark.mllib.recommendation.ALS`.

ALS parameters and their default constructs an ALS instance with default parameters as follows:

```
{numBlocks: -1, rank: 10, iterations: 10, lambda: 0.
numBlocks: -1,
rank: 10,
iterations: 10,
lambda: 0.01,
implicitPrefs: false,
alpha: 1.0
```

Dealing with implicit input for training

There are times when the actual observations (ratings) are not available and one must deal with implied feedback parameters. This can be as simple as which audio track was listened to during an engagement to how long a movie was watched, or the context (indexed in advance) or what caused a switch (a Netflix movie abandoned in the beginning, middle, or near a specific scene). The example provided in the third recipe deals with explicit feedback via the use of `ALS.train()`.

The Spark ML library provides an alternative method, `ALS.trainImplicit()`, with four hyper parameters to control the algorithm and address the implicit data. If you are interested in testing this (it is very similar to the explicit method), you can use the 1,000,000 song dataset for easy training and prediction purposes. You can download the dataset for experimentation from the `http://labrosa.ee.columbia.edu/millionsong/` URL.

The collaborative filtering pros and cons are as follows:

Pros	Cons
Scalable	Cold start problem • New items added to the inventory • New users added to the ecosystem
Discovers hard to find and often illusive data properties without profiles	Requires a decent amount of data
More accurate	
Portable	

14
Unsupervised Clustering with Apache Spark 2.0

In this chapter, we will cover:

- Building a KMeans classification system in Spark 2.0
- Bisecting KMeans, the new kid on the block in Spark 2.0
- Using Gaussian Mixture and Expectation Maximization (EM) in Spark 2.0 to classify data
- Classifying the vertices of a graph using Power Iteration Clustering (PIC) in Spark 2.0
- Using Latent Dirichlet Allocation (LDA) to classify documents and text into topics
- Streaming KMeans to classify data in near real time

Introduction

Unsupervised machine learning is a type of learning technique in which we try to draw inferences either directly or indirectly (through latent factors) from a set of unlabeled observations. In simple terms, we are trying to find the hidden knowledge or structures in a set of data without initially labeling the training data.

While most machine learning library implementation break down when applied to large datasets (iterative, multi-pass, a lot of intermediate writes), the Apache Spark Machine Library succeeds by providing machine library algorithms designed for parallelism and extremely large datasets using memory for intermediate writes out of the box.

At the most abstract level, we can think of unsupervised learning as:

- **Clustering systems**: Classify the inputs into categories either using hard (only belonging to a single cluster) or soft (probabilistic membership and overlaps) categorization.
- **Dimensionality reduction systems**: Find hidden factors using a condensed representation of the original data.

The following figure shows the landscape of machine learning techniques. In the previous chapters, we focused on supervised machine learning techniques. In this chapter, we concentrate on unsupervised machine learning techniques ranging from clustering to latent factor models using Spark's ML/MLIB library API:

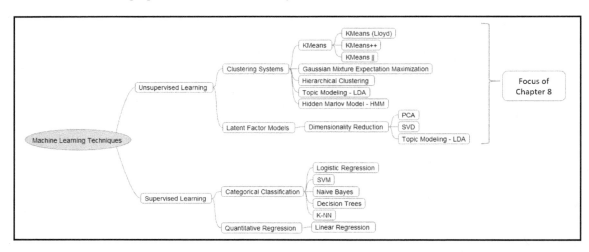

The clusters are often modeled using intra-cluster similarity measurement, such as Euclidian or probabilistic techniques. Spark provides a complete and high-performing set of algorithms which lend themselves to parallel implementation at scale. They not only provide APIs, but also provide full source code which is very helpful for understanding bottlenecks and resolving them (forking to GPU) to fit your needs.

The applications of machine learning are vast and as limitless as you can imagine. Some of the most widely known examples and use cases are:

- Fraud detection (finance, law enforcement)
- Network security (intrusion detection, traffic analysis)
- Pattern recognition (marketing, intelligence community, banking)
- Recommendation systems (retail, entertainment)
- Affinity marketing (e-commerce, recommenders, deep personalization)
- Medical informatics (disease detection, patient care, asset management)
- Image processing (object/sub-object detection, radiology)

A word of caution on ML versus MLIB usage and future direction in Spark:

While the MLIB is and will remain viable for the time being, there is a gradual movement towards Spark's ML library for future development rather than MLIB in Spark. The `org.apache.spark.ml.clustering` is a high-level machine learning package and the API is more focused on the DataFrame. The `org.apache.spark.mllib.clustering` is a lower-level machine learning package and the API is directly on RDD. While both packages will get the benefit of Spark's high performance and scalability, the main difference is the DataFrame. The `org.apache.spark.ml` will be the preferred method going forward.

For example, we encourage the developer to look at why the introduction of KMeans classifying system exists in both ML and MLLIB: `org.apache.spark.ml.clustering` and `org.apache.spark.mllib.clustering`

Building a KMeans classifying system in Spark 2.0

In this recipe, we will load a set of features (for example, x, y, z coordinates) using a LIBSVM file and then proceed to use KMeans() to instantiate an object. We will then set the number of desired clusters to three and then use kmeans.fit() to action the algorithm. Finally, we will print the centers for the three clusters that we found.

It is really important to note that Spark *does not* implement KMeans++, contrary to popular literature, instead it implements KMeans || (pronounced as KMeans Parallel). See the following recipe and the sections following the code for a complete explanation of the algorithm as it is implemented in Spark.

How to do it...

1. Start a new project in IntelliJ or in an IDE of your choice. Make sure the necessary JAR files are included.

2. Set up the package location where the program will reside:

   ```
   package spark.ml.cookbook.chapter8
   ```

3. Import the necessary packages for Spark context to get access to the cluster and Log4j.Logger to reduce the amount of output produced by Spark:

   ```
   import org.apache.log4j.{Level, Logger}
   import org.apache.spark.ml.clustering.KMeans
   import org.apache.spark.sql.SparkSession
   ```

4. Set the output level to ERROR to reduce Spark's logging output:

   ```
   Logger.getLogger("org").setLevel(Level.ERROR)
   ```

5. Create Spark's Session object:

   ```
   val spark = SparkSession
    .builder
   .master("local[*]")
    .appName("myKMeansCluster")
    .config("spark.sql.warehouse.dir", ".")
    .getOrCreate()
   ```

6. We create a training dataset from a file in the `libsvm` format and display the file on the console:

```
val trainingData =
spark.read.format("libsvm").load("../data/sparkml2/chapter8/my_kmea
ns_data.txt")

trainingData.show()
```

From the console, you will see:

```
+-----+--------------------+
|label|            features|
+-----+--------------------+
|  1.0|(3,[0,1,2],[1.0,1...|
|  2.0|(3,[0,1,2],[1.1,1...|
|  3.0|(3,[0,1,2],[1.0,1...|
|  4.0|(3,[0,1,2],[1.0,1...|
|  5.0|(3,[0,1,2],[3.1,3...|
|  6.0|(3,[0,1,2],[3.3,3...|
|  7.0|(3,[0,1,2],[4.0,4...|
|  8.0|(3,[0,1,2],[3.4,3...|
|  9.0|(3,[0,1,2],[8.3,8...|
| 10.0|(3,[0,1,2],[9.3,9...|
| 11.0|(3,[0,1,2],[9.2,9...|
| 12.0|(3,[0,1,2],[9.5,9...|
+-----+--------------------+
```

The following formula visualizes the data via contour maps that depict each feature vector (each row) versus the three unique features in both a 3D and flat contour map:

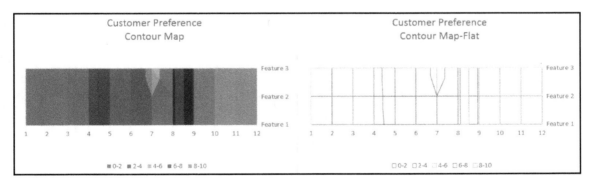

7. We then create a KMeans object and set some key parameters to the KMeans model and set parameters.

In this case, we set the K value to 3 and set the *feature* column as column "features", which was defined in the previous step. This step is subjective and the optimal value would vary based on specific datasets. We recommend that you experiment with values from 2 to 50 and examine the cluster centers for a final value.

We also set the maximum iteration count to 10. Most of the values have a default setting as the comments as shown in the following code:

```
// Trains a k-means model
val kmeans = new KMeans()
.setK(3) // default value is 2
.setFeaturesCol("features")
.setMaxIter(10) // default Max Iteration is 20
.setPredictionCol("prediction")
.setSeed(1L)
```

8. We then train the dataset. The fit() function will then run the algorithm and perform the calculations. It is based on the dataset created in the previous steps. These steps are common among Spark's ML and do not usually vary from algorithm to algorithm:

```
val model = kmeans.fit(trainingData)
```

We also display the model's prediction on the console:

```
model.summary.predictions.show()
```

From the console:

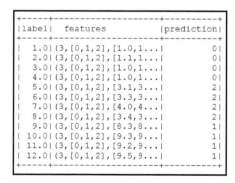

9. We then calculate the cost, using the included `computeCost(x)` function.

10. The KMeans Cost is calculated **Within Set Sum of Squared Errors (WSSSE)**. The value will be printed out in the program's console:

```
println("KMeans Cost:" +model.computeCost(trainingData))
```

The console output will show the following information:

```
KMeans Cost:4.137499999999979
```

11. We then print out the cluster's center based on the calculation of the model:

```
println("KMeans Cluster Centers: ")
 model.clusterCenters.foreach(println)
```

12. The console output will show the following information:

```
The centers for the 3 cluster (i.e. K= 3)
KMeans Cluster Centers:
[1.025,1.075,1.15]
[9.075,9.05,9.025]
[3.45,3.475,3.55]
```

Based on the setting of the KMeans clustering, we set the K value to 3; the model will calculate three centers based on the training dataset that we fit in.

13. We then close the program by stopping the Spark context:

```
spark.stop()
```

How it works...

We read a LIBSVM file with a set of coordinates (can be interpreted as a tuple of three numbers) and then created a `KMean()` object, but changed the default number of clusters from 2 (out of the box) to 3 for demonstration purposes. We used the `.fit()` to create the model and then used `model.summary.predictions.show()` to display which tuple belongs to which cluster. In the last step, we printed the cost and the center of the three clusters. Conceptually, it can be thought of as having a set of 3D coordinates as data and then assigning each individual coordinate to one of the three clusters using KMeans algorithms.

KMeans is a form of unsupervised machine learning algorithm, with its root in signal processing (vector quantization) and compression (grouping similar vectors of items together to achieve a higher compression rate). Generally speaking, the KMeans algorithm attempts to group a series of observations $\{X_1, X_2, \ldots, X_n\}$ into a series of clusters $\{C_1, C_2 \ldots C_n\}$ using a form of distance measure (local optimization) that is optimized in an iterative manner.

There are three main types of KMeans algorithm that are in use. In a simple survey, we found 12 specialized variations of the KMeans algorithm. It is important to note that Spark implements a version called KMeans || (KMeans Parallel) and *not* KMeans++ or standard KMeans as referenced in some literature or videos.

The following figure depicts KMeans in a nutshell:

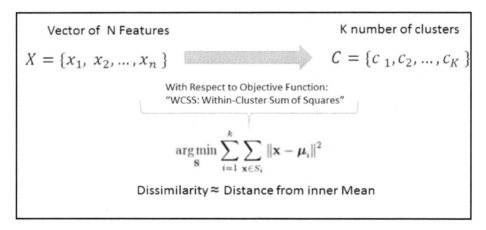

Source: Spark documentation

KMeans (Lloyd Algorithm)

The steps for basic KMeans implementation (Lloyd algorithm) are:

1. Randomly select K datacenters from observations as the initial centroids.
2. Keep iterating till the convergence criteria is met:
   - Measure the distance from a point to each centroid
   - Include each data point in a cluster which is the closest centroid
   - Calculate new cluster centroids based on a distance formula (proxy for dissimilarity)
   - Update the algorithm with new center points

The three generations are depicted in the following figure:

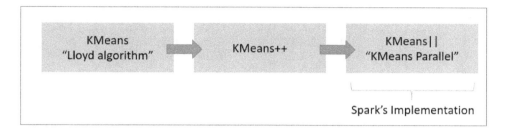

KMeans++ (Arthur's algorithm)

The next improvement over standard KMeans is the KMeans++ proposed by David Arthur and Sergei Vassilvitskii in 2007. Arthur's algorithm improves the initial Lloyd's KMeans by being more selective during the seeding process (the initial step).

KMeans++, rather than picking random centres (random centroids) as starting points, picks the first centroid randomly and then picks the data points one by one and calculates D(x). Then it chooses one more data point at random and, using proportional probability distribution D(x)2, it then keeps repeating the last two steps until all *K* numbers are picked. After the initial seeding, we finally run the KMeans or a variation with the newly seeded centroid. The KMeans++ algorithm is guaranteed to find a solution in an *Omega= O(log k)* complexity. Even though the initial seeding takes extra steps, the accuracy improvements are substantial.

KMeans|| (pronounced as KMeans Parallel)

KMeans || is optimized to run in parallel and can result in one-two orders of magnitude improvement over Lloyd's original algorithm. The limitation of KMeans++ is that it requires K-passes over the dataset, which can severely limit the performance and practicality of running KMeans with large or extreme datasets. Spark's KMeans|| parallel implementation runs faster because it takes fewer passes (a lot less) over the data by sampling m points and oversampling in the process.

The core of the algorithm and the math is depicted in the following figure:

Algorithm 2 k-means$\|$ (k, ℓ) initialization.

1: $C \leftarrow$ sample a point uniformly at random from X
2: $\psi \leftarrow \phi_X(C)$
3: **for** $O(\log \psi)$ times **do**
4:      $C' \leftarrow$ sample each point $x \in X$ independently with probability $p_x = \frac{\ell \cdot d^2(x, C)}{\phi_X(C)}$
5:      $C \leftarrow C \cup C'$
6: **end for**
7: For $x \in C$, set w_x to be the number of points in X closer to x than any other point in C
8: Recluster the weighted points in C into k clusters

Source: http://theory.stanford.edu/~sergei/papers/vldb12-kmpar.pdf
Stanford University : Bahman Bahmani plus others

In a nutshell, the highlight of the KMeans | | (Parallel KMeans) is the course-grain sampling which repeats in *log(n)* rounds and at the end we are left with *k * log(n)* remaining points that are a C (constant) distance away from the optimal solution! This implementation is also less sensitive to outlier data points that can skew the clustering results in KMeans and KMeans++.

For a deeper understanding of the algorithm, the reader can access the paper by Bahman Bahmani at `http://theory.stanford.edu/~sergei/papers/vldb12-kmpar.pdf`.

There's more...

There is also a streaming version of KMeans implementation in Spark that allows you to classify the features on the fly.

There is also a class that helps you to generate RDD data for KMeans. We found this to be very useful during our application development process:

```
def generateKMeansRDD(sc: SparkContext, numPoints: Int, k: Int, d: Int, r:
Double, numPartitions: Int = 2): RDD[Array[Double]]
```

This call uses Spark context to create RDDs while allowing you to specify the number of points, clusters, dimensions, and partitions.

A useful related API is: `generateKMeansRDD()`. Documentation for `generateKMeansRDD` can be found at `http://spark.apache.org/docs/latest/api/scala/index.html#org.apache.spark.mllib.util.KMeansDataGenerator$` for generate an RDD containing test data for KMeans.

See also

We need two pieces of objects to be able to write, measure, and manipulate the parameters of the KMeans | | algorithm in Spark. The details of these two pieces of objects can be found at the following websites:

- `KMeans()`:
  `http://spark.apache.org/docs/latest/api/scala/index.html#org.apache.spark.ml.clustering.KMeans`
- `KMeansModel()`: `http://spark.apache.org/docs/latest/api/scala/index.html#org.apache.spark.ml.clustering.KMeansModel`

Bisecting KMeans, the new kid on the block in Spark 2.0

In this recipe, we will download the glass dataset and try to identify and label each glass using a bisecting KMeans algorithm. The Bisecting KMeans is a hierarchical version of the K-Mean algorithm implemented in Spark using the `BisectingKMeans()` API. While this algorithm is conceptually like KMeans, it can offer considerable speed for some use cases where the hierarchical path is present.

The dataset we used for this recipe is the Glass Identification Database. The study of the classification of types of glass was motivated by criminological research. Glass could be considered as evidence if it is correctly identified. The data can be found at NTU (Taiwan), already in LIBSVM format.

How to do it...

1. We downloaded the prepared data file in LIBSVM
   from: `https://www.csie.ntu.edu.tw/~cjlin/libsvmtools/datasets/multiclass/glass.scale`

   The dataset contains 11 features and 214 rows.

2. The original dataset and data dictionary is also available at the UCI
   website: `http://archive.ics.uci.edu/ml/datasets/Glass+Identification`
   - ID number: 1 to 214
   - RI: Refractive index
   - Na: Sodium (unit measurement: weight percent in corresponding oxide, as are attributes 4-10)
   - Mg: Magnesium
   - Al: Aluminum
   - Si: Silicon
   - K: Potassium
   - Ca: Calcium
   - Ba: Barium
   - Fe: Iron

   Type of glass: Will find our class attributes or clusters using
   `BisectingKMeans()`:

- `building_windows_float_processed`
- `building_windows_non-_float_processed`
- `vehicle_windows_float_processed`
- `vehicle_windows_non-_float_processed` (none in this database)
- `Containers`
- `Tableware`
- `Headlamps`

3. Start a new project in IntelliJ or in an IDE of your choice. Make sure the necessary JAR files are included.

4. Set up the package location where the program will reside:

   ```
   package spark.ml.cookbook.chapter8
   ```

5. Import the necessary packages:

```
import org.apache.spark.ml.clustering.BisectingKMeans
import org.apache.spark.sql.SparkSession
import org.apache.log4j.{Level, Logger}
```

6. Set the output level to ERROR to reduce Spark's logging output:

```
Logger.getLogger("org").setLevel(Level.ERROR)
```

7. Create Spark's Session object:

```
val spark = SparkSession
 .builder
.master("local[*]")
 .appName("MyBisectingKMeans")
 .config("spark.sql.warehouse.dir", ".")
 .getOrCreate()
```

8. We create a dataset from a file in the libsvm format and display the dataset on the console:

```
val dataset =
spark.read.format("libsvm").load("../data/sparkml2/chapter8/glass.s
cale")
 dataset.show(false)
```

From the console, you will see:

```
+-----+----------------------------------------------------------------------------------------------------------+
|label|features                                                                                                  |
+-----+----------------------------------------------------------------------------------------------------------+
|1.0  |(9,[0,1,2,3,4,5,6,7,8],[-0.134323,-0.124812,1.0,-0.495327,-0.296429,-0.980676,-0.3829,-1.0,-1.0])         |
|1.0  |(9,[0,1,2,3,4,5,6,7,8],[-0.432839,-0.0496238,0.603564,-0.333333,0.0428581,-0.845411,-0.553903,-1.0,-1.0]) |
|1.0  |(9,[0,1,2,3,4,5,6,7,8],[-0.55838,-0.157895,0.581292,-0.221184,0.135713,-0.874396,-0.563197,-1.0,-1.0])    |
|1.0  |(9,[0,1,2,3,5,6,7,8],[-0.428443,-0.254135,0.643653,-0.376947,-0.816425,-0.481413,-1.0,-1.0])              |
|1.0  |(9,[0,1,2,3,4,5,6,7,8],[-0.449511,-0.23609,0.612472,-0.4081,0.167857,-0.822866,-0.509294,-1.0,-1.0])      |
|1.0  |(9,[0,1,2,3,4,5,6,7,8],[-0.577701,-0.380451,0.608018,-0.17134,0.128572,-0.793881,-0.509294,-1.0,0.0196078])|
|1.0  |(9,[0,1,2,3,4,5,6,7,8],[-0.448643,-0.227067,0.603564,-0.470405,0.171427,-0.813205,-0.490706,-1.0,-1.0])   |
|1.0  |(9,[0,1,2,3,4,5,6,7,8],[-0.437224,-0.27218,0.608018,-0.52648,0.224999,-0.816425,-0.477695,-1.0,-1.0])     |
|1.0  |(9,[0,1,2,3,4,5,6,7,8],[-0.294989,-0.00451109,0.594655,-0.327103,-0.189285,-0.819646,-0.466543,-1.0,-1.0])|
|1.0  |(9,[0,1,2,3,4,5,6,7,8],[-0.438103,-0.317293,0.603564,-0.333333,0.135713,-0.816425,-0.447955,-1.0,-0.568627])|
|1.0  |(9,[0,1,2,3,4,5,6,7,8],[-0.599648,-0.401504,0.541203,-0.208723,0.210713,-0.784219,-0.505576,-1.0,-0.0588235])|
|1.0  |(9,[0,1,2,3,4,5,6,7,8],[-0.43108,-0.377443,0.63029,-0.389408,0.142858,-0.806763,-0.418216,-1.0,-1.0])     |
|1.0  |(9,[0,1,2,3,4,5,6,7,8],[-0.583844,-0.353383,0.52784,-0.308411,0.239285,-0.777778,-0.513011,-1.0,-0.0588235])|
|1.0  |(9,[0,1,2,3,4,5,6,7,8],[-0.444247,-0.359398,0.585746,-0.389408,0.214285,-0.826087,-0.451673,-1.0,-0.333333])|
|1.0  |(9,[0,1,2,3,4,5,6,7,8],[-0.43108,-0.434586,0.599109,-0.364486,0.242857,-0.813205,-0.429368,-1.0,-1.0])    |
|1.0  |(9,[0,1,2,3,4,5,6,7,8],[-0.432839,-0.374436,0.576837,-0.41433,0.224999,-0.813205,-0.449814,-1.0,-1.0])    |
|1.0  |(9,[0,1,2,3,4,5,6,7,8],[-0.412639,-0.413534,0.634744,-0.457944,0.178571,-0.803543,-0.392193,-1.0,-1.0])   |
|1.0  |(9,[0,1,2,3,4,5,6,7,8],[-0.0509179,0.0917294,0.714922,-0.626168,-0.446428,-0.951691,-0.30855,-1.0,-1.0])  |
|1.0  |(9,[0,1,2,3,4,5,6,7,8],[-0.301143,-0.0466165,0.66147,-0.445483,-0.174999,-0.980676,-0.356877,-1.0,-1.0])  |
|1.0  |(9,[0,1,2,3,4,5,6,7,8],[-0.455665,-0.311278,0.576837,-0.127726,0.0428581,-0.826087,-0.440521,-1.0,-0.72549])|
+-----+----------------------------------------------------------------------------------------------------------+
only showing top 20 rows
```

9. We then split the dataset randomly into two parts in the ratio of 80% and 20%:

```
val splitData = dataset.randomSplit(Array(80.0, 20.0))
val training = splitData(0)
val testing = splitData(1)

println(training.count())
println(testing.count())
```

From the console output (total count is 214):

```
180
34
```

10. We then create a `BisectingKMeans` object and set some key parameters to the model.

In this case, we set the `K` value to `6` and set the `Feature` column as column "features", which was defined in the previous step. This step is subjective and the optimal value will vary based on specific datasets. We recommend you experiment with values from 2 to 50 and examine the cluster centers for a final value.

11. We also set the maximum iteration count to `65`. Most of the values have a default setting, as shown in the following code:

```
// Trains a k-means model
val bkmeans = new BisectingKMeans()
    .setK(6)
    .setMaxIter(65)
    .setSeed(1)
```

12. We then train the dataset. The `fit()` function will then run the algorithm and do the calculations. It is based on the dataset created in the previous steps. We also print out the model parameters:

```
val bisectingModel = bkmeans.fit(training)
println("Parameters:")
println(bisectingModel.explainParams())
```

From the console output:

```
Parameters:
featuresCol: features column name (default: features)
k: The desired number of leaf clusters. Must be > 1. (default:
4, current: 6)
maxIter: maximum number of iterations (>= 0) (default: 20,
```

```
current: 65)
minDivisibleClusterSize: The minimum number of points (if >=
1.0) or the minimum proportion of points (if < 1.0) of a
divisible cluster. (default: 1.0)
predictionCol: prediction column name (default: prediction)
seed: random seed (default: 566573821, current: 1)
```

13. We then calculate the cost, using the included computeCost(x) function:

```
val cost = bisectingModel.computeCost(training)
println("Sum of Squared Errors = " + cost)
```

The console output will show the following information:

```
Sum of Squared Errors = 70.38842983516193
```

14. Then, we print out the cluster's center based on the calculation of the model:

```
println("Cluster Centers:")
val centers = bisectingModel.clusterCenters
centers.foreach(println)
```

The console output will show the following information:

```
The centers for the 6 cluster (i.e. K= 6)
KMeans Cluster Centers:
```

```
Cluster Centers:
[-0.46260928765432086,-0.26111557395061724,0.5348786182716052,-
0.30964194814814805,0.05978796913580248,-0.817260111111111,-
0.4476571234567898,-0.9895747530864197,-0.9544904320987653]

[-0.04337657000000001,-0.041694967272727264,0.6138895227272727,-
0.6060604999999999,-0.3409090454545454,-0.9455423181818183,-
0.23056775045454544,-0.976912,-0.9447415000000001]

[-0.5077198235294117,-0.3592215294117648,0.5011136470588234,-
0.3384643647058823,0.15168052352941175,-0.8168040588235292,-
0.42444800000000005,-0.9902894705882354,-0.0288350470588235532]

[-0.2522087266666667,-0.21162887333333336,0.5634743933333334,-
0.4600208666666667,-0.11619064000000001,-0.8570048666666668,-
0.3346964,-0.9784126666666667,-0.2575163]

[-0.5328278250000001,0.1389904357142857,-
0.8722557857142856,0.14753011428571428,0.16109662499999997,-
0.8543823571428572,-0.43892724642857156,-0.3585034142857142,-
0.964986]

[0.07246095882352938,-0.38911972941176465,-0.8026987647058825,-
0.33076779941176465,-0.07563012941176467,-
0.8959931764705884,0.2749834882352941,-0.8733893529411765,-
0.6009227823529412]
```

15. We then use the trained model to make a prediction on the testing dataset:

```
val predictions = bisectingModel.transform(testing)
predictions.show(false)
```

From the console output:

```
+-----+------------------------------------------------------------------------------------------------------------------+----------+
|label|features                                                                                                          |prediction|
+-----+------------------------------------------------------------------------------------------------------------------+----------+
|1.0  |(9,[0,1,2,3,4,5,6,7,8],[-0.599648,-0.401504,0.541203,-0.208723,0.210713,-0.784219,-0.505576,-1.0,-0.0588235])|2        |
|1.0  |(9,[0,1,2,3,4,5,6,7,8],[-0.468832,-0.203007,0.55902,-0.464174,0.0857134,-0.838969,-0.442379,-1.0,-1.0])      |0        |
|1.0  |(9,[0,1,2,3,4,5,6,7,8],[-0.445126,-0.365413,0.55902,-0.470405,0.235713,-0.819646,-0.420074,-1.0,-1.0])       |0        |
|1.0  |(9,[0,1,2,3,4,5,6,7,8],[-0.444247,-0.359398,0.585746,-0.389408,0.214285,-0.826087,-0.451673,-1.0,-0.333333])|2        |
|1.0  |(9,[0,1,2,3,4,5,6,7,8],[-0.442488,-0.371428,0.581292,-0.252336,0.0499997,-0.826087,-0.42565,-1.0,-0.254902])|2        |
|1.0  |(9,[0,1,2,3,4,5,6,7,8],[-0.438103,-0.317293,0.603564,-0.333333,0.135713,-0.816425,-0.447955,-1.0,-0.568627])|0        |
|1.0  |(9,[0,1,2,3,4,5,6,7,8],[-0.426685,-0.422556,0.585746,-0.370717,0.167857,-0.803543,-0.394052,-1.0,-0.45098]) |2        |
|1.0  |(9,[0,1,2,3,4,5,6,7,8],[-0.417035,-0.254135,0.510022,-0.352025,0.0535719,-0.809984,-0.412639,-1.0,-1.0])    |0        |
|1.0  |(9,[0,1,2,3,4,5,6,7,8],[-0.404737,-0.254135,0.550111,-0.302181,0.0107138,-0.809984,-0.442379,-1.0,-1.0])    |0        |
|1.0  |(9,[0,1,2,3,4,5,6,7,8],[-0.391571,-0.18797,0.278396,-0.439252,0.0821412,-0.822866,-0.330855,-1.0,-1.0])     |0        |
|1.0  |(9,[0,1,2,3,4,5,6,7,8],[-0.338015,-0.26015,0.501114,-0.445483,0.0392859,-0.816425,-0.36803,-1.0,-0.372549]) |3        |
|1.0  |(9,[0,1,2,3,4,5,6,7,8],[0.0579511,-0.100752,0.657016,-0.862928,-0.307143,-0.971014,-0.139405,-1.0,-0.372549])|3       |
|2.0  |(9,[0,1,2,3,4,5,6,7,8],[-0.582965,-0.371428,0.567929,0.00311525,0.0892856,-0.777778,-0.527881,-1.0,-1.0])   |0        |
|2.0  |(9,[0,1,2,3,4,5,6,7,8],[-0.562776,-0.0406013,0.567929,-0.401869,0.0964273,-0.880837,-0.533457,-1.0,-0.45098])|3       |
|2.0  |(9,[0,1,2,3,4,5,6,7,8],[-0.546972,-0.215037,0.5902,-0.202492,0.0928578,-0.803543,-0.542751,-1.0,-1.0])      |0        |
|2.0  |(9,[0,1,2,3,4,5,6,7,8],[-0.53907,-0.452631,0.550111,-0.0155763,0.221429,-0.797101,-0.507435,-1.0,-0.647059])|0       |
|2.0  |(9,[0,1,2,3,4,5,6,7,8],[-0.509221,-0.380451,0.567929,-0.221184,0.267857,-0.78744,-0.540892,-1.0,-1.0])      |0        |
|2.0  |(9,[0,1,2,3,4,5,6,7,8],[-0.495175,-0.218045,0.576837,-0.17757,-0.0249999,-0.780998,-0.501859,-1.0,-1.0])    |0        |
|2.0  |(9,[0,1,2,3,4,5,6,7,8],[-0.48024,-0.172932,0.550111,-0.115265,-0.0321442,-0.800322,-0.524164,-1.0,-1.0])    |0        |
|2.0  |(9,[0,1,2,3,4,5,6,7,8],[-0.476734,-0.350376,0.612472,-0.202492,0.124999,-0.803543,-0.501859,-1.0,-1.0])     |0        |
+-----+------------------------------------------------------------------------------------------------------------------+----------+
only showing top 20 rows
```

16. We then close the program by stopping the Spark context:

```
spark.stop()
```

How it works...

In this session, we explored the Bisecting KMeans model, which is new in Spark 2.0. We utilized the glass dataset in this session and tried to assign a glass type using `BisectingKMeans()`, but changed k to 6 so we have sufficient clusters. As usual, we loaded the data into a dataset with Spark's libsvm loading mechanism. We split the dataset randomly into 80% and 20%, with 80% used to train the model and 20% used for testing the model.

We created the `BiSectingKmeans()` object and used the `fit(x)` function to create the model. We then used the `transform(x)` function for the testing dataset to explore the model prediction and printed out the result in the console output. We also output the cost of computing the clusters (sum of error squared) and then displayed the cluster centers. Finally, we printed the features with their assigned cluster number and stop operation.

Approaches to hierarchical clustering include:

- **Divisive**: Top down approach (Apache Spark implementation)
- **Agglomerative**: Bottom up approach

There's more...

More about the Bisecting KMeans can be found at:

- http://spark.apache.org/docs/latest/api/scala/index.html#org.apache.sp
  ark.ml.clustering.BisectingKMeans
- http://spark.apache.org/docs/latest/api/scala/index.html#org.apache.sp
  ark.ml.clustering.BisectingKMeansModel

We use clustering to explore the data and get a feel for what the outcome looks like as clusters. The bisecting KMeans is an interesting case of hierarchical analysis versus KMeans clustering.

The best way to conceptualize it is to think of bisecting KMeans as a recursive hierarchical KMeans. The bisecting KMeans algorithm divides the data using similarity measurement techniques like KMeans but uses a hierarchical scheme to increase accuracy. It is particularly prevalent in text mining where a hierarchical approach will minimize the intra-cluster dependencies of the corpus body among documents.

The Bisecting KMeans algorithm starts by placing all observations in a single cluster first but then breaks up the cluster into n partition (K=n) using the KMeans method. It then proceeds to select the most similar cluster (the highest inner cluster score) as the parent (the root cluster) while recursively splitting the other clusters until the target number of clusters is derived in a hierarchical manner.

The Bisecting KMeans is a powerful tool used in text analytics to reduce the dimensionality of feature vectors for intelligent text/subject classification. By using this clustering technique, we end up grouping similar words/text/document/evidence into similar groups. Ultimately, if you start exploring text analytics, topic propagation, and scoring (for example, what article would go viral?), you are bound to encounter this technique in the early stages of your journey.

A white paper describing the use of Bisecting KMeans for text clustering is available at http://www.ijarcsse.com/docs/papers/Volume_5/2_February2015/V5I2-0229.pdf

See also

There are two approaches to implementing hierarchical clustering--Spark uses a recursive top-down approach in which a cluster is chosen and then splits are performed in the algorithm as it moves down the hierarchy:

- Details about the hierarchical clustering approach can be found
  at `https://en.wikipedia.org/wiki/Hierarchical_clustering`
- Spark 2.0 documentation for Bisecting K-Mean can be found
  at `http://spark.apache.org/docs/latest/ml-clustering.html#bisecting-k-means`
- A paper describing how to use Bisecting KMeans to classify web logs can be found
  at `http://research.ijcaonline.org/volume116/number19/pxc3902799.pdf`

Using Gaussian Mixture and Expectation Maximization (EM) in Spark to classify data

In this recipe, we will explore Spark's implementation of **expectation maximization** (**EM**) `GaussianMixture()`, which calculates the maximum likelihood given a set of features as input. It assumes a Gaussian mixture in which each point can be sampled from K number of sub-distributions (cluster memberships).

How to do it...

1. Start a new project in IntelliJ or in an IDE of your choice. Make sure the necessary JAR files are included.

2. Set up the package location where the program will reside:

   ```
   package spark.ml.cookbook.chapter8.
   ```

3. Import the necessary packages for vector and matrix manipulation:

   ```
   import org.apache.log4j.{Level, Logger}
   import org.apache.spark.mllib.clustering.GaussianMixture
   import org.apache.spark.mllib.linalg.Vectors
   import org.apache.spark.sql.SparkSession
   ```

4. Create Spark's session object:

```
val spark = SparkSession
  .builder
 .master("local[*]")
  .appName("myGaussianMixture")
  .config("spark.sql.warehouse.dir", ".")
  .getOrCreate()
```

5. Let us take a look at the dataset and examine the input file. The Simulated SOCR Knee Pain Centroid Location Data represents the centroid location for the hypothetical knee-pain locations for 1,000 subjects. The data includes the X and Y coordinates of the centroids.

> This dataset can be used to illustrate the Gaussian Mixture and Expectation Maximization. The data is available
> at: http://wiki.stat.ucla.edu/socr/index.php/SOCR_Data_KneePainData _041409

The sample data looks like the following:

- **X**: The *x* coordinate of the centroid location for one subject and one view.
- **Y**: The *y* coordinate of the centroid location for one subject and one view.

      X, Y

      11 73

      20 88

      19 73

      15 65

      21 57

      26 101

      24 117

      35 106

      37 96

35 147

41 151

42 137

43 127

41 206

47 213

49 238

40 229

The following figure depicts a knee-pain map based on the SOCR dataset from `wiki.stat.ucla`:

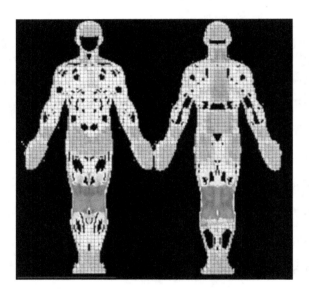

6. We place the data file in a data directory (you can copy the data file to any location you prefer).

    The data file contains 8,666 entries:

```
val dataFile ="../data/sparkml2/chapter8/socr_data.txt"
```

7. We then load the data file into RDD:

```
val trainingData = spark.sparkContext.textFile(dataFile).map { line
=>
Vectors.dense(line.trim.split(' ').map(_.toDouble))
}.cache()
```

8. We now create a GaussianMixture model and set the parameters for the model. We set the K value to 4, since the data was collected by four views: **Left Front (LF)**, **Left Back (LB)**, **Right Front (RF)**, and **Right Back (RB)**. We set the convergence to the default value of 0.01, and the maximum iteration counts to 100:

```
val myGM = new GaussianMixture()
.setK(4 ) // default value is 2, LF, LB, RF, RB
.setConvergenceTol(0.01) // using the default value
.setMaxIterations(100) // max 100 iteration
```

9. We run the model algorithm:

```
val model = myGM.run(trainingData)
```

10. We print out the key values for the GaussianMixture model after the training:

```
println("Model ConvergenceTol: "+ myGM.getConvergenceTol)
println("Model k:"+myGM.getK)
println("maxIteration:"+myGM.getMaxIterations)

for (i <- 0 until model.k) {
println("weight=%f\nmu=%s\nsigma=\n%s\n" format
(model.weights(i), model.gaussians(i).mu,
model.gaussians(i).sigma))
}
```

11. Since we set the K value to 4, we will have four sets of values printed out in the console logger:

```
Model ConvergenceTol: 0.01
Model k:4
maxIteration:100
weight=0.540515
mu=[147.30681254850833,208.6939884522598]
sigma=
4006.19815647266    -57.93614932156636
-57.93614932156636 662.9821920805127

weight=0.069784
mu=[351.3373566850737,231.83105600780897]
sigma=
33107.731896750345 57.84808144351749
57.84808144351749  4970.810900358368

weight=0.169685
mu=[507.34834190901864,194.47534268192427]
sigma=
4718.979203758771   13.290847642742316
13.290847642742316  178.16831733002988

weight=0.220017
mu=[155.24241473988965,218.9842905595943]
sigma=
3919.96712946773    37.75178487899691
37.75178487899691   149.10605322136172
```

12. We also print out the first 50 cluster-labels based on the GaussianMixture model predictions:

```scala
println("Cluster labels (first <= 50):")
val clusterLabels = model.predict(trainingData)
clusterLabels.take(50).foreach { x =>
print(" " + x)
}
```

13. The sample output in the console will show the following:

```
Cluster labels (first <= 50):
 1 1 1 1 1 1 1 1 1 0 0 0 0 0 0 0 0 0 0 0 0 0 0 0 0 0 0 0 0 0 0 0 0 0
 0 0 0 0 0 0 0 0 0 0 0 0 0 0 0 0
```

14. We then close the program by stopping the Spark context:

```
spark.stop()
```

How it works...

In the previous recipe, we observed that KMeans can discover and allocate membership to one and only one cluster based on an iterative method using similarity (Euclidian, and so on). One can think of KMeans as a specialized version of a Gaussian mixture model with EM models in which a discrete (hard) membership is enforced.

But there are cases that have overlap, which is often the case in medicine or signal processing, as depicted in the following figure:

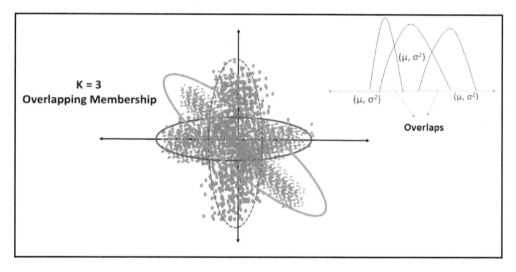

In such cases, we need a probability density function that can express the membership in each sub-distribution. The Gaussian Mixture models with **Expectation Maximization (EM)** is the algorithm `GaussianMixture()` available in Spark that can deal with this use case.

Here is Spark's API for implementing Gaussian Mixture with Expectation Maximization (the maximization of log likelihood).

New GaussianMixture()

This constructs a default instance. The default parameters that control the behavior of the model are:

> K: number of desired clusters, default value 2
>
> convergenceTol: Tolerance value for convergence, default 0.01
>
> maxIterations: Maximum number of Iterations, default 100
>
> seed: seeding at the initialization, default 'random'

The Gaussian Mixture models with Expectation Maximization are a form of soft clustering in which a membership can be inferred using a log maximum likelihood function. In this scenario, a probability density function with mean and covariance is used to define the membership or likelihood of a membership to K number of clusters. It is flexible in the sense that the membership is not quantified which allows for overlapping membership based on probability (indexed to multiple sub-distributions).

The following figure is a snapshot of the EM algorithm:

$$X \sim N(\mu, \sigma^2) \dots \dots X \sim N(\mu, \sigma^2)$$

Here are the steps to the EM algorithm:

1. Assume N number of Gaussian distribution.
2. Iterate until we have convergence:
   1. For each point Z drawn with conditional probability of being drawn from distribution Xi written as $P (Z \mid Xi)$
   2. Adjust the parameter's mean and variance so that they fit the points that are assigned to the sub-distribution

For a more mathematical explanation, including detailed work on maximum likelihood, see the following link:
http://www.ee.iisc.ernet.in/new/people/faculty/prasantg/downloads/GMM_Tutorial_Reynolds.pdf

There's more...

The following figure provides a quick reference point to highlight some of the differences between hard versus soft clustering:

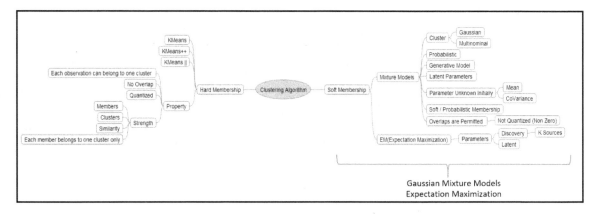

See also

- Documentation for constructor GaussianMixture can be found at http://spark.apache.org/docs/latest/api/scala/index.html#org.apache.spark.mllib.clustering.GaussianMixture

- Documentation for constructor GaussianMixtureModel can be found at http://spark.apache.org/docs/latest/api/scala/index.html#org.apache.spark.mllib.clustering.GaussianMixtureModel

Classifying the vertices of a graph using Power Iteration Clustering (PIC) in Spark 2.0

This is a classification method for the vertices of a graph given their similarities as defined by their edges. It uses the GraphX library which is ships out of the box with Spark to implement the algorithm. Power Iteration Clustering is similar to other Eigen Vector/Eigen Value decomposition algorithms but without the overhead of matrix decomposition. It is suitable when you have a large sparse matrix (for example, graphs depicted as a sparse matrix).

GraphFrames will be the replacement/interface proper for the GraphX library going forward (https://databricks.com/blog/2016/03/03/introducing-graphframes.html).

How to do it...

1. Start a new project in IntelliJ or in an IDE of your choice. Make sure the necessary JAR files are included.

2. Set up the package location where the program will reside:

   ```
   package spark.ml.cookbook.chapter8
   ```

3. Import the necessary packages for Spark context to get access to the cluster and `Log4j.Logger` to reduce the amount of output produced by Spark:

   ```
   import org.apache.log4j.{Level, Logger}
   import org.apache.spark.mllib.clustering.PowerIterationClustering
   import org.apache.spark.sql.SparkSession
   ```

4. Set up the logger level to ERROR only to reduce the output:

   ```
   Logger.getLogger("org").setLevel(Level.ERROR)
   ```

5. Create Spark's configuration and SQL context so we can have access to the cluster and be able to create and use a DataFrame as needed:

   ```
   // setup SparkSession to use for interactions with Spark
   val spark = SparkSession
    .builder
   .master("local[*]")
    .appName("myPowerIterationClustering")
    .config("spark.sql.warehouse.dir", ".")
    .getOrCreate()
   ```

6. We create a training dataset with a list of datasets and use the Spark `sparkContext.parallelize()` function to create Spark RDD:

   ```
   val trainingData =spark.sparkContext.parallelize(List(
   (0L, 1L, 1.0),
   (0L, 2L, 1.0),
   (0L, 3L, 1.0),
   (1L, 2L, 1.0),
   ```

```
(1L,  3L,  1.0),
(2L,  3L,  1.0),
(3L,  4L,  0.1),
(4L,  5L,  1.0),
(4L,  15L, 1.0),
(5L,  6L,  1.0),
(6L,  7L,  1.0),
(7L,  8L,  1.0),
(8L,  9L,  1.0),
(9L,  10L, 1.0),
(10L,11L, 1.0),
(11L, 12L, 1.0),
(12L, 13L, 1.0),
(13L,14L, 1.0),
(14L,15L, 1.0)
))
```

7. We create a `PowerIterationClustering` object and set the parameters. We set the K value to 3 and max iteration count to 15:

```
val pic = new PowerIterationClustering()
 .setK(3)
 .setMaxIterations(15)
```

8. We then let the model run:

```
val model = pic.run(trainingData)
```

9. We print out the cluster assignment based on the model for the training data:

```
model.assignments.foreach { a =>
 println(s"${a.id} -> ${a.cluster}")
 }
```

10. The console output will show the following information:

```
14 -> 1
4 -> 2
8 -> 2
0 -> 0
13 -> 0
11 -> 0
15 -> 0
5 -> 0
1 -> 0
7 -> 0
6 -> 2
12 -> 1
2 -> 0
10 -> 2
3 -> 0
9 -> 0
```

11. We also print out the model assignment data in a collection for each cluster:

```
val clusters =
model.assignments.collect().groupBy(_.cluster).mapValues(_.map(_.id
))
 val assignments = clusters.toList.sortBy { case (k, v) => v.length
}
 val assignmentsStr = assignments
.map { case (k, v) =>
s"$k -> ${v.sorted.mkString("[", ",", "]")}"
}.mkString(", ")
 val sizesStr = assignments.map {
_._2.length
}.sorted.mkString("(", ",", ")")
println(s"Cluster assignments: $assignmentsStr\ncluster sizes:
$sizesStr")
```

12. The console output will display the following information (in total, we have three clusters which were set in the preceding parameters):

```
Cluster assignments: 1 -> [12,14], 2 -> [4,6,8,10], 0 ->
[0,1,2,3,5,7,9,11,13,15]
 cluster sizes: (2,4,10)
```

13. We then close the program by stopping the Spark context:

```
spark.stop()
```

How it works...

We created a list of edges and vertices for a graph and then proceeded to create the object and set the parameters:

```
new PowerIterationClustering().setK(3).setMaxIterations(15)
```

The next step was the model of training data:

```
val model = pic.run(trainingData)
```

The clusters were then outputted for inspection. The code near the end prints out the model assignment data in a collection for each cluster using Spark transformation operators.

At the core **PIC (Power Iteration Clustering)** is an eigenvalue class algorithm which avoids matrix decomposition by producing an Eigen Value plus an Eigen Vector to satisfy $Av = \lambda v$. Because PIC avoids the decomposition of the matrix A, it is suitable when the input matrix A (describing a graph in the case of Spark's PIC) is a large sparse matrix.

An example of PIC in image processing (post enhanced for paper) is depicted in the following figure:

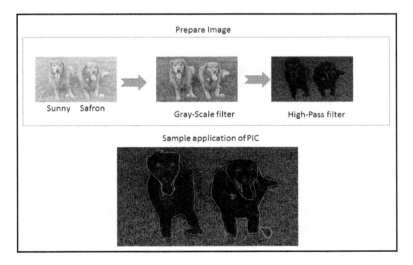

The Spark implementation of the PIC algorithm is an improvement over the previous common implementation (NCut) by computing a pseudo Eigen Vector of the similarities defined as edges given N number of vertices (like an affinity matrix).

The input as depicted in the following figure is a trinary tuple of RDDs describing the graph. The output is a model with a cluster assignment for each node. The algorithm similarities (edges) are assumed to be positive and symmetrical (not shown):

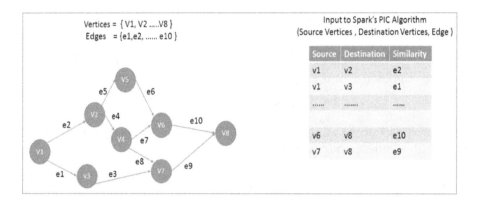

There's more...

For a more detailed mathematical treatment of the subject (power iteration), see the following white paper from Carnegie Mellon University: http://www.cs.cmu.edu/~wcohen/postscript/icml2010-pic-final.pdf

See also

- Documentation for the constructor PowerIterationClustering() can be found
  at http://spark.apache.org/docs/latest/api/scala/index.html#org.apache.spark.mllib.clustering.PowerIterationClustering

- Documentation for the constructor PowerIterationClusteringModel() can be found
  at http://spark.apache.org/docs/latest/api/scala/index.html#org.apache.spark.mllib.clustering.PowerIterationClusteringModel

Latent Dirichlet Allocation (LDA) to classify documents and text into topics

In this recipe, we will explore the **Latent Dirichlet Allocation** (**LDA**) algorithm in Spark 2.0. The LDA we use in this recipe is completely different from linear discrimination analysis. Both Latent Dirichlet Allocation and linear discrimination analysis are referred to as LDA, but they are extremely different techniques. In this recipe, when we use the LDA, we refer to Latent Dirichlet Allocation. The chapter on text analytics is also relevant to understanding the LDA.

LDA is often used in natural language processing which tries to classify a large body of the document (for example, emails from the Enron fraud case) into a discrete number of topics or themes so it can be understood. LDA is also a good candidate for selecting articles based on one's interest (for example, as you turn a page and spend time on a specific topic) in a given magazine article or page.

How to do it...

1. Start a new project in IntelliJ or in an IDE of your choice. Make sure the necessary JAR files are included.

2. Set up the package location where the program will reside:

   ```
   package spark.ml.cookbook.chapter8
   ```

3. Import the necessary packages:

   ```
   import org.apache.log4j.{Level, Logger}
   import org.apache.spark.sql.SparkSession
   import org.apache.spark.ml.clustering.LDA
   ```

4. We set up the necessary Spark Session to gain access to the cluster:

   ```
   val spark = SparkSession
    .builder
   .master("local[*]")
    .appName("MyLDA")
    .config("spark.sql.warehouse.dir", ".")
    .getOrCreate()
   ```

5. We have a sample LDA dataset, which is located at the following relative path (you can use an absolute path). The sample file is provided with any Spark distribution and can be found under the home directory of Spark inside the data directory (see the following). Assume the input is a set of features for input to the LDA method:

```
val input = "../data/sparkml2/chapter8/my_lda_data.txt"
```

Here is a sample of first 5 line of the file (file is in the libsvm format):

```
0 1:1 2:2 3:6 4:0 5:2 6:3 7:1 8:1 9:1 10:0 11:3
1 1:0 2:3 3:0 4:1 5:3 6:0 7:0 8:2 9:1 10:0 11:1
2 1:2 2:4 3:1 4:0 5:0 6:4 7:9 8:0 9:2 10:2 11:0
3 1:2 2:1 3:0 4:3 5:0 6:0 7:5 8:0 9:2 10:3 11:9
4 1:3 2:1 3:1 4:9 5:3 6:0 7:2 8:0 9:0 10:1 11:3
5 1:4 2:2 3:0 4:2 5:4 6:5 7:1 8:1 9:1 10:4 11:0
```

6. In this step, we read the file and create the necessary dataset from the input file and show the top five rows in the console:

```
val dataset = spark.read.format("libsvm").load(input)
dataset.show(5)
```

From the console output:

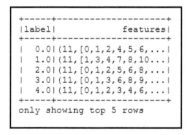

```
+-----+--------------------+
|label|            features|
+-----+--------------------+
|  0.0|(11,[0,1,2,4,5,6,...|
|  1.0|(11,[1,3,4,7,8,10...|
|  2.0|(11,[0,1,2,5,6,8,...|
|  3.0|(11,[0,1,3,6,8,9,...|
|  4.0|(11,[0,1,2,3,4,6,...|
+-----+--------------------+
only showing top 5 rows
```

7. We create the LDA object and set the parameters for the object:

```
val lda = new LDA()
.setK(5)
.setMaxIter(10)
.setFeaturesCol("features")
.setOptimizer("online")
.setOptimizeDocConcentration(true)
```

8. We then run the model using the high-level API from the package:

```
val ldaModel = lda.fit(dataset)


val ll = ldaModel.logLikelihood(dataset)
val lp = ldaModel.logPerplexity(dataset)

println(s"\t Training data log likelihood: $ll")
println(s"\t Training data log Perplexity: $lp")
```

From the console output:

```
Training data log likelihood: -762.2149142231476
Training data log Perplexity: 2.8869048032045974
```

9. We get the topics distribution from the LDA model for each set of features and show the topics.

10. We set the `maxTermsPerTopic` value as 3:

```
val topics = ldaModel.describeTopics(3)
  topics.show(false) // false is Boolean value for truncation for
the dataset
```

11. On the console, the output will show the following information:

```
+-----+-----------+------------------------------------------------------------+
|topic|termIndices|termWeights                                                 |
+-----+-----------+------------------------------------------------------------+
|0    |[2, 5, 7]  |[0.10590438713925907, 0.10552706453241487, 0.10414306358198831]|
|1    |[1, 6, 2]  |[0.10176875268567338, 0.09813701067499785, 0.09625065927903562]|
|2    |[10, 6, 9] |[0.224415590345134, 0.14259821198481398, 0.13437833678670488] |
|3    |[0, 4, 8]  |[0.10259611161709382, 0.09834614889684987, 0.09809818559264627]|
|4    |[9, 6, 4]  |[0.10443008806658334, 0.10406661341365932, 0.10092788028015136]|
+-----+-----------+------------------------------------------------------------+
```

12. We also transform the training dataset from the LDA model, and show the result:

```
val transformed = ldaModel.transform(dataset)
  transformed.show(false)
```

The output will display the following:

```
+-----+--------------------------------------------------------------------------+-------------------------------------------------------------+
|label|features                                                                  |topicDistribution                                            |
+-----+--------------------------------------------------------------------------+-------------------------------------------------------------+
|0.0  |(11,[0,1,2,4,5,6,7,8,10],[1.0,2.0,6.0,2.0,3.0,1.0,1.0,1.0,3.0])            |[0.6652875701333743,0.009021752920617748,...]                |
|1.0  |(11,[1,3,4,7,8,10],[3.0,1.0,3.0,2.0,1.0,1.0])                             |[0.01584997975758763,0.01581565024938826,...]                |
|2.0  |(11,[0,1,2,5,6,8,9],[2.0,4.0,1.0,4.0,9.0,2.0,2.0])                        |[0.007622470464432214,0.007627013290202738,...]              |
|3.0  |(11,[0,1,3,6,8,9,10],[2.0,1.0,3.0,5.0,2.0,3.0,9.0])                       |[0.007203235692928609,0.0072124840651476155,...]             |
|4.0  |(11,[0,1,2,3,4,6,9,10],[3.0,1.0,1.0,9.0,3.0,2.0,1.0,3.0])                 |[0.007851742406435247,0.0078622876385281,...]                |
|5.0  |(11,[0,1,3,4,5,6,7,8,9],[4.0,2.0,2.0,4.0,5.0,1.0,1.0,1.0,4.0])            |[0.007578630665190091,0.007575611615864504,...]              |
|6.0  |(11,[0,1,3,6,8,9,10],[1.0,1.0,3.0,5.0,2.0,2.0,9.0])                       |[0.007800362084464072,0.007809853027526702,...]              |
|7.0  |(11,[0,1,2,3,4,5,6,9,10],[2.0,2.0,2.0,9.0,2.0,1.0,2.0,1.0,3.0])           |[0.007564655969980252,0.007567856115057907,...]              |
|8.0  |(11,[0,1,3,4,5,6,7],[4.0,4.0,3.0,4.0,2.0,1.0,3.0])                        |[0.008607307662614899,0.008618046211724592,...]              |
|9.0  |(11,[0,1,2,4,6,8,9,10],[1.0,8.0,2.0,3.0,2.0,2.0,7.0,2.0])                 |[0.006723495485324213,0.006722272305280794,...]              |
|10.0 |(11,[0,1,2,3,5,6,9,10],[2.0,1.0,1.0,9.0,2.0,2.0,3.0,3.0])                 |[0.007892050842839225,0.007895033920912157,...]              |
|11.0 |(11,[0,1,4,5,6,7,9],[3.0,2.0,4.0,5.0,1.0,3.0,1.0])                        |[0.009491103339631072,0.0094727425025502,...]                |
+-----+--------------------------------------------------------------------------+-------------------------------------------------------------+
```

If the preceding method is changed to:

```
transformed.show(true)
```

13. The result will be displayed as truncated:

```
+-----+--------------------+--------------------+
|label|            features|   topicDistribution|
+-----+--------------------+--------------------+
|  0.0|(11,[0,1,2,4,5,6,...|[0.66525666771208...|
|  1.0|(11,[1,3,4,7,8,10...|[0.01584989652565...|
|  2.0|(11,[0,1,2,5,6,8,...|[0.00762242653921...|
|  3.0|(11,[0,1,3,6,8,9,...|[0.00720319194955...|
|  4.0|(11,[0,1,2,3,4,6,...|[0.00785171521188...|
|  5.0|(11,[0,1,3,4,5,6,...|[0.00757858435810...|
|  6.0|(11,[0,1,3,6,8,9,...|[0.00779999202859...|
|  7.0|(11,[0,1,2,3,4,5,...|[0.00756460520509...|
|  8.0|(11,[0,1,3,4,5,6,...|[0.00860724611808...|
|  9.0|(11,[0,1,2,4,6,8,...|[0.00672030365907...|
| 10.0|(11,[0,1,2,3,5,6,...|[0.00789214021488...|
| 11.0|(11,[0,1,4,5,6,7,...|[0.00948779706633...|
+-----+--------------------+--------------------+
```

14. We close the Spark context to end the program:

```
spark.stop()
```

How it works...

LDA assumes that the document is a mixture of different topics with Dirichlet prior distribution. The words in the document are assumed to have an affinity towards a specific topic which allows LDA to classify the overall document (compose and assign a distribution) that best matches a topic.

A topic model is a generative latent model for discovering abstract themes (topics) that occur in the body of documents (often too large for humans to handle). The models are a pre-cursor to summarize, search, and browse a large set of unlabeled documents and their contents. Generally speaking, we are trying to find a cluster of features (words, sub-images, and so on) that occur together.

The following figure depicts the overall LDA scheme:

Please be sure to refer to the white paper cited here for completeness http://ai.stanford.edu/~ang/papers/nips01-lda.pdf

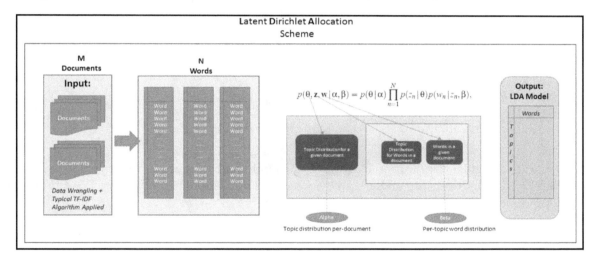

The steps for the LDA algorithm are as follows:

1. Initialize the following parameters (controls concentration and smoothing):

    1. Alpha parameter (high alpha makes documents more similar to each other and contain similar topics)

    2. Beta parameter (high beta means each topic is most likely to contain a mix of most of the words)

2. Randomly initialize the topic assignment.

3. Iterate:

    1. For each document.

        1. For each word in the document.

        2. Resample the topic for each word.

            1. With respect to all other words and their current assignment (for the current iteration).

4. Get the result.

5. Model evaluation

In statistics, Dirichlet distribution Dir(alpha) is a family of continuous multivariate probability distributions parameterized by a vector α of positive real numbers. For a more in-depth treatment of LDA, see the original paper in the

Journal of Machine Learning
at http://www.jmlr.org/papers/volume3/blei03a/blei03a.pdf

The LDA does not assign any semantics to a topic and does not care what the topics are called. It is only a generative model that uses the distribution of fine-grained items (for example, words about cats, dogs, fish, cars) to assign an overall topic that scores the best. It does not know, cares, or understand about topics called dogs or cats.

We often have to tokenize and vectorize the document via TF-IDF prior to input to an LDA algorithm.

There's more...

The following figure depicts the LDA in a nutshell:

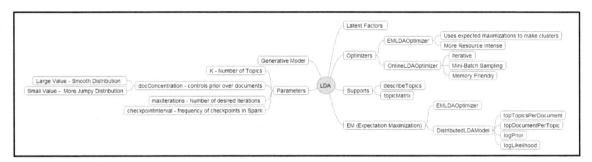

There are two approaches to document analysis. We can simply use matrix factorization to decompose a large matrix of datasets to a smaller matrix (topic assignments) times a vector (topics themselves):

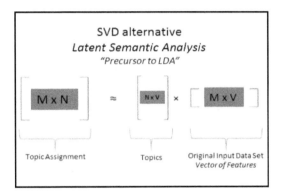

See also

- **LDA**: documentation for a constructor can be found
  at http://spark.apache.org/docs/latest/api/scala/index.html#org.apache.spark.ml.clustering.LDA
- **LDAModel:** documentation for a constructor can be found
  at http://spark.apache.org/docs/latest/api/scala/index.html#org.apache.spark.ml.clustering.LDAModel

See also, via Spark's Scala API, documentation links for the following:

- DistributedLDAModel
- EMLDAOptimizer
- LDAOptimizer
- LocalLDAModel
- OnlineLDAOptimizer

Streaming KMeans to classify data in near real-time

Spark streaming is a powerful facility which lets you combine near real-time and batch in the same paradigm. The streaming KMeans interface lives at the intersection of ML clustering and Spark streaming, and takes full advantage of the core facilities provided by Spark streaming itself (for example, fault tolerance, exactly once delivery semantics, and so on).

How to do it...

1. Start a new project in IntelliJ or in an IDE of your choice. Make sure the necessary JAR files are included.

2. Import the necessary packages for streaming KMeans:

   ```
   package spark.ml.cookbook.chapter14.
   ```

3. Import the necessary packages for streaming KMeans:

   ```
   import org.apache.log4j.{Level, Logger}
   import org.apache.spark.mllib.clustering.StreamingKMeans
   import org.apache.spark.mllib.linalg.Vectors
   import org.apache.spark.mllib.regression.LabeledPoint
   import org.apache.spark.sql.SparkSession
   import org.apache.spark.streaming.{Seconds, StreamingContext}
   ```

4. We set up the following parameters for the streaming KMeans program. The training directory will be the directory to send the training data file. The KMeans clustering model utilizes the training data to run algorithms and calculations. The `testDirectory` will be the test data for predictions. The `batchDuration` is a number in seconds for a batch run. In the following case, the program will check every 10 seconds to see if there is any new data files for recalculations.

5. The cluster is set to `2`, and the data dimensions will be `3`:

```
val trainingDir = "../data/sparkml2/chapter8/trainingDir"
val testDir = "../data/sparkml2/chapter8/testDir"
val batchDuration = 10
 val numClusters = 2
 val numDimensions = 3
```

6. With the preceding settings, the sample training data will contain data like the following (in the format of [X_1, X_2, ...X_n], where *n* is `numDimensions`:

[0.0,0.0,0.0]

[0.1,0.1,0.1]

[0.2,0.2,0.2]

[9.0,9.0,9.0]

[9.1,9.1,9.1]

[9.2,9.2,9.2]

[0.1,0.0,0.0]

[0.2,0.1,0.1]

....

The test data file will contain data like the following (in the format of (*y*, [*X1*, *X2*, .. *Xn*]), where *n* is `numDimensions` and `y` is an identifier):

(7,[0.4,0.4,0.4])

(8,[0.1,0.1,0.1])

(9,[0.2,0.2,0.2])

    (10,[1.1,1.0,1.0])

    (11,[9.2,9.1,9.2])

    (12,[9.3,9.2,9.3])

7. We set up the necessary Spark context to gain access to the cluster:

```
val spark = SparkSession
 .builder
.master("local[*]")
 .appName("myStreamingKMeans")
 .config("spark.sql.warehouse.dir", ".")
 .getOrCreate()
```

8. Define the streaming context and micro-batch window:

```
val ssc = new StreamingContext(spark.sparkContext,
Seconds(batchDuration.toLong))
```

9. The following code will create data by parsing the data file in the preceding two directories into `trainingData` and `testData` RDDs:

```
val trainingData =
ssc.textFileStream(trainingDir).map(Vectors.parse)
 val testData = ssc.textFileStream(testDir).map(LabeledPoint.parse)
```

10. We create the `StreamingKMeans` model and set the parameters:

```
val model = new StreamingKMeans()
 .setK(numClusters)
 .setDecayFactor(1.0)
 .setRandomCenters(numDimensions, 0.0)
```

11. The program will train the model using the training dataset and predict using the test dataset:

```
model.trainOn(trainingData)
 model.predictOnValues(testData.map(lp => (lp.label,
lp.features))).print()
```

12. We start the streaming context, and the program will run the batch every 10 seconds to see if a new dataset is available for training and if there is any new test dataset for prediction. The program will exit if a termination signal is received (exit the batch running):

```
ssc.start()
ssc.awaitTermination()
```

13. We copy the `testKStreaming1.txt` data file into the preceding `testDir` set and see the following printed out in the console logs:

```
----------------------------------------
Time: 1481750570000 ms|
----------------------------------------
(1.0,1)
(2.0,1)
(3.0,0)
(4.0,0)
(5.0,0)
(6.0,0)
```

14. For a Windows machine, we copied the `testKStreaming1.txt` file into the directory: `C:\spark-2.0.0-bin-hadoop2.7\data\sparkml2\chapter8\testDir\`.

15. We can also check the SparkUI for more information: `http://localhost:4040/`.

The job panel will display streaming jobs, as shown in the following figure:

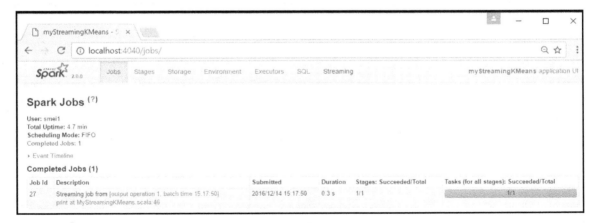

As shown in the following figure, the streaming panel will show the preceding Streaming KMeans matrix as the matrix displayed, the batch job running every 10 seconds in this case:

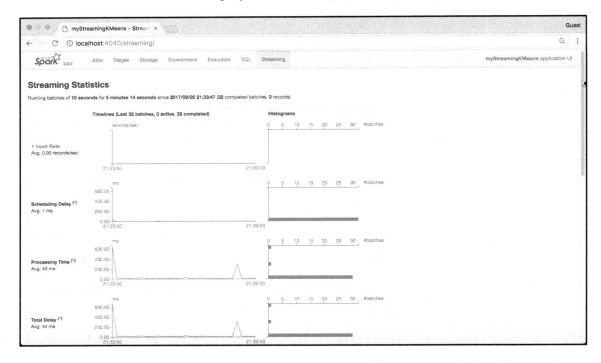

You can get more details on the streaming batch by clicking on any of the batches, as shown in the following figure:

How it works...

In certain situations, we cannot use batch methods to load and capture the events and then react to them. We can use creative methods of capturing events in the memory or a landing DB and then rapidly marshal that over to another system for processing, but most of these systems fail to act as streaming systems and often are very expensive to build.

Spark provides a near real-time (also referred to as subjective real time) that can receive incoming sources, such as Twitter feeds, signals, and so, on via connectors (for example, a Kafka connector) and then process and present them as an RDD interface.

These are the elements needed to build and construct streaming KMeans in Spark:

1. Use the streaming context as opposed to the regular Spark context used so far:

    ```
    val ssc = new StreamingContext(conf, Seconds(batchDuration.toLong))
    ```

2. Select your connector to connect to a data source and receive events:

    - Twitter
    - Kafka
    - Third party
    - ZeroMQ
    - TCP
    - ....

3. Create your streaming KMeans model; set the parameters as needed:

    ```
    model = new StreamingKMeans()
    ```

4. Train and predict as usual:

    - Have in mind that K cannot be changed on the fly

5. Start the context and await for the termination signal to exit:

    - ssc.start()

    - ssc.awaitTermination()

There's more...

Streaming KMeans are special cases of KMeans implementation in which the data can arrive at a near real-time and be classified into a cluster (hard classification) as needed. For a reference to Voronoi diagrams, see the following
URL: https://en.wikipedia.org/wiki/Voronoi_diagram

Currently, there are other algorithms besides streaming KMeans in the Spark Machine Library, as shown in the following figure:

See also

- Documentation for Streaming KMeans can be found
  at http://spark.apache.org/docs/latest/api/scala/index.html#org.apache.spark.mllib.clustering.StreamingKMeans

- Documentation for Streaming KMeans Model can be found
  at http://spark.apache.org/docs/latest/api/scala/index.html#org.apache.spark.mllib.stat.test.StreamingTest

- Documentation for Streaming Test--very useful for data generation--can be found
  at http://spark.apache.org/docs/latest/api/scala/index.html#org.apache.spark.mllib.clustering.StreamingKMeansModel

15
Implementing Text Analytics with Spark 2.0 ML Library

In this chapter, we will cover the following recipes:

- Doing term frequency with Spark - everything that counts
- Displaying similar words with Spark using Word2Vec
- Downloading a complete dump of Wikipedia for a real-life Spark ML project
- Using Latent Semantic Analysis for text analytics with Spark 2.0
- Topic modeling with Latent Dirichlet allocation in Spark 2.0

Introduction

Text analytics is at the intersection of machine learning, mathematics, linguistics, and natural language processing. Text analytics, referred to as text mining in older literature, attempts to extract information and infer higher level concepts, sentiment, and semantic details from unstructured and semi-structured data. It is important to note that the traditional keyword searches are insufficient to deal with noisy, ambiguous, and irrelevant tokens and concepts that need to be filtered out based on the actual context.

Ultimately, what we are trying to do is for a given set of documents (text, tweets, web, and social media), is determine what the gist of the communication is and what concepts it is trying to convey (topics and concepts). These days, breaking down a document into its parts and taxonomy is too primitive to be considered text analytics. We can do better.

Spark provides a set of tools and facilities to make text analytics easier, but it is up to the users to combine the techniques to come up with a viable system (for example, KKN clustering and topic modelling).

It is worth mentioning that many of the commercially available systems use a combination of techniques to come up with the final answer. While Spark has a sufficient number of techniques that work very well at scale, it would not be hard to imagine that any text analytics system can benefit from a graphical model (that is, GraphFrame, GraphX). The following figure is a summary of the tools and facilities provided by Spark for text analytics:

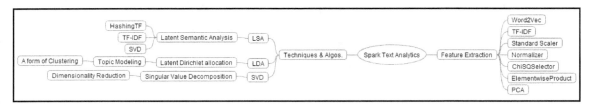

Text analytics is an upcoming and important area due to its application to many fields such as security, customer engagement, sentiment analysis, social media, and online learning. Using text analytics techniques, one can combine traditional data stores (that is, structured data and database tables) with unstructured data (that is, customer reviews, sentiments, and social media interaction) to ascertain a higher order of understanding and a more complete view of the business unit, which was not possible before. This is especially important when dealing with millennials that have chosen social media and unstructured text as their primary means of communication.

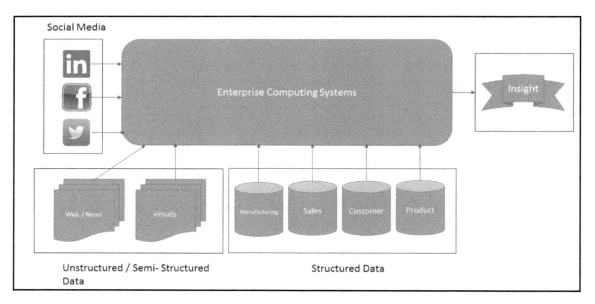

The main challenge with unstructured text is that you cannot use the traditional data platforming tools such as ETL to extract and force order on the data. We need new data wrangling, ML, and statistical methods combined with NLP techniques that can extract information and insight. Social media and customer interactions, such as transcriptions of calls in a call center, contain valuable information that can no longer be ignored without losing one's competitive edge.

We not only need text analytics to be able to address big data at rest but must also consider big data in motion, such as tweets and streams, to be effective.

There are several approaches to deal with unstructured data. The following figure given is a depiction of the techniques in today's toolkit. While the rule-based system can be a good fit for limited text and domains, it fails to generalize due to its specific decision boundaries designed to be effective in that particular domain. The newer systems use statistical and NLP techniques to achieve better accuracy and scale.

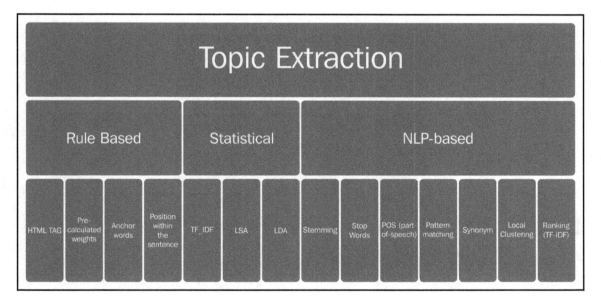

In this chapter, we cover four recipes and two real-life datasets to demonstrate Spark's facilities for handling unstructured text analytics at scale.

First, we start with a simple recipe to not only mimic the early days of web search (keyword frequency) but also to provide insight into TF-IDF in raw code format. This recipe attempts to find out how often a word or phrase occurs in a document. As unbelievable as it sounds, there was a US patent issued for this technique!

Second, we proceed with a well-known algorithm, Word2Vec, which attempts to answer the question, *if I give you a word, can you tell me the surrounding words, or what is in its neighborhood?* This is a good way to ask for synonyms inside a document using statistical techniques.

Third, we implement a **Latent Semantic Analysis (LSA)** which is a form of topic extraction. This method was invented at the University of Colorado Boulder and has been the workhorse in social sciences.

Fourth, we implement a **Latent Dirichlet Allocation (LDA)** to demonstrate topic modelling in which abstract concepts are extracted and associated with phrases or words (that is, less primitive constructs) in a scalable and meaningful way (for example, home, happiness, love, mother, family pet, children, shopping, and parties can be extracted into a single topic).

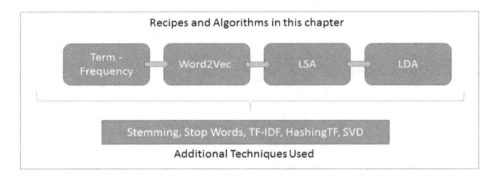

Doing term frequency with Spark - everything that counts

For this recipe, we will download a book in text format from Project Gutenberg, from http://www.gutenberg.org/cache/epub/62/pg62.txt.

Project Gutenberg offers over 50,000 free eBooks in various formats for human consumption. Please read their terms of use; let us not use command-line tools to download any books.

When you look at the contents of the file, you will notice the title and author of the book is *The Project Gutenberg EBook of A Princess of Mars* by Edgar Rice Burroughs.

This eBook is for the use of anyone, anywhere, at no cost, and with almost no restrictions whatsoever. You may copy it, give it away, or reuse it under the terms of the Project Gutenberg License included with this eBook online at http://www.gutenberg.org/.

We then use the downloaded book to demonstrate the classic word count program with Scala and Spark. The example may seem somewhat simple at first, but we are beginning the process of feature extraction for text processing. Also, a general understanding of counting word occurrences in a document will go a long way to help us understand the concept of TF-IDF.

How to do it...

1. Start a new project in IntelliJ or in an IDE of your choice. Make sure the necessary JAR files are included.

2. The `package` statement for the recipe is as follows:

```
package spark.ml.cookbook.chapter12
```

3. Import the necessary packages for Scala, Spark, and JFreeChart:

```
import org.apache.log4j.{Level, Logger}
import org.apache.spark.sql.SQLContext
import org.apache.spark.{SparkConf, SparkContext}
import org.jfree.chart.axis.{CategoryAxis, CategoryLabelPositions}
import org.jfree.chart.{ChartFactory, ChartFrame, JFreeChart}
import org.jfree.chart.plot.{CategoryPlot, PlotOrientation}
import org.jfree.data.category.DefaultCategoryDataset
```

4. We will define a function to display our JFreeChart within a window:

```
def show(chart: JFreeChart) {
val frame = new ChartFrame("", chart)
  frame.pack()
  frame.setVisible(true)
}
```

5. Let us define the location of our book file:

```
val input = "../data/sparkml2/chapter12/pg62.txt"
```

6. Create a Spark session with configurations using the factory builder pattern:

```
val spark = SparkSession
 .builder
 .master("local[*]")
 .appName("ProcessWordCount")
 .config("spark.sql.warehouse.dir", ".")
 .getOrCreate()
import spark.implicits._
```

7. We should set the logging level to warning, otherwise output will be difficult to follow:

```
Logger.getRootLogger.setLevel(Level.WARN)
```

8. We read in the file of stop words which will be used as a filter later:

```
val stopwords =
scala.io.Source.fromFile("../data/sparkml2/chapter12/stopwords.txt"
).getLines().toSet
```

9. The stop words file contains commonly used words which show no relevant value in matching or comparing documents, therefore they will be excluded from the pool of terms by a filter.

10. We now load the book to tokenize, analyze, apply to stop words, filter, count, and sort:

```
val lineOfBook = spark.sparkContext.textFile(input)
 .flatMap(line => line.split("\\W+"))
 .map(_.toLowerCase)
 .filter( s => !stopwords.contains(s))
 .filter( s => s.length >= 2)
 .map(word => (word, 1))
 .reduceByKey(_ + _)
 .sortBy(_._2, false)
```

11. We take top 25 words which have the highest frequency:

```
val top25 = lineOfBook.take(25)
```

12. We loop through every element in the resulting RDD, generating a category dataset model to build our chart of word occurrences:

```
val dataset = new DefaultCategoryDataset()
top25.foreach( {case (term: String, count: Int) =>
dataset.setValue(count, "Count", term) })
```

Display a bar chart of the word count:

```
val chart = ChartFactory.createBarChart("Term frequency",
  "Words", "Count", dataset, PlotOrientation.VERTICAL,
  false, true, false)

val plot = chart.getCategoryPlot()
val domainAxis = plot.getDomainAxis();
domainAxis.setCategoryLabelPositions(CategoryLabelPositions.DOWN_45
);
show(chart)
```

The following chart displays the word count:

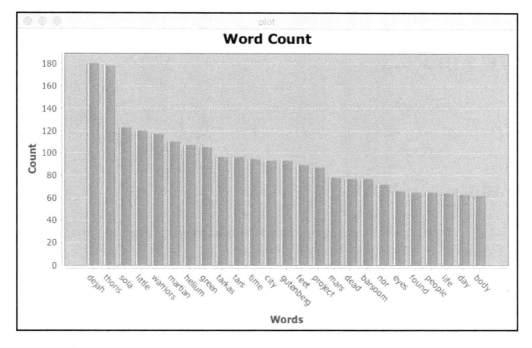

13. We close the program by stopping the SparkContext:

```
spark.stop()
```

How it works...

We began by loading the downloaded book and tokenizing it via a regular expression. The next step was to convert all tokens to lowercase and exclude stop words from our token list, followed by filtering out any words less than two characters long.

The removal of stop words and words of a certain length reduce the number of features we have to process. It may not seem obvious, but the removal of particular words based on various processing criteria reduce the number of dimensions our machine learning algorithms will later process.

Finally, we sorted the resulting word count in descending order, taking the top 25, which we displayed a bar chart for.

There's more...

In this recipe, we have the base of what a keyword search would do. It is important to understand the difference between topic modelling and keyword search. In a keyword search, we try to associate a phrase with a given document based on the occurrences. In this case, we will point the user to a set of documents that has the most number of occurrences.

See also

The next step in the evolution of this algorithm, that a developer can try as an extension, would be to add weights and come up with a weighted average, but then Spark provides a facility which we explore in the upcoming recipes.

Displaying similar words with Spark using Word2Vec

In this recipe, we will explore Word2Vec, which is Spark's tool for assessing word similarity. The Word2Vec algorithm is inspired by the *distributional hypothesis* in general linguistics. At the core, what it tries to say is that the tokens which occur in the same context (that is, distance from the target) tend to support the same primitive concept/meaning.

The Word2Vec algorithm was invented by a team of researchers at Google. Please refer to a white paper mentioned in the *There's more...* section of this recipe which describes Word2Vec in more detail.

How to do it...

1. Start a new project in IntelliJ or in an IDE of your choice. Make sure the necessary JAR files are included.

2. The `package` statement for the recipe is as follows:

   ```
   package spark.ml.cookbook.chapter12
   ```

3. Import the necessary packages for Scala and Spark:

   ```
   import org.apache.log4j.{Level, Logger}
   import org.apache.spark.ml.feature.{RegexTokenizer,
   StopWordsRemover, Word2Vec}
   import org.apache.spark.sql.{SQLContext, SparkSession}
   import org.apache.spark.{SparkConf, SparkContext}
   ```

4. Let us define the location of our book file:

   ```
   val input = "../data/sparkml2/chapter12/pg62.txt"
   ```

5. Create a Spark session with configurations using the factory builder pattern:

   ```
   val spark = SparkSession
             .builder
   .master("local[*]")
             .appName("Word2Vec App")
             .config("spark.sql.warehouse.dir", ".")
             .getOrCreate()
   import spark.implicits._
   ```

6. We should set the logging level to warning, otherwise output will be difficult to follow:

   ```
   Logger.getRootLogger.setLevel(Level.WARN)
   ```

7. We load in the book and convert it to a DataFrame:

```
val df = spark.read.text(input).toDF("text")
```

8. We now transform each line into a bag of words utilizing Spark's regular expression tokenizer, converting each term into lowercase and filtering away any term which has a character length of less than four:

```
val tokenizer = new RegexTokenizer()
 .setPattern("\\W+")
 .setToLowercase(true)
 .setMinTokenLength(4)
 .setInputCol("text")
 .setOutputCol("raw")
 val rawWords = tokenizer.transform(df)
```

9. We remove stop words by using Spark's `StopWordRemover` class:

```
val stopWords = new StopWordsRemover()
 .setInputCol("raw")
 .setOutputCol("terms")
 .setCaseSensitive(false)
 val wordTerms = stopWords.transform(rawWords)
```

10. We apply the Word2Vec machine learning algorithm to extract features:

```
val word2Vec = new Word2Vec()
 .setInputCol("terms")
 .setOutputCol("result")
 .setVectorSize(3)
 .setMinCount(0)
 val model = word2Vec.fit(wordTerms)
```

11. We find ten synonyms from the book for *martian*:

```
val synonyms = model.findSynonyms("martian", 10)
```

12. Display the results of ten synonyms found by the model:

```
synonyms.show(false)
```

```
+-----------+------------------+
|word       |similarity        |
+-----------+------------------+
|fool       |0.399660404463996 |
|friendships|0.3995726061226465|
|recently   |0.399537090796303 |
|belongings |0.3995208890222543|
|passageway |0.39947730349854393|
|dignified  |0.3993753331167374|
|entry      |0.3993680127191416|
|maximum    |0.3993070923891028|
|tongue     |0.3992951179510815|
|groundless |0.39928608744352556|
+-----------+------------------+
```

13. We close the program by stopping the SparkContext:

```
spark.stop()
```

How it works...

Word2Vec in Spark uses skip-gram and not **Continuous Bag of Words** (**CBOW**) which is more suitable for a **Neural Net** (**NN**). At its core, we are attempting to compute the representation of the words. It is highly recommended for the user to understand the difference between local representation versus distributed presentation, which is very different to the apparent meaning of the words themselves.

If we use distributed vector representation for words, it is natural that similar words will fall close together in the vector space, which is a desirable generalization technique for pattern abstraction and manipulation (that is, we reduce the problem to vector arithmetic).

What we want to do for a given set of words *{Word₁, Word₂, ..., Wordₙ}* that are cleaned and ready for processing, is define a maximum likelihood function (for example, log likelihood) for the sequence, and then proceed to maximize likelihood (that is, typical ML). For those familiar with NN, this is a simple multi class softmax model.

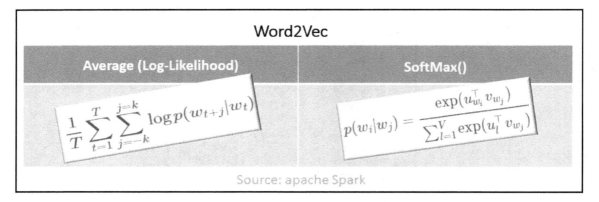

We start off with loading the free book into the memory and tokenizing it into terms. The terms are then converted into lowercase and we filter out any words less than four. We finally apply the stop words followed by the Word2Vec computation.

There's more...

How would you find similar words anyhow? How many algorithms are there that can solve this problem, and how do they vary? The Word2Vec algorithm has been around for a while and has a counterpart called CBOW. Please bear in mind that Spark provides the skip-gram method as the implementation technique.

The variations of the Word2Vec algorithm are as follows:

- **Continuous Bag of Words (CBOW)**: Given a central word, what are the surrounding words?
- **Skip-gram**: If we know the words surrounding, can we guess the missing word?

There is a variation of the algorithm that is called **skip-gram model with negative sampling (SGNS)**, which seems to outperform other variants.

The co-occurrence is the fundamental concept underlying both CBOW and skip-gram. Even though the skip-gram does not directly use a co-occurrence matrix, it is using it indirectly.

In this recipe, we used the *stop words* techniques from NLP to have a cleaner corpus before running our algorithm. The stop words are English words such as "*the*" that need to be removed since they are not contributing to any improvement in the outcome.

Another important concept is *stemming*, which is not covered here but will be demonstrated in later recipes. Stemming removes extra language artifacts and reduces the word to its root (for example, *Engineering*, *Engineer*, and *Engineers* become *Engin* which is the root).

The white paper found at the following URL should provide a deeper explanation for Word2Vec:

```
http://arxiv.org/pdf/1301.3781.pdf
```

See also

Documentation for the Word2Vec recipe:

- `Word2Vec()`: http://spark.apache.org/docs/latest/api/scala/index.html#o rg.apache.spark.ml.feature.Word2Vec
- `Word2VecModel()`: http://spark.apache.org/docs/latest/api/scala/index. html#org.apache.spark.ml.feature.Word2VecModel
- `StopWordsRemover()`: http://spark.apache.org/docs/latest/api/scala/ind ex.html#org.apache.spark.ml.feature.StopWordsRemover

Downloading a complete dump of Wikipedia for a real-life Spark ML project

In this recipe, we will be downloading and exploring a dump of Wikipedia so we can have a real-life example. The dataset that we will be downloading in this recipe is a dump of Wikipedia articles. You will either need the command-line tool **curl**, or a browser to retrieve a compressed file, which is about 13.6 GB at this time. Due to the size, we recommend the curl command-line tool.

How to do it...

1. You can start with downloading the dataset using the following command:

   ```
   curl -L -O
   http://dumps.wikimedia.org/enwiki/latest/enwiki-latest-pages-articl
   es-multistream.xml.bz2
   ```

2. Now you want to decompress the ZIP file:

   ```
   bunzip2 enwiki-latest-pages-articles-multistream.xml.bz2
   ```

   This should create an uncompressed file which is named `enwiki-latest-pages-articles-multistream.xml` and is about 56 GB.

3. Let us take a look at the Wikipedia XML file:

   ```
   head -n50 enwiki-latest-pages-articles-multistream.xml
   <mediawiki xmlns=http://www.mediawiki.org/xml/export-0.10/
   xmlns:xsi="http://www.w3.org/2001/XMLSchema-instance"
   xsi:schemaLocation="http://www.mediawiki.org/xml/export-0.10/
   http://www.mediawiki.org/xml/export-0.10.xsd" version="0.10"
   xml:lang="en">

     <siteinfo>
       <sitename>Wikipedia</sitename>
       <dbname>enwiki</dbname>
       <base>https://en.wikipedia.org/wiki/Main_Page</base>
       <generator>MediaWiki 1.27.0-wmf.22</generator>
       <case>first-letter</case>
       <namespaces>
         <namespace key="-2" case="first-letter">Media</namespace>
         <namespace key="-1" case="first-letter">Special</namespace>
         <namespace key="0" case="first-letter" />
         <namespace key="1" case="first-letter">Talk</namespace>
         <namespace key="2" case="first-letter">User</namespace>
         <namespace key="3" case="first-letter">User talk</namespace>
         <namespace key="4" case="first-letter">Wikipedia</namespace>
         <namespace key="5" case="first-letter">Wikipedia
   talk</namespace>
         <namespace key="6" case="first-letter">File</namespace>
         <namespace key="7" case="first-letter">File talk</namespace>
         <namespace key="8" case="first-letter">MediaWiki</namespace>
         <namespace key="9" case="first-letter">MediaWiki
   talk</namespace>
         <namespace key="10" case="first-letter">Template</namespace>
         <namespace key="11" case="first-letter">Template
   ```

```
talk</namespace>
      <namespace key="12" case="first-letter">Help</namespace>
      <namespace key="13" case="first-letter">Help talk</namespace>
      <namespace key="14" case="first-letter">Category</namespace>
      <namespace key="15" case="first-letter">Category
talk</namespace>
      <namespace key="100" case="first-letter">Portal</namespace>
      <namespace key="101" case="first-letter">Portal
talk</namespace>
      <namespace key="108" case="first-letter">Book</namespace>
      <namespace key="109" case="first-letter">Book
talk</namespace>
      <namespace key="118" case="first-letter">Draft</namespace>
      <namespace key="119" case="first-letter">Draft
talk</namespace>
      <namespace key="446" case="first-letter">Education
Program</namespace>
      <namespace key="447" case="first-letter">Education Program
talk</namespace>
      <namespace key="710" case="first-
letter">TimedText</namespace>
      <namespace key="711" case="first-letter">TimedText
talk</namespace>
      <namespace key="828" case="first-letter">Module</namespace>
      <namespace key="829" case="first-letter">Module
talk</namespace>
      <namespace key="2300" case="first-letter">Gadget</namespace>
      <namespace key="2301" case="first-letter">Gadget
talk</namespace>
      <namespace key="2302" case="case-sensitive">Gadget
definition</namespace>
      <namespace key="2303" case="case-sensitive">Gadget definition
talk</namespace>
      <namespace key="2600" case="first-letter">Topic</namespace>
    </namespaces>
  </siteinfo>
  <page>
    <title>AccessibleComputing</title>
    <ns>0</ns>
    <id>10</id>
    <redirect title="Computer accessibility" />
```

There's more...

We recommend working with the XML file in chunks, and using sampling for your experiments until you are ready for a final job to submit. It will save a tremendous amount of time and effort.

See also

Documentation for Wiki download is available at `https://en.wikipedia.org/wiki/Wikipedia:Database_download`.

Using Latent Semantic Analysis for text analytics with Spark 2.0

In this recipe, we will explore LSA utilizing a data dump of articles from Wikipedia. LSA translates into analyzing a corpus of documents to find hidden meaning or concepts in those documents.

In the first recipe of this chapter, we covered the basics of the TF (that is, term frequency) technique. In this recipe, we use HashingTF for calculating TF and use IDF to fit a model into the calculated TF. At its core, LSA uses **singular value decomposition** (**SVD**) on the term frequency document to reduce dimensionality and therefore extract the most important concepts. There are other cleanup steps that we need to do (for example, stop words and stemming) that will clean up the bag of words before we start analyzing it.

How to do it...

1. Start a new project in IntelliJ or in an IDE of your choice. Make sure the necessary JAR files are included.

2. The package statement for the recipe is as follows:

```
package spark.ml.cookbook.chapter12
```

3. Import the necessary packages for Scala and Spark:

```
import edu.umd.cloud9.collection.wikipedia.WikipediaPage
import
edu.umd.cloud9.collection.wikipedia.language.EnglishWikipediaPage
import org.apache.hadoop.fs.Path
import org.apache.hadoop.io.Text
import org.apache.hadoop.mapred.{FileInputFormat, JobConf}
import org.apache.log4j.{Level, Logger}
import org.apache.spark.mllib.feature.{HashingTF, IDF}
import org.apache.spark.mllib.linalg.distributed.RowMatrix
import org.apache.spark.sql.SparkSession
import org.tartarus.snowball.ext.PorterStemmer
```

The following two statements import the `Cloud9` library toolkit elements necessary for processing Wikipedia XML dumps/objects. `Cloud9` is a library toolkit that makes accessing, wrangling, and processing the Wikipedia XML dumps easier for developers. See the following lines of code for more detailed information:

```
import edu.umd.cloud9.collection.wikipedia.WikipediaPage
import
edu.umd.cloud9.collection.wikipedia.language.EnglishWikipediaPage
```

Wikipedia is a free body of knowledge that can be freely downloaded as a dump of XML chunks/objects via the following Wikipedia download link:

```
https://en.wikipedia.org/wiki/Wikipedia:Database_download
```

The complexity of text and its structure can be easily handled using the `Cloud9` toolkit which facilitates accessing and processing the text using the `import` statements listed previously.

The following link provides some information regarding the `Cloud9` library:

- Main page is available
  at `https://lintool.github.io/Cloud9/docs/content/wikipedia.html`.
- Source code is available
  at `http://grepcode.com/file/repo1.maven.org/maven2/edu.umd/cloud9/2.0.0/edu/umd/cloud9/collection/wikipedia/WikipediaPage.java`
  and `http://grepcode.com/file/repo1.maven.org/maven2/edu.umd/cloud9/2.0.1/edu/umd/cloud9/collection/wikipedia/language/EnglishWikipediaPage.java`.

Next, perform the following steps:

1. We define a function to parse a Wikipedia page and return the title and content text of the page:

```
def parseWikiPage(rawPage: String): Option[(String, String)] = {
 val wikiPage = new EnglishWikipediaPage()
 WikipediaPage.readPage(wikiPage, rawPage)

 if (wikiPage.isEmpty
 || wikiPage.isDisambiguation
 || wikiPage.isRedirect
 || !wikiPage.isArticle) {
 None
 } else {
 Some(wikiPage.getTitle, wikiPage.getContent)
 }
 }
```

2. We define a short function to apply the Porter stemming algorithm to terms:

```
def wordStem(stem: PorterStemmer, term: String): String = {
 stem.setCurrent(term)
 stem.stem()
 stem.getCurrent
 }
```

3. We define a function to tokenize content text of a page into terms:

```
def tokenizePage(rawPageText: String, stopWords: Set[String]):
Seq[String] = {
 val stem = new PorterStemmer()

 rawPageText.split("\\W+")
 .map(_.toLowerCase)
 .filterNot(s => stopWords.contains(s))
 .map(s => wordStem(stem, s))
 .filter(s => s.length > 3)
 .distinct
 .toSeq
 }
```

4. Let us define the location of the Wikipedia data dump:

```
val input = "../data/sparkml2/chapter12/enwiki_dump.xml"
```

5. Create a job configuration for Hadoop XML streaming:

```
val jobConf = new JobConf()
  jobConf.set("stream.recordreader.class",
"org.apache.hadoop.streaming.StreamXmlRecordReader")
  jobConf.set("stream.recordreader.begin", "<page>")
  jobConf.set("stream.recordreader.end", "</page>")
```

6. We set up the data path for Hadoop XML streaming processing:

```
FileInputFormat.addInputPath(jobConf, new Path(input))
```

7. Create a `SparkSession` with configurations using the factory builder pattern:

```
val spark = SparkSession
    .builder
.master("local[*]")
    .appName("ProcessLSA App")
    .config("spark.serializer",
"org.apache.spark.serializer.KryoSerializer")
    .config("spark.sql.warehouse.dir", ".")
    .getOrCreate()
```

8. We should set the logging level to warning, otherwise output will be difficult to follow:

```
Logger.getRootLogger.setLevel(Level.WARN)
```

9. We begin to process the huge Wikipedia data dump into article pages, taking a sample of the file:

```
val wikiData = spark.sparkContext.hadoopRDD(
  jobConf,
  classOf[org.apache.hadoop.streaming.StreamInputFormat],
  classOf[Text],
  classOf[Text]).sample(false, .1)
```

10. Next, we process our sample data into an RDD containing a tuple of title and page context text:

```
val wikiPages = wikiData.map(_._1.toString).flatMap(parseWikiPage)
```

11. We now output the number of Wikipedia articles we will process:

```
println("Wiki Page Count: " + wikiPages.count())
```

12. We load into memory the stop words for filtering the page content text:

```
val stopwords =
scala.io.Source.fromFile("../data/sparkml2/chapter12/stopwords.txt"
).getLines().toSet
```

13. We tokenize the page content text, turning it into terms for further processing:

```
val wikiTerms = wikiPages.map{ case(title, text) =>
tokenizePage(text, stopwords) }
```

14. We use Spark's `HashingTF` class to compute term frequency of our tokenized page context text:

```
val hashtf = new HashingTF()
 val tf = hashtf.transform(wikiTerms)
```

15. We take term frequencies and compute the inverse document frequency utilizing Spark's IDF class:

```
val idf = new IDF(minDocFreq=2)
 val idfModel = idf.fit(tf)
 val tfidf = idfModel.transform(tf)
```

16. We generate a `RowMatrix` using the inverse document frequency and compute singular value decomposition:

```
tfidf.cache()
val rowMatrix = new RowMatrix(tfidf)
val svd = rowMatrix.computeSVD(k=25, computeU = true)

println(svd)
```

U: The rows will be documents and the columns will be concepts.

S: The elements will be the amount variation from each concept.

V: The rows will be terms and the columns will be concepts.

17. We close the program by stopping the SparkContext:

```
spark.stop()
```

How it works...

The example starts off by loading a dump of Wikipedia XML using Cloud9 Hadoop XML streaming tools to process the enormous XML document. Once we have parsed out the page text, the tokenization phase invokes turning our stream of Wikipedia page text into tokens. We used the Porter stemmer during the tokenization phase to help reduce words to a common base form.

More details on stemming are available at `https://en.wikipedia.org/wiki/Stemming`.

The next step was to use Spark HashingTF on each page token to compute the term frequency. After this phase was completed, we utilized Spark's IDF to generate the inverse document frequency.

Finally, we took the TF-IDF API and applied a singular value decomposition to handle factorization and dimensionality reduction.

The following screenshot shows the steps and flow of the recipe:

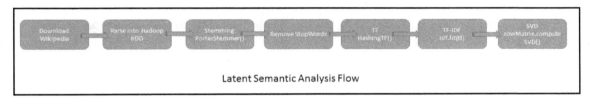

Latent Semantic Analysis Flow

The Cloud9 Hadoop XML tools and several other required dependencies can be found at:

- `bliki-core-3.0.19.jar`: `http://central.maven.org/maven2/info/bliki/wiki/bliki-core/3.0.19/bliki-core-3.0.19.jar`

- `cloud9-2.0.1.jar`: `http://central.maven.org/maven2/edu/umd/cloud9/2.0.1/cloud9-2.0.1.jar`

- `hadoop-streaming-2.7.4.jar`: `http://central.maven.org/maven2/org/apache/hadoop/hadoop-streaming/2.7.4/hadoop-streaming-2.7.4.jar`

- `lucene-snowball-3.0.3.jar`: `http://central.maven.org/maven2/org/apache/lucene/lucene-snowball/3.0.3/lucene-snowball-3.0.3.jar`

There's more...

It should be obvious by now that even though Spark does not provide a direct LSA implementation, the combination of TF-IDF and SVD will let us construct and then decompose the large corpus matrix into three matrices, which can help us interpret the results by applying the dimensionality reduction via SVD. We can concentrate on the most meaningful clusters (similar to a recommendation algorithm).

SVD will factor the term frequency document (that is, documents by attributes) to three distinct matrices that are much more efficient to extract to *N* concepts (that is, *N=27* in our example) from a large matrix that is hard and expensive to handle. In ML, we always prefer the tall and skinny matrices (that is, *U* matrix in this case) to other variations.

The following is the technique for SVD:

$$M = U\Sigma V^*$$

The primary goal of SVD is dimensionality reduction to cure desired (that is, top *N*) topics or abstract concepts. We will use the following input to get the output stated in the following section.

As input, we'll take a large matrix of *m x n* (*m* is the number of documents, *n* is the number of terms or attributes).

This is the output that we should get:

- Matrix 1 (m by n) ----> U [topics]
- Matrix 2 (n by n) ----> S [Eigenvalues are in diagonal of Matrix S]
- Matrix 3 (n by n) ------> V [proportion of contribution]

For a more detailed example and short tutorial on SVD, please see the following links:

- http://home.iitk.ac.in/~crkrish/MLT/PreRequisites/linalgWithSVD.pdf
- http://davetang.org/file/Singular_Value_Decomposition_Tutorial.pdf

You can also refer to a write up from RStudio, which is available at the following link:

`http://rstudio-pubs-static.s3.amazonaws.com/222293_1c40c75d7faa42869cc59df87954`
`7c2b.html`

See also

More details on `SingularValueDecomposition()` can be found
at `http://spark.apache.org/docs/latest/api/scala/index.html#org.apache.spark.ml`
`lib.linalg.SingularValueDecomposition`.

Please refer to `http://spark.apache.org/docs/latest/api/scala/index.html#org.`
`apache.spark.mllib.linalg.distributed.RowMatrix` for more details on `RowMatrix()`.

Topic modeling with Latent Dirichlet allocation in Spark 2.0

In this recipe, we will be demonstrating topic model generation by utilizing Latent Dirichlet Allocation to infer topics from a collection of documents.

We have covered LDA in previous chapters as it applies to clustering and topic modelling, but in this chapter, we demonstrate a more elaborate example to show its application to text analytics using more real-life and complex datasets.

We also apply NLP techniques such as stemming and stop words to provide a more realistic approach to LDA problem-solving. What we are trying to do is to discover a set of latent factors (that is, different from the original) that can solve and describe the solution in a more efficient way in a reduced computational space.

The first question that always comes up when using LDA and topic modelling is *what is Dirichlet?* Dirichlet is simply a type of distribution and nothing more. Please see the following link from the University of Minnesota for details: `http://www.tc.umn.edu/`
`~horte005/docs/Dirichletdistribution.pdf`.

How to do it...

1. Start a new project in IntelliJ or in an IDE of your choice. Make sure the necessary JAR files are included.

2. The `package` statement for the recipe is as follows:

   ```
   package spark.ml.cookbook.chapter12
   ```

3. Import the necessary packages for Scala and Spark:

   ```
   import edu.umd.cloud9.collection.wikipedia.WikipediaPage
   import
   edu.umd.cloud9.collection.wikipedia.language.EnglishWikipediaPage
   import org.apache.hadoop.fs.Path
   import org.apache.hadoop.io.Text
   import org.apache.hadoop.mapred.{FileInputFormat, JobConf}
   import org.apache.log4j.{Level, Logger}
   import org.apache.spark.ml.clustering.LDA
   import org.apache.spark.ml.feature._
   import org.apache.spark.sql.SparkSession
   ```

4. We define a function to parse a Wikipedia page and return the title and content text of the page:

   ```
   def parseWikiPage(rawPage: String): Option[(String, String)] = {
   val wikiPage = new EnglishWikipediaPage()
   WikipediaPage.readPage(wikiPage, rawPage)

   if (wikiPage.isEmpty
   || wikiPage.isDisambiguation
   || wikiPage.isRedirect
   || !wikiPage.isArticle) {
   None
   } else {
   Some(wikiPage.getTitle, wikiPage.getContent)
   }
   }
   ```

5. Let us define the location of the Wikipedia data dump:

   ```
   val input = "../data/sparkml2/chapter12/enwiki_dump.xml"
   ```

6. We create a job configuration for Hadoop XML streaming:

   ```
   val jobConf = new JobConf()
   jobConf.set("stream.recordreader.class",
   ```

```
            "org.apache.hadoop.streaming.StreamXmlRecordReader")
        jobConf.set("stream.recordreader.begin", "<page>")
        jobConf.set("stream.recordreader.end", "</page>")
```

7. We set up the data path for Hadoop XML streaming processing:

```
        FileInputFormat.addInputPath(jobConf, new Path(input))
```

8. Create a `SparkSession` with configurations using the factory builder pattern:

```
        val spark = SparkSession
            .builder
        .master("local[*]")
            .appName("ProcessLDA App")
            .config("spark.serializer",
        "org.apache.spark.serializer.KryoSerializer")
            .config("spark.sql.warehouse.dir", ".")
            .getOrCreate()
```

9. We should set the logging level to warning, otherwise, output will be difficult to follow:

```
        Logger.getRootLogger.setLevel(Level.WARN)
```

10. We begin to process the huge Wikipedia data dump into article pages taking a sample of the file:

```
        val wikiData = spark.sparkContext.hadoopRDD(
        jobConf,
        classOf[org.apache.hadoop.streaming.StreamInputFormat],
        classOf[Text],
        classOf[Text]).sample(false, .1)
```

11. Next, we process our sample data into an RDD containing a tuple of title and page context text to finally generate a DataFrame:

```
        val df = wiki.map(_._1.toString)
         .flatMap(parseWikiPage)
         .toDF("title", "text")
```

12. We now transform the text column of the DataFrame into raw words using Spark's `RegexTokenizer` for each Wikipedia page:

```
        val tokenizer = new RegexTokenizer()
         .setPattern("\\W+")
         .setToLowercase(true)
         .setMinTokenLength(4)
         .setInputCol("text")
```

```
      .setOutputCol("raw")
    val rawWords = tokenizer.transform(df)
```

13. The next step is to filter raw words by removing all stop words from the tokens:

```
val stopWords = new StopWordsRemover()
  .setInputCol("raw")
  .setOutputCol("words")
  .setCaseSensitive(false)

val wordData = stopWords.transform(rawWords)
```

14. We generate term counts for the filtered tokens by using Spark's CountVectorizer class, resulting in a new DataFrame containing the column features:

```
val cvModel = new CountVectorizer()
  .setInputCol("words")
  .setOutputCol("features")
  .setMinDF(2)
  .fit(wordData)
val cv = cvModel.transform(wordData)
cv.cache()
```

The "MinDF" specifies the minimum number of different document terms that must appear in order to be included in the vocabulary.

15. We now invoke Spark's LDA class to generate topics and the distributions of tokens to topics:

```
val lda = new LDA()
  .setK(5)
  .setMaxIter(10)
  .setFeaturesCol("features")
val model = lda.fit(tf)
val transformed = model.transform(tf)
```

The "K" refers to how many topics and "MaxIter" maximum iterations to execute.

16. We finally describe the top five generated topics and display:

```
val topics = model.describeTopics(5)
 topics.show(false)
```

```
|topic|          termIndices|          termWeights|
+-----+--------------------+--------------------+
|    0|[712, 2706, 155, ...|[0.00156744184517...|
|    1|[0, 1991, 1, 712,...|[0.00164906709185...|
|    2|[155, 74, 56, 974...|[0.00142808800646...|
|    3|[2473, 3487, 1, 9...|[0.00121717433276...|
|    4|[712, 155, 4533, ...|[0.00145563043495...|
+-----+--------------------+--------------------+
```

17. Now display, topics and terms associated with them:

```
val vocaList = cvModel.vocabulary
topics.collect().foreach { r => {
 println("\nTopic: " + r.get(r.fieldIndex("topic")))
 val y =
r.getSeq[Int](r.fieldIndex("termIndices")).map(vocaList(_))
 .zip(r.getSeq[Double](r.fieldIndex("termWeights")))
 y.foreach(println)

 }
}
```

The console output will be as follows:

```
Topic: 0
(insurance,0.0015674418451765248)
(samba,0.0011258608853073513)
(rights,0.0010481989926593705)
(spyware,8.513540441748018E-4)
(time,8.01287339366417E-4)


Topic: 3
(belarus,0.001217174332760276)
(interlingua,9.702547559148557E-4)
(used,8.767760726675688E-4)
(city,5.509786244008334E-4)
(embassy,5.30830057520273E-4)
```

```
Topic: 1
(american,0.0016490670918540016)
(netscape,0.0014955491401855165)
(used,9.353119763794209E-4)
(insurance,8.560486990185497E-4)
(analog,6.742308290569271E-4)


Topic: 4
(Insurance, 0.0014556304349531235)
(rights,0.0011301614983826025)
(voight,7.854171410474698E-4)
(human,7.751093184402613E-4)
(world,6.139408988550648E-4)
```

```
Topic: 2
(rights,0.0014280880064640189)
(human,0.001249116068564253)
(party,9.28780904037864E-4)
(labor,8.218773234641597E-4)
(mail,8.203236523858697E-4)
```

18. We close the program by stopping the SparkContext:

```
spark.stop()
```

How it works...

We began with loading the dump of Wikipedia articles and parsed the page text into tokens using Hadoop XML leveraging streaming facilities API. The feature extraction process utilized several classes to set up the final processing by the LDA class, letting the tokens flow from Spark's `RegexTokenize`, `StopwordsRemover`, and `HashingTF`. Once we had the term frequencies, the data was passed to the LDA class for clustering the articles together under several topics.

The Hadoop XML tools and several other required dependencies can be found at:

- `bliki-core-3.0.19.jar`: `http://central.maven.org/maven2/info/bliki/wiki/bliki-core/3.0.19/bliki-core-3.0.19.jar`
- `cloud9-2.0.1.jar`: `http://central.maven.org/maven2/edu/umd/cloud9/2.0.1/cloud9-2.0.1.jar`
- `hadoop-streaming-2.7.4.jar`: `http://central.maven.org/maven2/org/apache/hadoop/hadoop-streaming/2.7.4/hadoop-streaming-2.7.4.jar`
- `lucene-snowball-3.0.3.jar`: `http://central.maven.org/maven2/org/apache/lucene/lucene-snowball/3.0.3/lucene-snowball-3.0.3.jar`

There's more...

Please see the recipe LDA to classify documents and text into topics in `Chapter 8`, *Unsupervised Clustering with Apache Spark 2.0* for a more detailed explanation of the LDA algorithm itself.

The following white paper from the *Journal of Machine Learning Research (JMLR)* provides a comprehensive treatment for those who would like to do an extensive analysis. It is a well-written paper, and a person with a basic background in stat and math should be able to follow it without any problems.

Refer to the `http://www.jmlr.org/papers/volume3/blei03a/blei03a.pdf` link for more details of JMLR; an alternative link is `https://www.cs.colorado.edu/~mozer/Teaching/syllabi/ProbabilisticModels/readings/BleiNgJordan2003.pdf`.

See also

- Documentation for the constructor is available
  at `http://spark.apache.org/docs/latest/api/scala/index.html#org.apache.spark.ml.clustering.LDA`
- Documentation for LDAModel is available at `http://spark.apache.org/docs/latest/api/scala/index.html#org.apache.spark.ml.clustering.LDAModel`

See also Spark's Scala API documentation for the following:

- DistributedLDAModel
- EMLDAOptimizer
- LDAOptimizer
- LocalLDAModel
- OnlineLDAOptimizer

16
Spark Streaming and Machine Learning Library

In this chapter, we will cover the following recipes:

- Structured streaming for near real-time machine learning
- Streaming DataFrames for real-time machine learning
- Streaming Datasets for real-time machine learning
- Streaming data and debugging with queueStream
- Downloading and understanding the famous Iris data for unsupervised classification
- Streaming KMeans for a real-time online classifier
- Downloading wine quality data for streaming regression
- Streaming linear regression for a real-time regression
- Downloading Pima Diabetes data for supervised classification
- Streaming logistic regression for an on-line classifier

Introduction

Spark streaming is an evolving journey toward unification and structuring of the APIs in order to address the concerns of batch versus stream. Spark streaming has been available since Spark 1.3 with **Discretized Stream (DStream)**. The new direction is to abstract the underlying framework using an unbounded table model in which the users can query the table using SQL or functional programming and write the output to another output table in multiple modes (complete, delta, and append output). The Spark SQL Catalyst optimizer and Tungsten (off-heap memory manager) are now an intrinsic part of the Spark streaming, which leads to a much efficient execution.

In this chapter, we not only cover the streaming facilities available in Spark's machine library out of the box, but also provide four introductory recipes that we found useful as we journeyed toward our better understanding of Spark 2.0.

The following figure depicts what is covered in this chapter:

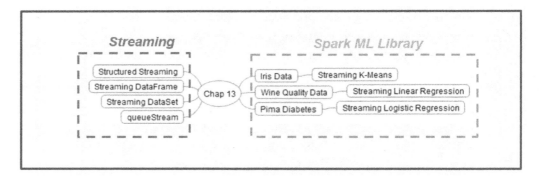

Spark 2.0+ builds on the success of the previous generation by abstracting away some of the framework's inner workings and presenting it to the developer without worrying about *end-to-end write only once* semantics. It is a journey from DStream based on RDD to a structured streaming paradigm in which your world of streaming can be viewed as infinite tables with multiple modes for output.

The state management has evolved from `updateStateByKey` (Spark 1.3 to Spark 1.5) to `mapWithState` (Spark 1.6+) to the third generation state management with structured streaming (Spark 2.0+).

A modern ML streaming system is a complex continuous application that needs to not only combine various ML steps into a pipeline, but also interact with other subsystems to provide a real-life useful, end-to-end information system.

The following figure depicts a minimum viable streaming system that is the foundation of most streaming systems (over simplified for presentation):

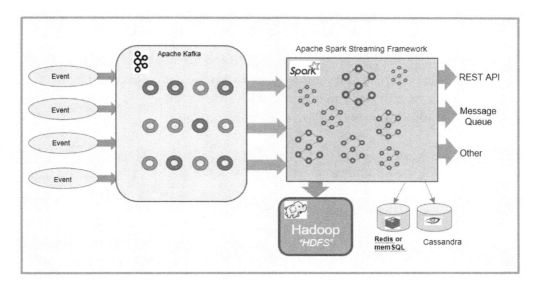

As seen in the preceding figure, any real-life system must interact with batch (for example, offline learning of the model parameters) while the faster subsystem concentrates on real-time response to external events (that is, online learning).

Spark's structured streaming full integration with ML library is on the horizon, but meanwhile, we can create and use streaming DataFrames and streaming Datasets to compensate, as will be seen in some of the following recipes.

The new structured streaming has several advantages, such as:

- Unification of Batch and Stream APIs (no need to translate)
- Functional programming with more concise expressive language
- Fault-tolerant state management (third generation)
- Significantly simplified programming model:
    - Trigger
    - Input
    - Query
    - Result
    - Output
- Data stream as a unbounded table

The following figure depicts the basic concepts beyond a data stream being modeled as an infinite unbounded table:

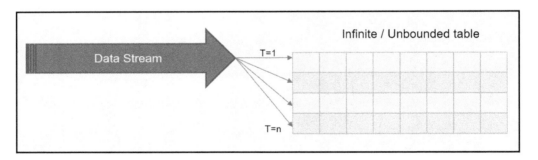

The pre-Spark 2.0 paradigm advanced the DStream construct, which modeled the stream as a set of discrete data structures (RDDs) that was very difficult to deal with when we had late arrivals. The inherent late arrival problem made it difficult to build systems that had a real-time chargeback model (very prominent in the cloud) due to the uncertainty around the actual charges.

The following figure depicts the DStream model in a visual way so it can be compared accordingly:

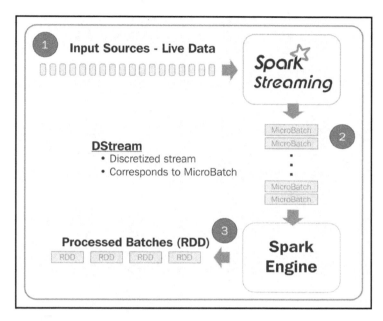

In comparison, by using the new model, there are fewer concepts that a developer needs to worry about and there is no need to translate the code from a batch model (often ETL like code) to a real-time stream model.

Currently, due to the timeline and legacy, one must know both models (DStream and structured streaming) for a while before all pre-Spark 2.0 code is replaced. We found the new structured streaming model particularly simple compared to DStream and have tried to demonstrate and highlight the differences in the four introductory recipes covered in this chapter.

Structured streaming for near real-time machine learning

In this recipe, we explore the new structured streaming paradigm introduced in Spark 2.0. We explore real-time streaming using sockets and structured streaming API to vote and tabulate the votes accordingly.

We also explore the newly introduced subsystem by simulating a stream of randomly generated votes to pick the most unpopular comic book villain.

 There are two distinct programs (`VoteCountStream.scala` and `CountStreamproducer.scala`) that make up this recipe.

How to do it...

1. Start a new project in IntelliJ or in an IDE of your choice. Make sure that the necessary JAR files are included.

2. Set up the package location where the program will reside:

   ```
   package spark.ml.cookbook.chapter13
   ```

3. Import the necessary packages for the Spark context to get access to the cluster and `log4j.Logger` to reduce the amount of output produced by Spark:

   ```
   import org.apache.log4j.{Level, Logger}
   import org.apache.spark.sql.SparkSession
   import java.io.{BufferedOutputStream, PrintWriter}
   import java.net.Socket
   import java.net.ServerSocket
   import java.util.concurrent.TimeUnit
   import scala.util.Random
   import org.apache.spark.sql.streaming.ProcessingTime
   ```

4. Define a Scala class to generate voting data onto a client socket:

   ```
   class CountSreamThread(socket: Socket) extends Thread
   ```

5. Define an array containing literal string values of people to vote for:

   ```
   val villians = Array("Bane", "Thanos", "Loki", "Apocalypse", "Red
   Skull", "The Governor", "Sinestro", "Galactus",
    "Doctor Doom", "Lex Luthor", "Joker", "Magneto", "Darth Vader")
   ```

6. Now we will override the `Threads` class `run` method to randomly simulate a vote for a particular villain:

```scala
override def run(): Unit = {

println("Connection accepted")
val out = new PrintWriter(new
BufferedOutputStream(socket.getOutputStream()))

println("Producing Data")
while (true) {
out.println(villians(Random.nextInt(villians.size)))
Thread.sleep(10)
}

println("Done Producing")
}
```

7. Next, we define a Scala singleton object to accept connections on a defined port `9999` and generate voting data:

```scala
object CountStreamProducer {

def main(args: Array[String]): Unit = {

val ss = new ServerSocket(9999)
while (true) {
println("Accepting Connection...")
new CountSreamThread(ss.accept()).start()
}
}
}
```

8. Don't forget to start up the data generation server, so our streaming example can process the streaming vote data.

9. Set output level to ERROR to reduce Spark's output:

```scala
Logger.getLogger("org").setLevel(Level.ERROR)
Logger.getLogger("akka").setLevel(Level.ERROR)
```

10. Create a `SparkSession` yielding access to the Spark cluster and underlying sessions object attributes such as the `SparkContext` and `SparkSQLContext`:

```
val spark = SparkSession
.builder
.master("local[*]")
.appName("votecountstream")
.config("spark.sql.warehouse.dir", ".")
.getOrCreate()
```

11. Import spark implicits, therefore adding in behavior with only an import:

```
import spark.implicits._
```

12. Create a streaming DataFrame by connecting to localhost on port `9999`, which utilizes a Spark socket source as the source of streaming data:

```
val stream = spark.readStream
.format("socket")
.option("host", "localhost")
.option("port", 9999)
.load()
```

13. In this step, we group streaming data by villain name and count to simulate user votes streaming in real time:

```
val villainsVote = stream.groupBy("value").count()
```

14. Now we define a streaming query to trigger every 10 seconds, dump the whole result set into the console, and invoke it by calling the `start()` method:

```
val query = villainsVote.orderBy("count").writeStream
.outputMode("complete")
.format("console")
.trigger(ProcessingTime.create(10, TimeUnit.SECONDS))
.start()
```

The first output batch is displayed here as batch 0:

```
------------------------------------------------
Batch: 0
------------------------------------------------
+------------+-----+
|       value|count|
+------------+-----+
|        Bane|   57|
|   Red Skull|   58|
|      Thanos|   60|
|The Governor|   62|
|     Magneto|   68|
| Doctor Doom|   69|
|    Sinestro|   72|
| Darth Vader|   72|
|    Galactus|   75|
|   Apocalypse|  76|
|        Loki|   77|
|       Joker|   77|
|   Lex Luthor|  78|
+------------+-----+
```

An additional batch result is displayed here:

```
------------------------------------------------
Batch: 51
------------------------------------------------
+------------+-----+
|       value|count|
+------------+-----+
|   Red Skull| 3805|
|        Bane| 3814|
| Doctor Doom| 3830|
|        Loki| 3852|
|    Sinestro| 3880|
|       Joker| 3885|
| Darth Vader| 3886|
|   Apocalypse| 3896|
|The Governor| 3901|
|     Magneto| 3906|
|      Thanos| 3913|
|   Lex Luthor| 3923|
|    Galactus| 4021|
+------------+-----+
```

15. Finally, wait for termination of the streaming query or stop the process using the `SparkSession` API:

```
query.awaitTermination()
```

How it works...

In this recipe, we created a simple data generation server to simulate a stream of voting data and then counted the vote. The following figure provides a high-level depiction of this concept:

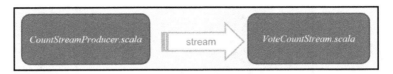

First, we began by executing the data generation server. Second, we defined a socket data source, which allows us to connect to the data generation server. Third, we constructed a simple Spark expression to group by villain (that is, bad superheroes) and count all currently received votes. Finally, we configured a threshold trigger of 10 seconds to execute our streaming query, which dumps the accumulated results onto the console.

There are two short programs involved in this recipe:

- `CountStreamproducer.scala`:
    - The producer - data generation server
    - Simulates the voting for itself and broadcasts it
- `VoteCountStream.scala`:
    - The consumer - consumes and aggregates/tabulates the data
    - Receives and count votes for our villain superhero

There's more...

The topic of how to program using Spark streaming and structured streaming in Spark is out of scope for this book, but we felt it is necessary to share some programs to introduce the concepts before drilling down into ML streaming offering for Spark.

For a solid introduction to streaming, please consult the following documentation on Spark:

- Information of Spark 2.0+ structured streaming is available
  at https://spark.apache.org/docs/latest/structured-streaming-programmin
  g-guide.html#api-using-datasets-and-dataframes
- Information of Spark 1.6 streaming is available
  at https://spark.apache.org/docs/latest/streaming-programming-guide.htm
  l

See also

- Documentation for structured streaming is available
  at `https://spark.apache.org/docs/latest/api/scala/index.html#org.apache`
  `.spark.sql.streaming.package`
- Documentation for DStream (pre-Spark 2.0) is available
  at `https://spark.apache.org/docs/latest/api/scala/index.html#org.apache`
  `.spark.streaming.dstream.DStream`
- Documentation for `DataStreamReader` is available
  at `https://spark.apache.org/docs/latest/api/scala/index.html#org.apache`
  `.spark.sql.streaming.DataStreamReader`
- Documentation for `DataStreamWriter` is available
  at `https://spark.apache.org/docs/latest/api/scala/index.html#org.apache`
  `.spark.sql.streaming.DataStreamWriter`
- Documentation for `StreamingQuery` is available
  at `https://spark.apache.org/docs/latest/api/scala/index.html#org.apache`
  `.spark.sql.streaming.StreamingQuery`

Streaming DataFrames for real-time machine learning

In this recipe, we explore the concept of a streaming DataFrame. We create a DataFrame consisting of the name and age of individuals, which we will be streaming across a wire. A streaming DataFrame is a popular technique to use with Spark ML since we do not have a full integration between Spark structured ML at the time of writing.

We limit this recipe to only the extent of demonstrating a streaming DataFrame and leave it up to the reader to adapt this to their own custom ML pipelines. While streaming DataFrame is not available out of the box in Spark 2.1.0, it will be a natural evolution to see it in later versions of Spark.

How to do it...

1. Start a new project in IntelliJ or in an IDE of your choice. Make sure that the necessary JAR files are included.

2. Set up the package location where the program will reside:

   ```
   package spark.ml.cookbook.chapter13
   ```

3. Import the necessary packages:

   ```
   import java.util.concurrent.TimeUnit
   import org.apache.log4j.{Level, Logger}
   import org.apache.spark.sql.SparkSession
   import org.apache.spark.sql.streaming.ProcessingTime
   ```

4. Create a `SparkSession` as an entry point to the Spark cluster:

   ```
   val spark = SparkSession
   .builder
   .master("local[*]")
   .appName("DataFrame Stream")
   .config("spark.sql.warehouse.dir", ".")
   .getOrCreate()
   ```

5. The interleaving of log messages leads to hard-to-read output, therefore set the logging level to warning:

   ```
   Logger.getLogger("org").setLevel(Level.ERROR)
   Logger.getLogger("akka").setLevel(Level.ERROR)
   ```

6. Next, load the person data file to infer a data schema without hand coding the structure types:

   ```
   val df = spark.read
   .format("json")
   .option("inferSchema", "true")
   .load("../data/sparkml2/chapter13/person.json")
   df.printSchema()
   ```

   From the console, you will see the following output:

   ```
   root
   |-- age: long (nullable = true)
   |-- name: string (nullable = true)
   ```

7. Now configure a streaming DataFrame for ingestion of the data:

```
val stream = spark.readStream
.schema(df.schema)
.json("../data/sparkml2/chapter13/people/")
```

8. Let us execute a simple data transform, by filtering on age greater than 60:

```
val people = stream.select("name", "age").where("age > 60")
```

9. We now output the transformed streaming data to the console, which will trigger every second:

```
val query = people.writeStream
.outputMode("append")
.trigger(ProcessingTime(1, TimeUnit.SECONDS))
.format("console")
```

10. We start our defined streaming query and wait for data to appear in the stream:

```
query.start().awaitTermination()
```

11. Finally, the result of our streaming query will appear in the console:

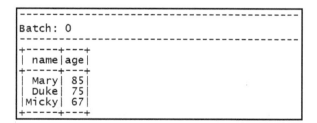

```
-------------------------------------------
Batch: 0
-------------------------------------------
+-----+---+
| name|age|
+-----+---+
| Mary| 85|
| Duke| 75|
|Micky| 67|
+-----+---+
```

How it works...

In this recipe, we first discover the underlying schema for a person object using a quick method (using a JSON object) as described in step 6. The resulting DataFrame will know the schema that we subsequently impose on the streaming input (simulated via streaming a file) and treated as a streaming DataFrame as seen in step 7.

The ability to treat the stream as a DataFrame and act on it using a functional or SQL paradigm is a powerful concept that can be seen in step 8. We then proceed to output the result using `writestream()` with append mode and a 1-second batch interval trigger.

There's more...

The combination of DataFrames and structured programming is a powerful concept that helps us to separate the data layer from the stream, which makes the programming significantly easier. One of the biggest drawbacks with DStream (pre-Spark 2.0) was its inability to isolate the user from details of the underlying details of stream/RDD implementation.

Documentation for DataFrames:

- `DataFrameReader`: https://spark.apache.org/docs/latest/api/scala/index.html#org.apache.spark.sql.DataFrameReader
- `DataFrameWriter`: https://spark.apache.org/docs/latest/api/scala/index.html#org.apache.spark.sql.DataFrameWriter

See also

Documentation for Spark data stream reader and writer:

- DataStreamReader: https://spark.apache.org/docs/latest/api/scala/index.html#org.apache.spark.sql.streaming.DataStreamReader
- DataStreamWriter: https://spark.apache.org/docs/latest/api/scala/index.html#org.apache.spark.sql.streaming.DataStreamWriter

Streaming Datasets for real-time machine learning

In this recipe, we create a streaming Dataset to demonstrate the use of Datasets with a Spark 2.0 structured programming paradigm. We stream stock prices from a file using a Dataset and apply a filter to select the day's stock that closed above $100.

The recipe demonstrates how streams can be used to filter and to act on the incoming data using a simple structured streaming programming model. While it is similar to a DataFrame, there are some differences in the syntax. The recipe is written in a generalized manner so the user can customize it for their own Spark ML programming projects.

How to do it...

1. Start a new project in IntelliJ or in an IDE of your choice. Make sure that the necessary JAR files are included.

2. Set up the package location where the program will reside:

```
package spark.ml.cookbook.chapter13
```

3. Import the necessary packages:

```
import java.util.concurrent.TimeUnit
import org.apache.log4j.{Level, Logger}
import org.apache.spark.sql.SparkSession
import org.apache.spark.sql.streaming.ProcessingTime
```

4. Define a Scala case class to model streaming data:

```
case class StockPrice(date: String, open: Double, high: Double,
low: Double, close: Double, volume: Integer, adjclose: Double)
```

5. Create SparkSession to use as an entry point to the Spark cluster:

```
val spark = SparkSession
.builder
.master("local[*]")
.appName("Dataset Stream")
.config("spark.sql.warehouse.dir", ".")
.getOrCreate()
```

6. The interleaving of log messages leads to hard-to-read output, therefore set the logging level to warning:

```
Logger.getLogger("org").setLevel(Level.ERROR)
Logger.getLogger("akka").setLevel(Level.ERROR)
```

7. Now, load the general electric CSV file inferring the schema:

```
val s = spark.read
.format("csv")
.option("header", "true")
.option("inferSchema", "true")
.load("../data/sparkml2/chapter13/GE.csv")
s.printSchema()
```

You will see the following in console output:

```
root
|-- date: timestamp (nullable = true)
|-- open: double (nullable = true)
|-- high: double (nullable = true)
|-- low: double (nullable = true)
|-- close: double (nullable = true)
|-- volume: integer (nullable = true)
|-- adjclose: double (nullable = true)
```

8. Next, we load the general electric CSV file into a dataset of type `StockPrice`:

```
val streamDataset = spark.readStream
            .schema(s.schema)
            .option("sep", ",")
            .option("header", "true")
            .csv("../data/sparkml2/chapter13/ge").as[StockPrice]
```

9. We will filter the stream for any close price greater than $100 USD:

```
val ge = streamDataset.filter("close > 100.00")
```

10. We now output the transformed streaming data to the console that will trigger every second:

```
val query = ge.writeStream
.outputMode("append")
.trigger(ProcessingTime(1, TimeUnit.SECONDS))
.format("console")
```

11. We start our defined streaming query and wait for data to appear in the stream:

```
query.start().awaitTermination()
```

12. Finally, the result of our streaming query will appear in the console:

```
------------------------------------------
Batch: 0
------------------------------------------
+--------------------+---------+---------+---------+---------+--------+--------+
|                date|     open|     high|      low|    close|  volume|adjclose|
+--------------------+---------+---------+---------+---------+--------+--------+
|2000-05-05 00:00:...|153.999996|159.999996|153.500004|158.000004|20685900|31.356408|
|2000-05-04 00:00:...|157.437504|     157.5|152.750004|153.999996|15411000|30.562573|
|2000-05-03 00:00:...|159.500004|159.999996|154.562496|156.062496|16594800|30.971894|
|2000-05-02 00:00:...|     159.0|  161.8125|158.187504|  161.0625|12725100|31.964186|
|2000-05-01 00:00:...|     159.0|     162.0|157.749996|   159.375|12486600|31.629287|
|2000-04-28 00:00:...|161.375004|     162.0|  156.5625|157.250004|14133900|31.207564|
|2000-04-27 00:00:...|     160.5|161.937504|158.187504|161.499996|20227200|32.051011|
|2000-04-26 00:00:...|   166.125|167.937504|161.312496|163.250004|21333300|32.398314|
|2000-04-25 00:00:...|162.249996|  166.3125|  160.875|165.999996|22854600|32.944073|
|2000-04-24 00:00:...|156.999996|163.937496|156.312504|162.062496|24014700|32.162643|
|2000-04-20 00:00:...|156.062496|158.499996|155.499996|158.499996|17056800|31.455636|
|2000-04-19 00:00:...|156.062496|156.812496|   154.125|155.499996|14150400|30.860261|
|2000-04-18 00:00:...| 152.8125|157.937496|151.937496|156.500004|25437900|31.058721|
|2000-04-17 00:00:...|   144.375|153.249996|143.874996|152.000004|31951500|30.165658|
|2000-04-14 00:00:...|147.999996|150.125004| 143.0625|145.749996|31645500|28.925293|
|2000-04-13 00:00:...|157.374996|157.437504|     150.0|150.500004|25497000|29.867971|
|2000-04-12 00:00:...|162.624996|163.250004|     156.0|   156.75|19443000|31.108334|
|2000-04-11 00:00:...|158.312496|   163.875|157.625004|   161.625|21002400|32.075819|
|2000-04-10 00:00:...|   159.375|161.000004|   157.875|159.437496|14234400| 31.64169|
|2000-04-07 00:00:...|157.625004|159.812496|  156.1875|   158.8125|13326600|31.517655|
+--------------------+---------+---------+---------+---------+--------+--------+
only showing top 20 rows
```

How it works...

In this recipe, we will be utilizing the market data of closing prices for **General Electric (GE)** dating back to 1972. To simplify the data, we have preprocessed for the purposes of this recipe. We use the same method from the previous recipe, *Streaming DataFrames for real-time machine learning*, by peeking into the JSON object to discover the schema (step 7), which we impose on the stream in step 8.

The following code shows how to use the schema to make the stream look like a simple table that you can read from on the fly. This is a powerful concept that makes stream programming accessible to more programmers. The schema(s.schema) and as[StockPrice] from the following code snippet are required to create the streaming Dataset, which has a schema associated with it:

```
val streamDataset = spark.readStream
        .schema(s.schema)
        .option("sep", ",")
        .option("header", "true")
        .csv("../data/sparkml2/chapter13/ge").as[StockPrice]
```

There's more...

Documentation for all the APIs available under Dataset
at `https://spark.apache.org/docs/latest/api/scala/index.html#org.apache.spark.sql.Dataset` website.

See also

The following documentation is helpful while exploring the streaming Dataset concept:

- `StreamReader`: `https://spark.apache.org/docs/latest/api/scala/index.html#org.apache.spark.sql.streaming.DataStreamReader`
- `StreamWriter`: `https://spark.apache.org/docs/latest/api/scala/index.html#org.apache.spark.sql.streaming.DataStreamWriter`
- `StreamQuery`: `https://spark.apache.org/docs/latest/api/scala/index.html#org.apache.spark.sql.streaming.StreamingQuery`

Streaming data and debugging with queueStream

In this recipe, we explore the concept of `queueStream()`, which is a valuable tool while trying to get a streaming program to work during the development cycle. We found the `queueStream()` API very useful and felt that other developers can benefit from a recipe that fully demonstrates its usage.

We start by simulating a user browsing various URLs associated with different web pages using the program `ClickGenerator.scala` and then proceed to consume and tabulate the data (user behavior/visits) using the `ClickStream.scala` program:

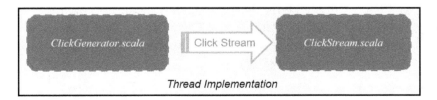

Thread Implementation

We use Spark's streaming API with `Dstream()`, which will require the use of a streaming context. We are calling this out explicitly to highlight one of the differences between Spark streaming and the Spark structured streaming programming model.

There are two distinct programs (`ClickGenerator.scala` and `ClickStream.scala`) that make up this recipe.

How to do it...

1. Start a new project in IntelliJ or in an IDE of your choice. Make sure that the necessary JAR files are included.

2. Set up the package location where the program will reside:

```
package spark.ml.cookbook.chapter13
```

3. Import the necessary packages:

```
import java.time.LocalDateTime
import scala.util.Random._
```

4. Define a Scala `case class` to model click events by users that contain user identifier, IP address, time of the event, URL, and HTTP status code:

```
case class ClickEvent(userId: String, ipAddress: String, time:
String, url: String, statusCode: String)
```

5. Define status codes for generation:

```
val statusCodeData = Seq(200, 404, 500)
```

6. Define URLs for generation:

```
val urlData = Seq("http://www.fakefoo.com",
 "http://www.fakefoo.com/downloads",
 "http://www.fakefoo.com/search",
 "http://www.fakefoo.com/login",
 "http://www.fakefoo.com/settings",
 "http://www.fakefoo.com/news",
 "http://www.fakefoo.com/reports",
 "http://www.fakefoo.com/images",
 "http://www.fakefoo.com/css",
 "http://www.fakefoo.com/sounds",
 "http://www.fakefoo.com/admin",
 "http://www.fakefoo.com/accounts"
 )
```

7. Define IP address range for generation:

```scala
val ipAddressData = generateIpAddress()
def generateIpAddress(): Seq[String] = {
 for (n <- 1 to 255) yield s"127.0.0.$n"
}
```

8. Define timestamp range for generation:

```scala
val timeStampData = generateTimeStamp()

def generateTimeStamp(): Seq[String] = {
val now = LocalDateTime.now()
for (n <- 1 to 1000) yield LocalDateTime.of(now.toLocalDate,
now.toLocalTime.plusSeconds(n)).toString
}
```

9. Define user identifier range for generation:

```scala
val userIdData = generateUserId()

def generateUserId(): Seq[Int] = {
for (id <- 1 to 1000) yield id
}
```

10. Define a function to generate one or more pseudo-random events:

```scala
def generateClicks(clicks: Int = 1): Seq[String] = {
0.until(clicks).map(i => {
val statusCode = statusCodeData(nextInt(statusCodeData.size))
val ipAddress = ipAddressData(nextInt(ipAddressData.size))
val timeStamp = timeStampData(nextInt(timeStampData.size))
val url = urlData(nextInt(urlData.size))
val userId = userIdData(nextInt(userIdData.size))

s"$userId,$ipAddress,$timeStamp,$url,$statusCode"
})
}
```

11. Define a function to parse a pseudo-random `ClickEvent` from a string:

```scala
def parseClicks(data: String): ClickEvent = {
val fields = data.split(",")
new ClickEvent(fields(0), fields(1), fields(2), fields(3),
fields(4))
}
```

12. Create Spark's configuration and Spark streaming context with 1-second duration:

```
val spark = SparkSession
.builder
.master("local[*]")
 .appName("Streaming App")
 .config("spark.sql.warehouse.dir", ".")
 .config("spark.executor.memory", "2g")
 .getOrCreate()
val ssc = new StreamingContext(spark.sparkContext, Seconds(1))
```

13. The interleaving of log messages leads to hard-to-read output, therefore set logging level to warning:

```
Logger.getRootLogger.setLevel(Level.WARN)
```

14. Create a mutable queue to append our generated data onto:

```
val rddQueue = new Queue[RDD[String]]()
```

15. Create a Spark queue stream from the streaming context passing in a reference of our data queue:

```
val inputStream = ssc.queueStream(rddQueue)
```

16. Process any data received by the queue stream and count the total number of each particular link users have clicked upon:

```
val clicks = inputStream.map(data =>
ClickGenerator.parseClicks(data))
 val clickCounts = clicks.map(c => c.url).countByValue()
```

17. Print out the 12 URLs and their totals:

```
clickCounts.print(12)
```

18. Start our streaming context to receive micro-batches:

```
ssc.start()
```

19. Loop 10 times generating 100 pseudo-random events on each iteration and append them our mutable queue so they materialize in the streaming queue abstraction:

```
for (i <- 1 to 10) {
  rddQueue +=
ssc.sparkContext.parallelize(ClickGenerator.generateClicks(100))
  Thread.sleep(1000)
  }
```

20. We close the program by stopping the Spark streaming context:

```
ssc.stop()
```

How it works...

With this recipe, we introduced Spark Streaming using a technique many overlook, which allows us to craft a streaming application utilizing Spark's QueueInputDStream class. The QueueInputDStream class is not only a beneficial tool for understanding Spark streaming, but also for debugging during the development cycle. In the beginning steps, we set up a few data structures, in order to generate pseudo-random clickstream event data for stream processing at a later stage.

It should be noted that in step 12, we are creating a streaming context instead of a SparkContext. The streaming context is what we use for Spark streaming applications. Next, the creation of a queue and queue stream is done to receive streaming data. Now steps 15 and 16 resemble a general Spark application manipulating RDDs. The next step starts the streaming context processing. After the streaming context is started, we append data to the queue and the processing begins with micro-batches.

Documentation for some of the related topics is mentioned here:

- StreamingContext and queueStream(): https://spark.apache.org/docs/latest/api/scala/index.html#org.apache.spark.streaming.StreamingContext
- DStream: https://spark.apache.org/docs/latest/api/scala/index.html#org.apache.spark.streaming.dstream.DStream
- InputDStream: https://spark.apache.org/docs/latest/api/scala/index.html#org.apache.spark.streaming.dstream.InputDStream

See also

At its core, `queueStream()` is just a queue of RDDs that we have after the Spark streaming (pre-2.0) turns into RDD:

- Documentation for structured streaming (Spark 2.0+): https://spark.apache.org/docs/2.1.0/structured-streaming-programming-guide.html

- Documentation for streaming (pre-Spark 2.0): https://spark.apache.org/docs/latest/streaming-programming-guide.html

Downloading and understanding the famous Iris data for unsupervised classification

In this recipe, we download and inspect the well-known Iris dataset in preparation for the upcoming streaming KMeans recipe, which lets you see classification/clustering in real-time.

The data is housed on the UCI machine learning repository, which is a great source of data to prototype algorithms on. You will notice that R bloggers tend to love this dataset.

How to do it...

1. You can start by downloading the dataset using either two of the following commands:

```
wget
https://archive.ics.uci.edu/ml/machine-learning-databases/iris/iris
.data
```

You can also use the following command:

```
curl
https://archive.ics.uci.edu/ml/machine-learning-databases/iris/iris
.data -o iris.data
```

You can also use the following command:

```
https://archive.ics.uci.edu/ml/machine-learning-databases/iris/iris
.data
```

2. Now we begin our first step of data exploration by examining how the data in `iris.data` is formatted:

```
head -5 iris.data
5.1,3.5,1.4,0.2,Iris-setosa
4.9,3.0,1.4,0.2,Iris-setosa
4.7,3.2,1.3,0.2,Iris-setosa
4.6,3.1,1.5,0.2,Iris-setosa
5.0,3.6,1.4,0.2,Iris-setosa
```

3. Now we take a look at the iris data to know how it is formatted:

```
tail -5 iris.data
6.3,2.5,5.0,1.9,Iris-virginica
6.5,3.0,5.2,2.0,Iris-virginica
6.2,3.4,5.4,2.3,Iris-virginica
5.9,3.0,5.1,1.8,Iris-virginica
```

How it works...

The data is made of 150 observations. Each observation is made of four numerical features (measured in centimeters) and a label that signifies which class each Iris belongs to:

Features/attributes:

- Sepal length in cm
- Sepal width in cm
- Petal length in cm
- Petal width in cm

Label/class:

- Iris Setosa
- Iris Versicolour
- Iris Virginic

There's more...

The following image depicts an Iris flower with Petal and Sepal marked for clarity:

See also

The following link explores the Iris dataset in more detail:

`https://en.wikipedia.org/wiki/Iris_flower_data_set`

Streaming KMeans for a real-time on-line classifier

In this recipe, we explore the streaming version of KMeans in Spark used in unsupervised learning schemes. The purpose of streaming KMeans algorithm is to classify or group a set of data points into a number of clusters based on their similarity factor.

There are two implementations of the KMeans classification method, one for static/offline data and another version for continuously arriving real-time updating data.

We will be streaming iris dataset clustering as new data streams into our streaming context.

How to do it...

1. Start a new project in IntelliJ or in an IDE of your choice. Make sure that the necessary JAR files are included.

2. Set up the package location where the program will reside:

```
package spark.ml.cookbook.chapter13
```

3. Import the necessary packages:

```
import org.apache.spark.mllib.linalg.Vectors
import org.apache.spark.mllib.regression.LabeledPoint
import org.apache.spark.rdd.RDD
import org.apache.spark.SparkContext
import scala.collection.mutable.Queue
```

4. We begin by defining a function to load iris data into memory, filtering out blank lines, attaching an identifier to each element, and finally returning a tuple of type string and long:

```
def readFromFile(sc: SparkContext) = {
 sc.textFile("../data/sparkml2/chapter13/iris.data")
 .filter(s => !s.isEmpty)
 .zipWithIndex()
 }
```

5. Create a parser to take the string portion of our tuple and create a label point:

```
def toLabelPoints(records: (String, Long)): LabeledPoint = {
 val (record, recordId) = records
 val fields = record.split(",")
 LabeledPoint(recordId,
 Vectors.dense(fields(0).toDouble, fields(1).toDouble,
 fields(2).toDouble, fields(3).toDouble))
 }
```

6. Create a lookup map to convert the identifier back to the text label feature:

```
def buildLabelLookup(records: RDD[(String, Long)]) = {
 records.map {
 case (record: String, id: Long) => {
 val fields = record.split(",")
 (id, fields(4))
 }
 }.collect().toMap
```

```
}
```

7. Create Spark's configuration and Spark streaming context with 1-second duration:

```scala
val spark = SparkSession
 .builder
.master("local[*]")
 .appName("KMean Streaming App")
 .config("spark.sql.warehouse.dir", ".")
 .config("spark.executor.memory", "2g")
 .getOrCreate()

val ssc = new StreamingContext(spark.sparkContext, Seconds(1))
```

8. The interleaving of log messages leads to hard-to-read output, therefore set logging level to warning:

```scala
Logger.getRootLogger.setLevel(Level.WARN)
```

9. We read in the Iris data and build a lookup map to display the final output:

```scala
val irisData = IrisData.readFromFile(spark.sparkContext)
val lookup = IrisData.buildLabelLookup(irisData)
```

10. Create mutable queues to append streaming data onto:

```scala
val trainQueue = new Queue[RDD[LabeledPoint]]()
val testQueue = new Queue[RDD[LabeledPoint]]()
```

11. Create Spark streaming queues to receive data:

```scala
val trainingStream = ssc.queueStream(trainQueue)
 val testStream = ssc.queueStream(testQueue)
```

12. Create streaming KMeans object to cluster data into three groups:

```scala
val model = new StreamingKMeans().setK(3)
 .setDecayFactor(1.0)
 .setRandomCenters(4, 0.0)
```

13. Set up KMeans model to accept streaming training data to build a model:

```scala
model.trainOn(trainingStream.map(lp => lp.features))
```

14. Set up KMeans model to predict clustering group values:

```
val values = model.predictOnValues(testStream.map(lp => (lp.label,
lp.features)))
 values.foreachRDD(n => n.foreach(v => {
 println(v._2, v._1, lookup(v._1.toLong))
 }))
```

15. Start streaming context so it will process data when received:

```
 ssc.start()
```

16. Convert Iris data into label points:

```
val irisLabelPoints = irisData.map(record =>
IrisData.toLabelPoints(record))
```

17. Now split label point data into training dataset and test dataset:

```
val Array(trainData, test) = irisLabelPoints.randomSplit(Array(.80,
.20))
```

18. Append training data to streaming queue for processing:

```
trainQueue += irisLabelPoints
 Thread.sleep(2000)
```

19. Now we split test data into four groups and append to streaming queues for processing:

```
val testGroups = test.randomSplit(Array(.25, .25, .25, .25))
 testGroups.foreach(group => {
 testQueue += group
 println("-" * 25)
 Thread.sleep(1000)
 })
```

20. The configured streaming queues print out the following results of clustered prediction groups:

```
-------------------------
(0,78.0,Iris-versicolor)
(2,14.0,Iris-setosa)
(1,132.0,Iris-virginica)
(0,55.0,Iris-versicolor)
(2,57.0,Iris-versicolor)
-------------------------
(2,3.0,Iris-setosa)
```

```
(2,19.0,Iris-setosa)
(2,98.0,Iris-versicolor)
(2,29.0,Iris-setosa)
(1,110.0,Iris-virginica)
(2,39.0,Iris-setosa)
(0,113.0,Iris-virginica)
(1,50.0,Iris-versicolor)
(0,63.0,Iris-versicolor)
(0,74.0,Iris-versicolor)
-------------------------
(2,16.0,Iris-setosa)
(0,106.0,Iris-virginica)
(0,69.0,Iris-versicolor)
(1,115.0,Iris-virginica)
(1,116.0,Iris-virginica)
(1,139.0,Iris-virginica)
-------------------------
(2,1.0,Iris-setosa)
(2,7.0,Iris-setosa)
(2,17.0,Iris-setosa)
(0,99.0,Iris-versicolor)
(2,38.0,Iris-setosa)
(0,59.0,Iris-versicolor)
(1,76.0,Iris-versicolor)
```

21. We close the program by stopping the SparkContext:

```
ssc.stop()
```

How it works...

In this recipe, we begin by loading the iris dataset and using the `zip()` API to pair data with a unique identifier to the data for generating *labeled points* data structure for use with the KMeans algorithm.

Next, the mutable queues and `QueueInputDStream` are created for appending data to simulate streaming. Once the `QueueInputDStream` starts receiving data then the streaming k-mean clustering begins to dynamically cluster data and printing out results. The interesting thing you will notice here is we are streaming the training dataset on one queue stream and the test data on another queue stream. As we append data to our queues, the KMeans clustering algorithm is processing our incoming data and dynamically generating clusters.

There's more...

Documentation for *StreamingKMeans()*:

- `StreamingKMeans`: https://spark.apache.org/docs/latest/api/scala/index.html#org.apache.spark.mllib.clustering.StreamingKMeans

- `StreamingKMeansModel`: https://spark.apache.org/docs/latest/api/scala/index.html#org.apache.spark.mllib.clustering.StreamingKMeansModel

See also

The hyper parameters defined via a builder pattern or `streamingKMeans` are:

```
setDecayFactor()
setK()
setRandomCenters(,)
```

Downloading wine quality data for streaming regression

In this recipe, we download and inspect the wine quality dataset from the UCI machine learning repository to prepare data for Spark's streaming linear regression algorithm from MLlib.

How to do it...

You will need one of the following command-line tools `curl` or `wget` to retrieve specified data:

1. You can start by downloading the dataset using either of the following three commands. The first one is as follows:

```
wget
http://archive.ics.uci.edu/ml/machine-learning-databases/wine-quali
ty/winequality-white.csv
```

You can also use the following command:

```
curl
http://archive.ics.uci.edu/ml/machine-learning-databases/wine-quali
ty/winequality-white.csv -o winequality-white.csv
```

This command is the third way to do the same:

```
http://archive.ics.uci.edu/ml/machine-learning-databases/wine-quali
ty/winequality-white.csv
```

2. Now we begin our first steps of data exploration by seeing how the data in `winequality-white.csv` is formatted:

```
head -5 winequality-white.csv

"fixed acidity";"volatile acidity";"citric acid";"residual
sugar";"chlorides";"free sulfur dioxide";"total sulfur
dioxide";"density";"pH";"sulphates";"alcohol";"quality"
7;0.27;0.36;20.7;0.045;45;170;1.001;3;0.45;8.8;6
6.3;0.3;0.34;1.6;0.049;14;132;0.994;3.3;0.49;9.5;6
8.1;0.28;0.4;6.9;0.05;30;97;0.9951;3.26;0.44;10.1;6
7.2;0.23;0.32;8.5;0.058;47;186;0.9956;3.19;0.4;9.9;6
```

3. Now we take a look at the wine quality data to know how it is formatted:

```
tail -5 winequality-white.csv
6.2;0.21;0.29;1.6;0.039;24;92;0.99114;3.27;0.5;11.2;6
6.6;0.32;0.36;8;0.047;57;168;0.9949;3.15;0.46;9.6;5
6.5;0.24;0.19;1.2;0.041;30;111;0.99254;2.99;0.46;9.4;6
5.5;0.29;0.3;1.1;0.022;20;110;0.98869;3.34;0.38;12.8;7
6;0.21;0.38;0.8;0.02;22;98;0.98941;3.26;0.32;11.8;6
```

How it works...

The data is comprised of 1,599 red wines and 4,898 white wines with 11 features and an output label that can be used during training.

The following is a list of features/attributes:

- Fixed acidity
- Volatile acidity
- Citric acid
- Residual sugar
- Chlorides

- Free sulfur dioxide
- Total sulfur dioxide
- Density
- pH
- Sulphates
- Alcohol

The following is the output label:

- quality (a numeric value between 0 to 10)

There's more...

The following link lists datasets for popular machine learning algorithms. A new dataset can be chosen to experiment with as needed.

Alternative datasets are available at https://en.wikipedia.org/wiki/List_of_datasets_for_machine_learning_research.

We selected the Iris dataset so we can use continuous numerical features for a linear regression model.

Streaming linear regression for a real-time regression

In this recipe, we will use the wine quality dataset from UCI and Spark's streaming linear regression algorithm from MLlib to predict the quality of a wine based on a group of wine features.

The difference between this recipe and the traditional regression recipes we saw before is the use of Spark ML streaming to score the quality of the wine in real time using a linear regression model.

How to do it...

1. Start a new project in IntelliJ or in an IDE of your choice. Make sure that the necessary JAR files are included.

2. Set up the package location where the program will reside:

```
package spark.ml.cookbook.chapter13
```

3. Import the necessary packages:

```
import org.apache.log4j.{Level, Logger}
import org.apache.spark.mllib.linalg.Vectors
import org.apache.spark.mllib.regression.LabeledPoint
import
org.apache.spark.mllib.regression.StreamingLinearRegressionWithSGD
import org.apache.spark.rdd.RDD
import org.apache.spark.sql.{Row, SparkSession}
import org.apache.spark.streaming.{Seconds, StreamingContext}
import scala.collection.mutable.Queue
```

4. Create Spark's configuration and streaming context:

```
val spark = SparkSession
 .builder
.master("local[*]")
 .appName("Regression Streaming App")
 .config("spark.sql.warehouse.dir", ".")
 .config("spark.executor.memory", "2g")
 .getOrCreate()

import spark.implicits._

val ssc = new StreamingContext(spark.sparkContext, Seconds(2))
```

5. The interleaving of log messages leads to hard-to-read output, therefore set logging level to warning:

```
Logger.getRootLogger.setLevel(Level.WARN)
```

6. Load the wine quality CSV using the Databricks CSV API into a DataFrame:

```
val rawDF = spark.read
 .format("com.databricks.spark.csv")
 .option("inferSchema", "true")
 .option("header", "true")
 .option("delimiter", ";")
 .load("../data/sparkml2/chapter13/winequality-white.csv")
```

7. Convert the DataFrame into an `rdd` and `zip` a unique identifier onto it:

```
val rdd = rawDF.rdd.zipWithUniqueId()
```

8. Build a lookup map to compare predicted quality against actual quality value later:

```
val lookupQuality = rdd.map{ case (r: Row, id: Long)=> (id,
r.getInt(11))}.collect().toMap
```

9. Convert wine quality into label points for use with the machine learning library:

```
val labelPoints = rdd.map{ case (r: Row, id: Long)=>
LabeledPoint(id,
 Vectors.dense(r.getDouble(0), r.getDouble(1), r.getDouble(2),
r.getDouble(3), r.getDouble(4),
 r.getDouble(5), r.getDouble(6), r.getDouble(7), r.getDouble(8),
r.getDouble(9), r.getDouble(10))
 )}
```

10. Create a mutable queue for appending data to:

```
val trainQueue = new Queue[RDD[LabeledPoint]]()
val testQueue = new Queue[RDD[LabeledPoint]]()
```

11. Create Spark streaming queues to receive streaming data:

```
val trainingStream = ssc.queueStream(trainQueue)
val testStream = ssc.queueStream(testQueue)
```

12. Configure streaming linear regression model:

```
val numFeatures = 11
 val model = new StreamingLinearRegressionWithSGD()
 .setInitialWeights(Vectors.zeros(numFeatures))
 .setNumIterations(25)
 .setStepSize(0.1)
 .setMiniBatchFraction(0.25)
```

13. Train regression model and predict final values:

```
model.trainOn(trainingStream)
val result = model.predictOnValues(testStream.map(lp => (lp.label,
lp.features)))
result.map{ case (id: Double, prediction: Double) => (id,
prediction, lookupQuality(id.asInstanceOf[Long])) }.print()
```

14. Start Spark streaming context:

```
ssc.start()
```

15. Split label point data into the training set and test set:

```
val Array(trainData, test) = labelPoints.randomSplit(Array(.80,
.20))
```

16. Append data to training data queue for processing:

```
trainQueue += trainData
 Thread.sleep(4000)
```

17. Now split test data in half and append to queue for processing:

```
val testGroups = test.randomSplit(Array(.50, .50))
 testGroups.foreach(group => {
 testQueue += group
 Thread.sleep(2000)
 })
```

18. Once data is received by the queue stream, you will see the following output:

```
------------------------------------------------
Time: 1465787342000 ms
------------------------------------------------
(22.0,2.518480861677331E74,5)
(26.0,3.4381438546729306E74,7)
(30.0,2.643700071474678E74,7)
(42.0,2.3743054548852376E74,7)
(44.0,2.935242117306453E74,8)
(46.0,3.854792342218932E74,5)
(88.0,3.5913920501881546E74,6)
(90.0,3.9063252778715705E74,7)
(98.0,3.5023649503686865E74,5)
(110.0,4.3840477190802075E74,6)
...

------------------------------------------------
Time: 1465787344000 ms
------------------------------------------------
(4.0,2.330551425952938E74,6)
(24.0,1.7639001479680153E74,5)
(38.0,3.1418032599086679E74,5)
(50.0,5.728473063697256E74,6)
(64.0,2.397328318539249E74,6)
(68.0,4.093243263541032E74,5)
(74.0,3.2704706499920196E74,6)
(78.0,3.565065843042807E74,5)
(84.0,3.7021298012378077E74,6)
(96.0,3.7021298012378077E74,6)
...
```

19. Close the program by stopping the Spark streaming context:

```
ssc.stop()
```

How it works...

We started by loading the wine quality dataset into a DataFrame via Databrick's `spark-csv` library. The next step was to attach a unique identifier to each row in our dataset to later match the predicted quality to the actual quality. The raw data was converted to labeled points so it can be used as input for the streaming linear regression algorithm. In steps 9 and 10, we created instances of mutable queues and Spark's `QueueInputDStream` class to be used as a conduit into the regression algorithm.

We then created the streaming linear regression model, which will predict wine quality for our final results. We customarily created training and test datasets from the original data and appended them to the appropriate queue to start our model processing streaming data. The final results for each micro-batch display the unique generated identifier predicted quality value, and the quality value contained in the original dataset.

There's more...

Documentation for
`StreamingLinearRegressionWithSGD()`: `https://spark.apache.org/docs/latest/api` `/scala/index.html#org.apache.spark.mllib.regression.StreamingLinearRegressionWi` `thSGD`.

See also

Hyper parameters for `StreamingLinearRegressionWithSGD():`

- `setInitialWeights(Vectors.zeros())`
- `setNumIterations()`
- `setStepSize()`
- `setMiniBatchFraction()`

There is also a `StreamingLinearRegression()` API that does not use the **stochastic gradient descent (SGD)** version:

`https://spark.apache.org/docs/latest/api/scala/index.html#org.apache.spark.mlli` `b.regression.StreamingLinearAlgorithm`

The following link provides a quick reference for linear regression:

`https://en.wikipedia.org/wiki/Linear_regression`

Downloading Pima Diabetes data for supervised classification

In this recipe, we download and inspect the Pima Diabetes dataset from the UCI machine learning repository. We will use the dataset later with Spark's streaming logistic regression algorithm.

How to do it...

You will need one of the following command-line tools `curl` or `wget` to retrieve the specified data:

1. You can start by downloading the dataset using either two of the following commands. The first command is as follows:

   ```
   http://archive.ics.uci.edu/ml/machine-learning-databases/pima-india
   ns-diabetes/pima-indians-diabetes.data
   ```

   This is an alternative that you can use:

   ```
   wget
   http://archive.ics.uci.edu/ml/machine-learning-databases/pima-india
   ns-diabetes/pima-indians-diabetes.data -o pima-indians-
   diabetes.data
   ```

2. Now we begin our first steps of data exploration by seeing how the data in `pima-indians-diabetes.data` is formatted (from Mac or Linux Terminal):

   ```
   head -5 pima-indians-diabetes.data
   6,148,72,35,0,33.6,0.627,50,1
   1,85,66,29,0,26.6,0.351,31,0
   8,183,64,0,0,23.3,0.672,32,1
   1,89,66,23,94,28.1,0.167,21,0
   0,137,40,35,168,43.1,2.288,33,1
   ```

3. Now we take a look at the Pima Diabetes data to understand how it is formatted:

   ```
   tail -5 pima-indians-diabetes.data
   10,101,76,48,180,32.9,0.171,63,0
   2,122,70,27,0,36.8,0.340,27,0
   5,121,72,23,112,26.2,0.245,30,0
   1,126,60,0,0,30.1,0.349,47,1
   1,93,70,31,0,30.4,0.315,23,0
   ```

How it works...

We have 768 observations for the dataset. Each line/record is comprised of 10 features and a label value that can be used for a supervised learning model (that is, logistic regression). The label/class is either a 1, meaning tested positive for diabetes and 0 if the test came back negative.

Features/Attributes:

- Number of times pregnant
- Plasma glucose concentration a 2 hours in an oral glucose tolerance test
- Diastolic blood pressure (mm Hg)
- Triceps skin fold thickness (mm)
- 2-hour serum insulin (mu U/ml)
- Body mass index (weight in kg/(height in m)^2)
- Diabetes pedigree function
- Age (years)
- Class variable (0 or 1)

```
Label/Class:
        1 - tested positive
        0 - tested negative
```

There's more...

We found the following alternative datasets from Princeton University very helpful:

```
http://data.princeton.edu/wws509/datasets
```

See also

The dataset that you can use to explore this recipe has to be structured in a way that the label (prediction class) has to be binary (tested positive/negative for diabetes).

Streaming logistic regression for an on-line classifier

In this recipe, we will be using the Pima Diabetes dataset we downloaded in the previous recipe and Spark's streaming logistic regression algorithm with SGD to predict whether a Pima with various features will test positive as a diabetic. It is an on-line classifier that learns and predicts based on the streamed data.

How to do it...

1. Start a new project in IntelliJ or in an IDE of your choice. Make sure that the necessary JAR files are included.

2. Set up the package location where the program will reside:

   ```
   package spark.ml.cookbook.chapter13
   ```

3. Import the necessary packages:

   ```
   import org.apache.log4j.{Level, Logger}
   import
   org.apache.spark.mllib.classification.StreamingLogisticRegressionWi
   thSGD
   import org.apache.spark.mllib.linalg.Vectors
   import org.apache.spark.mllib.regression.LabeledPoint
   import org.apache.spark.rdd.RDD
   import org.apache.spark.sql.{Row, SparkSession}
   import org.apache.spark.streaming.{Seconds, StreamingContext}
   import scala.collection.mutable.Queue
   ```

4. Create a `SparkSession` object as an entry point to the cluster and a `StreamingContext`:

   ```
   val spark = SparkSession
    .builder
   .master("local[*]")
    .appName("Logistic Regression Streaming App")
    .config("spark.sql.warehouse.dir", ".")
    .getOrCreate()


   import spark.implicits._

   val ssc = new StreamingContext(spark.sparkContext, Seconds(2))
   ```

5. The interleaving of log messages leads to hard-to-read output, therefore set the logging level to warning:

   ```
   Logger.getLogger("org").setLevel(Level.ERROR)
   ```

6. Load the Pima data file into a Dataset of type string:

```
val rawDS = spark.read
.text("../data/sparkml2/chapter13/pima-indians-
diabetes.data").as[String]
```

7. Build an RDD from our raw Dataset by generating a tuple consisting of the last item into a record as the label and everything else as a sequence:

```
val buffer = rawDS.rdd.map(value => {
val data = value.split(",")
(data.init.toSeq, data.last)
})
```

8. Convert the preprocessed data into label points for use with the machine learning library:

```
val lps = buffer.map{ case (feature: Seq[String], label: String) =>
val featureVector = feature.map(_.toDouble).toArray[Double]
LabeledPoint(label.toDouble, Vectors.dense(featureVector))
}
```

9. Create mutable queues for appending data to:

```
val trainQueue = new Queue[RDD[LabeledPoint]]()
val testQueue = new Queue[RDD[LabeledPoint]]()
```

10. Create Spark streaming queues to receive streaming data:

```
val trainingStream = ssc.queueStream(trainQueue)
val testStream = ssc.queueStream(testQueue)
```

11. Configure the streaming logistic regression model:

```
val numFeatures = 8
val model = new StreamingLogisticRegressionWithSGD()
.setInitialWeights(Vectors.zeros(numFeatures))
.setNumIterations(15)
.setStepSize(0.5)
.setMiniBatchFraction(0.25)
```

12. Train the regression model and predict final values:

```
model.trainOn(trainingStream)
val result = model.predictOnValues(testStream.map(lp => (lp.label,
lp.features)))
 result.map{ case (label: Double, prediction: Double) => (label,
prediction) }.print()
```

13. Start Spark streaming context:

```
ssc.start()
```

14. Split label point data into the training set and test set:

```
val Array(trainData, test) = lps.randomSplit(Array(.80, .20))
```

15. Append data to training data queue for processing:

```
trainQueue += trainData
 Thread.sleep(4000)
```

16. Now split test data in half and append to the queue for processing:

```
val testGroups = test.randomSplit(Array(.50, .50))
 testGroups.foreach(group => {
 testQueue += group
 Thread.sleep(2000)
 })
```

17. Once data is received by the queue stream, you will see the following output:

```
-------------------------------------------
Time: 1488571098000 ms
-------------------------------------------
(1.0,1.0)
(1.0,1.0)
(1.0,0.0)
(0.0,1.0)
(1.0,0.0)
(1.0,1.0)
(0.0,0.0)
(1.0,1.0)
(0.0,1.0)
(0.0,1.0)
...
-------------------------------------------
Time: 1488571100000 ms
-------------------------------------------
(1.0,1.0)
```

```
(0.0,0.0)
(1.0,1.0)
(1.0,0.0)
(0.0,1.0)
(0.0,1.0)
(0.0,1.0)
(1.0,0.0)
(0.0,0.0)
(1.0,1.0)
...
```

18. Close the program by stopping the Spark streaming context:

```
ssc.stop()
```

How it works...

First, we loaded the Pima Diabetes Dataset into a Dataset and parsed it into a tuple by taking every element as a feature except the last one, which we used as a label. Second, we morphed the RDD of tuples into labeled points so it can be used as input to the streaming logistic regression algorithm. Third, we created instances of mutable queues and Spark's `QueueInputDStream` class to be used as a pathway into the logistic algorithm.

Fourth, we created the streaming logistic regression model, which will predict wine quality for our final results. Finally, we customarily created training and test datasets from original data and appended it to the appropriate queue to trigger the model's processing of streaming data. The final results for each micro-batch displays the original label and predicted label of 1.0 for testing true positive as a diabetic or 0.0 as true negative.

There's more...

Documentation for `StreamingLogisticRegressionWithSGD()` is available at https://spark.apache.org/docs/latest/api/scala/index.html#org.apache.spark.m llib.classification.StreamingLogisticRegressionWithSGD

See also

The hyper parameters for the model:

- `setInitialWeights()`
- `setNumIterations()`
- `setStepSize()`
- `setMiniBatchFraction()`

Other Books You May Enjoy

If you enjoyed this book, you may be interested in these other books by Packt:

Modern Scala Projects
Ilango Gurusamy

ISBN: 9781788624114

- Create pipelines to extract data or analytics and visualizations
- Automate your process pipeline with jobs that are reproducible
- Extract intelligent data efficiently from large, disparate datasets
- Automate the extraction, transformation, and loading of data
- Develop tools that collate, model, and analyze data
- Maintain the integrity of data as data flows become more complex
- Develop tools that predict outcomes based on "pattern discovery"
- Build really fast and accurate machine-learning models in Scala

Apache Spark Deep Learning Cookbook
Ahmed Sherif and Amrith Ravindra

ISBN: 9781788474221

- Set up a fully functional Spark environment
- Understand practical machine learning and deep learning concepts
- Apply built-in machine learning libraries within Spark
- Explore libraries that are compatible with TensorFlow and Keras
- Explore NLP models such as Word2vec and TF-IDF on Spark
- Organize dataframes for deep learning evaluation
- Apply testing and training modeling to ensure accuracy
- Access readily available code that may be reusable

Leave a review - let other readers know what you think

Please share your thoughts on this book with others by leaving a review on the site that you bought it from. If you purchased the book from Amazon, please leave us an honest review on this book's Amazon page. This is vital so that other potential readers can see and use your unbiased opinion to make purchasing decisions, we can understand what our customers think about our products, and our authors can see your feedback on the title that they have worked with Packt to create. It will only take a few minutes of your time, but is valuable to other potential customers, our authors, and Packt. Thank you!

Index

www.ingramcontent.com/pod-product-compliance
Lightning Source LLC
LaVergne TN
LVHW081506050326
832903LV00025B/1400